The Rise of
Gridiron University

CultureAmerica

Erika Doss
Philip J. Deloria
Series Editors

Karal Ann Marling
Editor Emerita

The Rise of
Gridiron University

Higher Education's Uneasy
Alliance with Big-Time
Football

BRIAN M. INGRASSIA

UNIVERSITY PRESS OF KANSAS

Published by the University Press of Kansas (Lawrence, Kansas 66045), which was organized by the Kansas Board of Regents and is operated and funded by Emporia State University, Fort Hays State University, Kansas State University, Pittsburg State University, the University of Kansas, and Wichita State University

Parts of chapters 2 and 4 were previously published in "Public Influence inside the College Walls: Progressive Era Universities, Social Scientists, and Intercollegiate Football Reform," by Brian M. Ingrassia, *The Journal of the Gilded Age and Progressive Era*, Vol. 10, No. 1 (January 2011), pp. 59–88, Copyright © 2011 Society for Historians of the Gilded Age and Progressive Era. Reprinted with the permission of Cambridge University Press.

Library of Congress Cataloging-in-Publication Data
Ingrassia, Brian M.
  The rise of gridiron university : higher education's uneasy alliance with big-time football / Brian M. Ingrassia.
      p. cm. — (CultureAmerica)
  Includes bibliographical references and index.
  ISBN 978-0-7006-1830-9 (cloth : alk. paper)
  1. Football—United States. 2. College sports—United States. 3. Education, Higher—Aims and objectives—United States. 4. College athletes—Education—United States.
  I. Title.
  GV959.5.I64 2011
  796.332'630973—dc23   2011042398

British Library Cataloguing-in-Publication Data is available.

Printed in the United States of America

10 9 8 7 6 5 4 3 2 1

The paper used in this publication is recycled and contains 30 percent postconsumer waste. It is acid free and meets the minimum requirements of the American National Standard for Permanence of Paper for Printed Library Materials Z39.48-1992.

TO MY PARENTS,

MARIO AND BETTY INGRASSIA

Contents

Illustrations

Acknowledgments

The research and writing of this book have taken me from New England to California, as well as from Illinois to Georgia to Tennessee, over the course of the last decade. A number of individuals and institutions have guided or assisted me along the way, and I would like to take the opportunity to thank some of them here.

This project began at the University of Illinois, where Kathryn Oberdeck was an excellent mentor. Kathy's copious intellect and challenging questions helped make this a much more interesting book. Adrian Burgos, Bruce Levine, and Mark Micale read an early draft of the manuscript and gave crucial feedback. I particularly thank Chip Burkhardt for introducing me to the fascinating character of David Starr Jordan. Jim Barrett, Clare Crowston, Kristin Hoganson, Craig Koslofsky, Leslie Reagan, and Carol Symes also read portions of the project and offered comments, as did Will Cooley, Rebecca McNulty, Mike Rosenow, Jason Kozlowski, Greg Goodale, and Amanda Brian. My colleagues at Georgia State University in downtown Atlanta—a school with its own intriguing football story—provided a congenial and stimulating environment in which to finish the book. My fellow lecturers, including Robin Conner, Larry Grubbs, Scott Matthews, Mike O'Connor, Karen Phoenix, Mary Rolinson, and Walter Ward, helped make GSU a good place to work. Larry Youngs was kind enough to go above and beyond the call of duty by taking time out of his busy schedule to read the entire manuscript and provide helpful comments and encouragement. I also benefitted from feedback and advice from GSU colleagues Rob Baker, Isa Blumi, Michelle Brattain, Denis Gainty, Cliff Kuhn, Joe Perry, David Sehat, and Kate Wilson. Most recently, the history department at Middle Tennessee State University has provided office space as well as a warm welcome to Murfreesboro.

The Bentley Historical Library at the University of Michigan funded this project through a Mark C. Stevens Travel Grant, which allowed me to spend an extended period of time combing the Bentley's well-managed collections in Ann Arbor. Throughout the early stages of the project, the University of Illinois history department provided substantial funding for travel, research, and writing. I particularly thank Fred Hoxie and Vernon Burton for their assistance in helping me secure productive time for reflection at key points in the process.

A number of scholars have contributed their insights over the years. In particular, Murray Sperber and an anonymous reviewer carefully read and critiqued the entire manuscript before it went to press. Alan Lessoff, editor of *The Journal of the Gilded Age and Progressive Era,* provided thoughtful and incisive critiques on a related piece. At conferences and in correspondence, Victoria Bissell Brown, Steve Bullock, Court Carney, Daniel J. Clark, Elliott Gorn, Tim Lacy, Thomas Laqueur, Adam R. Nelson, Michael Oriard, Jeanne Petit, and David K. Robinson provided insights, critiques, and encouragement. While I may not have not been able to take all of their advice into account—or to resolve all of their questions—I believe that the book is a better project for their input.

Staffers at a number of university libraries aided this project by making their collections accessible. I especially thank Karen Jania and the rest of the staff at the Bentley Historical Library in Ann Arbor, Polly Armstrong and Margaret Kimball at Stanford, and Michelle Gachette and Barbara Maloney at Harvard. David McCartney (Iowa), Brad Cook (Indiana), and Mary Stuart and Chris Prom (Illinois) were also very helpful. A host of other librarians and archivists, too numerous to name here, were instrumental in helping me gather the research, images, and permissions. The production team at the University Press of Kansas has been stellar, and I particularly thank editor Ranjit Arab for all of his efforts, as well as his consummate professionalism and his enthusiasm for the project.

On my journeys to archives and conferences, several friends graciously shared their homes. I especially thank Linsey Griffith and Ken Doughman in Columbus, Ohio; Josh Carter in Alexandria, Virginia; Jared and Edit Hansen in San Francisco; Zina Lewis in Iowa City; Marshal Cooley in Omaha; and Paul Ruth and Debbie Hughes in Lafayette, Indiana. Paul, who is not a historian but is a sports fan with a keenly analytical mind, helped me to rethink the motivations of stadium builders. I also thank Vivian Schatz of Mountain View, California; Neile Rissmiller of Ann Arbor, Michigan; and Kirk Buggy of Somerville, Massachusetts. All three allowed me to lodge with them for extended research trips and listened to my musings; Vivian was kind enough to show me around the Bay Area and share her own recollections of the region's fascinating history. My cousin and fellow bibliophile, Donald Barclay, hosted me for a weekend at UC-Merced and enthusiastically discussed the project. While at Illinois, I was fortunate to spend time with a fun and smart bunch of people who made my time in Champaign-Urbana memorable. They include Jason Hansen; Cris Scarboro and Jill Baer; Mike and Kate Pedrotty; Paul, Ruth, and Debbie Hughes; Steve Hageman and Kerry Wynn; Dave Hageman and Beth Savage; Jamie Warren and Melissa Salrin; Will Cooley and Melissa Kath; Greg and Miha Wood; Andrew Cannon and Rosanna Yeh. From Illinois to points as distant as Nacogdoches and Macon. Jason Tebbe (along with Lori Perez) and Matt Jennings (and Susan and the boys) have proven to be wonderful friends and interlocutors; for their camaraderie I am especially thankful. And although Nicole Pasquarello came into my life just as I was wrapping up this project, she has kept me inspired at times when inspiration was not always easy to come by.

To a certain extent, any scholarly work transcends the words on the page and reflects the story of the person who has written it. My undergraduate mentor, Junius Rodriguez at Eureka College in central Illinois, was the first person to teach me the historian's craft; I hope that at least some of his efforts are evident in this book. But even before college, the experience of growing up in a working-class family fostered a distinct perspective on the relationship between institutions of academic life and the people located outside the metaphorical college walls. My parents, Mario (Marty) and Betty Ingrassia, provided years of love, support, and encouragement. Along with my older brother, Mark, they introduced me to libraries and the world of ideas at a young age. For these things, I am truly grateful.

The Cultural Cornerstone of the Ivory Tower

The Leland Stanford Junior University opened near Palo Alto, California, on October 1, 1891. Under a clear blue sky about 5,000 dignitaries, reporters, and local residents gathered at an event the *San Francisco Chronicle* noted for its tastefulness. Leland and Jane Stanford, who endowed the university named in memory of their son, had been enriched by the railroad's westward march, and the senator donated nearly $20 million and his roughly 8,000-acre stock-breeding farm to the project. To lead the enterprise, the Stanfords tapped an ambitious young administrator named David Starr Jordan, an ichthyologist who had studied with Harvard naturalist Louis Aggasiz and served as president of Indiana University since 1885. Jordan envisioned a great university at the Mission-style sandstone quadrangle then rising amidst the redwoods and coast oaks. Adhering to high academic standards, this university would support serious researchers—not just teachers—in a vast array of subjects. Although it would be coeducational, gender divisions would also permeate Stanford: "strong men" would make the university great and inspire male students, while women studying there (said Leland Stanford) could learn to be "mothers of a future generation." Quoting Aggasiz, Jordan assured the assembly that the funding of many fields of knowledge would benefit society more greatly than all the money spent to improve the masses.[1]

Despite this lofty rhetoric, some grumbled about the upstart university. One observer saw that it would rival the University of California, located on the other side of the Bay. The Stanfords, said such critics, might have done more good by donating their millions to the state university in Berkeley.[2] This complaint foreshadowed an athletic rivalry that blossomed the following spring in the city. On March 19, 1892, Stanford and Cal played their first football match at San Francisco's Haight Street baseball grounds, near Golden Gate Park. Hundreds of students, both men and women, along with professors and their families, joined the sizeable crowd. Berkeley's sophomores "secured a circus wagon and filled it to overflowing." Bookmakers set the

Opening ceremony, Leland Stanford Junior University, October 1891. David Starr Jordan is visible underneath the parasol, to the right. Courtesy of Stanford University Archives.

odds at 5 to 3 in favor of the blue and gold, but the cardinal-outfitted team from Palo Alto defied the odds and surprised the estimated 6,000 spectators by winning, 14–10. Stanford's opening ceremony the previous autumn was big news, but Stanford's victory was perhaps even bigger, and it prompted a major celebration. Afterward, students from both schools convened at the Bush Street Theater near Market Street. Several "pretty maids clad in tights" danced on stage and blew kisses, to the young men's delight. The *San Francisco Chronicle* reported that the noise was like "a couple of dozen steam calliopes all playing at once and out of tune": "How did they yell and stamp and whistle and abuse their din-creating instruments, the fish-horns, the bazoos, the devil's fiddles and the wooden rattles. They owned the theater, having bought it for the night, and they enjoyed their fill of harmless fun."[3]

These two very different events, Stanford's 1891 opening convocation and the 1892 football game, were sides of the same coin. One celebrated research carried out by professional scholars in academic disciplines at dignified campuses and appreciated by a serious public. The other featured a strenuous, popular game that amused a motley crowd. Each event represented essential, if seemingly contradictory, characteristics of America's emerging, industrial-era universities. These institutions, centers of a specialized modern intellectual culture,[4] were based in an industrial society with a booming economy and an increasingly diverse population that embraced popular culture while constructing new hierarchies of class, race, and gender. In this milieu, much academic knowledge was socially useful, but it was not nearly as accessible or as visible as commercial spectacle. Athletics, especially the prototypical big-time sport of football, filled this cultural gap by making universities appear meaningful to the public. If Jordan's speech at the beginning of the academic year outlined modern universities' academic orientation, the raucous scene in San Francisco during the spring term indicated a significant way that many universities would interact with the public for generations to come.

This book argues that intercollegiate football was maintained and reformed in the early 1900s because many university professors and administrators, as well as writers and politicians, saw it as a cultural ritual that, besides training young men in the strenuous ways of modern life, would publicize universities and disseminate prevailing ideas about the body and social order. In other words, they saw college sport as a type of *middlebrow* culture, a popular activity intended to make *highbrow* intellectual culture legible, or palatable, to the public. It would help to disseminate academic lessons or ideals to the American people.[5] In reality, though, these turn-of-the-century academics actually just institutionalized athletics as a university-sponsored *lowbrow* cultural ritual with its own permanent place on college campuses. Sport thus became a centerpiece of the modern university. In making this argument, I also seek to shed light on America's Progressive Era, the late 1800s and early 1900s period when reformers tried to solve or alleviate the problems of a rapidly growing, urban-industrial society.[6] Football reform and the concurrent rise of an academic ivory tower represented Progressive Era tensions between order and disorder, as well as Americans' love-hate relationship with chance, or risk. The game of football itself represented these tensions, as did the contours of the universities that embraced and reformed the sport. While Americans flocked to the gridiron, or football field, universities created a gridiron of research carried out in interconnected disciplines and departments. Football-sponsoring universities wanted to craft scientific scholarship that turned a blind eye to the commercial marketplace, yet still benefit from the risks of the market through semicommercial sport. As we will see, although many academics initially embraced properly regulated football at the turn of the century, many started to question this stance after World War I. In the post-progressive, interwar period of the 1920s and 1930s, the stereotypical ivory tower intellectual—alienated from the public and critical of popular sport—was essentially born.

It is important to note that while sport does not necessarily have to educate, nor must it attract paying spectators, both impulses have long been present in college football. This uneasy coexistence of pedagogy and market forces has led to a tension between reality and ideals, the seemingly paradoxical performance of a moneymaking cultural ritual by supposedly amateur students. This book analyzes football—rather than another game, such as basketball—because it was the prototypical big-time college sport: the lucrative, if not always profitable, spectacle that has dominated campus culture and the public's perception of many American universities since the early 1900s. Indeed, the origins of the term *big-time* help us understand college sport's cultural meanings. At the turn of the century, the same time when college football emerged, diverse crowds flocked to entertaining vaudeville variety shows. The companies that sponsored these popular events were dubbed either big-time or small-time, depending on how far they traveled, the size of the cities or theaters where they performed, and the numbers of tickets they sold.[7] Like the most famous vaudeville outfits, big-time football programs, by definition, attracted the most media attention, drew the largest number of paying spectators, and charged the highest ticket prices. Turn-of-the-century educators and scholars were both skeptical and optimistic about this cultural ritual, fearing that while football could injure players' bodies, minds, and morals, with the proper reforms it might actually strengthen students and benefit the crowd of spectators. But once football became a spectacle offered to paying spectators, its meanings—and the meanings of the university—moved beyond academic control. Like vaudeville performances or circus troupes, both of which attracted diverse crowds, football did not necessarily carry the meanings its most articulate proponents proclaimed. While sport might teach students and spectators a type of mental, moral, or physical discipline useful in modern society, it could also be an entertaining spectacle with nonacademic meanings.

By setting intellectual history and sport history side by side,[8] this book engages a key question of American history: What role do universities play in American culture, and what is the place of academic knowledge in a democratic society? I contend that institutions of higher education and research do not (and should not) constitute a so-called ivory tower hermetically sealed from outside influences. The lessons and spaces of the academy, which are incredibly relevant to the public, need to be accessible to the people they claim to serve. Yet it is folly to believe, as did some progressives, that a semiprofessional athletic spectacle such as intercollegiate football is an adequate form of public engagement.

We can see that some academics in the turn-of-the-century Progressive Era theorized ways that sport could make universities publicly relevant and visible, yet they merely created reforms that cemented football as a popular spectacle located uneasily between the academy and the public. This book, echoing historians who cite the anthropological theory of Clifford Geertz when examining college football as a cultural ritual, goes one step further to show how that ritual serves as a lens through which we can better analyze modern higher education. It also helps to illuminate the complicated relationship between modern American intellectuals and the public. Like Geertz, who famously accompanied his field-study subjects in Bali as they ran from a police raid on an illegal cockfight, we should run with the scholars and educators who were trying to understand the meanings of college sport at the same time they were forming and adopting their own social and academic roles.[9] By doing so, we can see that intercollegiate sport did not just originate as a popular appendage of the academy. Rather, it was the cultural cornerstone of the ivory tower, a popular ritual present at the creation of America's research universities. However, unlike those who defend big-time college athletics because of its central importance to major institutions of higher education, I offer this argument as a way to analyze critically the history of sport and its place within the ivory tower—not as a basis for sports advocacy. Indeed, this book more closely supports those scholars, such as Murray Sperber, who critique sport as a "circus" that diverts attention from higher education.[10] Taking this stance into consideration, though, it is ironic that Woodrow Wilson, who was then president of Princeton University, lamented in 1909 that academic "sideshows"—such as football—had "swallowed up the circus" of university life.[11] This book shows that progressives such as Wilson unintentionally initiated a process by which the football field, for many Americans, became the academic circus's central ring, while the classrooms and laboratories became the sideshows.

Upon close examination, it becomes apparent that the rise of big-time athletics was merely one symptom of a vast, nineteenth-century transformation in American higher education and intellectual culture. Before the Civil War, most colleges were local or regional institutions serving a small, usually elite student body. The curriculum, based in Christian morality, was designed to instill mental, moral, and physical discipline, so that male students could avoid the dangerous undercurrents of the capitalist market economy's murky waters. In this context, antebellum educators proclaimed the benefits of supervised physical training, yet decried team sports as potentially commercial. But both education and ideals of physical culture changed during the Civil War, when the federal government crafted legislation creating universities oriented around practical studies useful for building an industrial society. Shortly after the war, intercollegiate football competition began, with Rutgers and Princeton playing the first match in 1869. After 1880, Yale student Walter Camp (the so-called father of American football) reshaped the game in the image of an urban-industrial society. At the same time, universities were similarly retooling higher education. Aspiring American scholars traveled to Europe for academic training, and many returned with a new orientation. The typical industrial-era professor was not a teacher of *discipline* who taught students' bodies and morals. He was a teacher in an *academic discipline* who taught students one field of knowledge.[12]

The modern academy, based at campuses located in places such as Chicago, Palo Alto, or New Haven, consisted of disciplines—"communities of discourse" or "epistemic communities"—that were geographically expansive, yet largely abstract, aggregations of like-minded investigators. The expansion of disciplines and the development of autonomous departments represented the emergence of a fragmented, modern intellectual culture. For a scholar to compete successfully in this world and prove that he (for most professors at this time were male) was not a confidence man or trickster, he had to prove the ability to advance knowledge and craft scholarship aimed at academic, not popular, audiences. This process maximized the chances of creating accurate scholarship, but it also minimized the chance that knowledge would be accessible to people outside a particular discipline. Fields of study thus became narrower even as the number of scholars and the range of institutions sponsoring research grew. These changes in modern higher education represented a pragmatic mindset. Echoing the Darwinian theory of evolution by natural selection, which claimed that species emerged from a struggle for existence among large populations with great genetic diversity, pragmatists posited that truth was created by groups of intellectuals collaboratively testing a range of competing ideas. Many academic laborers had to be engaged in the process of making knowledge, and this process was facilitated by the growing number of universities and the increasing ease with which scholars could travel and communicate with one another. Intellectuals soon formed networks of academic disciplines based in autonomous departments. Some even saw sport as a way to unify fragmented campuses while protecting students' fragile nervous systems from the excessive rigors of education.[13]

In this modern intellectual landscape, universities—often seen as places of "manly"[14] striving—competed intensely for students, resources, and academic experts. Football became a public display of universities' relative strength and competitiveness, and it came to rival the commercial pastimes of professional baseball, the circus, world's fairs, and urban amusement parks.[15] Unlike other forms of popular culture, however, football was tied to institutions of higher learning that were seeking to produce useful ideas for an industrial society and train students in a wide variety of fields. At least in theory, said some Progressive Era psychologists and social scientists, football could teach young men physical, moral, mental, and social discipline; it might even offer instructive lessons to spectators. But soon, even football's proponents started to question the utility of college sport, especially because of its vast, seemingly unchecked popularity. Their analyses put a new spin on pre–Civil War concerns about physical culture, while also embodying debates or concerns about physiology and social organization. In turn, these intellectuals helped shape turn-of-the-century reforms—including athletic conferences, the National Collegiate Athletic Association (NCAA), professional coaches, and athletic departments—designed to protect, preserve, and oversee sport.

Yet ironically, at the same time scholars were creating reforms that would make the cultural ritual of sport safe for the academy, they were also crafting professional safeguards that would protect them from a disorderly society that embraced football. These academic reforms, which insulated scholars from potentially corrupting or damaging market forces, also had the unintended consequence of isolating professors from mainstream culture. In common parlance, America's universities and researchers were building an academic ivory tower. Of course, some early 1900s intellectuals still sought to create publicly relevant scholarship, but they were not always successful. Indeed, the stature of most of the academics employing popular media to reach the public in the early 1900s paled in comparison to the visibility of the football spectacle.[16] While academics still produced knowledge that was relevant to society, they had created structures of knowledge production largely inaccessible to most members of that society.

Football, though, was culturally accessible, and it was becoming more popular than ever. The game's appeal grew tremendously in the post–World War I "Golden Age of Sport," when Americans embraced bodily display and used their rising discretionary income and new media technologies to consume commodities of athletic celebrity.[17] Coaches exploited this consumer desire by placing one foot in academic culture while grounding the other firmly in popular culture. They benefited from the orderly stability of the university while also prospering from the economic and cultural risks and rewards inherent in the consumer marketplace. College football's paradoxical nature as a ritual located between the academy and commercial culture became manifested most concretely in campus stadiums, which, like the coaching profession, were a way for universities to maintain control— or at least the pretense of control—over athletics. Like the cultural marketplace it embodied, the football stadium was a *liminal* space, a ritual zone where meaning was malleable and represented a tension between structure and "anti-structure"—between rationality and irrationality.[18] Campus arenas, though, neither ensured academic control over the spectacle nor cemented football as middlebrow culture. They were merely university-controlled spaces for popular culture. Indeed, it was in the 1920s, when stadiums were popping up on campuses all over the country, that academics started questioning sport. Their critiques showed that their understandings of universities' public roles had changed. It was also apparent that some academics, in an attempt to reach out to the public sphere from which they had become isolated, had embraced new, or post-progressive, ideas about the appropriate form of middlebrow culture.

Concrete stadiums were a logical outgrowth of football's early 1900s popularity, reform, and institutionalization. By the 1920s, sport was a big business in America's universities, a business that nonetheless maintained an aura of respectability because it was supervised by trained experts who regularly proclaimed that sport was pedagogical in nature and pure in conduct. Big-time athletics represented modern universities' flawed attempt to maintain a connection to the public in an era of intellectual fragmentation and isolation. In the spaces of athletic spectacle and consumerism, the lines between academic and colloquial blurred. Many universities both bought and sold the tainted apple peddled by the serpent of popular culture, thus inviting the American people to engage in an awkward yet entertaining dance with academic institutions that, in many cases, only partially fulfilled the public roles they asserted. Scholars, administrators, coaches, and public critics can make any number of claims about the meaning of the spectacle occurring inside the stadium gates, as they have since the 1890s. But, ultimately, universities surrendered athletic control to spectators at the point of purchase, when ticket sales turned campus facilities into popular culture venues. Without a doubt, meaning is created in the arena, but that meaning does not necessarily reflect academic aims. Indeed, it is possible that Progressive Era reforms merely set in stone early 1900s ideas about football as an activity endorsing militarism and nationalism, as well as racial or gender hierarchies.

The intertwined history of football and the ivory tower is a distinctly American story that is nonetheless also immersed within global currents. The overseas origins of gymnastics, collegiate team sports, and much academic scholarship show the significance of transnational influences on American history.[19] Nevertheless, it is imperative to recognize that big-time intercollegiate athletics is a phenomenon unique to a specific nation, resulting from a peculiar higher educational structure rooted in America's political orientation and historical context. Since at least 1819, when Chief Justice John Marshall ruled in *Dartmouth College v. Woodward* that private corporations (including colleges) were not subject to state takeover or intervention, the United States has had a hybrid system of higher education. In this system a multitude of public and private institutions spread out over a large, expanding nation have existed side by side and competed with one another, with relatively little regulation or coordination by the federal government. In the late 1800s, when strenuous sport became popular throughout much of the globe, American colleges embraced football as a way to model this competitive spirit. The turn-of-the-century fascination with the muscular body, combined with America's democratic ethos that education should be widely accessible, provided a social terrain in which college sport thrived. Although Progressive Era reformers looked to Europe (or European empires) for inspiration, the rules and programs they ultimately adopted were fundamentally national in scope. Football reform was a consciously American project intended to strengthen the nation's male bodies and preserve social hierarchy while at the same time attempting to protect universities from corruption and counteract the realities of modern intellectual culture.

The story of football reform is a national one, but we must also acknowledge regional variations in the late 1800s and early 1900s. Football was born and first became popular in the elite colleges of the Northeast, but it soon spread to other areas with their own distinct characteristics or outlooks. Universities in the Midwest, California, and post-Reconstruction New South provided the terrain where many scholars trained in the East or in Europe competed for academic jobs, and they were also the places where athletics became an autonomous and permanent part of the university system. At the turn of the century, when football had become popular virtually everywhere in America, the United States was still solidifying its identity and consolidating separate regions into its national structure. Progressive Era struggles over football's meanings and forms resulted in the flattening of local differences, a process unavoidable when reformers attempted to shape national solutions for a large number of institutions located in diverse geographic contexts. After all, reformers were trying to create order by regulating chance, and they did so by making the policies of a wide variety of institutions conform to an acceptable common denominator. Although the most enduring reforms were national, several regional reforms—such as the Big Ten athletic conference in the Midwest and rugby reform on the West Coast—garnered varying degrees of success. To tell this regionally diverse story, this book draws upon published primary sources as well as archival sources at a number of major universities that invented both big-time football and modern academic research.[20]

The book is divided into seven chapters. Chapter 1 investigates changes in American society, intellect, higher education, and sport from the 1820s to the 1890s, especially the shift from small colleges and gymnastics in the antebellum era to large universities and competitive team sports in the late 1800s. It also explores the meaning of higher education in relation to America's shifting political economy, especially the rise of industry and cities. The second chapter examines how football grew in popularity during the 1890s, sparking debate about sport's place within Progressive Era universities. Scandals, injuries, and deaths prompted both critics and supporters to ask if the game was appropriate for colleges. Such debates resulted in major reforms, including the forward pass and the formation of the National Collegiate Athletic Association (NCAA). Chapters 3 (psychology) and 4 (social science) explore the intellectual basis of Progressive Era football reforms, while juxtaposing shifts in academic culture against football's emergence. Academic psychologists, who were then creating a fragmented academic terrain of specialized disciplines, saw football as a way to strengthen students' minds and bodies. If properly regulated, athletics could teach mental or physical discipline without damaging the nerves. At the same time, some social scientists—who would soon contribute to the progressive movement for permanent tenure and academic freedom—theorized sport's effects upon modern morals. They hoped to improve football by eliminating the crass professionalism that seemed to limit its educational potential. One way they did so was by proposing a national corps of coaches who would be respectable *professionals*, not undisciplined, trickster journeymen.

The fifth chapter investigates the coaches and athletic directors who turned sport into an autonomous university department tied to commercial culture. Fighting popular perceptions of physical culture as a field for confidence men, they dubiously promoted themselves as teachers who used spectator sport to instruct players, students, and spectators in the ways of physical, mental, and moral discipline. Chapter 6 examines how concrete stadiums, built on many campuses in the early 1900s, confirmed college sport's place as a permanent university activity that exploited consumerist desires, not necessarily pedagogical needs. Although alumni and athletic boosters commonly claimed football's educational and military importance, they built huge stadiums through fundraising campaigns that promised donors choice seats. The seventh chapter unearths the story of post–World War I football critics, especially intellectuals who had second thoughts about college football and the progressive-pragmatist universities created at the turn of the century. Some college leaders in the 1920s and 1930s hoped to abolish football and replace the fragmented curriculum with the liberal arts and Great Books. Others, many of whom were affiliated with the American Association of University Professors (AAUP), wanted to mute football commercialism. Both groups had limited influence, though, because big-time sport had become a permanent part of higher education by this time. Largely alienated from the public, moreover, many academics had lost social cachet and thus were no longer able to implement sweeping changes in athletic policy.

By analyzing the history of big-time intercollegiate athletics in light of its cultural, social, and institutional contexts, we can start to unravel the complicated historical relationship between academic intellectuals and the American public. Leading universities embraced strenuous sport, a seemingly irrational, nonacademic activity, because it seemed to provide a useful service for increasingly specialized higher education institutions. Athletics, by exploiting popular culture for quasi-academic ends, filled a void between the academy and the public sphere. As a cultural ritual easily enjoyed by the general public, intercollegiate football was one part of the academy consistently significant to the crowd located outside the university walls. Sport thus enabled academic institutions to appear culturally relevant to nonacademic constituencies at the same time academic life itself became sealed off within departments and disciplines. In turn, college sport began to emulate university structures, and the experts who orchestrated it claimed academic space by purporting to teach discipline to athletes, students, and the public. Yet the meanings of athletics were not limited to those crafted by professors or coaches. Rather, spectators and sportswriters crafted their own sets of meanings. Unlike the clearly pedagogical field of physical education, intercollegiate sport was a commercial spectacle that primarily fulfilled cultural and institutional, not educational, roles. Ultimately, reforms implemented in the Progressive Era cemented big-time football as just one more distinct university department with its own unique standards—standards that often owed more to lowbrow, popular culture than to highbrow, intellectual culture. They helped turn the academic circus inside out, relegating Woodrow Wilson's intellectual main tent to the fringes while bringing the athletic sideshow into the center ring. A cultural cornerstone of the ivory tower, big-time college football was a popular diversion that allowed America's institutions of higher education to maintain public visibility at the same time they invented an esoteric modern intellectual culture not easily consumed by the American public.

CHAPTER 1 *Physical Culture, Discipline, and Higher Education in 1800s America*

Francis Amasa Walker, a Civil War veteran and president of the Massachusetts Institute of Technology, spoke on college physical culture in his 1893 Phi Beta Kappa oration in Harvard's Sanders Theatre. Walker argued that the nation needed efficient, healthy, and vigorous male bodies to fuel commerce and industry. Thinking back to his student days at Amherst College before the Civil War, Walker recalled that students then did not develop their bodies. Instead, each strove to display a large forehead, combing back his hair to reveal a "remarkable phrenological development." Students back then had cared only for mind, not muscles. As a result of this disdain for physique, the body had become "but a shell, a prison in which the soul was confined." Thankfully, the war intervened and successfully demonstrated the superiority of body over soul, the importance of action over rhetoric.[1] Walker's memory, while vivid, was only partially correct. He was right that antebellum educators usually did not value strenuous athletics. Most were Whig moral or mental philosophers, immersed in a moment when Scottish Common Sense philosophy reigned in American colleges. As such, they argued that a proper education—including gymnastics—taught manly self-control. Collegians contended that individual physical culture, not team sports, might teach young men moral and mental, as well as physical, discipline. But both American society and education were in flux at midcentury. By the late 1800s, some academics began to embrace football, the prototypical intercollegiate sport. They saw athletics as a way that increasingly large, rational universities could train young men's bodies, minds, and morals for modern life.

Early American colleges stressed a curriculum that trained men for the ministry and other professions. Into the 1800s, colleges usually emphasized the divine unity of knowledge by structuring courses around three branches of philosophy: moral, mental, and natural. The college president, often a Protestant minister, taught ethics, political economy, and a rudimentary version of psychology within a capstone course designed to instill mental discipline and self-control. But as American society changed in the 1820s, so did colleges. Influenced by new communications and transportation technologies, America underwent what historians call a "market revolution." New colleges appeared in areas where the market economy (and Second Great Awakening religious revivals) flourished, including upstate New York and northern Ohio. In this context, some colleges served as focal points for vibrant, local intellectual cultures, and they also started attracting students who sought practical skills that would help them thrive in an increasingly market-oriented society. In the 1820s, a few budding universities even experimented with practical elective curricula. Some, though, disdained such innovations, fearing that the market would destabilize the nation's social life, politics, and morality. Therefore, they created or reinvented cultural institutions to mitigate the new economy's moral effects without negating its economic benefits. Middle-class moralists fashioned a "sentimental" culture of open and honest self-presentation, to protect against the social tricksters who profited from capitalism and urban anonymity. But even those who claimed to resist the market economy were often ensnared within its web. Tension grew as colleges tried to maintain a traditional emphasis on discipline in the face of the increasing desire for practical studies. Some educators feared that young men would learn to reap material rewards without becoming responsible citizens. Colleges thus had to find the right mix of utility and morality. Colleges could only responsibly build the economy if they taught students to resist the market's temptations.[2]

To do this, antebellum college educators, typically followers of the Whig Party, adhered to the "faculty psychology" of the Scottish Enlightenment. They stressed self-control, preaching a balance among mechanical, animal, and rational faculties. New England educators, in particular, argued that each individual had to suppress the passions while cultivating virtues. In this way, he could shape a disciplined self that could resist temptations of the "lower nature."[3] Most famously, Yale College's faculty articulated this pedagogical ideal in its influential 1828 report on a "Course of Liberal Instruction." Yale's professors argued that students needed to learn mental discipline in order to maintain faith and morality in an era of social instability. Responding to critics who charged them with "monkish ignorance," the Yale Report's authors explained that colleges must teach self-control, not offer practical studies—they had to train "mental faculties" to provide minds with *"discipline,"* not *"furniture."* Thus educated, graduates would contribute to political, economic, and social life. By contrast, a less rigorous education would turn students into mere confidence men, their schooling having hardly provided them with broader horizons than they would have gained through "conversation in stages and steam boats; or the reading of newspapers, and a volume or two of elegant extracts." Americans needed well-tutored intelligence, not just commerce. Yale's professors even analogized instruction to physical culture. They wrote, "As the bodily frame is brought to its highest perfection, not by one simple and uniform motion, but by a variety of exercises; so the mental faculties are expanded and invigorated, and adapted to each other, by familiarity with different departments of science." As bodies needed gymnastics, minds had to be exposed early to a regimen cultivating "proper symmetry and balance of character."[4]

That the Yale Report used this analogy is not surprising, considering the gymnastics craze sweeping New England at that time. Although student sports, including early versions of football, date to the colonial period, most educators did not start endorsing physical culture until the 1800s. Modern gymnastics originated with the nationalist *Turner* movement in Prussia. To cultivate nationalism and military strength during Napoleon's 1806–1814 occupation, Friedrich Ludwig *"Vater"* Jahn encouraged his countrymen to study German history, literature, and physical training. He promoted athletic fields as spaces for popular military training and nation building. Student gymnasts, subsequently, became cultural icons during the 1813–1814 wars of liberation. Their ideology, however, threatened the post-Napoleonic governments, and several German states banned gymnastics after 1818. Jahn, who published a treatise on physical culture in 1816, was imprisoned. Some of his followers were also persecuted. In 1824, two student radicals, Karl (Charles) Follen and Karl (Charles) Beck, fled Europe. Upon arriving in America these, men with help from German-educated Americans George Ticknor and George Bancroft, located teaching positions. Follen became German instructor at Harvard, while Beck taught Latin at the Round Hill School in Northampton, Massachusetts.

In addition to language instruction, both taught gymnastics. Follen influenced a generation of students by leading drills in Harvard's dining halls, while Beck established a gymnastics field at Round Hill. Soon, other schools built their own fields or gymnasia where students could learn bodily poise and stamina.[5]

This Germanic brand of physical culture was similar to the manual labor colleges of market revolution–era America, another antebellum educational phenomenon that was rooted in European models and transformed dramatically after the Civil War. Based on Johann Heinrich Pestalozzi's Hofwyl School in Switzerland, America's manual labor colleges first appeared in places most affected by the 1820s market revolution. Schools like Oberlin College (in Ohio) and Knox College (Illinois) offered instruction in farming and woodworking, alongside academic courses. The goods produced were rarely of artisanal quality and competed poorly in local markets, but educators claimed students benefited from the process. Manual labor proponents argued that college-educated men needed to combine powers of body and mind to survive the stressful mental work they would perform after graduation. Besides benefiting students' health, this type of education would, supposedly, "provide them with good habits, improve their studies, offer them a means for paying for their schooling, give them a trade to fall back on should difficult times demand it, and undo the tension between people who worked in the professions and people who worked in the trades." A student trained in manual labor would better appreciate the physical labor of his neighbors, perhaps even if those neighbors were of a different race. The manual labor colleges, like gymnasia or playing fields, were intended to bolster American society's ability to profit from the market without succumbing to its negative effects. Nevertheless, the manual labor curriculum largely disappeared by 1850—and it goes without saying that these few colleges were not successful in creating a classless, or racially harmonious, society.[6]

Charles Beck and Charles Follen, echoing manual labor proponents, argued that athletic fields could help tear down rigid barriers of social hierarchy. In 1828, Beck translated Jahn's gymnastics treatise for Americans. He wrote that physical training, carried out in simple linen uniforms, would bring together "all the different classes of peo-

ple, and thus [form] a new tie for those who . . . are widely separated by their different education and pursuits of life." Exercise could also unite physique with morality. Two afternoons of physical activity per week, accompanied by simple rations of bread and water, could teach young men to restrain their bodily impulses. The gymnasium, in other words, was both a radical and a conservative place, promoting liberty while preserving morality. This duality was based in the Prussian Turner movement itself, which was designed to serve both the individual and the state by cultivating bodies and morals, especially through teaching youth to avoid laziness and unrestrained sexuality.[7] Such prescriptions indicated the inherent paradox of physical culture: exercise could promote social leveling, but only if it were conducted in an approved manner. In the long run, the question of how to achieve proper balance between democracy and restraint would haunt educators and football reformers well into the early 1900s and beyond.

In the 1820s, gymnasia were established in many American cities. Follen, who founded Boston's first public gymnasium in 1826, argued that gymnastics allowed city-dwellers who worked office or factory jobs to participate in mentally stimulating physical activities. In 1827, he predicted that gymnastics would become a standard part of education and would be "a source of health, strength, and gracefulness" for those whose lifestyles led them "to neglect the cultivation of their physical powers."[8] Follen's writings and speeches embodied a common nineteenth-century belief about exercise: it was only beneficial if it was educational. In 1835, he proclaimed that exercise should neither provide mere "sensual enjoyment" nor be a popular spectacle that provided a diversion for workers bored by tending machinery. It must elevate society and strengthen the economy by giving workers both mental and physical outlets. Although he alluded to concerns about prostitution and gambling, Follen was optimistic that clerks or laborers could strengthen their bodies to resist urban temptations. He compared mind and body to management and labor, analogizing an athlete's body to the crew of a commercial sailing vessel, which obeyed the orders of the ship's captain (or "directing mind"). Workers should balance mental and physical functions the way managers coordinated labor, said Follen. Physical culture provided this balance. Work and play enabled head and hand to interact literally and metaphorically, thus promoting both individual and social harmony. But ironically, although Follen wanted to keep workers from becoming cogs in the capitalist machine, he promoted a system that turned workers into cogs and inspired them to find fulfillment in other activities. Urban amusements, including sport, usually served a different purpose than educational gymnastics, by enabling individuals to transgress traditional or prescribed social roles.[9]

Educators said that because physical training could easily become popular culture, and since popular culture could break down social norms, collegiate physical culture had to be carefully contained in a space located outside the marketplace. Otherwise, exercise could become spectator sport, turning students into performers for nonacademic consumers. The community had to be vigilant and prevent popular spectacle from undermining gymnastics' educational purity. In a passage that football coaches would echo (and invert) a century later, Beck described a gymnasium's proper location and specified who could congregate there. The ideal gymnasium was located outdoors in an elevated wooded area, away from the city, near fresh air and water. It should be surrounded by a fence or ditch denoting where the public realm ended and the educational realm began. After all, said Beck, "A gymnasium is no theatre, and no one has a right to expect a spectacle." Even though a gymnasium was not a secret place, it had to be constructed so as to separate the gymnast "from the mere spectator." The field had to be "arranged in such a manner as to afford a perfect view" for the citizens gathered there, so that everyone had "an opportunity to obtain a correct idea of the character and value of gymnastick exercises." Educators thus walked a fine line between cultivating men and creating spectacle. Instructors and qualified members of the public had to carefully watch or examine play and expel any athlete who refused to follow the rules. In this way, members of the "publick" could serve as the "overseers of morals." But they could not just be seeking entertainment.[10] Physical culture was pedagogically useful because it could discipline body and mind, teach morality, and prevent social fragmentation—as long as it did not cross into the realm of spectacle. The rise of late 1800s industrial society, however, would soon make it difficult for colleges to maintain pure, nonspectator sport. Yet educators would still try to control the spaces where intercollegiate sport was exhibited, as well as the meanings that spectators crafted in those spaces.

The gymnasium, said physical culture proponents, was a place of surveillance. Like educational institutions more generally—as well as the Panopticon, an Enlightenment-era prison intended to reform inmates' minds and bodies through constant supervision—playing fields instilled discipline by correcting the wayward behavior of deviant individuals. This idea, which had emerged in Europe, also permeated American culture in the 1830s, at a time when reformers (including educators such as Francis Wayland and Jahn-protégé Francis Lieber) founded penitentiaries and insane asylums that would presumably promote social order. The 1828 Yale Report even declared that collegiate lessons in discipline extended well beyond the classroom to all places on campus located near the watchful eyes, trained minds, and tutored morals of college officials.[11] School sports should *not* be open to those who sought a show, but they *should* be open to all who might help teach discipline. Gymnasia were not theaters—they were places where communities gathered to help students learn morality and self-control. The public's presence ensured that young men shaped virtuous selves, learned to live in harmony with one another, and followed the rules of the playing field, which mirrored those of the larger society. The nation's future, after all, depended on physical strength, mental discipline, and moral purity. Although the parameters of the debate and the type of sport changed dramatically, tension between egalitarian physical activity and moral development continued after the 1800s. The precarious balance between the playing field's inclusivity and exclusiveness, though, would be more difficult to maintain when college sport was carried out in a gray area located between modern academic institutions and the marketplace of commercial culture.

Despite the energies of its early proponents, enthusiasm for gymnastics faded in the 1830s. Historians attribute this decline to class stratification, the rise of other bodily reform movements, resistance to gymnastics' military origins, and workers' unwillingness to seek additional physical activity. Also, other sports gained popularity around this time. In the 1840s, baseball and cricket became common, while prizefighting gripped urban workers, who often preferred violent, spectacular contests.[12] Yet gymnastics resurged. The Pittsburgh Gymnasium opened in 1840, at about the same time *Turnvereine*, or gymnastics clubs, sprang up throughout Germany. When Germanic states suppressed these organizations after the 1848 revolutions, many people fled to America and founded *Turnvereine* in booming cities like Cincinnati or in smaller urban centers such as Peoria and Jacksonville, Illinois. America's first national Turner convention met in Philadelphia in 1851. Around this time, collegiate gymnastics started to regain popularity. New England colleges like Yale, Bowdoin, and Amherst built gymnasia, as did Oberlin College and Miami University in Ohio. Educators saw gymnastics as better than team sports, which could be violent and even scandalous. In October 1852, Yale students participated in a bloody interclass football game that seemed to mock collegiate discipline. According to the *New York Times*, this contest, witnessed by hundreds, resembled the Mexican-American War, and one player was even taken "bleeding from the field."[13]

Within a few years, Amherst College would document the reasons why educators established gymnasia at the same time they spurned team sports. Nathan Allen, a physician, college trustee, and member of Amherst's Gymnasium Committee, articulated the logic behind its new gymnasium—and its (nontenured) physical education professor—in 1869. Fourteen years earlier, in 1855, President William Stearns, who had studied gymnastics with Follen at Harvard in the 1820s, expressed his desire for a physical culture department that might save young men from overtaxing their bodies and minds through too vigorous study. Amherst hired Dr. Edward Hitchcock, Jr., an alumnus and recent Harvard Medical School graduate, to oversee the Barrett Gymnasium and direct the physical education department. Sounding like a typical Whig educator, Hitchcock noted his strict rules and his firm belief in surveillance and self-control; students should work off their "animal spirits" "under the eye of a college officer." In this light, Allen observed that Amherst intended physical culture to become part of the curriculum, just like Latin, Greek, or mathematics. This, he claimed—perhaps inaccurately, as some women's seminaries already stressed physical culture by this time—was the first instance when bodily development had been made equal to academic subjects. Such equal status was significant because physical education developed body and brain in tandem, while also teaching the discipline that any "professional man" needed (in part, by preventing the "nameless" vice of masturbation). Gymnasium exercises were also better than team sports, Allen said, because they were less susceptible to commercialism or spectatorship. Yet it turned out that even daily physical exercises could draw spectators. Hitchcock reported 4,787 spectators in 1869–1870, and 3,635 (including 842 "ladies") in 1876–1877, although usually only a few were present in the gallery at any one time.[14] Soon, much larger crowds would pay to watch intercollegiate football, inspiring much soul-searching amongst educators.

When Amherst initiated physical education, its leaders had already noticed team sports contending for student attention. They did not like intercollegiate athletics because competition between colleges put students in a space not easily regulated by either college, and it would make physical culture open to a crowd of diverse spectators possessing unregulated desires. So why did such contests originate? Historian Ronald Smith shows that students created athletic competition as a way to resist the all-encompassing mental and physical discipline of the antebellum college, and thus embodied America's democratic ideals.[15] This is a sound argument, especially for explaining an earlier period when football had few, lightly enforced rules, and college authorities opposed it. But the rise and acceptance of organized athletics also signified a shift in mid-1800s education, intellectual life, and culture. While pre–Civil War educators thought gymnastics fostered self-control and were superior to team sports, postwar students began to argue that athletics assuaged the monotony of the industrial-era curriculum. Eventually, this argument would be appropriated by coaches, educators, and progressive reformers who saw football as a way to teach teamwork and disciplined efficiency to the nation's future leaders.

First, though, we should be aware that collegiate team sports began in England, at Oxford and Cambridge, in the early 1800s, when students organized rowing crews and football teams. Some observers, including Harvard's Ralph Waldo Emerson, compared Cambridge's students to steam-powered machinery and likened the university's curriculum to an engineer's apprenticeship. Organized sport seemed to emulate modern education's competitiveness while fortifying bodies against its rigors. But games soon became so demanding that some students longed for the days when they had been encouraged to develop their minds as well as their bodies.[16] English athletic culture came to the United States a decade before the Civil War. America's first intercollegiate athletic competition was the 1852 Harvard-Yale crew race, modeled on the Oxford-Cambridge regatta. Seven years later, in 1859, students at Amherst and Williams Colleges inaugurated intercollegiate baseball. Yet this development prompted critiques, especially from some educators. John Bascom, a Williams College professor (and future University of Wisconsin president), complained that Amherst students demonstrated an "exact and laborious discipline" in their training and play. Such single-mindedness seemed to contradict a more holistic vision of physical culture in which individual development was much more important than spectator sport. But by 1860, when the Harvard and Yale gymnasium directors staged a "scientific" gymnastics exhibition alongside a regatta, the carefully managed pedagogical exercise of gymnastics was clearly in the process of becoming a sideshow.[17]

This transformation was representative of larger changes in post–Civil War American society. In a time of rapid industrial growth and intense nationalism, meanings of time and discipline shifted. Modern warfare, which came of age at this time, instilled a new kind of rigid time discipline in soldiers, many of whom shed premodern rhythms of labor after the conflict and became industrial workers—or else tramps who eschewed the daily grind of a time clock by refusing to work or by moving from job to job.[18] Postwar physical education reflected the new, more rigorous approach to discipline. By the 1870s, observers noted military drill's potential for instilling rigid manliness and nationalism, and some colleges even tried, with mixed results, to combine drill with gymnastics.[19] These changes—as well as reactions against those changes—prefigured college football's popularity as a strenuous, time-regimented game played by students (and a few "tramp" athletes) at increasingly rationalized universities.

The Civil War also contributed to a more complex understanding of humanity because the physicians who aided wounded soldiers studied the nervous system and came to comprehend it more thoroughly than ever before. Subsequently, new academic fields emerged as intellectuals restructured the meanings of mind, body, and social relations within a scientific, physiological framework. Mental philosophy fragmented into psychology and related disciplines, while moral philosophy splintered into the social sciences and natural philosophy became natural science. Late 1800s pragmatic thinkers even reimagined the nature of intellect by arguing that ideas were tools for crafting truths, not representations of divine, absolute truth. People who employed those tools were enmeshed in a complex social matrix, not souls beholden to God's unyielding will.[20] Modern scholars could not be expected to teach scientific truths alongside moral discipline because the professor was no longer a shaper of morals or a cultivator of student virtue. He was one individual in a network of truth seekers who read, experimented, and wrote, crafting new ideas representing the whole range of human thought and experience. In this context, even sport could serve a purpose in America's universities by knitting mind, body, and morals together. It could teach discipline to both athletes and the public, and it might even advertise those increasingly rational yet cumbersome institutions in which the production of knowledge had splintered into a wide range of individual fields.

But there was no guarantee that sport would only have academic meanings, or that its meanings could be controlled by those located within the college walls. After the Civil War, historians have demonstrated, competitive sport became increasingly popular throughout American society. Urban baseball clubs turned into professional teams by hiring "revolving" players, charging admission, and relegating wealthier, less talented members to the sidelines. Athletic teams— whether they were professional baseball clubs like the Cincinnati Red Stockings or collegiate teams like those at Amherst and Williams— were able to move between urban centers because of expanding railroad networks. Railway and streetcar companies were very conscious of their role in this process. They gladly transported spectators to urban athletic parks such as Manhattan's Polo Grounds as well as campus venues like Yale Field in New Haven (or even far-off Lake Winnipesaukee in New Hampshire for the 1852 Harvard-Yale regatta) in order to collect fares and even promote tourism or development. Sport also gained popularity because it made the new industrial order comprehensible at the same time it challenged modern labor's mores. The baseball diamond, for instance, reflected the disciplined coordinates of a commercial city at the same time it became a workplace rife with the language of labor and management. Yet in the same way that the prizefighting ring could symbolize an alternate shop floor that gave working-class men a sense of autonomy or artisanal identity, the diamond could also be a space for an enjoyable release from modern life. Even more simply, sport often appealed to working-class Americans who were becoming more strident in their demands for spare time. The ring and the diamond, like the theater or dance hall, were becoming urban spaces for leisure, recreation, and the forging of community bonds.[21]

By midcentury, when sport became a cultural terrain for urban spectators, thinkers like Charles Follen—who had warned against spectatorship in the 1830s—had been all but drowned out by the clanking of factory machinery and the cacophony of the urban crowd. In the intertwined urban industrial centers that created consumer sport, paying to watch others play became spectacular entertainment, not self-culture.[22] And when physical activity, whether professional or amateur, became spectacle, it took on unpredictable meanings and traveled routes that Jahn, Beck, and other antebellum college leaders had not endorsed. This point was clearly illustrated by Dudley Sargent, who later served as the director of Harvard's gymnasium. Sargent, like vaudeville pioneer B. F. Keith, toured with a circus in the 1860s. Reflecting on his big-top days, Sargent noted his gymnastics troupe's broad appeal and the diverse reactions they elicited from crowds filled with individuals of varying socioeconomic statuses and tastes. Some spectators appreciated the educational side of gymnastics, but others considered it mere "monkeyshines" similar to working-class billiards or bowling. Under a circus tent both literally and figuratively big, Sargent transformed physical culture from a display of educational discipline into a cultural commodity. He wrote, "In gymnastics, we used to win applause . . . in college or school towns, where the audience was familiar with the work of the gymnasium, and understood and appreciated the fine techni[que]. In small rural towns, the minstrels, clowns, and side-show freaks were the darlings of the public." A performer adjusted to the audience's expectations: "He may loaf before an unappreciative crowd, or exert himself to the utmost before people who show interest and enthusiasm." The exigencies of performing for a paying crowd shaped physical culture, turning an activity once intended for a watchful community into mass entertainment.[23]

The tension between spectacle and pedagogy became apparent in the late 1800s universities that invented big-time football at the same time they pioneered a new type of higher education focused on research and training large numbers of students in specialized fields. In 1862, during the Civil War, Congress, dominated by the Republicans (successors to the Whigs), passed the Morrill Land Grant Act, which gave each state at least 90,000 acres of land to endow "agricultural and mechanical" (A&M) colleges. Universities funded by this law, like Cornell, Wisconsin, Illinois, and Ohio State, taught scientific farming and engineering, subjects essential to the Republican "free labor" platform. While antebellum manual labor colleges had intended to thwart social hierarchy by training head and hand in unison, advocates of A&M universities openly promoted universities as places for facilitating social mobility within class-stratified society. Moreover, the curriculum was not limited to farming and engineering, as many of these colleges taught a wide range of practical fields, including the sciences and military drill. This law served as a catalyst that eventually changed American higher education. By the 1870s, industrialists started endowing universities focused on specialized research, such as Johns Hopkins in Baltimore, Stanford in California, and John Rockefeller's University of Chicago. Some older colleges also turned themselves into universities. By forming academic departments and embracing the elective system, which allowed students to select courses of study, these higher education institutions became centers for producing and teaching knowledge in an array of academic *disciplines*, rather than for teaching fewer students traditional modes of *disci - pline*.[24]

In 1869, Harvard, the nation's oldest college, inaugurated President Charles William Eliot, a former MIT chemistry professor. His tenure lasted an influential forty years, in which time Harvard solidified its place as a leading university and developed a big-time football team. An educational innovator, Eliot was a prototypical (to use Thorstein Veblen's memorable phrase) "captain of erudition" who promoted electives and organized departments designed to produce scholarship that could build the national economy.[25] In his inaugural address, the thirty-five-year-old Eliot explicitly stated that a college could not manage itself like a railroad or textile mill, yet he nonetheless advocated industrial methods for higher education. Eliot proclaimed, "When millions are to be fed where formerly there were but scores, the single fish-line must be replaced by seines and trawls, the human shoulders by steam-elevators, and the wooden-axled ox-cart on a corduroy road by the smooth-running freight train." The most highly developed societies had the greatest variety of tools, Harvard's new president argued, and Americans needed to develop the multitude of minds that would work together to build the economy. The new curriculum, in other words, was another version of the division of labor.[26] But not all agreed with Eliot. James McCosh, a fifty-seven-year-old Scottish moral philosopher and president of the College of New Jersey (Princeton), criticized proposals like Eliot's as a mere path to indulgence. Colleges should teach discipline and tame animal spirits, not train students to gain material prosperity. McCosh echoed the 1828 Yale Report, stating that colleges should strengthen a student's faculties rather than stocking him with knowledge. In an era when too many men pursued wealth, a college should not try "to make its students artizans or merchants, or manufacturers, or farmers, or shipowners"; it must instill morality. Noah Porter, a Yale moral philosopher, also warned against tailoring education to the practical fulfillment of basic social needs.[27]

Despite such protests, Eliot's influence was profound. Although he retained some of the university's traditional features, Eliot changed its aims and methods. He pragmatically calculated that teaching should remain Harvard's main focus, since that was the only way to support most research programs, but he also argued that Harvard had to cultivate academic disciplines and scientific knowledge instead of focusing on the "petty discipline" that ruled prewar colleges. Eliot even implied that thorough precollege education would teach discipline, thus preparing young men to study specific fields at university. Therefore, Harvard could "advance the grade of its teaching" to instruct "men instead of boys." Eliot, claiming that the college would teach mature men of twenty to twenty-five years, was perhaps taking into account the increased age of returning veterans, who had already learned discipline in the army. Nevertheless, he belied his mistrust in student maturity when stating that Harvard should remain an all-male institution. The university could eliminate "boyishness" and promote "manliness" through the elective system, but the presence of women would inspire men to misbehave and renew the need for onerous rules and surveillance. One day women might study at Harvard, said Eliot, but for now it should merely construct a separate institution for women.[28] Such ambivalence about male students' maturity would continue to manifest itself in Progressive Era debates about football.

The specter of biological determinism, an idea common in a post-Darwin era, also loomed in Eliot's inaugural. Promoting an educational philosophy that rejected the Yale Report, he argued that students should choose courses fitting innate capabilities, rather than adhering to a prescribed curriculum. An elective system tailored to "natural preferences and inborn aptitudes" relied on enthusiasm, not duty. Students were better suited to some subjects than others, and they did not need to learn *discipline*. They should just study the specialized *disciplines* for which they showed aptitude. The new Harvard, though, was not only filled with drudgery. As a student in the 1850s, Eliot had rowed at Harvard, and his postwar address contended that sport could help transform the university. He proclaimed, "There is an aristocracy to which the sons of Harvard have belonged, and let us hope will ever aspire to belong,—the aristocracy which excels in manly sports, carries off the honors and prizes of the learned professions, and bears itself with distinction in all fields of intellectual labor and combat; the aristocracy which in peace stands firmest for the public honor and renown, and in war rides first into the murderous thickets." Eliot posited that athletics and academics, like war, were two realms where the strongest, fittest, most educated men always placed first.[29]

By connecting academic success to sports victories, Eliot used an athletic metaphor very different from that of James McCosh, Princeton's president. Once again sounding like Follen or the Yale Report, McCosh saw education as a way to unify body and mind. He said that education should "be a gymnastic to all our powers, not overlooking those of the body; that every muscle may be braced to its manly use; that our students may be able to assume the natural posture, and make proper use of their arms and limbs, which so many of our best scholars feel, in their public appearances, to be inconvenient appendages." Education should "strengthen by exercising the intellectual powers."[30] Though both McCosh and Eliot appealed to robust manliness, the older Scottish philosopher's concept was very different from that of the younger American chemist. For McCosh, manliness entailed proper posture and the ability to function gracefully in public, like a skilled, evenly developed gymnast. To Eliot, manliness indicated ability to win strenuous competitions on the athletic field or battlefield, in the academy or the commercial economy. This contrast represented a distinction between a *manliness* based on self-control and a *masculinity* based on aggressive physicality, a transition that developed late in the 1800s. In modern society, force and victory counted more than self-restraint or virtue. Even though Eliot cherished the nonutilitarian undergraduate college at the heart of Harvard University,[31] and he later appealed to discipline in Progressive Era debates over football, in 1869 he invoked a brutal version of manliness, a vision that represented the changing aims of late 1800s universities.

Specialized academic fields dominated the changing institutional framework that stressed *disciplines* over *discipline*. Industrial-era universities, like the rest of modern society, fragmented into smaller pieces. Each discipline comprised a community of discourse spread out over a broad geographic space but connected via journals and professional associations. In turn, universities created departments, campus units that were institutional nodes of disciplines. Modern intellectual laborers had to adhere to high academic and scientific standards to maintain scholarly credibility. But this rigor often had the unintended effect of placing academics in a place removed from the general public. Scholars were based at university campuses, but their work was not always tied to local conditions or problems. Even though many universities would claim a mantle of progressive social utility, ideas or research produced in academic departments were not always publicly accessible. Obedience to scholarly methods and modes of thought led to the creation of an academic world located in, but not always of, the communities it served. By the 1900s, scholars created esoteric knowledge in narrow disciplines and departments, while administrators used sport to make universities relevant to Americans.

Alienation was particularly evident in the humanities and social sciences by the early 1900s. In philosophy, for example, scholars retreated into esoteric mathematical proofs and became removed from public discourse. Meanwhile, social scientists created specialized, nonhistorical disciplines, while historians prioritized objectivity over social utility.[32] These modern scholars were not necessarily trying to create an ivory tower located beyond the layman's grasp. Rather, they embraced specialization because they had to produce accurate, cutting-edge knowledge in order to prove to employers within a national academic market that they were true intellectuals. Progressive Era psychologists and social scientists worked in this academic matrix, as did early male physical educators and coaches, who eventually carved out an analogous space of their own.

The nationalization of research created intense competition, and it even inspired some educators to theorize a Darwinian university system in which stronger scholars and institutions survived at the expense of weaker ones. Cornell's Andrew Dickson White analogized the university to nature, as did Chicago's William Rainey Harper and White's protégé, David Starr Jordan.[33] Stanford's first president, Jordan was a biologist who promoted the Darwinian theory of evolution by natural selection; he also pioneered eugenics and often used scientific analogies in his popular writings. In 1887, while the president of Indiana University, Jordan wrote that the "law of the survival of the fittest" would eventually eliminate extraneous colleges. He called this double-edged process "the evolution of the college curriculum." First, it weeded out small colleges that could not compete in a national market. Second, via innovations like the elective curriculum, competition would eliminate "incompetent, superficial, or fossilized" scholars. As academics struggled for funds and thwarted less productive peers, universities would evolve into mature, competitive institutions able to produce competitive ideas and graduates. Jordan said that the "struggle for existence" was a natural law that permeated all of society— even education.[34]

In a modern society that determined the value of knowledge and truth in a marketplace that was becoming consolidated on state, regional, and national levels, universities struggled for funding, students, and publicity. Some fields, scholars, and institutions thrived while others perished. The survival of an instructor, discipline, or college typically depended upon the ability to prove value in both a figurative marketplace of ideas and a literal one of dollars and cents. America's late 1800s universities were pragmatic institutions insofar as each was a tool—or a collection of tools—designed to produce knowledge and provide graduates with the skills or ideas they needed to survive modern life. In most contexts, a university or field of knowledge could not survive by appealing to divine authority or absolute truth. It had to prove its ability to withstand withering competition. Universities therefore had to maximize their ability to produce accurate research and knowledgeable graduates, while minimizing the chance that ideas or students would prove unable to compete in the market economy. This was the basic problem that Harvard pragmatist William James documented in his 1903 article called "The Ph.D. Octopus." Comparing universities to industry (in particular the railroad trusts), James lamented that colleges had become so fixated upon the Ph.D. that true intellectual life suffered because university departments would rather hire a man with credentials than one with talent. The doctorate was a way of proving competency and marketability, not brilliance.[35] Although James did not admit it, this method of training scholars was truly pragmatic. The successful academic, by earning a Ph.D., had not necessarily proven his ability to think; he had demonstrated his ability to survive in a marketplace of thought. The competitiveness of higher education reflected the spirit of late 1800s American society, a spirit that eventually led university leaders to engage in aggressive institution building and to embrace big-time intercollegiate sport.

The existence of a national educational marketplace was not lost on students, nor were they unaware of the significance of athletic competition within that marketplace. Before Jordan, White, or Harper ever proclaimed the relevance of natural selection for institutions of higher education, students at Harvard and Michigan crowed that their universities were the best and most modern, and thus would win the "struggle for existence" against smaller colleges that still clung to outdated, antebellum moral codes. Some even argued that once small colleges died out, their abandoned buildings would be used as factories to create flawless machines instead of anachronistic, or obsolete, undergraduates. In a society that valued strenuous competition, successful teams became an indirect way of signifying success in the struggle for academic existence. Students in Ann Arbor, for example, noted that competitive sports were a way to advertise colleges. They even said that once Michigan equaled eastern colleges' athletic success, public opinion would place it on a par with those competitors. "Besides excelling in popularity and in rigor of instruction," wrote one student, "our University ought to be champion in some of the manly sports." He eagerly anticipated an era when people everywhere recognized both the athletic and scholarly supremacy of Ann Arbor men.[36]

Students made this connection in an era when football's popularity and visibility were growing rapidly. On November 6, 1869, just three weeks after Eliot's inauguration, another turning point in American higher education occurred in New Brunswick, New Jersey. Before a crowd of 200 spectators, two teams of twenty-five students each, representing Princeton and Rutgers, played the first intercollegiate football match. The final score was 6–4, Rutgers. Although this match was played as a disorganized kicking game, it foreshadowed the rise of American football, which adapted the game to the realities of industrial society.[37] The sport quickly caught on, eventually spreading from the Northeast to the Midwest, California, and the post-Reconstruction New South, drawing tens of thousands to games in city parks or university athletic fields. For many students it gave release, while for the public it provided recreation and spectatorship. But football was not just fun and games. Commentators would eventually see it as a mirror of modern industrial society, a tonic for modern manliness and culture, and a tool for American universities to publicize themselves and strengthen their competitive advantage.

Although interclass football matches took place in antebellum colleges, intercollegiate football was a post–Civil War phenomenon. While Union officers widely encouraged soldiers to play baseball (New York rules) during the war, troops also played a type of "foot ball." By the 1870s, baseball professionalized, while football started to become the predominant collegiate game.[38] We have already seen that railroads abetted intercollegiate play, but transportation alone does not explain the rise of football. We can also see that the postwar curriculum caused young men to find a healthy escape in physical recreation. In 1867, Michigan students claimed that university coursework depleted "manhood" and physical strength. Worried that mental development would outstrip physique, one writer argued that modern students needed exercise. Neither cricket nor baseball was adequate, since each only provided release for a few of the university's 1,200 physically "needy" students. Describing a game very different from the carefully measured and timed sport that took hold less than fifteen years later, the writer contended that football would provide physical activity for many:

> What we need . . . is something more republican in its form than either [cricket or baseball]. What shall it be? Of all the many games played for the health and strength they give, there is no one which admits of such universal participation as Foot Ball.—In this game there is respect paid neither to rank nor person. The veriest lubber may often add *materially* either to the interest or amusement of the game, by kicking the ball or something else, or by being accidentally kicked by some blind zealot because he happens to be where the ball was but an instant before.

This description seems tongue-in-cheek, the writer ironically connecting republican virtue with lack of skill. Nonetheless, he indicated that football engaged more players ("the more the merrier") than other sports. It was democratic because it did not require special grounds; a field could accommodate several games at once; and players did not need special clothing.[39]

In this account football, like antebellum gymnastics, connoted equality. But unlike gymnastics, it was not designed to discipline bodies, minds, or morals. It was simply a way for college men to unwind and enjoy a physical activity that would supposedly save their minds from too much study. Unlike the game created in the 1880s, early football was not a particularly "rational" form of recreation.[40] Players did not occupy special positions or wear protective equipment; referees did not measure downs or keep time. In fact, it is not apparent that there were even goal markers or clear rules. The game was an intramural romp for men who hoped to preserve their strength and manliness. It was also exclusionary. By citing the need to preserve manhood, students implied fear that women would soon take their places. This was a real concern for students at universities like Michigan, where both women and racial minorities were being admitted for the first time, thus challenging a then-prevalent notion that higher education was reserved for white males. Indeed, many continued to see the turn-of-the-century academy as a gendered place of competition. When assessing potential faculty members, some university leaders considered a scholar's manliness, his mental and physical stamina, his ability to build strong academic programs, and even his former athletic successes. Universities often excluded female professors, arguing that scholarship required manly strength and would drain women's reproductive energy—or would take time away from their roles as wives and mothers. Both research and sport seemed to be manly pursuits that demonstrated institutional virility.[41]

Although McCosh's Princeton participated in the first intercollegiate football game, Eliot's Harvard initiated the dramatic transformation whereby the sport became rational. In 1874, Harvard and McGill University staged a dual football match in Cambridge, playing one game under Harvard rules and another under rugby rules. The next year Tufts and Yale began playing rugby. But in the early 1880s, football changed once again. Walter Camp, a Yale student who later served for decades as Yale's graduate football advisor (amateur coach), introduced new rules. The so-called father of American football, Camp disliked unorganized recreation. In 1878, he suggested that teams be reduced from fifteen players to eleven to facilitate field tactics and team travel. Some New England colleges adopted this change in 1880. They also introduced another Camp innovation, "downing" the ball. According to historian John Watterson, this rule "marked the great gridiron divide that led American football down the opposite slope from British rugby." Instead of massing in a disorderly scrum, the player with the ball set it on the ground to start play anew. This innovation foreshadowed the modern scrimmage. But the new rule created new problems. In an 1881 Yale-Princeton game, neither team tried to cross the goal line, for fear of losing the ball and thus losing the game. To close this loophole, Camp insisted that each team get only three opportunities, or *downs*, to move the ball forward five yards, or backward ten. This rule resulted in measured plays and yardage lines, the field becoming a *gridiron*. American football, afterward, was "less like the

Walter Camp, captain of the Yale football team, circa 1880. This photograph was taken around the time that Camp suggested reducing the number of players on each team and "downing" the ball. Camp, Walter, Pps, Manuscripts & Archives, Yale University.

spontaneous game that had appeared in the 1870s and more tied to discipline and organization." It was, in other words, rational—just like the rest of American society, and just like the universities in which it was taking root.[42]

Why did Walter Camp introduce these innovations, and why did they last? Camp's professional career and historical context illustrate how social and cultural transformations may have caused football's rationalization. The late 1800s was a time of rational factory management, or Taylorism. Industrialist Frederick W. Taylor (who may have been inspired by a mathematics teacher who gave timed tests) fostered efficiency by timing workers and breaking production into small steps. As some historians note, turn-of-the-century Americans were engaged in a "search for order" that facilitated the rise of urban-industrial society, while taming its growth and disorderliness with progressive reforms. Industrialists and reformers sought to minimize the unruly effects of chance in a multitude of ways. Time zones made trains run efficiently; reformers tried to remove gambling from politics; and insurance policies protected businesses and investors. Minimizing risk ensured social and economic stability, as well as geographical consistency.[43] Camp, reputedly, possessed an orderly mind and disdained gambling, and he applied his distaste for chance or luck to football. Each down represented a rational unit of score production, giving the team with the ball an opportunity to stop play and impose order on the game. The time clock and yard measurements made the game progress efficiently, with precision. Scholar Michael Oriard notes that American football has shown a historical tendency toward a rigorous division of labor, and innovators like Camp sought to lessen chance's role in deciding the game. New rules limited loss of possession, thus increasing the possibility of consistent scoring and victory. The downed ball and the scrimmage helped tame modern society by taming the way it played. (The scrimmage's military analogue, trench warfare, similarly restructured warfare by minimizing the effects of powerful new technologies like the rifled musket.) New rules were a type of risk management. By stressing rational measurement and strength over chance and disorder, football was a form of leisure that appealed to modern society. Like Eliot, who applied industrial methods to education, Camp applied them to sport. Not surprisingly, Camp was also an industrialist. After leaving Yale in 1882, he worked for a New York clock manufacturer. The following year he went to the New Haven Clock Company, one of the nation's largest timepiece manufacturers; in 1903, he became its president.[44]

The transformation of sport into work was especially visible in Ann Arbor. In 1889, less than a decade after Camp's new rules were introduced, Michigan students discussed football's new character in terms that eerily echoed the prevailing industrial order:

> The players no longer rush about as of old, each playing his own game, but every individual has a definite place to fill, and the captain, by means of signals, manages so as to have all his men act as a unit. The game of college football suffers somewhat from the ignorance of its principles in the public mind, but remains, nevertheless, one of the most fascinating and scientific of the heavy sports. It trains and brings into play the highest physical powers and manliness, and at the same time cultivat[es] decision and self-command even under the most trying circumstances.[45]

This version of football differed greatly from the simple, "republican" game students played two decades earlier. The writer stressed manly physique while at the same time invoking science. The game was thoroughly organized, no longer consisting of throngs of students kicking multiple balls in an undisciplined fashion. Perhaps it was too complex for some spectators, but it was still capable of developing physical and mental prowess—perhaps, some would argue, even more so.

Football's emphasis on team strategies, rational order, and intercollegiate competition represented a dramatic shift in the training of minds and bodies. Academic life was moving away from the small, antebellum colleges and toward the intellectual hegemony of large research universities that competed in a larger marketplace transcending the local community. The tasks of industry, academic production, and sport had been rationalized and broken into smaller components to produce consistent results. Whereas earlier scholars such as the Yale faculty had claimed to teach students a holistic philosophy of mental and moral discipline in harmony with God's will, industrial-era scholars theorized the meaning of the modern mind and social ethics within their respective academic disciplines and departments. On a multitude of campuses, academic laborers conducted research based on rigorous scientific standards, and they disseminated findings to other specialists in the same discipline. This academic organization established a rational framework for scholarship and represented the triumph of modernism, a transnational cultural and intellectual movement in which fields of knowledge splintered and proclaimed independence from one another.[46]

By the early 1900s, only those writers who looked back to nineteenth-century education with humorous nostalgia could see higher education in a different light. George Fitch's "Old Siwash" stories, loosely based on his undergraduate experience at Knox College, lampooned dumb football players (the most prominent of whom was Ole Skjarsen, a barely literate Scandinavian immigrant) and saw the faculty as an anachronistic, uptight bunch. In a 1910 Siwash novel, Fitch's narrator called the faculty "a collection of brains tied together" in the job of disciplining students' lives; the professors sought to snuff out the excitement of college at the same time they acted like a "hypodermic syringe through which the student is supposed to get wisdom." They could understand Latin grammar or German folktales, but they did not know what made young men tick.[47] This was a largely outdated view by 1910, but the language Fitch chose was telling. At many larger American universities in the twentieth century, professors were not necessarily expected to teach students discipline; however, they did comprise a network of minds designed to fill students with knowledge in a number of different fields. Since too much attention to extracurricular activities could stifle the learning process, administrators and faculty members would soon turn to departments of athletics and physical culture as a way to impose order in student life and to find a way to teach the discipline that was no longer the purview of the faculty. By the 1920s, though, coaches would become particularly well versed at turning college boys into the celebrities of big-time intercollegiate athletics.

Antebellum colleges had aspired to develop bodies through gymnastics, teaching physical discipline to complement the mental and moral discipline learned in coursework. Such training was essential to preserve virtue in an era when the expansive market economy seemed to be taking over American life. By contrast, post–Civil War universities fed the growing industrial economy and established intercollegiate football. Team sports, unlike gymnastics, reflected the rational order of modern industrial society, and they also seemed to provide relief from intense, specialized mental work. Although antebellum collegians had warned against turning physical culture into spectacle, postwar universities transformed football into popular spectator sport. The next chapter shows how universities tried to justify and reform a game that could supposedly teach manliness, cultivate the strenuous life for an industrial and imperial nation, and help advertise and unify universities. But it soon became clear that sport's meanings were not easily controlled in the commercial marketplace. Eventually, educators and the public realized that the football spectacle was problematic. Matches might possibly teach students discipline, but the attention and demands of paying spectators might also corrupt young men or institutions of higher education. This concern resulted in an array of Progressive Era movements to reform football. Through progressive action that crossed local or state boundaries, reformers hoped, sport's worst elements might be eliminated so its most promising aspects could be preserved.

CHAPTER 2

Progressive Era Universities and Football Reform

In the 1880s football was a rational, orderly game for college men in the Northeast. But within a decade it gained national popularity and threatened to bring irrationality into the academy. Football joined an array of leisure activities, such as vaudeville, major league baseball, and amusement parks, which embodied Americans' penchant for play and desire for diversion. As football became more popular and brutal in the 1890s, journalists, politicians, physicians, and academics clamored for reform. They recognized the game's many problems, yet still saw its educational value. Football might be a commercial activity that could corrupt universities while destroying young men's bodies, minds, and morals; but if properly reformed and regulated, it might publicize the academy while bolstering American masculinity. Although a few outspoken critics suggested intercollegiate football's abolition in the 1890s, most saw the sport as a strenuous tonic benefiting both students and academic institutions. To purify football, progressives created multiple reforms. Some of these were local or regional, although the most long-lasting were national. Some also had unintended consequences, as reformers constructed regulations and agencies that eventually turned football into a permanent university ritual.

Harvard, Yale, Princeton, and other New England colleges embraced rugby football in the 1870s, before Walter Camp turned it into American football around 1880. Then the sport moved west and south, mirroring a migration of scholars from the academic establishment to newer institutions. Industrialists built universities in Chicago and Palo Alto, while states like Wisconsin, Illinois, and Minnesota pumped money into burgeoning public colleges. Both types of institutions strove for social utility: teaching students, disseminating knowledge, sponsoring social settlements, pioneering university extension, and filling state government with university-trained experts.[1] This was the institutional context in which football flourished, quickly becoming virtually indispensable for any institution aspiring to university sta-

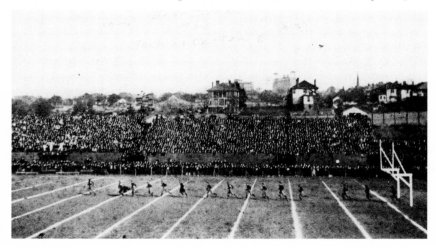

Grant Field at Georgia Tech, 1920. Georgia Tech, along with Auburn, Vanderbilt, and the University of Georgia, was an institution that pioneered southern college football by the 1890s. Permission of the Georgia Institute of Technology Library and Information Center, Archives and Records Management Department.

tus. The sport spread throughout the Midwest in the decade following Michigan's first intercollegiate game in 1879. In the West, Stanford and California embraced football by the 1890s, at roughly the same time the universities of the urban, industrial New South (especially Georgia, Georgia Tech, and Auburn) began play. At two of these southern schools, football was introduced by professors trained at Johns Hopkins—University of Georgia chemist Charles Herty and Auburn historian George Petrie. Georgia and Auburn played the South's first big game in Atlanta in February 1892, at what is now Piedmont Park. Vanderbilt University became a power after 1904, when Michigan assistant coach Dan McGugin moved to Nashville, where he coached for nearly three decades.[2]

Intercollegiate sport was visible and entertaining, but while football joined the late 1800s pop-culture pantheon, its connection to institutions of higher education put it in a unique position. Progressive Era universities had to decide if football was a "manly" pedagogical tool or a dangerous spectacle that threatened higher learning. For those who saw football as beneficial, sport provided publicity and instant tradition. The University of Chicago fielded a team virtually from its opening day, in large part because President William Rainey Harper saw it as a way to advertise the raw institution. In 1912, the University of Illinois's President Edmund J. James claimed that sport could make taxpayers aware of state-funded higher education institutions. He also hoped that athletic spectacle would unite these increasingly large, unwieldy, and fragmented universities, which were becoming full of new disciplines with specialized terminologies, organizations, and departments. James noted, "We are falling into sections and factions and are wrapped up in the proceedings of our own colleges and laboratories to such an extent that any force that . . . bring[s] us out of that tendency, professors as well as students, is of value." While antebellum educators had expected physical culture to produce disciplined men, progressives now gave it the new task of providing a common ground for expanding universities.[3]

Although the sport started in predominantly white institutions, football's perceived advantages did not stop at the color line. According to turn-of-the-century proponents of African-American higher education, football might demonstrate the effectiveness and equality of black schools like Morehouse College, Atlanta University, Fisk University, and Tuskegee Institute. To some, black squads seemed so well trained and disciplined that they might even silence white critics. In 1908, Atlanta and Claflin Universities played a match in Augusta during the Georgia-Carolina Negro Fair. One account recorded that the contest, which drew both black and white spectators to the fairgrounds racetrack, showed that black sport was "orderly" and comparable to white sport. Those spectators who "expect[ed] to see a game where there was an exhibition of brute strength . . . having none of the elements of modern and scientific football, were rudely disappointed, for the qualities of football displayed by the two Negro teams compared favorably with those displayed" recently by Clemson and Georgia.[4]

As football swelled in popularity, tens of thousands paid to attend and watch the games. Most spectators, at least initially, were upper- and middle-class white males. Thus it is not surprising that big-time money accompanied the first big-time college sport. For example,

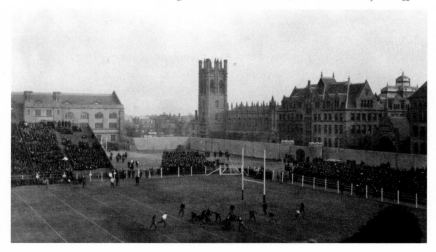

Stagg Field (formerly Marshall Field) at the University of Chicago. This undated view from the early 1900s shows the Gothic quadrangles located across 57th Street. Special Collections Research Center, University of Chicago Library.

Yale's 1892–1893 athletic receipts totaled over $36,000, while its expenditures were little more than $13,000. At first, this money enriched the university. Except for $4,000 used to service the Yale Field debt, the remainder of the profits (about $19,000) was handed over to Yale's Financial Union. But over time, the money went back into sport. By 1903, football took in over $56,000 of Yale's nearly $93,000 of athletic receipts, but the year's athletic profit was just a little over $1,000. In addition to regular expenditures on athletics, nearly $23,000 was spent to construct new stands at Yale Field. Harvard also had a lucrative program that eventually used ticket sales to build a large stadium. The Crimson grossed over $40,000 in 1894; by 1901 gate receipts totaled nearly $56,000, and the Harvard Athletic Association delivered $29,000 in surplus to Harvard's treasurer. Soon, these funds would help construct Harvard Stadium.[5]

Many claimed that football ticket sales funded physical education, and at many colleges this was apparently true.[6] Yet much money collected at the gates (or provided by alumni) never entered college coffers. Athletes received sinecures or loans, while coaches received payments that were barely, if at all, disguised. In 1905 Harvard hired alumnus William T. Reid, Jr., to turn the Crimson eleven into a winner. While Harvard advertised Reid as a nonprofessional graduate coach hired to maintain athletic purity, it paid him a $7,000 salary.[7] Some money went to stadiums and coaches, but other revenues bypassed the gates entirely, going instead to gamblers and hustlers, who thrived by exploiting the elusive promise of luck. Football gambling thrived because it mocked rational, middle-class morals and restored disorder to what could seem an overly orderly contest. Newspapers sometimes even reported the odds for major contests, including the 1892 Big Game in San Francisco, the 1894 Harvard-Yale game, and the Yale Bowl's first game in 1914. By the early 1900s, progressives worried that young men learned wasteful habits by squandering their fathers' money on betting, and athletic conferences sought, without much success, to quell wagering. In the 1920s, Big Ten Commissioner John Griffith stated that betting showed how disreputable members of the public were willing to undermine higher education by ruining the otherwise morally uplifting ritual of football. Illinois athletic director George Huff warned that the gambler was usually a hoodlum "in a class with the saloonkeeper and only above the confidence man and the burglar."[8]

Commercialism and gambling were unsavory aspects of turn-of-the-century football, but the game also threatened to corrupt universities in other ways. The tramp athlete, a significant concern at this time, transcended monetary issues. Like hobos, whose lack of homes destabilized society, tramp football players destabilized colleges by rendering academic standards meaningless. They enrolled for the season, helped secure key victories, and then disappeared. Others never enrolled at all. Stanford's President David Starr Jordan complained that football "ringers" were "a drag" on universities.[9] How could the academy maintain rigor in an era of electives if unqualified students enrolled just to play (or watch) a game? Sport was also dangerous because it crossed institutional boundaries. Football pitted colleges with varying standards against one another. If one school had lower admissions requirements, even properly enrolled students might give its team an unfair advantage. To add to the confusion, spectators often had little investment in academic aims. Even alumni were sometimes more interested in entertainment than in collegiate purity. Since football was not entirely contained within one college, administrators or faculty could not easily regulate it. Unlike classrooms or gymnasia, intercollegiate contests were not subject to one school's rules. Players, teams, and coaches were beholden to the cultural marketplace. Football was subject to the desires of those who enjoyed victories, spectacle, and profit—not just those who operated under university auspices.

Additionally, football was becoming a violent and brutal game by the 1890s. Since Camp had introduced rational rules a decade earlier, coaches and players devised tactics to reduce the risk of losing the ball, enhance the chance of scoring, and increase the possibility of victory. One tactic was the mass play, in which players grouped together to gain yardage through brute force. Such plays were the harbingers of "scientific" football, played with strict rules and complex strategies. Such play was epitomized by the notorious flying wedge formations, pioneered by Lorin Deland, a Boston businessman (and admirer of Napoleon), in 1892. In one variety of the wedge, six offensive players began moving before the ball was snapped, and then surrounded the ball carrier in a V that swept down the field with "half a ton of bone and muscle," crushing defenders. "The victim," said one newspaper critic, "is generally sent sprawling with his nose broken or his chest crushed, and if the man with the ball gets through the line for ten or twenty yards the critics all exclaim: 'What a grand play!'" In effect, the wedge helped teams win by minimizing the chance of losing the ball and maximizing the chance of attaining the goal line. Conversely, though, it also led to risks that had little to do with victory. The *New York Times* noted, "every time a youth steps on the field to uphold the reputation of his college he assumes nearly the same risk that a soldier does on the battle field. Every day one hears of broken heads, fractured skulls, broken necks, wrenched legs, dislocated shoulders, and many other accidents of a more or less serious nature." One writer even quipped that a player who perused a book on naval history would recognize the diagrams and the dictum to overwhelm the "enemy's line." If Admiral Horatio Nelson "had lived a little later we should have found him playing his ships in a Princeton V or in a Deland revolving wedge."[10]

Rule makers, responding to the public outcry, legislated against the wedge in February 1894. Representatives from Harvard, Yale, Princeton, Columbia, and Dartmouth conferred with New York's University Athletic Club to eliminate dangerous plays. Yale's Walter Camp, then an executive at the New Haven Clock Company, was part of a committee charged with making specific changes. Since these reformers were from the Northeast, the dominant region in both academic life and college football, they believed they were legislating for the entire country. Camp and his cronies abolished the flying wedge, yet did not end mass play altogether. Soon, coaches crafted plays to follow the law's letter, if not its intent. Even with reforms, therefore, injuries did not cease. Indeed, dangerous plays persisted in distant parts of the country where teams did not observe rules agreed upon by the "Big Three"—Harvard, Yale, and Princeton.[11]

As the Big Three tried to eliminate dangerous plays, Harvard's President Charles William Eliot drew attention to football in his annual report. At first, Eliot merely proposed six reforms: eliminate freshman squads, limit games to college-owned grounds, ban graduate students, allow each student to play only one sport per year, reduce brutality, and hold contests only in alternating years. Some of his proposals were more practical than others, but some members of Harvard's Board of Overseers were receptive. Industrialist Charles Francis Adams agreed that something should be done, since college men spent too much time and energy on football, but he was sure it would not be abolished. Some critics interpreted Eliot's proposals as a call for abolition, and some accused him of effeminacy or immaturity.[12] Even some who supported Eliot misinterpreted him. Yale law professor Simeon Baldwin commented that Eliot had "struck a hard blow" against football. The game, said Baldwin, besides being nearly as "dangerous to life and limb" as prizefighting, had "tended to lower the grade of scholarship and literary achievements" by distracting students and elevating athletes to a level of prestige formerly held only by scholarly young men. Soon, Philadelphia's Art Club held a debate where Princeton's Woodrow Wilson squared off against Cornell's Burt Wilder. Wilson, who supported football, said the game developed morality. Wilder, who opposed football, thought it had deteriorated since he played in the 1850s; yet even he believed that appropriate reforms might fix the controversial game.[13]

Eliot's 1894 critiques were not as strident as some imagined them to be, but his attack became harsher after several highly publicized, violent games. In November 1894, Yale beat Harvard in a game at Springfield, Massachusetts, characterized by an "unusual amount of bad blood and foul play." Injuries included broken bones, a "contusion of the brain," and other head wounds. By comparison, prizefighting seemed tame.[14] The next Thursday, Thanksgiving, Georgetown halfback George "Shorty" Bahen was seriously injured in a game against the Columbian Athletic Club of Washington, D.C. Bahen fractured two cervical vertebrae, with his spinal cord crushed in between. Georgetown's faculty reacted quickly and immediately banned football until new rules could reduce the risk of serious injury. Meanwhile, Bahen lingered for four months in the hospital, where surgeons operated on his spine and restored some sensation to his limbs. Fellow students organized a benefit to pay the medical bills, but by spring Bahen had become irrational and was succumbing to "nervous chills." He died on March 26. Despite the Georgetown Alumni Association's stated intent to sue, a District of Columbia coroner's jury refused to pin the blame for Bahen's death on one specific player. Although the situation was complicated by the fact that the death had occurred in a game with a noncollegiate team, it was not easy for Georgetown to maintain a high moral stance in the dispute. As the Columbians' Captain Bivens pointed out, both teams had simply played to win.[15]

More critiques ensued. Two months after Bahen's injury and the Harvard-Yale debacle, Eliot issued his 1894 annual report. He scathingly wrote that football was unsuited to college life. The rules led to "a large number of broken bones, sprains, and wrenches" and helped those who played "with reckless violence or with shrewd violations of the rules to gain thereby great advantages." The game had become too risky, and the public no longer believed that coaches could fix the sport. In fact, said Eliot, the public was part of the problem, since players were "swayed by a tyrannical public opinion" to which even the worst "gamblers and rowdies" contributed. The possibility of death was ever present, and urban spectators resembled "the throngs which enjoy the prize fight, cock fight, or bull fight, or which, in other centuries, delighted in the sports of the Roman arena." Eliot criticized the belief that more officials or penalties would solve football's problems. Not only was it difficult to find impartial officials, but a game that required such scrutiny was "not fit for genuine sportsmen." Eliot did not oppose physical culture. He merely disdained the sensationalism and expense of collegiate athletics, which now repulsed proponents of "simple and rational manly sports."[16]

By 1895, Eliot had been Harvard's president for over two decades and was one of the nation's most influential educators. His words echoed through the press, inspiring strenuous defenses of football. Walter Camp was one apologist. In 1894, after mass play reform and Eliot's initial critiques, Camp wrote *Football Facts and Figures*, a book of sympathetic testimonials and doctored statistics. Camp claimed that carriage-riding and sailing were more lethal than football, and he cited numerous authorities, including school headmasters, football players, and college professors, who proclaimed the sport's physical, mental, and moral benefits. For example, Yale mathematician Eugene Lamb Richards argued that the game made students healthier, instilled self-control, reduced discipline problems, strengthened religious faith, and created citizens who could defend their nation. Even Harvard Law Professor James Barr Ames, a contributor who thought the game too brutal, conceded that Camp's statistics would certainly show that the public overstated the "physical risks" of the game. Football's defenders often invoked the book.[17]

Younger university leaders, especially William Rainey Harper and David Starr Jordan, tended to favor football, which resembled their strenuous university-building methods. Harper made Chicago into an imposing institution by raiding other faculties, and he promoted the new venture through football. Indeed, Coach Amos Alonzo Stagg turned Chicago's Maroons into a dominant midwestern program known as the "Monsters of the Midway" long before the NFL Chicago Bears inherited that moniker. Harper, realizing football's usefulness, took a pragmatic stance on brutality. He blithely proclaimed, "If the world can afford to sacrifice the lives of men for commercial gain, it can much more easily afford to make similar sacrifices upon the altar of vigorous and unsullied manhood." Meanwhile, at Stanford, Jordan proclaimed football's positive effects on character, bodies, and intellect. Football, he said, promoted "manliness." While there were "possibilities of evil and possibilities of excess," the game had not yet reached that point. Football was "manly" and it even counteracted debilitating fin de siècle culture by cultivating "bodies as well as brains."[18]

Harper and Jordan, like many late 1800s university leaders, were well-known public figures whose statements often appeared in the press. In 1894, Presidents James B. Angell of Michigan and Jacob G. Schurman of Cornell contributed to a roundtable discussion in *The Forum* regarding football's brutality and immorality. Both saw football as a valuable sport in need of reform. Angell said it instilled "temperate and regular habits of living, vigor and agility of body, quickness of perception, readiness of resource, manly courage, skill in planning, and subordination of the individual will to the cooperation of the team." Michigan's aging president echoed antebellum Whig educators' belief in moral discipline, but he had abandoned their distrust of team sports. By claiming that football taught teamwork, Angell thus foreshadowed twentieth-century coaches, such as Michigan's Fielding H. Yost, who expressed football's numerous benefits for players and spectators. Likewise, Schurman discussed the game's positive characteristics. Cornell's president thought that football should be less brutal and not distract from study, but he also contended that since strenuous sport had "deep roots in the nature of man," as many students as possible should participate in athletics. Football, he implied, echoed human development and thus adhered to the Darwinian order of modern society.[19]

Other commentators took this idea further by explicitly connecting football to racial development. Eugene Richards, the Yale professor quoted in Camp's book, argued that football was essentially a mental game that cultivated discipline. In an 1894 issue of *Popular Science Monthly*, he said that the sport developed muscular strength as well as manliness and "quickness of mind." Like Angell, Richards also embraced teamwork. He argued that football taught submission to authority and resembled military discipline. In this usage, *discipline* meant something different than in the 1828 Yale Report. While gymnastics supposedly tamed animal spirits and trained body and mind to work together, team sports trained multiple bodies and minds to act in concert. Richards, in fact, directly tied sport to American imperialism. "For a virile race, like the Anglo-Saxon," he noted in the *Yale Medical*

Journal, "the dangerous sports have always had the greatest fascination, because they call for just those qualities which make that race the dominant race of the world. Foot-ball is one of these sports." Like other turn-of-the-century scholars, Richards argued that football augmented American virility because the stress of urban life and the overwhelming mental work of university studies wore down nerves. "The circle of knowledge has become so wide that to keep pace with its increase, the minds of our children are crammed with knowledge from morning to night." Football corrected such evils, enabling colleges to graduate "men of force and energy" who combined "strong body, energetic will and mental culture." Through strenuous sport, colleges could save civilization by preventing overcivilization. Instead of blindly following writers who opposed football, the public should read more about the game and understand its suitability for colleges.[20]

Physicians also muted fears about football, stressing instead sport's ability to develop strong, educated men. In the 1894 *Boston Medical and Surgical Journal*, Dr. William Conant (who was also quoted in Camp's book) wrote that everyone knew that no young man with an underdeveloped body could think "great thoughts." Other prominent Bostonians—including public health officials, Cambridge's mayor, and MIT's Francis Walker, who had delivered his Phi Beta Kappa oration the previous year—argued that colleges should regulate, not abolish, sport.[21] While such concerns originated in the Northeast, a fatal brain injury nearly ended football in the South. In October 1897, the University of Georgia's Richard "Von" Gammon sustained a concussion before 5,000 spectators in Atlanta, and he died the following day. Georgia and some of its rivals immediately ended their season, while Atlanta's clergy condemned football as "uncivilized" and the state legislature quickly passed a bill banning it. Yet some lawmakers, including Gammon's hometown representative, thought football should be reformed. Professor Charles Herty proclaimed that the state university needed to keep football and build a better gymnasium, which would benefit mentally overworked students who spent all day cooped up in classrooms. If the present trend continued, students would lose "vitality" and become "sluggish in brain and torpid in liver, without muscle or energy." Gammon's mother even asked that her son's death not become an excuse to end the "manly sports" that he loved. When the press called for a veto, Governor William Atkinson obliged, defending football as a sport that developed "the highest and noblest type of our race." As the Olympics had once trained men of ancient Greece, football prepared "young men for the life of today." Echoing Richards, Atkinson proclaimed, "There is no quality that a nation can less afford to lose than its aggressive manliness."[22]

Critics cared about men's bodies, but they were also concerned about commercialism and its negative effects upon universities. Even proponents argued that the game's public exposure should be limited. By the 1890s, though, it was becoming apparent that sport's meanings could not be dictated by academics. Millions of Americans attended the contests or read about football. Although most were middle-class white males, the crowd was expanding to include a number of less educated Americans as well, and this multitude often possessed little formal connection to the academy or did not share upper-class conceptions of sport's meanings. Indeed, it is likely that many readers and spectators made scarce distinction between college athletes and popular entertainers. Americans were starting to imagine football as another cultural ritual around which to construct meanings of play, work, race, and gender relations. In this climate, press coverage could be problematic. University leaders like James Angell resented newspapers that criticized colleges for ineffectively regulating football, yet sold copy by exposing scandals. Angell contended that the sport's negative aspects originated largely from sensational media attention. Young athletes who had not yet mastered the art of disciplined self-control would take questionable risks when thousands of spectators and "millions of newspaper readers" were watching. Angell and Schurman, like Eliot, argued that matches should be limited to campus, not played in large, malevolent, and distant cities. Games were for students. When it was treated as commercial entertainment, football was effectively "prostituted."[23]

The desire to remove physical culture from the gaze of paying spectators recalled Charles Beck's 1828 English translation of *Vater* Jahn's gymnastics handbook. If sport became just an entertaining urban spectacle, it would tempt students to seek easy money and play to the crowd, rather than improving their physiques and morality. We can see, though, that most late 1800s football reformers were not so much adamant about eliminating commercialism but rather were interested in simply regulating it. Regulations were often forged in regional athletic conferences, agencies that transcended institutional or state boundaries and exemplified a late 1800s era when large associations took over American life. The first formal athletic conference was the Intercollegiate Conference of Faculty Representatives, later known as the Western Conference or (depending on its number of members) the Big Nine or Big Ten. In 1895, Purdue's President James Smart proposed that the leaders of major universities in the Midwest, including Chicago, Illinois, Minnesota, Northwestern, and Wisconsin, meet to discuss football. Smart, writes historian John Watterson, wanted to reform football without giving up access to urban spectators and their money. By initiating an interstate athletic conference, he used the same logic as the 1887 Interstate Commerce Act, which regulated railroads by closing loopholes resulting from varying state policies. The Western Conference restricted competition to member institutions and crafted eligibility rules, thus protecting universities' academic reputations while at the same time monopolizing ticket sales. Other regions would later form similar regulatory agencies. Like 1800s gymnasts, the founders of the earliest athletic conferences claimed sport was pedagogy, not entertainment. They hoped to minimize corruption while preserving sport's presumptive benefits. Regional associations allowed similar educational institutions to band together, meet perpetually at regular intervals, and craft regulations to transcend local policies. But they did not necessarily try to quench Americans' desire for athletic spectacle.[24]

The unruly spectators who led universities to consolidate control over football caused problems—including injuries, deaths, or expensive lawsuits—when they crowded into fields designed primarily for profit, not safety. In the 1890s, the University of Chicago built stands on its campus athletic grounds, Marshall Field. Complications ensued when the university rented the field to other colleges, thus essentially turning it into a commercial venue located on campus. This arrangement became problematic when, in 1902, a section of the grandstands collapsed during a game between Wisconsin and Michigan. Sounding like newspaper accounts of a violent game, spectators (perhaps goaded, as one lawyer claimed, by the city's "ambulance chasers") reported broken bones and damaged nerves; some even requested free football tickets as compensation. Lawyers representing each university debated which institutions were liable: the host campus, the universities that scheduled the game, or all three? Chicago's lawyers thought it unfair that the university should receive a small sum for renting the grounds and then have to pay a greater sum in settlements. But Michigan law professor Victor Lane argued that the game was a three-way business venture. Chicago had clearly known the risks of selling tickets inviting the public into a facility located on its campus, while the Universities of Michigan and Wisconsin had acted responsibly by quickly settling claims out of court.[25] This incident proved to be a cautionary tale. Universities would eventually reduce the chance—or cost—of disaster by limiting contests to campus grounds, building sturdier structures, and buying insurance policies.

Football's popularity kept growing at the turn of the century, a time when it still had many academic proponents, such as University of California president Benjamin Ide Wheeler. More scandals, though, soon led some observers, including Wheeler and Stanford's David Starr Jordan, to change their opinions. After the turn of the century, Jordan argued that athletes who received intricate directions or special treatment could not learn football's true lessons. He did not want to ban football—he merely asked whether the game, as played, was living up to its potential. Sport should showcase players' strength and skill, not coaches' strategies. Jordan said he firmly believed in collegiate athletics, yet thought that sport lost its educational value when colleges hired "gladiators"; he would prefer that football be banished for a decade and "athletic fields closed . . . for fumigation than to see our colleges helpless in the hands of athletic professionalism," as they seemed to be in 1903. Supporters of military education also critiqued football. One observer contended that spectator sports placed Annapolis midshipmen under the "gaze" of the general public, thus distracting from their naval training.[26]

Reformers typically hoped to remove the taint of commercialism without eliminating strenuous college sport. One proposal flowed from the pen of Chicago's William Rainey Harper, who said that since football was a public relations tool, it could not be managed by students, and it should not be financed through ticket sales. It was problematic that the "physical culture and athletics" department was supported by the masses. "Shall the university depend for the support of one of its departments upon a crowd, a large proportion of which treats the game as it would treat the race-course, and patronizes it because of the opportunity which it furnishes for gambling?" Should the institution "cater thus to the lowest passions of the multitude?" The answer was no. Harper wanted to publicize the university, but he dreaded any influence the public exerted upon the academy. Not only did the wrong people patronize college sport, he argued, but the right people were no longer able to do so. Ticket prices had climbed so high that many students and faculty members could not even attend the games. The athletic department had to find a way to retain academic respectability while still paying its bills. As early as 1903, Harper broached a plan for athletic endowments to Presidents Angell (of Michigan) and Charles Van Hise (Wisconsin), and in 1904 he published a piece in *Harper's Weekly* where he reasoned that physical culture ("a regularly recognized department in many institutions, co-ordinate with other departments of the university") should receive institutional support equal to that of other departments. Such support would reduce college athletics' air of illegitimacy, reduce the intensity of rivalries, and "lift . . . physical education to a plane co-ordinate with that of intellectual education." In turn, football could become a true "gentleman's sport."[27]

Harper's desire to make football genteel was not uncommon, but his call for endowments was. Although his suggestion was idiosyncratic and did not gain many adherents, Harper seems to have understood the relationship among the academy, sport, and the public better than most of his contemporaries. Many progressives wanted to purify football and remove the taint of the crowd from college life, but they were loath to cut off the cash flow sport provided. Many seemed to want a profitable yet pure spectacle, a game that made huge sums of money while simultaneously demonstrating a commitment to discipline. But Harper was more realistic. He knew that the only way to preserve culturally valuable strenuous physical activity without corrupting universities was to find a steady revenue source not derived from the masses. Yet even if it demonstrated a realistic understanding of the complexity of intercollegiate athletics, Harper's proposal itself was un-

William Rainey Harper built the University of Chicago's academic reputation and also initiated big-time athletics at the institution. In the early 1900s, he proposed endowments for athletics so that college football could remain respectable as well as popular. Special Collections Research Center, University of Chicago Library.

realistic. Many universities dependent upon football revenue or publicity did not possess benefactors with pockets as bottomless as those of Chicago tycoons like John D. Rockefeller, Charles Yerkes, or Marshall Field. Indeed, the *Chicago Tribune* reported the laconic response from Ann Arbor and Madison: "Where can we get the $500,000?"[28]

As Harper's proposal for athletic endowments made little impact, anti-football opinion mounted in the early 1900s. Newspapers reported at least fifteen players dead in 1902, and another fourteen in 1903 (although many were high school students and several did not actually die). The year of crisis was 1905, when football, like pure food and drugs the following year, became a target of progressive reform. Some of the loudest voices calling for reform were familiar. Eliot continued to argue that sport distracted from academics; showcased "brawny" bodies rather than "slighter, quick witted men"; and encouraged immoral behavior.[29] One new critic was President Theodore Roosevelt, who had recently mediated an end to the Russo-Japanese War and supported the Hepburn Act, which bolstered the Interstate Commerce Act. In October 1905, Roosevelt called representatives from Harvard, Yale, and Princeton to the White House. This group included Walter Camp, who had attended Yale when Roosevelt was at Harvard. The president was particularly sensitive to football's dangers. His son, Ted, had recently been injured while playing on Harvard's freshman team. Roosevelt liked football, but thought his guests should work to reform the game so it embodied "fair play"—not brutality. He wanted young men to play manly sports, but he also hoped to protect them from the physical and moral effects of the strenuous life. He was aware that public opinion against football brutality was rising, and that gridiron deaths would eventually cause football's demise. Camp and others assured Roosevelt that they would implement reforms.[30]

Roosevelt's call for reform was widely publicized. And while Eliot was skeptical that men who had long been aware of the sport's negative aspects could successfully implement reform, others were more optimistic. Cornell's President Schurman argued that Roosevelt was an ideal leader for athletic reform and suggested that a convention of university representatives be held in Washington. Some commentators even proposed a national governing body, a "Supreme Court" or "National Board of Review" that would oversee amateur athletics. The members of this hypothetical body might include Roosevelt and Eliot, as well as Presidents Harper of Chicago, Jordan of Stanford, Angell of Michigan, Arthur Twining Hadley of Yale, Woodrow Wilson of Princeton, Nicholas Murray Butler of Columbia, and Francis Preston Venable of North Carolina. Amateur sport luminaries like James E. Sullivan and Luther Gulick of the Amateur Athletic Union and Caspar Whitney of *The Outing* might also serve on the board. This body would set eligibility standards and serve as a "court of final resort," thus protecting amateur sport's potential.[31] While this national, progressive agency was not actually formed, a national convention was soon held in New York City that would lead to sweeping changes.

Reforms happened, in large part, because of the 1905 season's sensational violence. That year, eighteen men died on college and high school gridirons. In the highly publicized Harvard-Yale game on November 25, a Yale defender broke a Harvard ball carrier's nose on a late hit. The same day, Union College's Harold Moore died of a cerebral hemorrhage in a contest against New York University. NYU's Chancellor Henry MacCracken, shocked at Moore's death and even more incensed at accusations against the NYU team, called for football's reform or abolition. He outlined three reasons for ending the sport as then played. First, it was murderous; while other sports might cause injuries or fatalities, football caused both deaths and "subtle injuries to the physical organs" that might prove to be even worse than death. Second, only a few large, skilled "gladiators" were able to play the game and benefit from exercise. Third, and most damningly, football had become a commercial spectacle unsuitable for institutions of higher learning. MacCracken made a striking comparison. Suppose Americans learned "that the great universities of Germany had decided to permit the student corps to fight their duels before grandstands full of spectators in Berlin or Vienna for $2 admission per head! Would it not degrade them at once from their high esteem?" Americans, said MacCracken, were so obsessed with moneymaking that they were willing to overlook the "sordid characteristics" of intercollegiate football and the shadow it was casting over the nation's universities.[32]

Football's critics were already primed for outrage, since the middle-class reform press had recently published muckraking articles about football. In summer 1905, *McClure's Magazine*, which had published Lincoln Steffens's influential "Shame of the Cities" municipal reform articles two years earlier, issued a piece by Henry Beach Needham on football's commercialism and professionalism. Needham critiqued the coaches who had to win at all costs. Along with alumni and undergraduates who were hungry for football victories, professional coaches and trainers were destroying college athletes. Equally critical of college football commercialism was Edward S. Jordan, a young Milwaukee newspaper reporter and University of Wisconsin alumnus who wrote four articles published in *Collier's* in November 1905 as "Buying Football Victories." This series, very similar to Steffens's earlier muckraking pieces, exposed midwestern football's impurity. Jordan wrote that coaches' recruiting practices turned players into "grafter[s]," and he uncovered an $80,000 slush fund at Chicago. Corruption permeated the region's colleges, he said, including the public universities that were supposed to be fostering progressive reforms on the state and municipal levels. He particularly targeted university administrators like Minnesota's Cyrus Northrup who prized popularity over morality and allied themselves with the "bleacher crowd" rather than with progressive ideals. Even worse, Jordan charged the University of Wisconsin in Madison, a bastion of progressivism, with fielding pro players and enrolling athletes in "snap" (or blow-off) courses. A law professor even arranged state sinecures for athletes who "packed political mass meetings, cheered and hissed speakers in turn, and gained a livelihood by a perversion of the fundamental principles of the service of the State." Clearly, college football was not living up to its progressive potential.[33]

The confluence of deaths, injuries, media outrage, and White House attention led to a movement, or a congeries of movements, to banish football's evils. The most enduring football reform was the creation of a national supervisory agency. In response to MacCracken's call, on December 8 (two weeks after the violence of November 25 and not long after the publication of Jordan's articles), representatives from thirteen colleges convened in New York City. Union College, NYU, and Columbia favored abolition, but they were in the minority. Delegates from the U.S. Military Academy at West Point, along with seven other colleges, rallied in favor of football. Three weeks later, sixty institutions from the East and Midwest convened at a larger conference, which created the Intercollegiate Athletic Association of the United States (IAAUS). This organization was renamed the National Collegiate Athletic Association (NCAA) in 1910. At the first annual meeting in 1906, the group's president, West Point's Major Palmer Pierce, articulated their progressive aim to make football safer and more moral. He observed that institutions all over the nation had "banded together to control more effectively college athletic sports in the interest of educational work, and of amateur standards"; by establishing a new rules committee, they had made "a vast improvement in the game of football, both in regard to the risks to life and limb [that] were felt to have been too great, and especially in the better moral tone of the play." Amos Alonzo Stagg, Chicago's head coach and professor of athletics, also touted that the organization would raise standards of "honesty, fair play, and manliness."[34] The IAAUS pursued this goal by proposing new rules and adding better officials. But the delegates were not satisfied with a few modifications. They wanted to construct an organization to perpetuate the process of reform. While the IAAUS's founders intended it as a *"governing* body," they soon realized the impossibility of imposing their will on many institutions. Instead, they shaped it into an *advisory* body that promoted amateurism and discouraged commercialism.[35]

The IAAUS created a new football rules committee, which cooperated with Camp's older group. Based on a suggestion from Bill Reid and others at Harvard, this joint rules committee considered several major reforms: increase the number of yards necessary for a first down from five to ten; raise the number of attempts to achieve a first down from three to four; add a neutral zone between the teams (so officials could spot rule infractions); and legalize the forward pass. According to sport historians, the forward pass, the most innovative of these new rules, was intended to reduce brutality and create a more "open" style of play, thus making football safer and more exciting.[36] But it was also about promoting disciplined play, reducing unethical conduct, and therefore making the game more honest and transparent. According to some proponents, the more open style of play would allow for more efficient surveillance by spreading players out on the field and subjecting the game to public scrutiny. One writer even argued that open play did not result in fewer injuries, but it still produced better football, since it enabled referees to "see the character of every man's play" and more easily punish players for breaking rules. In such a game, play would unfold in a disciplined, moral, and fair manner.[37] Like the 1906 Meat Inspection Act, the new rule was designed to make football's conduct visible to authorities and the public—and thus subject to regulation, reform, and punishment, if necessary. It also foreshadowed Woodrow Wilson's 1919 "Fourteen Points," which proclaimed that nations should conduct international relations via "open covenants." The forward pass would also minimize the effectiveness of sheer force, thus reducing the number of concussions and spinal injuries, while at the same time reintroducing the element of chance. Unlike mass plays, which helped teams retain possession of the ball and methodically gain ground a few yards at a time, the riskier forward pass could result in a range of outcomes: large or small amounts of gained yardage, an incomplete pass, or an interception. In this way, the new type of play was similar to Roosevelt's trust-busting efforts, which broke up monopolies and restored market competition. In 1908, *The Outlook* even argued that the open game gave smaller colleges a chance to compete; in 1914, the *New York Times* observed that "luck" was a major factor in the forward pass era.[38]

Initially, the impact of the 1905–1906 reforms was limited, mostly because of the continued presence of the old committee. Camp resisted the forward pass and critiqued it as an unscientific tactic that reintroduced an element of chance that his reforms had effectively eliminated in the 1880s. But by 1910, as younger rulemakers grew in national stature and influence and older ones became less prominent, even Camp grudgingly admitted that the forward pass had become scientific.[39] The IAAUS represented, in many ways, the triumph of Progressive Era reform over Gilded Age excesses. It was a national organization, created when universities banded together to reduce the influence of the market and untutored public opinion upon intercollegiate football. Through this agency, educators tried to limit popular influence on big-time sport, a lucrative university activity that individual institutions could not easily control. By providing a forum in which many institutions spread out over a large geographic area discussed reforms and collectively issued guidelines, the IAAUS was a national reform organization that resembled other progressive bodies. This analogy was not lost on its founders. Pierce explained:

This Association is the one means existing for organized effort for improvement of collegiate athletics throughout this country. Modern civilization demands concentration. As a result there have arisen all sorts of societies and associations. . . . There is scarcely a trade or profession which has not a general organization. The doctors, the lawyers, the dentists, the engineers, have organized with certain definite ends in view. . . . Labor and capital have found it advisable to form so-called unions and trusts. The latest addition is the proposed organization of a National Health Society, announced in the New Year's Papers.[40]

Modern society's greatest reforms did not happen via radical action, and the IAAUS was no exception. The apparatus of change in a nation connecting far-flung "island communities" together had to be bulky and, preferably, national in scope.[41] While the Western Conference was a regional attempt by several universities to reform football jointly, the IAAUS encompassed the whole nation. At its annual convention, delegates gathered to analyze college athletics and suggest regulations that regional conferences or individual institutions might adopt. The organization also encouraged all American colleges to join, so it could have the widest possible influence. If this goal were achieved, it would be nearly impossible for a few institutions to evade reform. At the time of the IAAUS's founding, the only significant progressive characteristic that college athletics lacked was a cadre of professional experts. But coaches and athletic directors, the experts who shaped a national profession with distinct standards, expectations, and specialized discourse, were already starting to appear at this time, as we will see.

The IAAUS/NCAA became the dominant voice in football reform, but it was not the only one. Several alternate reforms were suggested in the early 1900s. While some never took off, others lasted until the World War I era. In October 1905, shortly after Roosevelt called for reform, a British association football (soccer) team, the "Pilgrims," toured the United States and Canada, hoping to add international competition by persuading American colleges to convert to the kicking game.[42] While this potentially dramatic change to intercollegiate football was not implemented, a similar change did happen on the West Coast, where several colleges replaced the "American" game with rugby. This seismic shift was inspired by problems similar to those plaguing the East, but took a different turn in California, which had its own progressive attitudes and movements. A few days after the disastrous Saturday in November when Harold Moore died and the Harvard-Yale game was marred by the late hit, Benjamin Ide Wheeler wrote Yale and Harvard, calling for concerted action. West Coast universities could not easily go their own way because their students had to play the same sort of football embraced elsewhere in America. Californians were in a unique position because they wanted to preserve intersectional competition, but they had little say in national reforms because of their relatively isolated location. By December, unhappy with the direction of football, Stanford and Berkeley officials convened to discuss reform. They were particularly interested in adopting New Zealand–style rugby. Wheeler warned Yale that he would go so far as to create an entirely "separate Pacific Coast football game" and insisted in the *Los Angeles Times* that a new game should be created.[43]

A long-standing proponent of physical culture, Wheeler had served as a judge at the 1896 Olympics in Athens; and while a Cornell classics professor in the mid-1890s, he attended at least one Cornell-Harvard game in Manhattan. By 1906, though, he was done with football. In the *American Review of Reviews*, edited by Albert Shaw, Wheeler commented that although football could develop "manliness," it had become a sport of military violence and industrial precision. Teams were "rampart-like lines of human flesh," with the offense firing "a missile composed of four or five human bodies . . . with a maximum of initial velocity against the presumably weakest point in the opposing rampart." Such exertion was dangerous, its monotony demoralizing and stultifying to athletes who had become "cogs in a machine." Football was a spectacle maintained for its ability to generate revenue and ersatz "college spirit," not bona fide physical culture. The game had become a profit machine that endangered students.[44] Rugby, which was established and was known to entice many men onto the playing field, was Wheeler's solution. By contrast, he said, the post-1905 version of American football was an unknown quantity, a mere collection of scribbled-down rules that might or might not work on the field. Rugby also gave West Coast schools new outlets for competition. According to Wheeler, rugby was "played all around the globe: New Zealand, Australia, British Columbia, Canada, Scotland, Wales, England and Ireland." The game was common and tested; "hundreds of thousands" watched or enjoyed it regularly.[45]

In March 1906, a joint Stanford-Berkeley committee formally recommended switching to Canadian- or Australian-style rugby until American football was satisfactorily reformed.[46] It is not clear that rugby advocates originally intended this switch to be permanent, but by 1907 it was. Rugby's staying power may have been aided by the 1906 earthquake that rocked San Francisco less than four weeks after the decision to abandon football. The quake destroyed much of the city, as well as Stanford's campus. The post-catastrophe moment was a time of optimism. William James, then a visiting professor at Stanford, considered the earthquake a "'god-given' opportunity to re-launch" the university, and Jordan told students just hours after the tremor that Stanford would rebuild. New football rules were part of this process. By November, one Bay Area observer even suggested that Californians should create an entirely new game reflecting their determination to rebuild.[47] Although this game was never created, rugby did persist. Its partisans argued that rugby was more interesting and less injurious than football, involved more players, and was less commercial. Wheeler asked students to come down from their "sedentary" spot in the stands to "get health and fun and virility out of the heartiest and manliest of the Anglo-Saxon sports."[48] Jordan tapped Progressive Era discourses about the nervous system (as well as his own Darwinian peace eugenics) in arguing for rugby. He claimed that rugby injuries, unlike those in American football, were mostly superficial. In 1907, Jordan even traveled to Australia with two Stanford coaches to observe rugby. Subsequently, he waged a campaign, with Wheeler and Stanford psychology professor Frank Angell, to convert colleges and high schools in California, Nevada, Oregon, and Washington to the game. At first, many students resisted change, especially in Southern California, which had not felt the 1906 quake. But eventually much of the West shifted, albeit temporarily, to rugby.[49]

While many West Coast schools briefly replaced American-style football with rugby, other colleges responded differently to early 1900s scandals and reforms. The University of Michigan, to protest seemingly oppressive conference regulations, withdrew from the Big Nine. Michigan's Board in Control of Athletics was particularly upset about conference regulations that outlawed the training table, cut the season to five games, gave faculty control of athletics, and limited player eligibility to three years. Many Michigan partisans perceived these rules as a strategy for smaller colleges, like Purdue and Indiana, to limit the Wolverines' ability to train winning teams and garner athletic revenue. While some Ann Arbor faculty supported the new regulations, many students and trustees favored withdrawal. They wanted Michigan to compete against elite eastern institutions, like Harvard or Yale, rather than midwestern state universities. Michigan thus left the conference in January 1908 and would not return until the eve of America's involvement in the Great War. As the Chicago press pointed out, though, Michigan's independence posed its own problems. The University of Pennsylvania, apparently, was the lone northeastern power willing to play the Wolverines on their home field. Only a motley collection of football's "lesser lights" would play at Ann Arbor, including Vanderbilt, Oberlin (then a relatively large university), and Ohio State (not yet part of the Big Nine).[50]

Reactions or reforms like those in California and at Michigan turned out to be somewhat idiosyncratic, but this was not necessarily by design. David Starr Jordan, for instance, actually tried to convert all American colleges to rugby. In 1908, he sent Wisconsin's Charles Van Hise a letter proposing two major reforms. First, the whole nation should switch to rugby. This would virtually eliminate dangerous brain or spinal injuries, while at the same time strengthening a greater number of young men's bodies. Second, universities should band together to eliminate professional coaches, so as to banish monetary influence and the victory-at-all-costs mentality. After all, a paid coach often evaded the rules so he could "justify his existence" by winning more games. Jordan sent copies of his letter to hundreds of colleges, and the response was overwhelming. Most replies were positive, although a few were unintentionally comical (Jordan did not include a cover letter, and several recipients returned it upon seeing Van Hise's name). Many encouraged Jordan's efforts or expressed interest in rugby; a few even reported that they had already abolished the game. But it is clear that resignation lurked in the pens of several college administrators who did not believe that substantial changes could occur, or that they could last. Ohio University's president agreed it was time to "curb" athletics, but he also noted that he had recently given up the fight at his own institution and merely focused on "mitigating the evils of the professional athletics" by controlling the football team's finances. The head of a Missouri college noted that small schools could not reform sport without help from larger universities.[51] Such skeptics understood that the modern academy was based in institutional networks led by increasingly research-oriented universities, and that reform was led by groups. Progressive change happened via orchestrated action, not drastic or sudden shifts at a few institutions. Indeed,

Stanford's rural West Coast location and persistent financial problems left it too weak to lead a movement challenging mainstream football. By contrast, reforms introduced via national organizations mitigated football's biggest problems, even if they could not truly solve them.

Like other college leaders, Van Hise was hesitant to make the major changes Jordan proposed because he believed that reform would only result from widespread cooperation and gradual change within established structures, including the Big Nine athletic conference. Van Hise noted that if Wisconsin adopted rugby and abolished professional coaches while the rest of the conference did not, the only remaining course of action would be to leave the Big Nine. This was an extreme action that Wisconsin was not willing to take.[52] Van Hise's caution in embracing Jordan's rugby reform was telling. Administrators wanted to clean up football, the same way politicians and muckrakers tried to purify consumer goods such as pharmaceuticals or meat. But they did not want to get left behind, and they did not want reforms to thwart ambition. For example, an institution that did not field a team playing by standard rules limited the scope of its competition and could not compete in postseason games like the Pasadena Rose Bowl (first held in 1902 and played annually after 1916). Regionally, if Wisconsin dropped football for rugby, while Minnesota or Chicago did not, both the state and its university would cut off possibilities to demonstrate manly sporting merit. While some saw football's brutality and commercialism as threatening, others understood that the game's ability to attract spectators and media attention held potential. University leaders chose a course that seemed safer than scrapping the game and replacing it with a different one. Since national and regional associations seemed to be improving football, there was little incentive to follow a solitary or narrow path toward reform.

Jordan's proposal also found little support because coaching, by 1908, was becoming a semirespectable profession of trained and earnest athletic experts. Jordan would pay coaches only if they were alumni or students, and then only under a contract limited to four years. But Charles Van Hise was less concerned about professional coaches because he did not necessarily see them as journeymen not dedicated to academic ideals. Rather, echoing a professional self-image that coaches consciously cultivated, Van Hise optimistically concluded that the situation was looking up because the "present group of men who are connected with athletics in the university seem to be a very nice set of fellows." While Jordan wanted to keep coaches from gaining permanent positions, Van Hise would embrace professional coaches as long as they became a part of the university.[53] This ambivalence over coaching would soon be expressed in the NCAA. In 1910, the national organization rejected professional coaches, recommending instead that universities place sport (as important "as any other line of university or college work") under faculty auspices. Presumably, faculty control would banish "all taint of professionalism and commercial spirit" from college athletics.[54] But some NCAA delegates, like Purdue social scientist Thomas Moran, were at this time taking the recommendation for faculty control in a different direction. As we will see, Moran proposed that professional coaches could be like faculty members. Once coaches constituted a respectable class equal to academic scholars, he argued, they would make college athletics safe for students, universities, and the public.

David Starr Jordan's call for the national adoption of rugby and elimination of coaches was not particularly influential. As it turns out, moreover, West Coast rugby was more susceptible to commercialization than its idealistic proponents would have admitted. As Walter Camp (Stanford's occasional football coach in the 1890s) pointed out, American football had originated as rugby in the 1870s. There was no guarantee that rugby would not change again, or succumb once more to professional coaching. Moreover, it is ironic, considering rugby proponents' amateur idealism, that Stanford and Berkeley invited professional teams from Vancouver and New Zealand to play exhibition games and teach students how to play. Thus, at the same time these universities were withdrawing from mainstream college football partly because of its popular appeal, they were forging ties to commercial sport in Britain's Pacific Rim empire. In 1906, A. H. Baskerville, a professional rugby player, author, and the self-proclaimed "Walter Camp of New Zealand," sent a long, rambling message to Jordan that encouraged him to send Stanford's team to play a game before 30,000 spectators in Sydney. Baskerville even implored Stanford's president to hire him as coach at a $5,000 annual salary, a rate at which he guaranteed his "organisation" could beat any eastern team (or even Oxford and

Cambridge, for that matter). It seems that Jordan seriously entertained Baskerville's proposal. Apparently, New Zealand's premier footballer was not aware that rugby was inherently an amateur game—and Jordan may not have been totally convinced, either.[55]

For some observers, the switch from the American game to the healthier and ostensibly more relaxing game of rugby was a step forward in the natural progression of college sport. In 1907, Dr. T. M. Williams, a former Stanford football player, joked that under the old rules the only players killed were the best athletes, who were intentionally targeted by opposing players. Since this type of play defied David Starr Jordan's peace activism—which, based in Darwinian biology and eugenics, said that the end of warfare would result in a better and stronger human population—rugby reform demonstrated that West Coast society was following the mandate of evolutionary biology and had thus "advanced one step further on the road to civilization." One might debate whether or not rugby was truly evidence of civilization's forward progress, but for a decade many West Coast schools played it exclusively. Stanford and Cal held their Big Game as a rugby match from 1906 to 1914, and Santa Clara College also became a Bay Area rugby power. These colleges, though, returned to the old game during the World War I era.[56]

Even with all of the reform movements that emerged after 1905, not all of American football's problems disappeared; neither did its critics. The 1909 season was particularly bad. Earlier reforms like the forward pass did not eliminate mass play, so ball carriers were still injured when they were pushed and pulled by fellow players. Injuries and deaths were once more on the rise. In all, eleven college players died that season, including the well-publicized deaths of West Point's Eugene Byrne (spinal injury versus Harvard) and Virginia's Archer Christian (brain hemorrhage against Georgetown). Quarterback Edwin Wilson of the Naval Academy nearly died from injuries sustained in a game with Villanova. The fact that two of these deaths happened to student athletes at the service academies led to renewed critique of football's role in officer training. In *The Independent*, William Everett Hicks lambasted football as "detrimental" to cadets. The game was injurious, and it was possible that damage caused by a concussion would lie hidden for years before showing its effects. The army

Army-Navy game at the Polo Grounds in New York, 1916. Service academy football was controversial by the early 1900s, because it might injure cadets or midshipmen, thus making them unfit for military service. Library of Congress, Prints & Photographs Division.

needed strong bodies to win battles, and football was not achieving this end. He noted that the modern military employed all kinds of precautions that soldiers had once scorned, such as mosquito nets and flannel bandages. Similar protective practices should be extended to sport so that men's bodies and minds were preserved on the athletic field. Soccer would even be a better sport for West Point, Hicks argued, since it would allow men to survive to fight on actual battlefields one day.[57]

University presidents once again weighed the need for football reform in the middle-class muckraking journals. *Collier's* cited Brown's clergyman president William H. P. Faunce, who sounded like a pre–Civil War Whig moral philosopher when he argued that football aroused the "baser passions"; the magazine also quoted Ohio State University president William O. Thompson, who saw football's "moral risks" as problematic as its "physical dangers." Gridiron carnage, combined with this academic soul searching, inspired more reforms. In 1909, the presidents of the Big Three (A. Lawrence Lowell of Harvard, Arthur T. Hadley of Yale, and Woodrow Wilson of Princeton) conferred. They knew that the rules and reforms they shaped would apply to football in the Northeast, but they also expected to affect national policy. Wilson thought that the game was too dangerous and brutal. It would be best if the Big Three "could meet public opinion in this matter and effect some reform that would save a very noble game." Wilson's optimistic expectation may have been true five or ten years earlier. But even though the Big Three were still very influential in shaping both academics and athletics in 1909, times were changing. Hadley distrusted Palmer Pierce and blamed him for the shortcomings of the 1905 reforms, but even he must have noticed that the soon-to-be-renamed IAAUS was gaining influence. Harvard had joined the association in 1909, news that had stirred unease in New Haven, but Lowell assured Hadley—perhaps disingenuously—that Harvard's IAAUS membership did not affect the rules under which the Crimson played football.[58]

In any case, the early NCAA certainly did reshape intercollegiate athletics. Although critics still spoke against football, the vast public outcry of 1905 dissipated, and the modern form of college football and athletic control began to emerge by 1910. The NCAA's new rules committee, influenced by younger coaches like Minnesota's Henry Williams and Princeton's Bill Roper, finally gained power over aging pioneers like Camp. By 1910, new rules made the forward pass a more effective offensive field tactic. Once limited to the middle of the field and restricted near the goals, now teams could pass anywhere on the gridiron. To accommodate expanded usage of the forward pass, end zones were carved out of the existing field. So that colleges with permanent stands, like Harvard, would not have to reconfigure or abandon their stadiums, the field was shortened by ten yards, thus absorbing the end zones. In addition, the ball was elongated so it would be easier to pass. Because of these reforms and the increasing influence of the NCAA, after about 1911, there would be fewer challenges to college football, and fewer major attempts to overhaul its fundamental rules.[59]

Football's rise and reform reflected the state of American culture, politics, and academic structure in the late 1800s. Its rules were the product of a rational, industrial approach to sport, a cultural orientation that helped explain football's widespread appeal. Although academic leaders touted the seemingly endless pedagogical benefits of sport and relished the attention it gave their institutions, they feared the influence of popular spectacle. Crowds and money could damage universities that were trying to exert positive public influence by creating useful, modern knowledge. The next two chapters show how academics working within modern, disciplinary universities theorized football's meanings and also contributed to discussions about reform. Psychologists focused on the nervous system, while social scientists discussed public morality. Both groups were engaged in debates over collegiate sport's utility at the same time they were helping to create the structures and safeguards of America's academic ivory tower. In the modern academy, each group of specialists created a discipline with its own epistemology, methodology, and discourse (or jargon). This fragmented intellectual milieu contributed to Progressive Era football reform, but it also created a realm where athletics became just one more university department—and popular culture started to gain a permanent place on campus.

CHAPTER 3

Psychologists: Body, Mind, and the Creation of Discipline

In 1888, University of Iowa philosophy professor George T. W. Patrick wrote that Americans needed to reshape their "notions about the relation of body and mind."[1] One of many middle-class men who suffered from the fin de siècle malady *neurasthenia*, or nervous exhaustion, Patrick explored the meanings of work, play, and mental health throughout his career. He identified sport as a way to counter the mentally draining effects of a rigorous, modern education that was becoming grounded in an overwhelming number of disciplines. This conclusion was only appropriate, since the scholars who worked to unlock the mysteries of the nervous system were themselves enmeshed in transatlantic webs of research and gaining academic positions in departments of psychology, philosophy, physiology, and pedagogy. Within these disparate yet related fields, modern intellectuals theorized a world where mind and body were intimately yet tenuously connected via the nerves. As such, they plumbed the meanings of physical culture and college athletics, arguing that strenuous games like football could aid society by building young men's bodies and thus preparing them for the stresses of modern life. It could also inspire white, male, middle-class spectators to participate in the strenuous physical activities that would help them maintain their supposed position at the top of an evolutionary hierarchy. But to be beneficial, sport had to be played safely, with no danger to the central nervous system. Football had to be reformed. Psychologists provided a key part of the intellectual foundation for Progressive Era football reforms, but the institutional and disciplinary structures they were simultaneously creating also signaled a change in the order of American higher education. Scholars were helping to turn the university into a rational and orderly gridiron of departments, presaging an era when the athletic field—itself measured and laid out in an orderly gridiron— would be one of the few campus spaces culturally accessible to most nonacademic Americans.

It helps to start out with the modern history of the discipline of psychology, which is rooted in the fields of philosophy and physiology. In the early nineteenth century, mental philosophers began studying the "science of the soul." By the late 1800s this field became the science of the nervous system, the organ where mind and body intersected. This materialistic approach originated in midcentury Germany, where scientists like Hermann von Helmholtz and Carl Ludwig crafted biological laws for the human body.[2] Charles Darwin's theory of natural selection, published in 1859, augmented this approach. *The Origin of Species* led thinkers to theorize the mind's organic, not supernatural, basis. The brain and nervous system had apparently evolved as individuals suited to the rigors of life reproduced and perpetuated their biological characteristics. This idea had serious implications. If the human mind developed and adapted as the result of chance mutations, not divine decrees, the likelihood of an immortal soul was seriously diminished. Once scholars saw the mind as a mere product of biology, it became difficult to believe in absolute, divine truth. Influenced by natural selection, thinkers such as William James laid the foundations of pragmatic philosophy and modern psychology. Each mind was not part of an entity with physical, mental, and spiritual elements—it existed in a physical body operating within social matrices.[3] The nerves, not the soul, were the seat of intellect, sensation, and volition. This idea made Whig faculty psychology obsolete. By the late 1800s, many scholars saw the mind as a survival tool rather than a collection of disciplined, rational faculties that deduced truth. The brain was an organic creator of thought and behavior, not the divine seat of righteousness. Scholarship was not a gateway to one heavenly truth. It was a means of crafting a multitude of truths through induction, observation, and experimentation.

According to late 1800s psychologists, the evolutionary mind was fragile, perhaps too fragile for modern mental work. One physician who made this argument was S. Weir Mitchell, a Philadelphia doctor who first gained fame by studying Civil War gunshot wounds and nervous injuries. Mitchell reiterated his findings in fiction and popular nonfiction, including *Wear and Tear* (1871). He also invented an infamous "rest cure" for hysterical women that was, in many cases, worse than the disease. Mitchell (like George Beard, who coined the term *neurasthenia* in 1869) explained that mental work fatigued the brain, not just the muscles.[4] Mental fatigue could quietly overtax minds, sap men of nervous energy and procreative capacity, and thus imperil Anglo-American civilization. Psychologists such as G. Stanley Hall even saw strenuous sport as a way to preserve young male bodies and minds from nervous fatigue. This argument echoed the refrain of *mens sana in corpore sano*, a Victorian credo that permeated both high-brow and lowbrow literature.[5] Many used this phrase, best translated as "a sound mind in a sound body," to explain the importance of exercise. They included President Theodore Roosevelt, whom *The Outlook* magazine dubbed the nation's best proponent of *mens sana in corpore sano*, as well as the German-born strongman Eugen Sandow, who coauthored the illustrated book *Sandow on Physical Training* (1894). Teachers also embraced the concept of strengthening the body to maintain the mind. When late 1800s educators split subjects into separate fields, students were confronted with an exponentially increasing amount of specialized information. This, in turn, led to mental fatigue, which inspired schools and colleges to prescribe physical culture.[6]

Late 1800s students often argued that sound minds needed sound bodies. For example, a Yale student warned in 1866 that a college man, if he did not have access to a gymnasium, could easily overtax his mind. But such pessimism did not last long, thanks to the rise of physical culture. A Harvard student, foreshadowing Francis Walker's 1893 Phi Beta Kappa speech, rejoiced in 1867 that a new "enthusiasm for sports" distinguished post–Civil War students, who no longer burned the "midnight oil" so intensely that they forgot they had bodies. In a similar vein, University of Michigan students, who posited a "close and sympathetic union" between body and mind, petitioned (albeit unsuccessfully) for a gymnasium that would rescue manly nervous systems from the insanity caused by rigorous studies.[7] An Ann Arbor student even made the extravagant claim in 1868 that a student who graduated with too much intellect would be a mere shell of a man. He would never "know full manhood nor have the courage of a woman; with a shattered nervous system" he would "tremble if a door slams, a dog barks, or child shouts." But exercise could prevent such mental wreckage. "We should exercise mind and body," he said, "developing them both together, [and] make the latter a perfect instrument for the use of the former." It should be shameful, he said, for "any institution of learning to send forth graduated, pale-faced, constitutionally ruined young men."[8]

Perhaps such proclamations were just grandstanding, overstatements so that administrators would give students facilities where they could play fun games. Even if this was the case, students successfully tapped real concerns by using the rhetoric of fragile nerves, and they may have even believed that physical culture would actually save their minds. Colleges responded favorably to these demands by building gymnasia or making older facilities more accessible. In 1873, for example, Harvard eliminated its gymnasium fee; in 1879 it built the state-of-the-art Hemenway Gymnasium. In 1892, Yale's new gymnasium, advertised as the world's best, debuted. Ten years later the University of Chicago built Bartlett Gymnasium, which even had a faculty exercise room. Athletic director Amos Alonzo Stagg proclaimed that this gymnasium would create mentally and physically sound men whose strong physiques and "robust" minds could tackle life's challenges. Meanwhile, Michigan and Stanford built separate gymnasia for men and women.[9] Physical education facilities were segregated by sex because of the era's prevailing beliefs about male-female physiology. Thinkers like S. Weir Mitchell and Harvard's Edward H. Clarke contended that female education diverted energy from reproductive organs, and thus could rob girls of their procreative capability. Such ideas met resistance, yet colleges still used them to limit the female curriculum. And separate spheres still reigned supreme in turn-of-the-century women's athletics, despite the efforts of female physical educators like Stanford's Dr. Clelia Mosher.[10]

Girls, according to physicians such as Mitchell, were not supposed to exercise, but these doctors endorsed men's sport because it could prepare men for business careers. Yet they still worried that improperly supervised activities—including overly strenuous football—might hinder bodily development. Addressing this concern, Morton Prince, a Boston City Hospital nerve specialist who had played football at Harvard in the 1870s, contributed a piece on "Possible Injuries to the Nervous System" to the 1896 book *Football* by Walter Camp and Lorin Deland. Prince declared football safe for brains and spinal cords (and received a complimentary copy of the book). Yet Prince remained ambivalent about football's effects upon nerves. Even though he acknowledged that hard hits might cause traumatic neuroses similar to "railway spine," a mental malady caused by railroad accidents, he claimed that team doctors had never seen such injuries.[11] In order to further examine this question, Prince surveyed six football programs and published the results in a *Boston Medical and Surgical Journal* article that appeared in 1898, a year after Georgia halfback Von Gammon died from a concussion. Prince argued that severe impacts were not likely to cause psychological damage, since football players knew in advance that they placed themselves in danger. Prince's argument was not convincing, and he even briefly acknowledged that one doctor had recently documented that football injuries led to neuroses. Yet his premises demonstrate why he made this contradictory claim: Prince was asking whether naval battles would cause neuroses in sailors. Unlike women who fainted after railroad accidents, he concluded, men remained stoic under the stress of war, industry, and sport.[12]

Football was a convenient analogy, a metaphor that seemed to prove men's combat readiness in an imperial era. It helps to recall that this was a time when Theodore Roosevelt touted the "strenuous life"; William James called for a "moral equivalent of war"; and Stephen Crane based his war story *The Red Badge of Courage* (1895) in part upon his college football experience.[13] Whether men worked in industry or served in the military, their nerves seemed to be conduits for the mental energy needed to build and expand modern society. This idea became common in turn-of-the-century discussions of football reform, at a time when psychologists began to inhabit the numerous college towns where the sport was played on autumn Saturdays. Many of these scholars trained in the laboratories of European researchers like Vienna physiologist Carl Ludwig or Leipzig psychologist Wilhelm Wundt, the so-called father of psychology.[14] Wundt's many students included Harvard physiologist Henry P. Bowditch, who also studied with Ludwig and taught noteworthy students like William James, G. Stanley Hall, and physiologist Warren Lombard. Wundt also directly taught Hall, Lombard, G. T. W. Patrick, Hugo Münsterberg, and Frank Angell. Hall, in turn, mentored Patrick, John Dewey, and William Lowe Bryan. These intellectuals were professional academics, immersed within a transatlantic network of physiological psychology.

They researched and taught within increasingly narrow academic disciplines. Due to this process of intellectual fragmentation, we will see, universities eventually sought novel forms of public engagement, such as intercollegiate athletics. And some of these thinkers were vocal proponents of college football.

Universities became fragmented and departmentalized because they were embracing the modern division of labor by the late 1800s. At this time, fields once occupied by lightly trained philosophers or clerics were becoming disciplines mastered by rigorously trained academics with earned doctorates and pragmatic orientations. The production of ideas, said late 1800s thinkers, could not be left to chance. It had to be carried out systematically, by scientists. Psychologists such as Hugo Münsterberg, imported from Leipzig to supervise Harvard's new laboratory, regularly stressed this scientific rigor. Upon his 1892 arrival in Cambridge, curious Bostonians asked Münsterberg about the nature of experimental psychology almost as often as they asked whether Germans played football. Harvard's new psychologist did not record his answer to the football question, but he did explain to curious readers that the budding field of psychology emulated natural science without engaging in speculative philosophy. Universities, Münsterberg said, should hire scholars who focused exclusively on experiments, not abstraction. Recently, he noted, psychologists had established labs in cities and university towns such as New York; Philadelphia; Madison, Wisconsin; and Champaign, Illinois. Through rigorous scholarship, he predicted, experimental psychologists would become true "men of science."[15]

One such experimentalist and self-conscious man of science was G. Stanley Hall, who earned America's first psychology Ph.D. at Harvard in 1878. He also studied with Wundt and Ludwig in Europe before becoming a professor at Johns Hopkins and, later, president of Clark University in Worcester, Massachusetts (Hall even lured Vienna psychologist Sigmund Freud to Clark for his only American visit in 1909). One of the era's most influential thinkers, Hall theorized psychology in terms of evolution and racial and gender hierarchy. Using Darwin's theories and the concept of biological recapitulation, which was pioneered by German scientist Ernst Häckel in the 1860s, Hall posited that children, women, and nonwhite races occupied lower stages in evolutionary hierarchy. He and his contemporaries saw sport as a relatively safe way for male children to reenact the evolutionary struggle for existence. Play trained children to withstand modern society's mental pressures, remain sexually viable, and reproduce white civilization. Football, he said, was a valuable form of "mental and moral training."[16] Hall also spread his ideas via his graduate students, including G. T. W. Patrick, a "promising" protégé who began teaching philosophy at Iowa in 1887.[17] Hall, as the founding editor of the *American Journal of Psychology*, even published Patrick's entire dissertation, "A Further Study of Heraclitus," in 1888. By today's standards Patrick's analysis, contrasting ancient Greek philosophers Heraclitus, Plato, and Socrates, seems out of place in an academic psychology journal. But the young scholar was writing at a time when modern intellectual culture was still under construction and disciplinary boundaries were not yet firm. Patrick showed that pre-Socratics like Heraclitus valued the relationship between body and mind, while the Platonists, like modern thinkers, did not appreciate such links. His sympathies clearly lay with the pre-Socratics.[18] Such academic border crossing was reflected, by necessity, in Patrick's job. He was the University of Iowa's lone philosophy professor until the early 1890s, teaching both experimental psychology and philosophy. He even studied with Wundt and Ludwig for six months in 1894 in Leipzig, where he purchased apparatus for Iowa's new psychology laboratory. As department chair, Patrick supervised the laboratory's construction, and he continued teaching psychology after experimentalist Carl Seashore joined Iowa's faculty.[19]

In a 1903 *American Journal of Psychology* article titled "The Psychology of Football," Patrick noted a gap in prevailing discussions of the popular collegiate sport. While he did not dispute the belief that football might teach players self-control, discipline, and manliness, he complained that those who discussed football's *ethics* were ignoring its *psychology*. Unlike muckrakers or social scientists who criticized football as a morally corrupt spectacle, Patrick gauged its effect on minds and bodies. He noted that English thinker Herbert Spencer had argued that play helped children expend "surplus energy," while German psychologist Karl Groos contended that it helped children prepare for adult life. Yet neither theory satisfied Patrick. He estimated, based on his cor-

G. T. W. Patrick in 1878, before earning his
doctorate in philosophy under G. Stanley Hall at
Johns Hopkins University. Frederick W. Kent
Photograph Collection, University of Iowa
Libraries, Iowa City, Iowa.

respondence with Walter Camp, that as many as 40,000 spectators attended college football games. Patrick wanted to explain this phenomenal spectatorship. He dismissed the claim that football embodied intercollegiate rivalry. After all, Patrick wryly noted, debates did not draw
crowds quite like gridiron contests. He thought football was popular
because it helped players and spectators return to evolutionary roots.
The modern world was a place of streets, railways, factories, banks, offices, schools, libraries, and laboratories. Paying homage to Hall, his
mentor, Patrick hypothesized that adult play, by reverting to earlier
phases of evolution, protected men from overcivilization. Football's
"primitive features"—"the bare heads and long hair; the dust and dirt
and grimy faces; the Indian-like blankets worn by the players when at

rest; the colored and decorated suits"—simulated steps in the struggle for existence. To top it all off, the prevailing style of football play even resembled "a scrimmage of savages."[20]

By implying that women, children, and nonwhites were located on lower biological planes, Patrick (like Hall) invoked recapitulation theory. Spectators at football games, like children and so-called savages, did not try "to restrain emotional expression."[21] By watching football, white men could release inhibitions by reenacting earlier evolutionary stages, and thus get a reinvigorating dose of the premodern struggle for existence. Patrick's argument seems paradoxical, though, if we recall that in the early 1900s, many Native American youths were force-fed modern American life, including football, at federal boarding schools. In highly publicized games against major colleges and military academies, these players—along with white coaches and journalists—challenged traditional manliness by turning football into a sport of trickery.[22] Who, we might ask, were the true savages: the Native Americans who figured out how to win at football, or the white Americans who invented this rational yet brutal game, tirelessly promoted it, and encouraged supposedly primitive peoples to play it?

While Patrick argued that white children resembled other races by instinctively *playing* games that helped counteract modern civilization, he implied that adult white men could get the necessary mental release by simply *watching* athletic sports—and that such spectatorship might be the only way for the crowd to relieve stress. Indeed, nonspectator sports sometimes puzzled him. Before publishing this article, Patrick, who was then president-elect of the Western Philosophical Association, became anxious and ill. He crossed the Atlantic to recover in Europe, where a German physician diagnosed neurasthenia. In Germany, Patrick observed a sporting mentality different from one he had seen in Iowa City. An association football game in Berlin seemed "childish" because the cheers of the mere 200 spectators compared poorly with the noise made by tens of thousands at American football games.[23] An aspect of football that made it manly, he implied, was the roar of the crowd. Where were all of the German men who should have been gathering for the psychological or physical release their monotonous jobs required? Such observations were logical to early 1900s experimental psychologists, but they would have made no sense to antebellum educators like Charles Beck, who warned against allowing untutored spectators to attend school athletic contests. If spectators had no serious interest in disciplining bodies, minds, and morals, they could corrupt physical culture. Many Progressive Era social scientists, as we will see, also found negative meanings in huge, unruly crowds. But even some social scientists worried that football developed neither mind nor body and argued that if sport caused nerve damage, it lost its practical utility. Certainly, exhausted athletes who left the field crying did not reflect "the best traditions of Anglo-Saxon manhood." If this was the case, could hysterical, "overstrained" male nerves be the true goal of college athletics?[24]

Psychologists often argued that football facilitated manly behaviors and mentalities, but they were not the only ones to do so. Students also portrayed football as a sport beneficial to the mind and senses.[25] They found encouragement from professors like Indiana University psychologist William Lowe Bryan, who liked to warn students about mental fatigue and nerve damage. A charter member of the American Psychological Association who counted both David Starr Jordan and G. Stanley Hall as mentors, Bryan advised students not to study too hard, lest they go insane. All should get enough sleep, shun drugs, eat properly, and play. "It is not enough for the five hundred and eighty to hurrah at the twenty's game," Bryan warned. "Go to the gymnasium. Or play tennis. Or saw wood."[26] Such words aptly captured turn-of-the-century Americans' belief that healthy nerves were a type of capital, an investment in the future of both the individual and the nation. The nervous system was a crucial symbol for embodied manliness, an obsession for a society that saw commercial and political success resting upon men's intact bodies and minds. Nerves and spinal cords were the threads holding together modern life and thought. Football could strengthen those threads, but it might also damage them beyond repair. Healthy nerves indicated robust manly character, but deficient nerves implied the opposite. Late 1800s jingoes branded peace advocates as spineless, and they criticized President William McKinley's lack of a "backbone." Magazines even illustrated lethal nerve injuries as a way to warn readers about football's dangers.[27] In *Collier's* in 1905, muckraker Edward S. Jordan declared that the University of Wisconsin faculty did not possess enough "nerve" to reform football. The athletic committee's incompetence reflected a "flabby faculty spine"; it would "take a big man with a strong nervous organism and more than a smattering of practical brains to save Wisconsin from herself." He even charged that men who entered universities only to play football would one day constitute "a flabby backbone" for their respective states.[28]

In this cultural context, psychologists were heavily invested in determining football's significance for the nerves. Another scientist who crossed both the Atlantic and early disciplinary lines to explore the relationship between body and mind was physiologist Warren Lombard. Like G. Stanley Hall, Lombard studied with Bowditch; like Morton Prince, he played football at Harvard in the 1870s. In 1881, Lombard traveled to Europe to study in Carl Ludwig's Institute of Physiology, a cosmopolitan Vienna laboratory where students explored the nervous system in experiments conducted upon the exposed nerves of dissected frogs. Lombard later attended Wundt's course at Leipzig, and Hall hired him in 1889 to teach at Clark. When William Rainey Harper raided Clark's faculty in 1892, luring many of its disillusioned professors to Chicago, Lombard left for Michigan's medical school. Like G. T. W. Patrick, Lombard wrote in the *American Journal of Psychology* about the mind-body relationship, but he used empirical evidence instead of philosophical reflection. His article, the journal's first, recounted an experiment in which Lombard's wife struck his knee 6,639 times for a month and measured each reflex. He concluded that his knee-jerk varied according to the effects of external stimuli. Without indicating the extent of Mrs. Lombard's contribution to this part of the experiment, the author recorded a "seminal emission" one morning, but stated that he was not sure whether the ejaculation had caused a subsequent depression in the strength of his reflex. Besides implying that sexual release lowered nervous energy, Lombard was also implying that manly, strenuous sports might actually affect the nerves positively. He would occasionally doze off and dream that he was "kicking a football [or] . . . performing some other vigorous action." His reflex, if induced at this time, was unusually violent.[29] These findings seemed to show that the mere *thought* of vigorous activity might actually *increase* nervous energy. In the next two decades, Lombard's research found a wide reception, attracting the at-

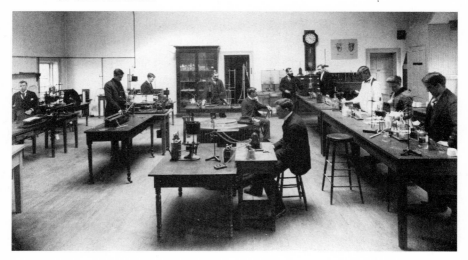

University of Michigan physiology laboratory, circa 1893. Medical School (University of Michigan) records, Box 136, Folder: Gibson Photos, 1893 (1), Bentley Historical Library, University of Michigan.

tention of scholars such as S. Weir Mitchell, John Dewey, and Edward Scripture, as well as Yale gymnasium director Jay Seaver.[30]

Throughout his career, Lombard argued that sport's benefits bridged stages in the life cycle, from childhood to sexual maturity to professional advancement. Addressing the University of Michigan Scientific Club in 1938, he claimed that the intertwined instincts of play and reproduction were necessary for an individual's growth as well as "the maintenance of the species." Second only to sexuality in importance, "motor activities" provided pleasure and developed muscle coordination. As a man grew older, said Lombard, he should continue to play so that he might continue to outcompete his rivals. He even compared the first physiology lecture he ever gave to sport. Even though he had misplaced his notes before the lecture, he succeeded because he recalled the detached attitude that had helped him win football games at Harvard. Lombard also applied his sporting fortitude and passion for athletics in institutional contexts in Ann Arbor. He served on Michigan's Board in Control of Athletics and spoke at student football mass meetings. On a Friday evening in October 1894, he addressed hundreds of students in a campus lecture hall, asserting the importance of manliness and honesty in athletics.[31] Although he was one of the most vocal, Lombard was not the only faculty proponent of athletics at Michigan's medical school. Charles B. G. de Nancrède, who provided free medical care for the team, also spoke at mass meetings, telling students to support the Athletic Board, since they would need responsive bodies in their professional lives.[32]

When professors like Lombard and Nancrède participated in university assemblies, they often did so in spaces that were sex-segregated. After all, they inhabited an academic world that, if it did not entirely *exclude* women, did not entirely *include* them, either. At Stanford, female students were restricted to the assembly hall's balcony, and one writer claimed in 1908 that each and every student "wearing trousers and claiming to be a man" should attend so they could listen to the "virile" speakers.[33] Rhetoric of manliness and sport was often tied to gendered understandings of the modern nervous system. At a 1901 Stanford rally, for instance, David Starr Jordan tied sportsmanship to the cultivation of manly nerves, noting that a good team could "take defeat like men." He endorsed football because it was "the best way of developing nerve."[34] At the same time, such commentators were ambivalent about athletics' implications for women's nerves. University of Michigan students and alumni agreed that women needed physical education, but they saw sport only as a way to prepare women to be "good wives" and "mothers of the race." Women needed physical training, but not competitive athletics. In 1915, Stanford psychologist Frank Angell explicitly warned women gathered at Stanford's Roble Gymnasium not to imitate strenuous, commercial men's sport.[35] After all, if college sport could corrupt men, how might it transform the mothers of the race? Yet this attitude implied a general ambivalence about athletics. If sport posed substantial dangers to mind, body, or morals, why was it part of college life at all?

For turn-of-the-century psychologists and physiologists, intercollegiate football was an essential aspect of modern universities because it seemed to hold pedagogical implications. It is therefore not surprising that as psychologists were starting to create the discipline of teacher education at this time, professors in that field also had something to say about the sport. The University of Illinois's Edwin G. Dexter, who completed his doctorate under Columbia psychologist James McKeen

Cattell (Wilhelm Wundt's first American Ph.D.), was chair of pedagogy at Illinois from 1899 until his appointment as education commissioner for Puerto Rico in 1907.[36] In the 1904 *Educational Review*, Dexter examined reports of serious football accidents and produced statistics dismissing the game's risks. His quantitative analysis of questionnaires completed by officials at various universities showed that less than 3 percent of players were injured seriously enough to lose time from study. The number of men killed or "permanently injured" was "practically a negligible quantity."[37] Two years later, when football underwent its most intense period of scrutiny, Dexter published figures in the *Popular Science Monthly* that dismissed most injuries as the mere product of sensational journalism. Real football, he claimed, was much less dangerous than "newspaper football."[38] Dexter defended college sport because he saw it as a way to instill mental and physical discipline, as well as a relatively safe way to replicate natural selection. In his 1904 article he quantified the opinions of fifty-eight college officers and athletic committee chairs. After weighing the responses proportionally to favor institutions with larger enrollments—a problematic analytical method that might have appealed to readers in an era when big universities were seen as more competitive or important than small colleges—Dexter declared that universities favored retaining football (or only slightly modifying it) at a ratio of 17:1. Among the officials quoted, many stated that football developed "manliness" and inculcated such characteristics as "discipline, brainwork, self-control, self-mastery, [and] self-measurement." Only a few responses stressed the game's disadvantages.[39]

Dexter, like Hall and Patrick, clearly based his ideas on Darwinian evolutionary theory. After watching his young son play, he concluded that a process mirroring natural selection shaped human behavior. He claimed (invoking German psychologist Karl Groos) that children retained and perfected only those actions that were fit for facilitating mental or physical development.[40] In 1906, furthermore, he asserted that even though football was not "gentle," it was not too dangerous for American men:

No youth of bone and muscle who hears even the faintest "Call of the Wild" echoing down from a thousand generations of fighting ancestors—and they must have been fighters or they would never have been ancestors—comes to his own without somewhere and somehow a chance at the physical try out with worthy adversaries. With the days of almost universal war superseded by days of as universal peace and the knight-errant and the tournament things of the past, if we emasculate football and attempt to eliminate entirely the danger element, we shall close the last safety valve to virile expression and may well expect an explosion.[41]

Play, for Dexter, was worth the minimal risk because it strengthened both mind and body. Football seemed a relatively safe way for boys to unleash violent impulses resonating from the earlier stages of evolution. This stance recalled Jack London's 1903 novel, *The Call of the Wild*; and by proclaiming the game a "safety valve," Dexter also anticipated William James's 1910 plea for a "moral equivalent of war." James, in his famous call for a humane type of strenuous conflict, contended that by creating institutions that mimicked war, Americans could improve future generations by teaching manliness and saving civilization from weakness. Even the tremendous bloodshed of the Civil War was worthwhile, said James, if it saved Americans from a world of rampant industry, monotonous mind-work, "co-education . . . and feminism unabashed." The Harvard psychologist and philosopher wrote that the "race" should never stop breeding "military character," nor should it ignore warfare's ability to teach discipline. Whether it involved mine labor or urban construction projects, this moral war-equivalent could strengthen young men, making good fathers who would be a positive example for coming generations. Though James did not explicitly discuss team sports, historians have interpreted football as one such equivalent for early 1900s readers.[42]

While some psychologists were discussing a moral equivalent of war, others were actually trying to find a moral, or at least safe, equivalent for football. Frank Angell, a longtime Stanford professor, helped lead the movement on the West Coast to replace football with rugby. A nephew of Michigan's president James Angell, Frank had played football and baseball while a student at the University of Vermont in the 1870s, before he completed his Ph.D. at Leipzig, under Wilhelm Wundt, in 1891. Angell was teaching at Cornell when David Starr Jordan invited him to become Stanford's first psychology professor in 1892. For thirty years (1895–1925) Angell was associate editor of Hall's *American Journal of Psychology*, and he chaired Stanford's Faculty Athletic Committee from 1892 to 1922. (Jordan liked to tell students that several Stanford professors, including Angell, were former athletes whose strong physiques had fueled their "mental machinery" and augmented their professional success.)[43] Angell was strident about the positive potential of sport. Early in his career, he had critiqued Charles William Eliot's widely disseminated 1894 critiques, claiming that Harvard's leader "belonged to that class of estimable old ladies of both sexes who classed football and prize fighting together, and invoked the aid of newspapers and legislatures to abolish the game." Unlike boxing, Angell implied, football was a respectable middle-class pastime, and anyone who opposed it was effeminate. Nonetheless, Angell did concede some of Eliot's points, agreeing that too much time spent on training could negatively affect studies. While he thought this was not a problem at Stanford, Angell did acknowledge that continuous discussions around the training table were "a drain on nervous energy," which players should instead channel into coursework.[44]

Along with David Starr Jordan and President Benjamin Ide Wheeler of Berkeley, Angell fought hard for the adoption of Australian-style rugby in America. The three touted rugby in part because of its relative safety for young men's nerves and internal organs. It was, in other words, a way to make college sport safe for students' minds and bodies. Angell extolled rugby's virtues in *The Independent* in 1910. He recalled that the faculty at Stanford and Berkeley had not objected to football in the 1890s, when both universities hired the best East Coast coaches: Walter Camp at Stanford and William "Pudge" Heffelfinger, a Yale All-American, at Cal. Professors at that time had avidly watched the "manly, vigorous" game. But Camp and Heffelfinger made California football a "dangerous and objectionable" contest of mass plays. Rugby was better sport, Angell argued, because it enticed more men onto the field and inspired them to keep playing later into the year. It enhanced the bodies and minds of the many rather than stultifying the intellects or damaging the physiques of the few. Rugby required rigorous conditioning, yet was still recreational and provided "exhilarating" exercise. Rugby players were faster and more skilled, he declared, and they were just as manly. It was a "rough game," not a "pink tea" game. Angell even boasted, somewhat perversely, that rugby caused its fair share of injuries. But, like Jordan, he thought that rugby injuries were not as serious as those in football. Angell also argued that rugby turned players into quick thinkers because it replaced "wearisome drill" with a quick style of play that demanded nimble minds. It should not be too surprising that Angell, who was head timer at Stanford track meets and authored academic studies on reaction time, observed that old football stars were "too slow in the head" for rugby. Even though Angell noted that rugby's quick pace led to large crowds, he assured readers that attracting spectators should not be the main goal. His biggest concern was to protect nerves. Angell wanted a game that was enjoyable and, if strenuous, did not cause broken spines and concussions. He cared little for the crowd, and he cared less for the "drill master" professional coach. He even called football "battleball," a term coined by one of the professional Vancouver players who taught Stanford students rugby. The older game, said Angell, was dangerous and interesting mainly to spectators and athletic associations.[45]

Based on the language that spectators used to talk about the game, football may have been appealing in large part because of its perceived effects upon the nervous system. At colleges with big-time football programs, aspiring athletic impresarios used the rhetoric of nerves to promote grand football shows at the turn of the century. Charles Baird, the student manager who later became Michigan's first athletic director, congratulated the university on the send-off it gave the Wolverines before a big game at Harvard in 1895. The farewell, he said, had helped to "nerve" the players for the big match. Some early 1900s commentators even contended that sport could positively affect *spectators'* nervous systems. Stanford professor Colbert Searles implored students and spectators to cheer "for the sake of those little ecstatic thrills that chase up and down all properly constructed vertebral columns when a comrade combines skill, nerve and grit to do what we would all love to do" on the athletic field.[46]

Football might thrill sedentary nerves, but some began to fear that it was actually causing mental distress. One anxiety-inducing game, apparently, was the 1902 Rose Bowl in Pasadena. After Stanford lost to

Michigan, 49–0, Cardinal football captain Ralph Fisher complained, in what must have been one of the first irate postgame interviews, about the Wolverines' late arrival. This tardiness seemed like a deliberate attempt to rattle Stanford's men. The players "were compelled to wait thirty minutes in the hot sun," and each player was thus "nerved to the highest pitch." Football was difficult enough for the nerves, and the anticipation of a pounding at the hands of Michigan's undefeated "point-a-minute" squad, led by former Stanford journeyman coach Fielding Yost, was nearly as bad. In response to this intense pressure, coaches soon began treating players and sequestering them at rural retreats. To counteract his players' anxiety, Chicago's Amos Alonzo Stagg took them to vaudeville shows and led them on an excursion to a Lake Forest, Illinois, country club in 1905. By this time, Stanford coach James Lanagan had already begun his annual ritual of taking players to a hillside resort a week before the Big Game against Cal. The season's strain tended to make the players nervous, so the off-campus trips were "intended to obviate any chance of nervous breakdowns, and to relieve the tension" caused by the pregame festivities. Ironically, the game that supposedly benefited nerves by providing release from the modern grind still proved to be intense work, a source of nervous tension that unnerved spectators. One of the 13,000 who attended the 1905 Big Game observed that Stanford's victory over California was a "nerve racking struggle."[47]

Even the advent of rugby, a game that was supposed to alleviate many of sport's physical and mental problems, may not have been as effective as reformers like Frank Angell wanted to believe. In fact, some Stanford students described rugby in a manner evoking the intensity of the old game. In 1908, one student called for each player to "grit his teeth for an ordeal of nerves, speed, and force" in a coming contest. Based on such statements, it seems that rugby may not have been all that different from the sport that aggravated players at the 1902 Rose Bowl, or the one that had inspired Stagg and Lanagan to take their players to far-off, relaxing retreats before big games. One student even berated the Stanford faculty in 1912 for trying to proclaim rugby's "mental, moral, and physical" benefits while openly continuing to seek profit and publicity. He doubted that rugby positively impacted the majority of students who did not play on the varsity team and went so far as to argue that the university leadership was letting the competition for athletic supremacy impede educa- tion.[48]

The struggle for football supremacy became an established part of America's colleges in the early 1900s, especially after the founding of the NCAA and the rise of professional coaching. As intercollegiate ath- letics became institutionalized, moreover, professors were less able to influence it directly. After 1910, few psychologists wrote about sport's place in university and society, or its effects upon students' minds and bodies. One exception was H. Addington Bruce, who published "The Psychology of Football" in *The Outlook* in 1910. Bruce, who studied with William James, Morton Prince, and psychologist Boris Sidis, au- thored popular books and articles but never held a formal university position. Bruce's article rehashed much of Patrick's 1903 piece, but he used even more belligerent terms to promote football. He also con- tended that the game helped spectators expend the "fund of nervous energy" they had accumulated. Although some spectators may have disagreed, Bruce even argued that football spectatorship relaxed the mind. The game led to "self-forgetfulness" and allowed spectators to "let go." Watching sports did more than just inspire the primitive be- havior that rescued men from modern civilization, said Bruce. Specta- torship actually relaxed the mind, an argument that reflected Bruce's position as one of Sigmund Freud's acolytes and anticipated Ameri- cans' twentieth-century fascination with psychotherapy.[49] Although Bruce was too late to contribute to progressive football reform, his ar- ticle did foreshadow the writings of University of Illinois coach Bob Zuppke, who would later portray football as a psychologically fulfill- ing game in the 1920s.

At the same time psychologists wrote about football's benefits and its reform, many of these scholars were becoming sequestered in a fragmented disciplinary landscape housed in a bewildering array of university departments. The process of fragmentation occurred gradu- ally as the disciplines adapted to institutional circumstances and cur- ricular needs. Some universities, such as Harvard, Michigan, and Iowa, still considered experimental psychology a branch of philoso- phy into the 1920s, long after German-trained scholars like Münster- berg and Hall had transformed it. But other universities, especially newer institutions in the Midwest or West, had already established psychology as a unique field at a much earlier date. At Illinois, for instance, psychology was originally part of Dexter's pedagogy department, but by 1904 the field had its own bailiwick. At Stanford, David Starr Jordan planned for experimental psychology to dominate philosophy virtually from the university's opening day. In the early 1890s, he hired Wundt's student Frank Angell while simultaneously trying to lure William Lowe Bryan, a Hall student, to Palo Alto as a second experimentalist disguised as a historian of philosophy. (Harvard's Josiah Royce, a native Californian, had already refused Jordan's advances.) But Bryan resisted Jordan's overtures, displaying his disciplinary integrity by claiming the need to retrain in Europe if he took the new position. He stayed at Indiana University.[50]

The split between psychology and philosophy became more obvious and widespread by 1930. While Harvard had recognized the two as separate fields within the same department in 1912, by 1934 it split the two fields that were then occupying one of the nation's last combined psychology-philosophy departments. Historian Bruce Kuklick has likened this process to a divorce. The separation was less acrimonious in Ann Arbor, where the death of Michigan's aging philosophy chair quietly prompted the formation of a separate psychology department in 1929. At Iowa, experimentalist Carl Seashore (who earned Yale's first psychology Ph.D. under philosopher-psychologist George Trumbull Ladd and experimentalist Edward Scripture, a Wundt student) recast his unit as the "department of philosophy and psychology" in 1905, soon after superseding G. T. W. Patrick as chair. After this intellectual shift, Iowa's department hired mostly experimental psychologists, who comprised over 80 percent of the department by the early 1920s. Although Seashore later stressed interdisciplinary scholarship as the dean of the graduate college at Iowa, he and other psychologists often maligned their nonexperimentalist colleagues, like Edwin Starbuck, for supposedly less rigorous research methods. Iowa's philosophers, bitter and tired of the acrimony, formed their own department in 1927.[51]

While psychology-related disciplines shared common intellectual roots, in the early 1900s they started becoming separate disciplines less amenable to what historians call "boundary work."[52] Psychology was no longer a deductive mode of inquiry led by mental philosophers at semi-isolated colleges, as it was in the antebellum era; nor was it a cross-disciplinary field with a wide range of epistemologies or methods. Rather, it was a rigorously experimental subject tightly focused on the nervous system, with research carried out in a multitude of narrow departments at large universities designed to generate practical knowledge. The academic laborers who filled these departments had trained at German universities or up-and-coming American research institutions. This reality represented a trend that was becoming evident in modern academic and intellectual life. The production of knowledge, although carried out on a vast geographical scale, was rational and standardized. As specialization grew, so too did the quality and quantity of scholarship. The chances that scientifically accurate knowledge would grow improved as more and more scholars used scientific methods and were employed in a growing number of university departments. Even though it was becoming less likely that knowledge would be accessible to nonacademics in the new academic order of things, this reality did not necessarily faze those who saw the athletic spectacle as a way to keep universities in the public spotlight while at the same time strengthening students' nervous systems for the rigors of modern life.

Academic specialization was a hallmark of the ivory tower. But, as it turned out, so was sport. Scholars who theorized the psychology of football within modern society and fragmented, disciplinary universities contributed to Progressive Era discussions about football reform. What did sport mean for modern minds and bodies, they asked, and what was physical culture's proper role within American higher education? Thinkers such as Patrick, Lombard, and Dexter saw football as an important exercise for developing men; Angell even directly shaped and promoted the briefly successful West Coast rugby reform. They were globe-hopping scholars who contributed to progressive reform, but they were also academic laborers, workers in increasingly specialized universities. As such, they helped create the academic disciplines and departments that colonized institutions of higher education and research. Universities, competing for resources and publicity, turned to a popular spectacle that attracted public attention, dollars, and spectators. But football's popularity also caused scandals and moral crises. Social scientists, in turn, addressed this problem, theorizing that if universities could minimize the impact of the crowd and the taint of its money, academics could use sport to teach students disciplined morality, while also reaching out to the public. Enmeshed within their own intellectual networks, disciplines, and departments, however, social scientists were also reframing the relationship between the academy and the American people. They did so by creating professional safeguards to protect academic specialists from the market-oriented world located beyond the college walls.

CHAPTER 4

Social Scientists: Making Sport Safe for a Rational Public

In 1908 Edward A. Ross, a University of Wisconsin sociologist, wrote that athletics helped players develop "moral as well as physical tone" and resist the "mob mind." Sports did not merely train the body or strengthen the nervous system; they molded individual and social ethics. Ross proclaimed that football taught athletes to follow training rules, subdue their tempers, and display "modest self-restraint in victory" as well as grace in defeat. This disciplined training demonstrated "the triumph of the will over suggestion."[1] For progressives like Ross, sport embodied the modern tension between order and disorder. Intercollegiate football, depending on how it was supervised, could create either a moral or an immoral populace. After all, ticket sales and the press seemed to be turning sport into a sensational spectacle that corrupted universities, students, and spectators. Reforms, including shielding athletics from corruption by the market and the media, might eliminate sport's vices while retaining its virtues. But to work, reforms had to be carried out on a national level. Universities had to band together to purify sport and protect higher learning. Social scientists did, ultimately, help shape athletic reforms. But, like psychologists, they also contributed to the construction of an academic ivory tower that was not always accessible to the general public. At the same time athletic reforms began to enshrine sport as a university department devoted to exploiting the commercial marketplace, academic scholars began creating professional safeguards to protect their labor from that very market.

As in the case of psychology, the modern social sciences were transformed greatly in the late 1800s. The fields of economics, political science, history, and sociology emerged from the ashes of moral philosophy following the Civil War. At first, scholars of social science formed broad associations bridging divergent fields of inquiry. For example, Richard T. Ely, who held a Heidelberg doctorate and carried German social reform traditions to America by challenging the hegemony of laissez-faire economic orthodoxy, founded the American Social Sci-

Edward Alsworth Ross, photographed around the time he
came to the University of Wisconsin, Madison (1906), wrote
about the importance of sport for college students. Photo
courtesy of UW Madison Archives.

ence Association in the 1890s. While teaching first at Johns Hopkins
and then at Wisconsin, Ely also supervised many graduate students
who went on to be professors of sociology, economics, history, and labor relations (as well as commentators on college football). By 1900,
though, practitioners of the various social sciences were creating special organizations for each discipline. Scholars, in short, like other professionals, embraced the modern division of labor.[2] These modern intellectuals tended to favor, at least explicitly, empirical observation
over philosophical deduction. They were particularly influenced by

Darwinian evolutionary theory, which reinforced scientific authority and established rational order in a modern age seemingly filled with disorder. In this brave new academic world, scholars no longer engaged in a priori discussions of society. They constructed truth through rigorous investigation. Nonetheless, social scientists did not entirely dissociate themselves from qualitative judgments or Christian morality. Academics like Ross often employed an admixture of scientific epistemology and Social Gospel moralism as a way to promote their view of social order and its reform.[3]

Some social scientists, including Francis A. Walker, the economist and MIT president who gave the 1893 Phi Beta Kappa oration on college athletics at Harvard, thought that football would help students understand and succeed in the modern industrial order. The son of antebellum thinker Amasa Walker, Francis Walker graduated from Amherst in 1860, during the era of the Barrett Gymnasium and Edward Hitchcock. Walker then enlisted in the Union army in 1861. It was apparent that collegiate gymnasium lessons were not lost on Walker, who cited Amherst's President William Stearns in his 1893 speech. Walker contended that industry, like modern war, required special skills and efficient cooperation. He echoed psychologists when he noted that strenuous physical activities like military training strengthened the body, but hard mental labor drained it. Walker touted competitive team sports as the solution. Games like football taught specialized efficiency, creating robust men who possessed "courage, coolness, steadiness of nerve, quickness of apprehension, resourcefulness, self-knowledge, [and] self-reliance." Yet sport's benefits were also social and moral, not just mental or physical. Athletics developed the ability to cooperate and sublimate one's personal desires to common goals—skills that were becoming essential in an industrial era when individuals were expected to contribute their specialized labor to the population. Walker also pondered the idea that sport benefited spectators. Football was so popular, he speculated, because it assuaged modern life's "monotony" and inspired men to leave their stuffy offices and engage in physical activity. Sport would provide relief from the cutthroat scramble for money and professional status.[4]

Other turn-of-the-century social scientists were more ambivalent than Walker about football's effects. Writing at the time of the 1894–

1895 football crisis initiated by Charles William Eliot's critiques, Harvard economist Frank W. Taussig (a member of the 1879 Harvard College class, which later contributed to the Harvard Stadium construction fund in 1902) argued that athletics might corrupt students and pervert education. While Taussig noted that sport could promote "loyalty and public spirit," he also feared that it would damage college men's morality and intellect, in addition to causing physical injury. The public's vast expenditures on football prompted students to spend too much time, energy, and money on the spectacle. As in modern party politics, vigorous enthusiasm was good, but it should not steal the show. The public's overemphasis on athletics, though, was dangerous insofar as sports like football were starting to overshadow universities' role "as training-places for educated, intelligent, public-spirited, rightly guided, and rightly ambitious men and citizens." Taussig contended that colleges had to teach discipline, but he was afraid that sport might limit their ability to do so. He implied that athletic leaders, like political campaign organizers, must not pander to the untutored masses.[5] It is not surprising that Taussig voiced such cautions. Concerns about lack of discipline in politics and social life were common in the late 1800s "Gilded Age" of industrial and urban expansion. Capitalist tycoons monopolized wealth in an era of scarce economic regulation, while "machine" politicians, represented most famously by Tammany Hall's Boss Tweed, seemed to control city politics. Meanwhile, national parties spawned spectacular electoral campaigns. In this large, disorderly, and apparently corrupt society, reformers hoped to curtail power brokers' influence and create a society with purer political conduct. To strengthen democracy, individuals needed moral discipline. This trait would supposedly steel the "best men" against the temptations of quick money and corrupt politics. Critics like Taussig pointed out that while college sport might teach self-control and promote genteel manliness, it might also corrupt college men and, as a result, American life.[6]

But there was a younger generation of scholars—many of whom were influenced by Richard T. Ely—who initially viewed college sport neither as a way to prepare young men for lives of industry nor as an activity that would corrupt the nation's politics. Rather, they saw games like football as a way to instill a progressive spirit that would help to reform a modern society dominated by large, capitalist corporations. In early 1893, not long after earning his Ph.D. in economics at Johns Hopkins, E. A. Ross—then a rising star of West Coast progressivism—told Stanford students that strong male bodies and morals would facilitate political reform. Ross deplored the "survival of the fittest" mentality that enabled investors and leaders of massive corporations like Standard Oil to stockpile riches, and he debunked the Social Darwinists like William Graham Sumner who justified social inequality as a natural result of competition for jobs, money, and resources. To counteract socially irresponsible corporations and the dog-eat-dog competitive mentality of Gilded Age America, said Ross, Americans had to build durable ethical consciences. At that time a young, idealistic economist, Ross insisted that "moral health" was better than wealth, and he implored students to become "manly" through reform-minded political activity. Athletic training was crucial to this process, since it produced the bodily stamina that would help young men save society from corrupt captains of industry.[7] One of Ross's colleagues, Stanford economist Burt Estes Howard, articulated a similar connection between football and public conscience. At a 1901 football rally after the annual athletic banquet, which Howard attended with psychology professor Frank Angell and Stanford president David Starr Jordan, Howard spoke on football's moral potential to hundreds of students in Stanford's crowded assembly hall. He expected Stanford to win the upcoming Big Game against California, yet implored the team to play only "clean football" and win via honest means. Howard warned, "Do not come back to us with a stain on our colors. An unclean victory is the worst possible defeat." After all, he noted, maintaining honorable manliness was more important than winning a football game. This theme was present throughout Howard's larger body of scholarship, including a 1901 book, *Education and Democracy*, in which he dismissed monetary disputes between Populists and conservatives as a superficial manifestation of a much deeper conflict. Society needed the right type of man, he said—not just the right type of money.[8]

Budding progressive social scientists like Howard and Ross held both great hopes and great fears for football. This perspective was not lost on students. In 1895, Michigan students observed that President Charles Kendall Adams of the University of Wisconsin argued that football taught players "manhood, self-restraint, [and] courage." Four years later, they heard from New York's Governor Theodore Roosevelt, the Spanish-American War hero who would soon be elected vice president and assume the presidency in 1901 upon William McKinley's assassination. During a visit to Ann Arbor, Roosevelt discussed sport in terms that anticipated his stances on antimonopoly trust-busting as well as pure food and drug legislation. While football was good for America, said Roosevelt, its positive effects were felt only because of successful reform movements, especially in the Midwest, which eradicated "taints of professionalism." He told Michigan students to "play fair and keep the money element out"; that was the only path to "honest, manly" athletics. Students also heard this refrain from professors who defended football as a way to raise the moral tone of the entire student body; yet teachers and other critics warned students that if college sport became a business carried out by mercenaries, its manly benefits would be lost.[9] Although such optimism ran high, students were not blind to sport's problems. Stanford students discussed football's potential for "manly self-control" as early as 1891, but they also realized that the extent to which the game cultivated manliness depended on how it was played. In 1900, a Stanford alumnus, sounding a lot like Burt Howard, implored players to follow training rules and to be "honest, manly, square fellows" in football, just as in life. University of Michigan students even printed a piece on sport by alumnus Delos Wilcox, a municipal reformer in Grand Rapids (and later New York), who equated trickster athletes with students who cheated or rigged class elections. Wilcox recommended that reformers remodel education to limit possibilities for dishonesty and ruthlessness.[10]

Football was good, but only if it improved young American men. For some turn-of-the-century observers, this meant that sport should promote a type of competition that would strengthen the white race and enable it to dominate the globe. Francis A. Walker—who had developed harsh Indian policies for the federal government in the 1870s and warned against the dangers of unchecked foreign immigration in the 1890s—insisted that sport might bolster the hereditary traits of the white race without depleting its ranks (as war might). He thus anticipated William James's call for a "moral equivalent" of war when he proclaimed that "the blood of the whole community is stirred by physical contests among the picked youth of the land, as once it was only stirred by battle." Isaac A. Loos, a University of Iowa political scientist and athletic booster who had studied with Yale Social Darwinist William Graham Sumner (Walter Camp's brother-in-law), boldly proclaimed that the "English race" was in the process of establishing political and cultural hegemony throughout the world because it played the "sturdiest" type of sports. Even in the early 1900s, more self-consciously progressive social scientists like Frederick Jackson Turner and E. A. Ross proclaimed football's racial benefits. Ross, for example, attributed white colonial success to athletics, saying that British military officers were able to keep their heads "in a Dervish charge or an Afghan rush" because they possessed the same coolness that a "seasoned football player" gained by having to make quick decisions on the football field when exposed to "the cheers of excited thousands" of spectators.[11]

Others saw football's racial meanings in a less positive light. In *The Theory of the Leisure Class* (1899), Thorstein Veblen, a University of Chicago sociologist, critiqued athletic spectacle as merely another variety of conspicuous consumption. Football was simply a way to shape players' "predatory temperament"; it was a means of instilling violence and trickery without teaching virtuous self-control. Veblen claimed that the game was more show than physical culture, and (in a typically dry yet colorful passage) insisted that conflating football with physical education was like confusing a bullfight with animal husbandry: "The material used, whether brute or human, is subjected to careful selection and discipline, in order to secure and accentuate certain aptitudes and propensities which are characteristic of the ferine state." The game reflected moral "arrested development" and taught "truculence" or "cunning" instead of developing "physique" and "manly spirit." It cultivated, said Veblen, a sort of competitive "barbarism" more useful in modern, capitalist society than in nature, yet still lacked "redeeming features of the savage character." This critique, in other words, read football's Darwinian influence in reverse. The game was unfit for students because it negated evolution, rather than echoing it. Not only did football *not* promote the discipline that would save modern society, but it actually *did* promote a kind of discipline that corrupted American culture.[12]

At a time when scholars made their reputation by critiquing each other's ideas and disciplinary boundaries were in flux, even members of the same department might not agree on the meanings of sport. William I. Thomas, an anthropologist and sociologist who taught alongside Veblen at Chicago, argued in the *American Journal of Sociology* in 1901 that physical play was one manifestation of the "gaming instinct," an innate trait that had resulted from millennia of natural selection. He contended that men and women in all societies and social classes expressed hereditary interest in risky or dangerous contests of "skill and chance," including bear-baiting, street fights, prizefights, bullfights, cockfights, and football. Thomas argued that "instincts developed in the struggle for food and rivalry for mates" had ingrained the desire for conflict in the human psyche. He warned, though, that modern advances had begun negating biological evolution. Life had become unchallenging and "artificial" for many. (Although he noted with relief that not everyone lived counterevolutionary lives: Chicago's gamblers, tramps, and "confidence men" eschewed modernity's monotony; some workers were still exposed to fighting at work, and even respectable men engaged in risky business, like the stock market.) If the "white race" did not embrace natural selection, said Thomas, it would fall behind other racial or ethnic groups. Atavistic behaviors like strenuous sport were a relatively safe way to introduce the risk and chance that were necessary to perpetuate America's predominant biological and cultural group. Sport, in other words, could serve as a ritual training ground for the primitive traits that American men seemed to need to develop.[13]

Thomas also promoted intercollegiate athletics as a positive force by portraying sport as a form of university extension, or public engagement, which could develop instinctive behaviors within tens of thousands of spectators who possessed an innate need for conflict. Unlike courses or academic scholarship, he wrote, virtually everyone in the city could appreciate college athletics. Competitive sport was "the only phase of university life which appeals directly and powerfully to the instincts, and it is consequently the only phase of university life which appeals equally to the man of culture, the artist, the businessman, the man about town, the all-around sport, and, in fact, to all the world." Football bridged social divisions by reaching deep into the human psyche. Therefore, it could bring the city together and teach important evolutionary lessons that modern society seemed to be forgetting. Unlike disciplinary scholarship, sport was relevant to a wide range of spectators located in the university's urban shadow because it provided some of the danger missing in civilized life.[14]

Thomas's idea reflected a key truth of the Progressive Era. Turn-of-the-century universities, whether publicly or privately endowed, were seen as being useful to the American public. So there had to be a way that their lessons could be extended to the broader society located outside the college walls. The University of Chicago, led by Chautauqua adult education proponent William Rainey Harper, was one of the major institutions (along with Wisconsin) to develop university extension. From its opening day, the University of Chicago sponsored academic scholarship yet also tried to reach out to nonacademics. In short, it wanted to be meaningful to the city. The campus was even located alongside the Midway Plaisance, the pop-culture center of the 1893 Columbian Exposition. Like Jane Addams and other middle-class, Windy City activists, men and women in the university's pioneering departments of social work and sociology analyzed Chicago with the hope of improving it. Indeed, university records show us that other scholars in Hyde Park shared the notion that football could bolster university extension. In 1897, several years before Thomas wrote his article on the "gaming instinct," Professor Ira W. Howerth of Chicago's sociology department proposed to bring Extension Division students as a group to a major football game. This excursion, presumably, would instill "a strong interest in the University" and make extension students feel like they were "sharers in its privileges." President Harper, always eager to publicize the university, endorsed the plan.[15]

Football, in other words, could help market America's budding universities. It could also teach both students and spectators some of the lessons regarding race and manliness that were being developed in departments of psychology and social science. But as the number of injuries, deaths, and scandals piled up, concerns about sport's negative effects on progressive universities also increased. In early 1905, in an influential piece in *The Outlook* magazine, Princeton history professor Paul Van Dyke defended football's timeless educational utility, writing that the game, which reflected the toughness of the "Saxon" race, could suppress student "vice" and thus cultivate disciplined morality. But he also wrote that any "reasonable" person could see that college athletics had become debased. Although some critics exaggerated football's faults, they were correct to point out that it had become filled with "evils" that reflected the sad state of American society. Football's problems, though, were not intrinsic to the game itself. They simply showed that unsavory aspects of nonacademic culture had infiltrated the academy. Football, Van Dyke reassured readers, no more caused gambling than did presidential elections. College sport, like American political life, was a victim of the nation's moral short-comings. Its failings were "not the native product of university soil"; they were the result of seeds that had been introduced from "outside" and had "grown into a noxious crop of weeds" that were "a disfigure-ment to the fields of university athletics." In particular, Americans' unhealthy fascination with chance—in the form of gambling, a special concern for progressives—had invaded football and sullied pure uni-versity campuses. Sport had to be rescued from the dissipated masses, who valued monetary gain and entertainment over education or ra-tional thought. One could not blame football when its "wildest" ex-cesses were no worse than "the senseless displays of 'enthusiasm' at great political conventions, when grown men declare[d] their attach-ment to political leaders by acting like maniacs for half an hour at a stretch."[16]

Van Dyke, like Thorstein Veblen and other Progressive Era com-mentators, saw consumerism as a major part of college athletics' prob-lem. To satisfy spectators, football's proponents had transformed it from a manly game into a complicated business. Van Dyke lamented that teams possessed their own budgets, just like university depart-ments. He especially targeted the media as a major reason for college sport's corruption. Van Dyke accused the popular press of feeding the desire for brutality, and he claimed that more readers wanted to con-sume stories about prizefights than about political orations, and *ten times* the number of boxing enthusiasts wanted to read about football. The root of sport's moral decline, therefore, was the popular desire for spectacle. No longer a skillful, educational contest, football had be-come a sport with "men of extraordinary weight and strength drilled to mechanical exactness in executing monotonous movements." Van Dyke used the common comparison with politics to make his point that the media caused football's downfall. The game, like so many other aspects of American life, was a victim of the crowd, and had become shrouded in "hysterical" reactions. The notion that an educational experience had become an irrational (even effeminate) end, rather than a sober and enlightening means to an end, was a public disgrace. Instead of embracing rational cooperation and responsible politics, Americans merely craved spectacle and profiteering.[17]

Football's most vocal critics were alarmed that commercialized sport would make universities less useful to the public by inhibiting their ability to develop students' morals. In his 1905 *Collier's* series, "Buying Football Victories," muckraker Edward Jordan targeted the state universities of the Midwest, whose students were often drawn from rural areas. These growing institutions had to produce graduates who were good citizens, or else risk endangering the state by "contaminat - [ing]" its "talent." Football was so dangerous because it had apparently become a business that just provided entertainment. At Wisconsin, charged Jordan, the athletic association rigged elections and fielded paid players. A professor even arranged sinecures for athletes who "packed political mass meetings, cheered and hissed speakers in turn, and gained a livelihood by a perversion of the fundamental principles of the service of the State." The players and coaches became admirers of trickery, which they taught to the rest of the undergraduates. This brand of morally reprehensible conduct needed progressive remedies, such as the "Australian," or secret, ballot election that eventually removed the corrupt professor from the athletic committee. (But even then, we can see that no one was immune from charges of corruption within a Progressive Era public sphere where money, print, and spectacle mixed. A Michigan professor accused Jordan of printing exaggerated rumors merely to secure a permanent job at *Collier's*.)[18]

It is not surprising that Jordan targeted Wisconsin, his alma mater, as one of the universities that needed to clean up football corruption. While the University of Chicago was trying to bring the benefits of knowledge to the urban masses in America's most quickly growing city, the University of Wisconsin was trying to bring education and expertise to an entire state. The university was located in the capital of

Madison, where progressives such as Robert M. LaFollette, Charles R. Van Hise, and state legislative librarian Charles McCarthy pioneered the "Wisconsin Idea." Those who developed this progressive concept argued that publicly funded universities should aid government by producing knowledge, encouraging faculty to serve on public commissions, and disseminating knowledge via university extension and public lectures. Key supporters of the Wisconsin Idea, such as Richard T. Ely (who came to Madison in 1892), E. A. Ross (1906), and historian Frederick Jackson Turner, contended that state universities could help form a rational and orderly public. They could do so by training experts in industry and government who would help protect the public against both the unthinking "mob" and unscrupulous capitalists. Properly maintained universities, in other words, were moderate places of social purity that would disseminate knowledge and higher learning so as to eliminate, or at least alleviate, the cultural dangers of greed, deprivation, and the crowd mentality.[19]

Public universities like Wisconsin, though, could not do their job if they were being corrupted by football and its irrational spectators. Concerned about the crowd's influence over rational universities, Wisconsin's Frederick Jackson Turner critiqued football at an alumni banquet in Madison in January 1906, at virtually the same time the IAAUS was being founded in New York City. Turner did have a few positive things to say about sport: he praised the "strenuous life" for giving formerly "pale and ascetic" students a healthy physical outlet, and he also maintained that college athletics would help develop the courage necessary to build America's national character. Yet Turner complained that the popularity of football had led some universities to conduct themselves inappropriately. "The public has pushed its influence inside the college walls," he proclaimed, thus "making it impossible for faculties and for the clean and healthy masses of the students to keep athletics honest and rightly related to a sane university life." Football was a professional business supported by taxpayers, with colleges recruiting athletic "gladiators" (or "mercenaries" or "experts") from distant locales for mere physical prowess. In the process of making money, it ruined "student ethics" and muddled "ideals of sport, manliness, and decency." Such "Tammany Hall methods" could not be used to educate college students. Turner assigned blame to the ticket-buying and newspaper-reading spectators who would apparently rather support a "football giant" than the hardworking students who would comprise a generation of progressive state leaders. (Ironically, though, some of those hardworking students hanged Turner in effigy and threatened to toss him into Lake Mendota after he supported a proposal that the Big Nine, Wisconsin's athletic conference, suspend football for two years.)[20] For a Wisconsin Idea proponent, the idea that universities were succumbing to sports enthusiasts and market forces—and letting nonacademics degrade the academy—was untenable. Unregulated football appealed to the lowest common denominator, thus allowing the uneducated multitude to corrupt an otherwise educational ritual.

Social scientists' concerns about football represented growing progressive concerns about the place of rationality within the public sphere, as well as universities' role within that public sphere. If not conducted properly, intercollegiate athletics could hinder social morals, and it could also limit universities' societal effectiveness. One critic of college life was Woodrow Wilson, the president of Princeton University, who had studied with Richard T. Ely (among others) while a graduate student at Johns Hopkins. In *Scribner's Magazine* (1909) Wilson asked, "What Is a College For?" Institutions of higher education, he said, had to be useful to the nation. Yet this usefulness could not be construed as mere practical utility. Rather, colleges had to train students' "faculties" in "mental discipline." Echoing antebellum moral philosophers, Wilson wrote that modern life needed *mental* athletes even more than it needed *physical* athletes. While extracurricular activities should be part of college life, insofar as they could help train students for life after college, they could not become the prime focus of America's budding universities. Wilson lamented that the modern American college had become a "teaching machine" that no longer taught men discipline. Athletics had to be just one part of a broader educational program designed to teach both "intellectual discipline and moral enlightenment" to students. So that they could be heard over the din, said Wilson, professors and college leaders had to figure out a way to "subordinate" the distracting sideshows—like athletics—to the larger academic circus.[21]

A critic who expressed a similar position and even corresponded with Wilson on the matter was Albert Shaw, another Johns Hopkins Ph.D. (and Ely student) who edited the *American Review of Reviews*. A well-known municipal reformer, in 1909 Shaw wrote a critique of athletics and student culture in which he pointed out that the taxpayers and philanthropists who were funding the phenomenal growth of Progressive Era universities needed to know that their millions were not being frittered away on a corrupt enterprise. Shaw claimed that American colleges had once been free of "drunkenness, gambling, lavish expenditure," and other deleterious activities. Pre–Civil War moral philosophers had taught and inspired young men, leading them to live disciplined lives rather than just filling students with information. But by the early 1900s, said Shaw, this older educational impulse had died off at the same time the rise of "social clubs and luxurious cliques" had transformed college youths into socialites carelessly spending their fathers' money on cocktails and fine living. Football distracted young men from study and encouraged gambling. In this way, it injured students' morals. Colleges, now filled with such temptations, might actually corrupt young men and prevent them from living "lives of real industry, real intellectual vigor, and real moral power."[22]

Shaw commented that universities were admitting too many students and growing excessively large. Institutions of higher education were reflecting the problems of larger society as they were becoming overrun by "cliques" that resembled urban "hoodlum" gangs. While athletics might provide a façade of institutional unity for massive universities, in reality they were only a poor substitute for a true "unified college spirit." Football, claimed Shaw, actually tore institutions apart and corrupted them. By exposing athletes to the desires of a heterogeneous crowd of thousands of spectators—some of whom were women—colleges were training students to take foolish chances and perform a brutal ritual that destroyed their vital organs. Even worse, daily papers had turned intercollegiate sport into a disorderly spectacle. Parents, said Shaw, did not want to see their sons' pictures on the sports pages next to "Jack Johnson, the negro pugilist heavy-weight," or professional baseball players. College men, he implied, should not be exposed to the public gaze in a racially mixed commercial sphere. Referring, like Taussig and others, to urban politics, he said that ath-

letics comprised "a network of commercialism that thoroughly Tam-
many-ize[d] what ought to be decorous and fine, like contests in the
English universities."[23]

By comparing football to British sport, Shaw demonstrated a notion
common among white, middle-class progressives who feared racial in-
tegration and working-class culture. After all, segregation and nativism were sometimes considered reform-minded in an era of anti–
African American violence and the arrival of millions of new
immigrants from southern and eastern Europe (who were hardly seen
as "white" upon landing in America). College sport, many progressive
critics maintained, should be amateur and white, not professional or
racially integrated. Moreover, football's commercial appeal, gambling
potential, and resemblance to violent modes of working-class leisure,
such as prizefighting, might damage student morality and taint public
life. Without proper regulation, sport could even create celebrity performers, turning progressive universities into corrupt sponsors of
spectacle and transforming both students and members of the public
into unthinking consumers. But with the right reforms, football might
uplift American society, preserve the utility of Progressive Era universities, and craft university students into upright, moral men who
could reshape industrial society along ethical lines.[24]

As Shaw and Wilson expounded upon the meanings of sport and
extracurricular activities for America's colleges, Wisconsin's E. A. Ross
continued to see sport as a pedagogical tool for creating moral, reform-
minded men. Ross argued in 1908 that sport was a "prophylactic"
against the mob mind, a means of protecting society by creating a
proper public attitude and teaching self-control. Education in rational
analysis would equip students with the critical tools needed to distin-
guish "objective truth" from popular fads. Sporting contests would
strengthen individual will, instill discipline, and train participants to
cooperate with one another without yielding to the crowd. For Ross,
football was useful only insofar as its less savory aspects prepared college men to resist cultural tricksters and ignore the crowd's desires.
College graduates, once thoroughly educated in mind, body, and
morals, would be able to protect themselves from "the sweep of popular delusion" and thus avoid the confidence men who peddled faulty
political or social panaceas.[25] Ross painted an appealing portrait of

sport and its educational possibilities, but he avoided a key question: How exactly would athletics help students develop self-restraint? Might students, without expert guidance, get swept up in the popular spectacle and succumb to the mob mind after all? This conundrum awaited a solution that turned out to be close at hand.

Some Americans claimed that athletic guidance would come from professional physical educators or coaches. In 1908, Harvard philosopher and social ethicist Josiah Royce called on physical educators to aid in the moral training of athletes, teams, and crowds. Using an argument that some coaches already employed, Royce claimed that physical training could "extend its influence to large bodies of boys who, as spectators of games or as schoolmates, are more or less influenced by the athletic spirit." Trained experts, in other words, could help shape the morality of those watching in the stands.[26] In this light, properly supervised spectator sport seemed like a magic bullet that could solve any number of social problems. Thomas F. Moran, an Ely student and longtime Purdue University professor of history and economics, advanced a similar theory. During his thirty-three-year tenure at Purdue, Moran served as the university's faculty representative to the IAAUS and NCAA, as well as the Big Nine. According to contemporaries, Moran represented a progressive stance on football that was influential in the Midwest.[27] But Moran broadened his sphere of influence when he spoke at the annual IAAUS convention in New York in late 1909. Echoing Royce and others who wanted to clean up American sport, he called for the moral leadership of professional athletic experts.

Moran noted that football reform would be difficult, since most spectators simply desired entertaining games and were uninterested in change. To make matters worse, most college presidents even wanted winning teams for advertising purposes. Football reform, therefore, had to be carefully crafted and widely implemented—what Moran called a "mutual disarmament" among colleges. To reform sport, universities needed a new kind of football leader. Too many coaches served only during the season, migrated from job to job, sought only victory, and were not sympathetic to collegiate ideals or goals. These journeymen employed dishonest means, either to retain their current jobs or to move to new positions with higher salaries. Instead of embracing such devious, shifty types, universities should seek the "right kind of men." A coach should be a well-paid, professional instructor, not a rover perpetually seeking money. He should be a teacher of mental, physical, and moral discipline. Men of unimpeachable character usually entered stable professions, said Moran, so universities should sign respectable men to full-year contracts: "Such a man is a fixture, not a transient. . . . He is a part of the college community and is interested in putting athletics on a sound and wholesome basis. He is usually a member of the instructional corps and as such has a feeling of responsibility." Moran, envisioning an institutional niche for coaches, advocated a football teacher with bona fide status. The new profession would have to exist throughout all of the nation's universities, though, since even coaches with high moral character had to compete against distant teams led by unethical tricksters. He anticipated an eager reception for his ideas about "clean and manly" athletics, since all of the IAAUS's members wanted "strenuous, manly" college sport and would presumably "be zealous in protecting intercollegiate athletics from all influences of a harmful character."[28]

Moran's approach to reform reflected a thought process typical of progressives. First it was national. Football's savior class, made up of scrupulous, truly professional coaches, would be created through structural reform carried out on a broad geographical level. This process could be left neither to chance nor to local or regional efforts. As modern transportation and communication networks tied distant communities together, reforms intended to circumvent graft and corruption must be all-encompassing. All institutions had to agree on changes that would, to use an athletic metaphor, level the intercollegiate playing field. Second, Moran's proposal negotiated a fine line between two kinds of professionalism: one that chased easy money, and one that sought a steady salary. Moran deplored the journeyman coach who desired profit and fame, but he exalted the resident expert who taught football and in return demanded only a respectable living. Itinerant showmen might enrich themselves and corrupt universities by appealing to the irrational mob, while expert coaches could enrich the university by serving the interests of a rational public. Athletic experts, presumably, would not be swayed by popular opinion. Unlike a coach who moved from job to job pursuing quick money, a truly professional coach would, like other university experts, possess respectable credentials and settle at one athletic department. These men would teach moral discipline and self-control, while simultaneously creating stability and respectability for lucrative football programs. Moran held faith in the public sphere. He thought that reason would persuade students and alumni to follow the "guiding hand" of the reformers who would save football by entrusting it to a group of expert coaches who would focus all of their time and attention on making football an honest game.[29]

Moran was probably not aware of it, but his proposal effectively brought social scientists' involvement in college football full circle. A generation earlier, before regional conferences and national regulatory agencies, a few scholars directly shaped the game that was permeating American culture and campuses. In the 1880s and 1890s, some of the first coaches were social scientists, men who were professional students of society but mere amateur athletes. Indiana University's first coach, for instance, was Arthur B. Woodford. Woodford was hired by Indiana's President David Starr Jordan in 1885, taught psychology and social science there for four years, and led the first Hoosier squad in 1887. He later completed a Ph.D. at Johns Hopkins in 1891 (the same year as E. A. Ross) with Ely, wrote on monetary policy, and advised the federal government on labor issues. Another Johns Hopkins social science graduate helped bring football to the South. George Petrie, who also earned a doctorate at Hopkins in 1891, invigorated athletics at Auburn, where he taught history. Petrie coached Auburn's squad and led it to the school's first victory against the University of Georgia in 1892. Five years later, Charles McCarthy, who had been a star fullback at Brown and articulated the Wisconsin Idea in the early 1900s, was Georgia's coach for two seasons, including the 1897 season shortened by Von Gammon's death.[30]

Each of these individuals earned prestige within his respective scholarly field, but none gained the same kind of notoriety that John Heisman or Knute Rockne did in the 1920s. Unlike well-known coaches, social scientists often had to show that they were practitioners of esoteric disciplines who were not interested in drawing notoriety. They had to prove that they were moderate and would not endanger universities' reputations as progressive institutions. For example, at Stanford, E. A. Ross developed a reputation as a prodigious public speaker, but incurred Jane Stanford's wrath in the 1890s by speaking out against imported Chinese labor and supporting the bimetallic, fiat monetary standard proposed by the Populists, which would have helped farmers and laborers. He also supported the Pullman strikers and other causes hostile to big industry. The wife of railroad magnate Leland Stanford might never have noticed Ross's remarks, except that newspapers reported (and perhaps exaggerated) his speeches. Ross later condemned the articles as sensational—another instance of the commercial press pandering to the mob mind—but he could not persuade the only audience that mattered. Jane Stanford, sole trustee of the university named in her son's memory, eventually convinced David Starr Jordan to fire Ross in 1900. Jordan portrayed Ross as an immature scholar who played to the crowd. Colleges could not indulge "the whims and fads of its clever young men who diffuse University ideas with their ears upon the mob and their eyes upon the newspapers." Josiah Royce agreed that Ross had ignored his public duty.[31] Jordan claimed that a true scholar subscribed to "sound and conservative opinion." He even dismissed Ross's professionalism, sneering that the sociologist possessed "little scientific training." Ross's real problem was not his beliefs, but his lack of rigor, decorum, and self-restraint. Jordan informed Yale's president, Arthur T. Hadley, that Ross was a stain on Stanford's reputation. "No right of free thought or free speech has been denied here," Jordan asserted, "but if a man's outside speech hurts or helps his own reputation, he must take the consequences as elsewhere in the world."[32]

Ross conceded the premises of Jordan's attacks, if not their substance, when he defended his academic reputation by employing a logical, if somewhat disingenuous, tactic. He protested accusations of substandard scholarship by claiming that his writings were uninteresting and had virtually no popular appeal. Thus the same scholar who had called young men to social activism when assailing laissez-faire economics and promoting strenuous sport in 1893 proclaimed in 1900 that he was a disinterested academic. Ross assured Jane Stanford that his work was "dry" and that he did not engage any "burning questions." He said that his articles, published in journals based at major research universities, proved he was not "dangerous." He even claimed that he was so far removed from contemporary politics that students could not discern his stances on pressing issues like bimetallism. Initially, Jordan backed these claims before he turned against Ross.[33] At various points, in other words, both Jordan and Ross said that he was such a good scholar because he was irrelevant. It was not quite true, but it was the right thing to say to try to get out of hot water with a politically conservative trustee. Professors in the new ivory tower, no matter the social or political relevance of their research, had to become, or at least look like, disinterested scientists. Unlike the football team, it was probably not a good thing if the sociology department made a splash in the local papers.

Ross's dismissal led to a national uproar, several indignant faculty resignations, and a major academic freedom controversy.[34] After leaving Palo Alto he moved on, first to the University of Nebraska in Lincoln, and then to Wisconsin, where he joined his Ph.D. advisor and mentor, Richard T. Ely. Public universities located in progressive state capitals welcomed ostensibly radical scholars like Ross more eagerly than had cloistered Stanford, but only if the professors tamed their public profiles and asserted identities as sensible scholars. Wisconsin had even put Ely on trial in 1894 for his support of organized labor. Although he held on to his professorship, the trial changed Ely's scholarly and political orientation. Formerly an outspoken radical unafraid to exhibit his Social Gospel inclinations, after the trial he became more conservative and reticent. As historian Ellen Schrecker notes, Ely then "stopped writing for a popular audience and developed an appropriately scholarly niche for himself in the relatively obscure field of land economics." Even the academic freedom statement that Wisconsin's board of regents issued after Ely's acquittal was mostly a publicity stunt formulated to advertise the university. Although the early 1900s was a golden age for Wisconsin progressivism, by 1914 conservatives led a backlash in state politics. They subsequently muted the influence of the university and of progressives like Robert LaFollette or Charles Van Hise.[35]

At this time some critical observers were starting to see that universities, by virtue of being public institutions, could never be immune from the less savory elements of public life. In 1918, Thorstein Veblen—near the end of an itinerant scholarly career marred by dis-

missals resulting in large part from his own disruptive professional behavior (not just his caustic opinions and the lack of tenure or academic
freedom protection)—published *The Higher Learning in America*. In
this book he once again critiqued football at the same time he called
for universities to seal themselves off from nonacademic influences.
Veblen argued that higher education should comprise a pure academic
sphere untainted by politics or money. Universities trained scholars,
and prolonged exposure to the gilded ways of the leisure class would
sully both men and the institutions designed to cultivate them. Football was merely a distraction. Veblen said that intercollegiate sport
brought the unreflective, backslapping culture of businessmen into
the academy, diverting attention from education. Veblen wanted universities to remain intellectual spaces, not become places for producing men adept in a modern perversion of the Darwinian struggle for
existence that was only useful for the unnatural selection of capitalist
functionaries. Football was less than desirable because it represented
the academy's willingness to sink to the base desires of a society that
did not appreciate the university's true, intellectual function.[36]

Veblen's 1918 critique of football and call for a reemphasis on intellectual life indicated a shift in the way some Americans thought about
universities. In order to be useful to the public, they had to be protected from that public. As chapter 7 will show, Ross's dismissal inspired American intellectuals to band together and create professional
safeguards, such as academic freedom, permanent tenure, and the
American Association of University Professors (a group that sought to
reform or eliminate football in the 1920s). These late Progressive Era
reforms did, in fact, provide some security for academics. We can see
that later in life, when Ross reflected on his career in Wisconsin he
praised the institution for disregarding prevailing systems of social
class and for tolerating outspoken professors. Indeed, he proclaimed,
Madison's hundreds of faculty members were so well protected from
American society's "ruthless commercialism" that they felt obligated
to be as critical as possible. By the 1920s, scholars like Ross were often
able to speak without fear of dismissal because of Progressive Era reforms. But other critics, as we will see, were then starting to observe
that such professional safeguards might also cause them to play it safe
and merely produce respectable—not provocative—scholarship. They

may have had a point, insofar as it is evident that Ross's fondness for Wisconsin's intellectual climate appears to have only been surpassed by loyalty to his discipline. Since the 1890s, he observed in 1936, sociology had become a scientific field with a "massive body of accepted doctrine." In turn, its practitioners were able to move between state-funded and privately endowed universities.[37] The communities of modern intellectual culture provided relatively safe cocoons within which scholars could communicate complicated ideas to each other via standard jargon without having to worry about threats from the outside world. At the same time, this disciplinary structure also provided national, transinstitutional structures for both vertical and horizontal promotion.

Turn-of-the-century social scientists wanted academic research and higher education to be useful to the American public. Studying a wide range of pressing issues, they crafted solutions to mitigate the problems of a growing urban-industrial society. In particular, they focused on morality in the public sphere, envisioning collegiate sport as one activity that, if regulated, could solve many of society's moral problems. By 1910, one solution was the professional coach, who might bring the same type of stature and expertise to athletics that university professors had brought to academic studies. Coaches, however, occupied a very different public space than the one that scholars were starting to occupy. While Ross and some other progressive social scientists were effective public intellectuals, the very circumstances about which they wrote—the "mob mind" and the influence of money or the sensational press—forced them to create a veritable ivory tower of esoteric or arcane academic structures. To pursue knowledge relevant to modern society, ironically, they had to be protected from that society—especially the market economy. Intercollegiate football, however, found itself in a different place. By contrast, coaches directly engaged the commercial sphere. At the same time they theorized a pedagogical identity as educators who understood the body, mind, and crowd psychology, coaches solidified their identity as pop-culture ingénues. College athletics' impresarios, in other words, successfully created a cultural space located squarely between the university and American consumers.

When Thomas Moran spoke at the IAAUS annual meeting in 1909, professional coaching was not an entirely new idea. Coaches were already working to present themselves as reputable teachers of physical education, a field that had been initiated in the mid-1800s. In the 1890s, they began writing and publishing football manuals that—besides providing play diagrams and tips for athletes and other coaches—stressed sport's pedagogical potential. Through such writings, which flourished in the 1920s, coaches tried to create *discipline* in multiple ways. First, they strove to show that sport taught self-control to players, students, and spectators. Second, they started to claim a quasi-disciplinary university space by arguing that they were athletic experts and educators, not agents of popular culture or mere entertainers. Nevertheless, despite some resemblances, there were crucial differences between football coaches and physical education instructors. Early 1900s intercollegiate sport was, in fact, a popular spectacle that attracted hundreds of thousands of paying spectators and millions of dollars to arenas throughout the nation. While coaches strenuously cultivated public personas as teachers of discipline not interested in personal gain, by necessity they also created close ties to the cultural marketplace.

Physical culture, as we have already seen, first became important in antebellum colleges and grew in prominence after the Civil War, when students clamored for relief from the intense mental work of modern higher education. At that time, the field had few clearly defined parameters or methodologies, so the men hired to teach physical education created them. Gymnasium directors such as Amherst's Edward Hitchcock and Harvard's Dudley Sargent contributed to the development of anthropometry, a post–Civil War physiological science that measured students to calculate median body types.[1] To standardize pedagogy and theory within their field as well as attain professional status, early physical educators also published textbooks: Hitchcock's *Elementary Anatomy and Physiology* (1860) and Sargent's *Handbook of Developing Exercises* (1889) were two of the earliest. Jay Seaver of Yale, who wrote *Anthropometry and Physical Examination* (1890), argued that for physical education to be science, it needed a gradable curriculum—a system to "[mark] physical excellence or deficiency in a numerical way that shall in some way correspond with the mark that is given on examination for intellectual accomplishments." Like psychologists, Seaver noted that the stress of modern life caused nervous disorders. Without exercise, Americans' "nerve fibres" and health would deteriorate, thus negating eons of evolutionary development. Since physical education was so important, it needed intelligent direction—by professional gymnasium experts—to be effective.[2]

But physical educators also ran into obstacles. Early gymnasium classes were optional; to keep students enrolled, teachers had to balance the curricular need for discipline with students' desire for recreation or enjoyment. In addition, gymnasium directors could not escape the fact that both real and perceived ties existed between physical culture and entertainment. Even Harvard's physical education displays at the 1893 Chicago Columbian Exposition, which included nude statues of anthropometrically ideal college students, may have appeared similar to the exotic bodies displayed on the Midway.[3] Pioneer physical educators, therefore, had to assert that they were professionals with high standards uninterested in making money or exploiting popular desires. They also had to overcome the taint of their eclectic training. For example, Dudley Sargent, hired in 1879 to direct Harvard's Hemenway Gymnasium, was a former circus gymnast who held a Yale medical degree and had directed Bowdoin College's gymnasium. This hybrid background initially helped him thrive both as a Harvard professor and as head of a profitable summer school for physical education teachers, but it eventually came to haunt him. Despite his assertions that his courses, including his patented physical culture apparatus, were purely scientific, some Harvard professors doubted Sargent's professional status and called for his removal. As athletic committee chair Charles Eliot Norton observed in 1884, Sargent's presence on the faculty was "obviously irritating" to some members. Harvard rescinded Sargent's professorial standing in 1889, yet he kept teaching there and his affiliation attracted many students. He even unsuccessfully argued that his prominence was a reason for reinstatement.[4] Sargent, even without faculty status, maintained an apparent association with popular culture that continued to raise eyebrows in Cambridge. In 1892, he incurred scrutiny by examining famous boxer John L. Sullivan and publishing an article about him. Critics implied that Sargent's willingness to be associated with the working-class art of prizefighting kept him from being a teacher or scientist. Sargent justified his actions by claiming that he had examined Sullivan (whom he called "a splendid animal") to further scholarship, not to promote spectatorship or aid gamblers. After all, Sargent had "made no allusions to the coming fight" and did not discuss Sullivan's odds of winning. As a physical trainer, Sargent's job was to understand the human physique and seek out "rare specimens"—even if they were famous pugilists.[5]

Responding to such challenges, physical educators like Sargent and Seaver eventually created a niche within universities by founding departments of physical culture. Coaching soon also entered the picture, although its relationship to physical education was not quite so clear (and there was often a tension between coaches and physical educators). In 1891, Chicago's President William Rainey Harper—in order to facilitate his goal of hiring the best faculty while also promoting the new university through intercollegiate sport—appointed his former Yale student Amos Alonzo Stagg as the nation's first tenured professor of physical culture and athletics. Hiring Stagg, though, was not easy. After lengthy negotiations, in which he hinted that a larger salary would help him forget more attractive offers from Yale and Penn, Stagg agreed to work at the raw campus next to the Midway.[6] Although Stagg ultimately accepted the lower salary at Chicago, he used this concession as leverage. He warned that if he tried to do too much work, it would "drain" his "nervous energy" and weaken his own health. So he would need more assistants and better equipment if the university expected him to direct the men's and women's gymnasia while simultaneously maintaining research in the quickly growing fields of physical culture and anthropometry. Despite being head of a physical culture department, however, Stagg served primarily as a coach and trainer for the intercollegiate athletic teams in baseball, football, track, and crew. His job was more publicity agent than physical education instructor. Stagg observed that if Chicago fielded a team to compete with rivals like Michigan or Northwestern, "*it must be a winning team* or one which will bring honor to the university." By combining physical cul-

Amos Alonzo Stagg of the University of Chicago, widely
recognized as America's first tenured professor of athletics
and physical education, circa 1912. Special Collections
Research Center, University of Chicago Library.

ture and intercollegiate athletics in one department, Chicago had
bridged education and popular culture. Other colleges, especially state
universities in the Midwest, soon followed this model. As early as 1892,
Stagg reported that Michigan was hotly pursuing Henry "Harry"
Williams, another former Yale athlete. If Ann Arbor hired Williams,
fretted Stagg, the Wolverines *"would lick us* almost certainly."[7]

Aspiring coaches often employed the rhetoric of science and pedagogy in an attempt to mask the language of victory and promotion.

Like academic scholars, they had to display impeccable credentials; universities, in turn, had to ensure that they were hiring professionals, not showmen cleverly posing as experts. For example, in 1909, candidates for Wisconsin's athletic director position displayed their character and earnestness as a way to win the position. Emmett Angell, head of the physical education department at Oregon Agricultural College (now Oregon State University), listed studies at Harvard, Yale, the YMCA school in Springfield, Massachusetts, as well as in Germany. He even mentioned his book manuscript then in press at Little, Brown. Angell and other aspirants insisted that athletic training was not a lark. It was a "profession" to which they had devoted their lives.[8] Since physical culture was equal to academics, they claimed, supervising athletics was not a job for a gymnast or a baseball player. It was a career for a disciplined professional. Candidates who asserted temperate habits underscored this assumption. One Spanish-American War veteran, a former Sargent student, even claimed that his students learned discipline in military-style drills.[9] Taking such factors into account, Wisconsin ultimately offered the job to the University of Missouri's Clark Hetherington. Luther Gulick called Hetherington a "scholar, a gentleman and a man of extraordinary executive ability"; Sargent considered him "one of the best qualified men" in America.[10] Such traits were important for Wisconsin, which hoped to consolidate athletics and physical culture in one department. Hetherington's academic expertise, especially his psychology training at Clark University, was also appealing. G. Stanley Hall wrote that Hetherington possessed "an unusually wiry, nervous, muscular organization" that prepared him "to stand any amount of work"; he was the only physical educator Hall knew who had a broadly "scientific" perspective on the field. While Hetherington was an athlete, said Hall, he was also able "to appeal to the intellect of students" and wanted to be a "professor" who taught degree candidates. Hetherington, who ultimately declined the position, added to Hall's view by noting the need for a rigorous physical education "curriculum" to train "experts."[11]

The duties of a turn-of-the-century athletic director or head coach—to supervise physical education, lead teams, build a department, and advertise a university—apparently required a great deal of energy. Or at least this seems to be the case if we examine coaches' salary demands. In 1905, Stagg requested a raise to $6,000, which he justified by noting that his year-round work was "extremely wearing nervously [and] physically." The university expected him to produce consistently victorious intercollegiate teams with reputable amateur athletes, a task that was especially difficult, considering the strict eligibility requirements. In addition, the recruiting of quality players was "a continuous moral as well as nervous strain." Such work was both stressful and never-ending. Stagg complained that he continually felt pressure from both the university and the public. He even worked during his vacations and received unpaid assistance from his wife because he was expected to do tasks for which other colleges might pay several men. With a significant salary raise to acknowledge his great efforts and sacrifices, his physical and mental condition would improve, and he could continue to oversee his department's growth.[12]

Stagg made his plea at a time when many universities were placing sport within a single department in order to make it conform to regional or national mandates. In the Northeast, where many colleges still proclaimed amateurism, some institutions quietly hired professional coaches and established athletic departments. In 1914, for example, Yale reorganized its Board of Athletic Control, hired a new coach, and joined the NCAA. Such reforms would apparently make sport respectable and place it on an equal footing with the rest of the university. Yale dean Robert Corwin (who called the athletic field a "great laboratory of clean living and clear thinking") wrote that athletics should command "the same constructive thought and attention" as other university departments.[13] This process happened even more openly in the Midwest. Before 1910, Ohio State University separated intercollegiate athletics from physical education, but it had to place both within the same department in order to join the Big Nine. Professor H. Shindle Wingert compared this transformation to reforms at progressive state universities like Wisconsin, Missouri, and Nebraska, where athletics inhabited *"a regular department"* and was treated like any other university department. This idea closely followed the 1910 NCAA recommendation that athletics maintain the same standards as other academic units. Coaches should be part of the instructional staff, said the NCAA, not mavericks without clearly defined status. Dissatisfaction surfaced, though, when it became clear that physical education and intercollegiate athletics fulfilled very different goals. Wingert later complained that big-time sports only benefited "strong, robust, perfectly healthy" men and had become overtly commercial. This was unlike physical education, which sought to instruct all students, especially the physically deficient. Health was its main goal, not entertainment.[14] The coexistence of these two disparate aims was difficult to maintain, but coaches eventually learned to minimize this tension by theorizing spectator sport as a public activity with virtually unlimited pedagogical possibilities.

Early 1900s coaches found numerous ways to claim that football could teach self-control to students, athletes, and spectators. The career of Harvard's semiprofessional coach, William T. "Bill" Reid, illuminates the process by which amateur coaching was associated with physical education before it became professional coaching. Before 1908, Harvard experimented with arrangements that might yield gridiron success without compromising a genteel reputation for amateur sport. Engineering professor Ira Hollis, who served on Harvard's athletic committee and later helped design its concrete stadium, stated in 1899 that by hiring professional coaches, universities risked exposing young men to the taint of commercial culture. Yet he conceded that if the coach was a respectable man chosen "by a responsible committee," he could be a positive influence no matter his rate of pay.[15] In 1905, two years after constructing the stadium, the university hired Reid, a recent alumnus and star baseball player, to coach the Crimson eleven. The university paid the ostensible amateur coach $7,000 per season for his ability to mentor young men. Reid aided this notion by stating his intention to build a winning team "cleanly."[16] Reid's father, William T. Reid, Sr. (a former University of California president), agreed that his son could lead efficient squads and build "a healthful and virile . . . sentiment" at Harvard by leading precise and efficient football squads. Yet the elder Reid only supported the vocation as a temporary one and expected his son to return to California, eventually, to teach.[17]

Reid, ultimately, did abandon coaching to teach at his father's academy near San Francisco. But before leaving Harvard he outlined his rationale for professional coaches. First and foremost, said Reid, the game must be conducted as a business. Harvard's team could not succeed if it had to continue relying on a mix of seasonal, journeyman coaches. Harvard had to either hire "a paid coach of the right type and self-respect" or settle for "charity coaching" and disrespect in the world of college sport.[18] Reid disliked journeyman coaches, but for different reasons than those Thomas Moran would offer in 1909. While Moran thought that temporary coaches corrupted universities, Reid thought they were unsuccessful. Also, Reid lived the lonely, itinerant life of a journeyman for several years and did not like it very much. But even though his coaching stint at Harvard was brief, Reid did help reform football. Besides meeting with Roosevelt, Camp, and others at the White House in 1905, he belonged to the Harvard committee that recommended reforms such as the neutral zone and the forward pass in January 1906. Formerly, said Reid, many offenses went undetected because they occurred when the action on the field was "hidden from the eyes of the umpire." The neutral zone and forward pass would help officials to see the players clearly and thus keep athletes from evading the rules. While a few critics thought the forward pass would make football worse, by leading to more injuries, some, such as Harvard's President Charles William Eliot, conceded its value in making the game more sportsmanlike.[19]

Even with the forward pass—which did not take its ultimate form until after 1910—reform was not yet complete. Later rule makers implemented other changes designed to stop teams from cheating. In 1911, for example, Stagg, based on the suggestion of a coach in Kirksville, Missouri, proposed a rule that would prevent one team from gaining an advantage by using an underinflated ball.[20] By World War I, moreover, teams began numbering uniforms, a reform seen as a way to track and restrain unsportsmanlike players or coaches. Parke Davis, an attorney, writer, and amateur statistician who operated a "Record Office of American Collegiate Football" out of his home in Easton, Pennsylvania, promoted uniform numbers in 1913 because the previous season several teams had been charged with improper player substitutions. He favored an 8- to 10-inch number "sewn securely upon the back of the jersey." Others thought numbers would help spectators prevent dishonest or incompetent referees from "discrediting" athletes. Herbert Reed, author of *Football for Public and Player*, noted that uniform numbers were common in Australian rugby, a sport that many saw as purer than American football. Reed argued that in order to keep the game honest, spectators should know all pun-ishable rule infractions and their penalties, and they should also watch in a disciplined manner that would help them better enjoy, un-derstand, and profit from football. In this way, spectator sport could be universally accessible and educational, teaching ethical self-control to all of society—not just developing a few bodies or providing enter-tainment for the masses. Reforms like uniform numbers might help everyone in the arena see the game and enforce sportsmanlike con-duct. In this way, they could enhance football's pedagogical potential and keep it corruption-free.[21]

Football proponents did not typically see the irony in the need to legislate against corruption in a game that was supposedly ideal for in-stilling self-control. Rather, they steadfastly argued that sport taught disciplined behavior by making athletes internalize rules. For some, including Amos Alonzo Stagg and Minnesota's Henry Williams—who quoted the Gospel of Luke when preaching athletic perseverance and "strict training" to his Gopher football players—this brand of disci-pline was based on Muscular Christianity. Along with Stagg, Williams was a prime example of how sport could assume a religious tone that was becoming less common in academic departments at the turn of the century.[22] But while some tied discipline to Christian ideals, others connected it to whiteness. In 1914, a Boston attorney informed Har-vard's president that athletes should act like civilized gentlemen; after all, he said, Americans admired "the man who plays the game white."[23] In colleges where most (if not all) students were white males, proper athletic conduct represented normative racial and gender stan-dards. Yet players and spectators did not always exhibit gracious be-havior toward minorities, especially the few black athletes at northern universities in the early 1900s, such as Paul Robeson of Rutgers and Frederick Douglass "Fritz" Pollard of Brown. Only through athleticism and hard work did these black players earn grudging respect from coaches, teammates, and opponents. Even then, the All-American Pol-lard withstood game-day taunts and backhanded compliments. Later in life, he reflected that his college experiences had, in his words, "niggerized" him.[24]

Even though football invited less than gentlemanly behavior, coaches stressed their ability to teach moral, mental, and physical discipline. But in truth, coaches were different from physical education instructors. Coaches trained a few men to perform with athletic precision before the crowd and publicize alma mater through victories. They earned their livelihood by winning, but to justify positions located in a space perched precariously between the academy and popular culture, these men created a quasi-academic community of discourse, the professional identity of which coalesced around the idea that athletics taught discipline to all. This pseudo-scholarly field—which, like academic disciplines, was based on specialized expertise and discourse—found its fullest expression in the didactic football manuals that first appeared in the 1890s and became common in the 1920s.[25] While early manuals stressed football's ability to discipline athletes, later books stressed spectatorship's effects upon the crowd itself. In the 1920s, when college football became a staple of American popular culture, famous coaches regularly touted sport's pedagogical potential at the same time they rose in the profession and made money through product endorsements and the mass media.

Walter Camp, not surprisingly, pioneered the didactic manual with play diagrams and reflections on the meanings of sport when he published *American Football* in 1891. Ever the rational manager, Camp noted that players must be disciplined, and he posited that self-control could be imposed from the outside, through strict training and obedience to the rules. He even listed fouls and penalties in a chapter for spectators. Two years later, Amos Alonzo Stagg and Henry Williams published a *Scientific and Practical Treatise on American Football for Schools and Colleges*. This book followed Camp's precedent of stressing the importance of skilled spectatorship. It ordered readers to learn the game's rules first before delving into training, strategy, or play diagrams. Not to be outdone, Camp coauthored an 1893 volume, *Football*, with Harvard's Lorin Deland. They argued that if players did not learn "strict discipline," a team would degenerate into a leaderless mob. They explained the importance of spectatorship and told readers where to find the best seats in the grandstands. Football was so complex that only well-prepared viewers sitting in the right place could "appreciate its real worth, both as a sport for sport's sake, and as a means of developing character."[26] Despite its authoritative tone, *Football* was not an unqualified success: by 1901, Camp and Deland agreed to allow Houghton Mifflin to sell discounted remainder copies. But lackluster sales did not augur hardship for the authors, businessmen whose livelihoods relied neither upon university salaries nor upon book royalties.[27] This would change, though, in the 1900s, when many football authors were professional coaches.

One early 1900s coach who wrote a successful football manual was Fielding Yost, whose Michigan Wolverines team included the "point-a-minute" squad that won the first Rose Bowl in 1902. *Football for Player and Spectator*, an illustrated volume published by the University of Michigan's press in 1905, went further than Camp, Stagg, or Williams in discussing the ways that spectators could benefit from football—not just the ways that they could assist players in learning discipline. Yost claimed that football developed a seemingly endless list of traits ("self-reliance, moral courage, 'sand,' determination, energy, discipline, judgment, self-restraint"), and he also argued that it taught moral and physical lessons to thousands of spectators. The players' disciplined example "extend[ed] in most surprising ways to the entire student body," and even mere viewers could be "moved to habits of temperance and regularity." In turn, football might benefit the whole university by helping spectators absorb the same lessons as the players, and thus forging "a spirit which reaches out from the athletic field through the campus and into the very recitation room."[28] This argument was novel. In the 1820s, Charles Beck had written that only members of the public with a vested interest in teaching students disciplined behavior could watch gymnasium work; in the 1890s, Camp also argued that spectators helped teach players discipline. Yost, though, claimed that watching sport could actually discipline *spectators*. He was turning the arena into a classroom of morality by saying that football's influence extended to everyone. This claim was both new and self-serving, insofar as it justified Yost's professional existence as a teacher who was not a popular entertainer. Also, it could not be proven false. Whether or not Yost's claim possessed a shred of truth, there was no way to ascertain whether thousands in the stands—who subsidized sport at the same time they formed a bond with the universities who sponsored the contests—actually learned discipline by watching football.

Football for Player and Spectator was a success. Michigan students

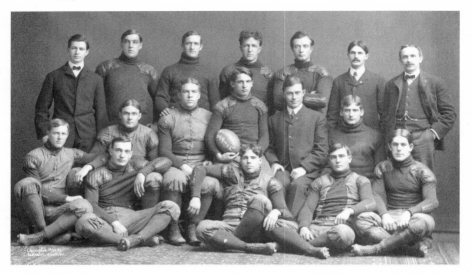

Fielding H. Yost, top left, with his famed "point-a-minute" 1902 Michigan Wolverines squad. Three years later, Yost would publish *Football for Player and Spectator,* which argued that college sport could teach discipline to spectators. Rentschler's Studio (Ann Arbor, Michigan) records, Box 47, Bentley Historical Library, University of Michigan.

crowed that Yost's "Text-Book," packed with play diagrams, photographs, and training tips, was essential reading. Quickly selling out its 3,000-copy first edition, it soon entered a second printing. The volume seemed certain to make both Yost and the university nationally known.[29] Practically speaking, this was Yost's last book, but the popular coach of the Michigan Wolverines neither stopped making pedagogical claims nor ceased portraying himself as an authority on both sport and education. In later speeches he stressed the importance of discipline, arguing that teams could only gain victory through honest means, with players who lived "clean" lives. Played properly, team sports were the best way of inculcating "good citizenship" and manliness. Sport was an important part of education, said Yost, but only if the crowd was disciplined and backed the referees who supervised the game and punished rule breakers. Yost even sounded like Eugene Richards and other turn-of-the-century football proponents when he stated that sport, like eugenics, could play a part in racial improvement. Football, he said, would remain the "national autumn sport . . . as long as Anglo-Saxon blood flow[ed] in the veins of the young American."[30]

Football's popularity grew tremendously in the 1920s, and coaches like Bill Roper, John Heisman, and Percy Haughton capitalized by publishing manuals with titles like *Winning Football*, *Principles of Football*, and *Football and How to Watch It*. This genre, by disclosing the way to produce winning teams and by asserting authors' mastery of the art of teaching discipline, served a practical purpose. Coaches, depending on their ambition, could use these books to attain professional status or monetary reward. Some so-called football mentors (especially in the Big Ten) parlayed their coaching expertise into stable faculty chairs or athletic department positions. Others used publications to secure lucrative contracts. Either way, they created a professional identity located at the crossroads of commercial culture and the academy.

Princeton's Bill Roper wrote one of the first 1920s manuals, *Winning Football*. In it, the well-known "Biff" coach called football "a splendid . . . preparatory school for life."[31] Legendary Georgia Tech coach John Heisman, whose resume included stints at half a dozen colleges, stressed a similar message in *Principles of Football* (1922), published while he coached at the University of Pennsylvania. Heisman called the athletic field "the best laboratory known where the young man can get the training, the discipline, [and] the experience" he needed. While many might perceive self-control as a "Sunday School" quality, Heisman saw it as a Saturday afternoon trait. In a dubious syllogism, Heisman reasoned that since football tempted players to cheat, and since temptation was the best way to learn discipline, football was a practical way for a player to learn "how to govern, to control, [and] to conquer" himself. Like physical educators, however, Heisman was careful to point out that this process required supervision by trained experts. The ideal coach was a "man of education and culture," not an unschooled brute seeking fame or fortune. He did not allow players to engage in "muckerism" (defined as cheating or profiteering). Heisman even claimed, extravagantly, that a coach could build character more successfully than the majority of ministers and fathers—or even professors.[32]

While Heisman professed anti-muckerism and discipline, statements made earlier in his career indicate that he may not have always held himself to such high standards. Heisman began coaching at Oberlin College before moving to Buchtel College (now the University of Akron), Auburn, and Clemson. Until his 1899 arrival, Clemson was a football lightweight. But the Atlanta press explained that Heisman turned Clemson's team into winners by 1903 by expecting players "to take desperate chances" and training them in the ways of trickery. Sewanee, Georgia, and other colleges protested that Clemson violated the rules and did not play "clean" football. Heisman denied the charges, claiming that his practice field was unequaled in "order" and "decorum." But he also defended himself by proclaiming the virtues of pigskin legerdemain and by redefining the terms of the debate. Heisman said that he did not plan to abandon his "tricks," since they helped "to run up the score and aid the team in many ways." While some saw tricks as dishonest, Heisman believed that football was just like war, "where all kinds of tricks go by the name of strategy"; he liked to call his style "strategical instead of trickery." Opposing teams who disdained Heisman's strategy must have also been impressed by it, because soon Heisman was entertaining offers from several southern schools. He went to Georgia Tech in 1904.[33]

Although Heisman apparently employed any means necessary to gain victories, he—like other coaches—claimed that sport was a discipline-building exercise for the whole university. Percy Haughton, a former Harvard coach (1908–1916) who published *Football and How to Watch It* in 1922, argued that team leaders had "to supervise the scholastic work" of all potential athletes. Surveillance ensured players' academic eligibility, and it also ensured proper decorum. To enforce proper ethics, each match required the presence of officials who maintained "law and order" on the field. Spectators could aid officials by watching closely and by knowing all the rules. Haughton wrote that spectators could learn the same mental habits and discipline as the quarterback, but only if they were serious and diligent. Although he conceded that some spectators were men who did not properly "study" the game, Haughton particularly criticized women who attended games for entertainment and were unaware of both football's "higher technique" and "simplest rudiments." Attention to detail and mental discipline, traits coded as male, were more important than en-

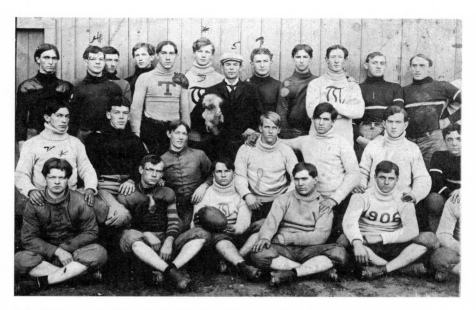

John Heisman (holding dog) with the 1906 Georgia Tech team. Just two years earlier, Heisman had come to Tech from Clemson College, despite having been accused of using trickery to win football games. Permission of the Georgia Institute of Technology Library and Information Center, Archives and Records Management Department.

joyment or relaxation—less demanding activities coded as female. Haughton told spectators to sit high in the stands, where they could see all the action. Removed from the social butterflies and the temptation to enjoy the game without learning from it, said Haughton, attentive spectators could concentrate on developing their minds.[34]

Heisman insisted that all students, not just athletes, had a sacred duty to report players who broke training rules. Not only did players have to follow a strict training regimen, but thousands of other students needed to follow the rules as well. This idea echoed an argument that Roper posited in *Winning Football*. Princeton's coach said that the proper campus "atmosphere" was necessary to keep players physically, mentally, and morally sound. Any student who aspired to participate in intercollegiate athletics had to "stand well in his classes and behave himself outside of them" throughout the whole year. In some cases, said Roper, only "public" pressure could have any effect on re-calcitrant athletes. He argued that the efforts of the entire student body helped create respectable teams, and these efforts, in turn, taught all students. Roper contended that his main goal was to instill a "winning football spirit" among all students in the college. While this claim may seem outlandish or fanciful, in 1927, James Harrison, a *New York Times* sportswriter, bought it. He recalled Roper's assertion that he taught the entire college. Princeton's coach had claimed "to make his domain not only the gridiron but the entire campus; to arouse col-lege spirit; to get the whole university behind the thirty or forty or fifty young men [on the field]." While some "modern young sophisti-cates" might reject such claims, Roper had thoroughly demonstrated his skills. Harrison claimed that if he were in control of a university and sought a football coach, Roper would be his first choice.[35]

At least one coach apparently employed this logic by using his book to build a reputation and gain employment at a university that wanted a coach expert at both winning and instilling discipline—or at least at promoting his ability to instill discipline. Percy Haughton be-gan his successful run at Harvard in 1908, but he left in 1916 to be-come president and part-owner of National League baseball's Boston Braves. By November 1922, the same month Frank J. "Buck" O'Neil re-signed as Columbia University's head coach, Haughton had published *Football and How to Watch It*. Four months later, after reviewing ap-plications from "America's greatest football mentors," Columbia ap-pointed Haughton as O'Neil's successor. The *New York Times* wrote that Haughton's name was universally known and that his recently published book showed he was skilled at "teaching" football. Colum-bia's President Nicholas Murray Butler seemed to agree, and he ex-pressed his pleasure with the appointment. He wrote that Columbia saw sport "as an integral part of the training and discipline" received by undergraduates. Butler was sure that Haughton would assist the university in this regard, and he wished the coach success in his "im-portant post." For his services, Haughton was well compensated. The terms of the contract were not revealed, but the press reported that Haughton would be one of America's most highly paid coaches—al-though, as it turned out, he was not successful in his brief tenure at Columbia, which was cut short by his death.[36]

Lavish salaries were available for master coaches in the 1920s because, as the decade unfolded and Americans became wealthier, college football became more popular than ever. Universities drew millions of spectators to the huge concrete arenas they constructed on campus, as well as to massive public sports palaces like the Los Angeles Coliseum, Chicago's Soldier Field, or Birmingham's Legion Field. Radio also helped increase the game's popularity. As the market for successful coaches and their books grew, midwestern football experts like Howard Jones, J. W. Wilce, Knute Rockne, and Bob Zuppke published their own manuals, in which they relied less on the rhetoric of surveillance and discipline than had Yost, Roper, Heisman, and Haughton. The football manual, it seemed, was becoming a standard genre. Coaches had a model from which to work and so they did not need to work quite so hard to develop pedagogical theory justifying their university positions. The manual, like college football itself, was becoming less a means to an instructional end and more a means unto itself. Soon, football's educational meanings would be subordinated to its proper execution and entertainment value.

Howard Jones, Iowa's head coach and athletic director from 1916 to 1923, published *How to Coach and Play Football* in 1923. The publisher bolstered Jones's status by stating his position on the title page (other football books, like Haughton's, included a similar tagline). Jones also indicated his achievements and credentials throughout the text, including his summer football courses at Iowa and the undefeated Big Ten champion teams he led in 1921 and 1922. "Successful coaching of football requires thought, and judgment," wrote Jones, "based upon as much knowledge of the game as it is possible for the coach to acquire." Most of the book just explained how to produce winning teams, yet in the final pages, almost as an afterthought, Jones dutifully asserted that football taught "sacrifice" through rigorous training rules and required "quick clear thinking"; only through "clean" and "fair" play could players learn character. Jones (or his editor) also felt the need to assert that college football was not a money-making activity. He warned that "boys who attempt to commercialize their athletic prowess" would not learn discipline.[37] At a time when the first professional football leagues were forming, and shortly before student-athletes started playing in them after graduating or quitting college, such anti-commercialism, although explicitly pedagogical, hid an essential truth of college sport: athletes were not supposed to play for money, since professionalism could corrupt education—but it was acceptable for universities or coaches to profit from intercollegiate football.

Whether or not Jones seriously believed the notion that he was a teacher of discipline, it is hard to tell. Nevertheless, he certainly was one of his generation's best coaches and successfully built a career. In 1924 he left Iowa City to become athletic director at North Carolina's Trinity College, which was then using tobacco money to transform itself into Duke University. According to several newspapers, Jones lived in Denver and only wanted to be in Iowa City during the season, but some Iowa faculty members opposed this arrangement. The Duke contract, supposed to last five years, was more flexible. But soon Jones received an offer that was even more appealing. In 1925, he signed with the University of Southern California (USC), whose president, Rufus B. von KleinSmid, eagerly used sport to build the university's reputation. This approach had mixed results. Before Jones, the dubious methods of Elmer "Gus" Henderson had tainted the program with scandal. USC tried to recover by buying out Henderson and luring Notre Dame's Knute Rockne to Los Angeles, but Rockne would not bite. So USC instead hired Jones to lead the Trojans. Duke could not believe that its new coach had jumped ship after just one season in the North Carolina Piedmont, but the Los Angeles press was delighted. Jones, a former Yale athlete (his brother, Tad, was a noteworthy coach at Yale), was known as a stellar football "tutor" and "a believer in the highest college ethics." Jones claimed that money did not lead him to accept the USC job, but one might wonder. Reputedly, his salary would be $10,000 per year, the same amount the university offered Rockne.[38]

Even though he did not accept USC's offer, Rockne dominated 1920s football. Like the era's other premier coaches, he also published a manual, *Coaching: The Way of the Winner* (1925, revised 1928). In this book, Rockne echoed other coaches by observing that a coach needed to teach "fair play," be "a strict disciplinarian," instill "sportsmanship," and not tolerate "muckerism." Sounding like early 1900s social scientists, he noted that coaches, as educators, were important to society, since they could shape citizens by teaching sportsmanship. Most of the book, though, was dedicated to play diagrams and game-day advice. Rockne also cowrote *Training, Conditioning and the Care of Injuries* (1931), in which he took a potshot at his rival Glenn S. "Pop" Warner by deriding Warner's practice-field equipment as "contraptions" that only served to puff him to admiring "players, faculty, alumni, or townspeople."[39] While this accusation may have been true, one might level the same criticisms at Rockne, who conducted a similar publicity campaign via his (often ghostwritten) publications, as well as his manipulation of local boosters and the regional and national press. Rockne was the prototypical big-time coach, a pop-culture celebrity who probably profited more from college football and consumer endorsements than any other person in the 1920s. He was pitchman for South Bend's Studebaker automobile company, signed an endorsement deal with Wilson sporting goods, and was flying to Los Angeles to sign a movie contract when he perished in a 1931 plane crash.[40]

Coaches, though, could not appear as though they were just interested in money. They had to stress their professionalism, honesty, and openness. Rockne's foil, Pop Warner—who had built his prodigious reputation as a football mentor by leading the "Redmen" at the Carlisle Indian School, a paternalistic boarding school intended to assimilate Native Americans—published *Football for Coaches and Players* in 1927 while "Director of Football" at Stanford. Twenty years had passed since his first book, which had sold out its press run, so it was time "for a new textbook on the game." Warner portrayed himself as a true professional writing an authoritative, trustworthy text—not a trickster selling useless books to an easily duped public. He aimed to show that he was a respectable teacher, not a confidence man, by asserting that everything in the book was based on his own experience, and he had not hidden from his readers any play that he had "found to be practical and effective" on the gridiron.[41] Such claims were essential, for without them coaches like Warner might just look like showmen out to make a quick buck.

Another 1920s coach who used this rhetorical flourish was Illinois's Bob Zuppke.[42] Zuppke only played football as a scrub at Wisconsin around 1905, but like other coaches, he professed that the teaching of

disciplined young men was his career goal. His books echoed such notions. *Football Technique and Tactics* (1922, revised 1924) was based on
Zuppke's popular summer course at Urbana, which he boasted had
trained 1,500 football coaches from thirty-seven states. Although
Zuppke stressed sport's educational value, including its ability to
teach sportsmanship, his books focused almost exclusively on play diagrams and coaching tips.[43] He even argued that it was acceptable for
sport to entertain, as long as it did so in a "clean" and "sportsmanlike" way. Yet while Zuppke mastered the rhetoric of discipline, he
also embraced the consumer marketplace and the popular media. He
endorsed a line of football products, including helmets, pads, and a
new, aerodynamic football, for Rawlings.[44] He also wrote a newspaper
column called "Follow the Ball." In one 1925 piece, Zuppke said that
football was "one of the most potent educational factors in school
life," since it represented the cultivation "of virility, of courage and of
character." Football heroes like Illinois's Harold "Red" Grange, said
the Illini coach, modeled the right way of living and inspired young
men to form healthy habits, such as eating spinach. Zuppke claimed
that football was socially important because, as G. Stanley Hall had
shown, physical and mental health were equally important. Football,
therefore, did not only benefit players. It also benefited spectators,
since it was a "mental stimulant."[45]

Zuppke was not the only coach to claim in the 1920s that football
was good because it stimulated spectators' nervous systems. In 1923,
Ohio State head coach J. W. Wilce admired the forward pass because it
"cause[d] more thrills and tingles up and down one's spine than any
other play."[46] Such statements enabled coaches to make football's benefits for spectators even more expansive. While Yost had argued in
1905 that football was good for spectators because it taught discipline,
Wilce and Zuppke contended that the game was beneficial because it
was a stimulant. Around 1900, coaches could only argue openly for
sport by citing its ability to cultivate discipline. But by 1925, football
was an established part of American culture. Moreover, the field of
psychology, influenced by Freud and his American disciples (like H.
Addington Bruce), had changed by becoming more focused on the
subconscious workings of the mind.[47] In the mid-1920s, Zuppke, who
had majored in psychology at Wisconsin and was renowned for his

practical mastery of sport psychology, discussed football's effects on spectators by making an argument about mental stimulation, not pedagogy. While Zuppke cited G. Stanley Hall in 1925, he was actually promoting an idea that mixed Hall's words with Freud's ideas.

Even though their rationale kept changing, coaches could always find ways to claim sport's benefits for both the university and the public. Yet it was becoming evident that the arena provided tangible rewards for coaches, benefits that easily surpassed the mere satisfaction of having taught players discipline or stimulated minds. This fact was not lost on players. In retrospect, it is ironic that Zuppke praised Red Grange's morals in 1925. Just two months later, the "Galloping Ghost" flouted traditional notions of amateur athletic purity by signing, moments after his last college game, a professional contract with the National Football League's Chicago Bears. Although Grange wanted to finish his degree, Zuppke assured his star player—and the public—that graduation was not an option. Grange saw such hatred of professional sport, which was common among older coaches like Stagg in the 1920s, as hypocritical. When Zuppke tried to talk his star player out of the decision to play pro sports, writes Grange biographer John Carroll, the football player reportedly "replied that Zuppke made a living out of teaching and coaching football, 'so what's the difference if I make a living playing football?'"[48]

Red Grange had a point. In the 1920s, college coaches found multiple ways to profit from college sport. One way was through salaries, which steadily rose throughout the early 1900s. This was particularly evident in the career of John Heisman, an ambitious coach unafraid to move from university to university in search of a better job or a bigger paycheck. Throughout the 1890s and early 1900s, Heisman held a series of increasingly lucrative positions. One biographer even notes that Heisman composed a "self-promotional pamphlet" in 1899 to land the Clemson post. Later, at Georgia Tech, Heisman negotiated several lucrative contracts. For example, a 1904 agreement paid him a base salary of $2,250 per year, plus 30 percent of Grant Field gate receipts. Perhaps to maintain a façade of respectability, the athletic association lowered his share of the gate receipts when it later raised his salary. Heisman built a successful team at Tech, but in 1920 he signed a three-year contract to coach at his alma mater, Penn, which was then a premier college football program. Heisman coached at Penn until 1922, when he published *Principles of Football*. After Penn, he briefly moved to Washington and Jefferson College, where he coached in 1923. In 1924 he became "Director of Athletics" and coach at Houston's new Rice Institute, where he received higher pay than any tenured faculty member: a five-year contract at the princely sum of $9,000 per year.[49] This high level of compensation might have seemed outrageous to some, but to many coaches and administrators it made perfect sense. Heisman had already promoted the dubious yet self-serving idea that a football coach was the college's single most important teacher of character, and administrators knew that successful coaches could very effectively advertise higher education institutions—even if they were not necessarily teaching discipline to all of the players and spectators in the arena.

Coaches at other universities, especially in the Midwest, forged a different path to reward and respectability. In 1923, Fielding Yost, then Michigan's athletic director, gained appointment as "Professor of the Theory and Practice of Athletic Coaching" in the university's college of education.[50] Meanwhile, other Big Ten schools created athletic departments that made sport a permanent part of the university structure. Ohio State established an athletic department (the one H. Shindle Wingert eventually criticized) that placed intercollegiate athletics under faculty control. It was led by athletic director Lynn St. John, "Professor of Competitive and Recreative Athletics" (and namesake of St. John Arena), from 1913 to 1947. In 1924, Iowa established a "Division of Physical Education" and provided "faculty ranking, tenure and salary" to all coaches. This unit resembled other departments, insofar as its faculty possessed professional status. But the relationship of Iowa's physical education division to the university was complicated by the fact that it served separate masters. In matters of physical education, it reported to the College of Liberal Arts, but in regard to intercollegiate athletics it reported directly to the university administration. In 1932—shortly after the Carnegie Report (discussed in chapter 7) and the reforms of President Thomas Gates at the University of Pennsylvania, who created a "Department for Health, Physical Education, and Athletics"—Illinois created a School of Physical Education that included physical culture, health, and intercollegiate athletics.

But athletics, not truly physical education, was also placed under the supervision of the Athletic Association.[51] In such arrangements, administrators tacitly acknowledged big-time college athletics' unique role as a generator of publicity and revenue. Although coaches might gain professional status, in reality they occupied a much different position than other professors, including physical educators. Sport enabled the university to engage the public in the lucrative, high-stakes arena of popular culture. It was convenient and necessary to place regulation of college sport in the hands of athletic professionals, but the money and publicity it generated were too great to remain unsupervised—or to be placed directly in the hands of men renowned for tricky plays or for their willingness to depart quickly for a contract with more favorable terms.

Opinion came down on both sides of these new departments. Some praised the structure for providing autonomy and status for athletic experts. Fielding Yost compared coaching to dentistry and engineering, two of Michigan's most successful professional programs. A major advantage of "departmentalized" universities, he claimed, was that they put "every faculty man . . . on more or less the self same plane." The expectation of equality was reasonable, he said, since athletics furnished an essential service. Athletic "departments are just one of the many departments of the modern university," Yost stated, "wherein all contribute in some manner to the betterment of those studying in them." These words echoed a prophecy that James Murfin, a Detroit attorney, athletic committee representative, and future University of Michigan regent, had made in 1907. Murfin predicted that he and athletic director Charles Baird would "live to see the day when the athletic department will be conducted the same as the department of Greek, the department of Physics or any other department on the campus. The parties having athletics in charge will be bound in honor to conduct their department and themselves honestly and as gentlemen."[52] Similar wisdom prevailed at Harvard. LeBaron Briggs, who later served as NCAA president, noted in 1922 that professors gladly placed sport in the hands of an athletic director with "legal training and . . . excellent business capacity." Such men were important, but they should not break the bank. In 1927, Harvard's Athletic Association frugally urged the university to engage "intelligent experts" at reasonable salaries, so as to keep the athletic budget in line with other departments.[53] Athletic expenses, of course, would later become a persistent problem, as coaches' successes—measured in victories and ticket sales—dictated their market value.

By the 1920s, athletic experts had established a permanent space within the academic structure. Athletic departments, though, flouted the intentions of progressives who had hoped to eliminate popular influence. In fact, they made commercial sport a permanent part of the university. This permanence became clearer when colleges built large arenas to accommodate the thousands of spectators who bought tickets and, supposedly, benefitted from the athletic spectacle. The process of stadium building began at the turn of the century, but it accelerated after World War I, when dozens of universities constructed reinforced-concrete arenas. Often dedicated as memorials to nationalism and spaces for training manly discipline, these structures were also places for popular spectacle and interinstitutional competition. Ultimately, though, stadiums proved to be dubious places for melding academic ideals with popular desires—or for teaching the multitude of students and nonacademic spectators lessons of discipline or self-control.

CHAPTER 6

Stadiums: Between Campus and Culture

In 1902, Ira Hollis, a Harvard engineering professor and athletic committee chairman, advised Charles William Eliot that the university should build a football arena at its Soldiers Field athletic grounds in Boston. The new facility was needed, said Hollis, since big-time spectator sport was "probably a lasting addition to modern universities." This prophecy—the accuracy of which Hollis would later come to regret—was self-fulfilling, for if athletics was not permanent at Harvard before the $310,000 stadium's construction in 1903, it certainly seemed so afterward. Completed less than a decade after the first modern Olympics in 1896, Harvard Stadium was modeled on the classical stadium at Olympia. To minimize costs, Harvard used the new technology of steel-reinforced concrete. America's first large concrete structure, Harvard Stadium was the prototype for dozens of large, early 1900s arenas, many of which were constructed for nationalistic or militaristic reasons.[1] While colleges often built such stadiums to fit campus plans, they could hardly disguise the fact that these venues cemented football as a ritual located in a gray area between campus and culture. To be sure, many administrators and coaches claimed that sport was an educational experience—a form of physical, mental, and moral training. But huge stadiums exposed the reality that football was commercial popular culture. By building permanent arenas, universities constructed liminal campus spaces, located in a semi-academic, semi-popular netherworld, where meaning was a saleable commodity. Higher education institutions thus ceded cultural control of athletics to the public. By the 1920s, the proliferation of campus arenas showed that sport's meanings, which were situated between commercial culture and the ivory tower, could be negotiated by consumers—not only by academics.

Since the 1880s, big games, especially on Thanksgiving, were played at urban athletic parks. Harvard and Yale played at the South End Grounds, home of the Boston Red Stockings (Braves) in 1878 and 1880, and at Manhattan's Polo Grounds, the field of baseball's New York Giants, in 1883 and 1887; Columbia and Princeton also played at the Polo Grounds. Stanford and Cal first met at the Haight Street base-ball grounds in 1891. Georgia and Auburn played at the Atlanta fair-grounds that later became Piedmont Park in 1892, before relocating their rivalry to Brisbane Park, home of the minor league Atlanta Crackers. At this time, some universities began building temporary wooden stands on campus. Chicago students constructed stands on Marshall Field (land that was donated by the retail magnate of the same name, at the request of William Rainey Harper) in 1893. Initially, the stands seated 1,200 spectators and cost $1,210; by 1898, they ac-commodated nearly 11,000. Such a facility required constant mainte-nance. The university kept a large stockpile of wooden boards, planks, and stringers on hand for repairs. Likewise, every summer until 1914, a group of carpenters fixed Yale Field's stands by replacing weakened or old boards that had been marked by their leader, dubbed "Blue Pencil Pete."[2]

While workers kept collegiate sports venues in a condition that al-lowed them to generate money and publicity, the large crowds that flooded rickety stands could still cause problems. Universities, like the owners of other entertainment venues, had to control the crowd and protect facilities from wear and tear. As early as 1896, Chicago's Presi-dent William Rainey Harper asked athletic director Amos Alonzo Stagg to employ a "special policeman" to patrol the stands during the game, in order to ensure that spectators did not smoke in nonsmoking areas or cause excessive wear to the seats. The condition of the stands was a sensitive issue at a university that consciously used football to raise funds and promote itself to potential donors. By the early 1900s, Harper even pleaded with Stagg to keep the grandstands presentable for the "down town people" who complained that that the bleachers were filthy and unsuitable for genteel patrons. While the university wanted to avoid alienating refined Chicagoans, it also had to consider the safety of the crowd. In 1902, temporary stands at Marshall Field collapsed during a game between Michigan and Wisconsin, leading to protracted and expensive legal battles.[3] To avoid a repeat of these nightmares, Chicago officials ensured there were enough ticket clerks and ushers for the 1905 Thanksgiving game. The Chicago police de-partment even dispatched 125 men to patrol the grounds, while jani-tors locked down nearby Hitchcock Hall to keep out nonpaying spectators. University lawyer Wallace Heckman, concerned about the possibility of another collapse, asked Stagg if the grandstands could support the weight of the crowd. To reduce the chance of tragedy, the athletic department erected wooden fences between sections and made sure not to sell more tickets than seats. After the game, Heckman lauded the "splendid work" that "with almost mathematical certainty" had made the contest a success.[4]

Just as games were won by systematically gaining yardage and minimizing the chance of losing the ball, successfully staged athletic drama did not happen by luck. Universities could also reduce the chance of catastrophe or litigation by building permanent stands. Beginning in the 1890s, nationalism and war memory often served as motivations, or convenient rationalizations, for constructing such arenas. Harvard's Soldiers Field was dedicated in 1890 to the memory of alumni who served in the Civil War. College officials intended the field, located on a reclaimed Charles River tidewater marsh, to stimulate martial manliness. Donor Henry Lee Higginson and President Eliot hoped it would promote "manly sports" and prepare students for their "duties as men and citizens of the Republic." Sport might heal the nation's metaphorical war wounds by allowing (white) men from distant regions to gather for strenuous athletics.[5] Half a continent away, the University of Wisconsin dedicated its field, Camp Randall, in 1893. At first, the state legislature considered purchasing the former Civil War training camp for the use of a veterans' organization, the Grand Army of the Republic. But a mass of students gathered in March of that year to demand that Camp Randall become part of the university campus. They cited Harvard's new "monumental and memorial" field and argued that the field could serve as a drill ground for the "university battalion," as well as a place for war monuments and athletics. The students did gain their field, and while some considered changing its name, those who insisted that the moniker "Camp Randall" was sacred, like the names of the Civil War battlefields, won.[6]

A decade after dedicating Soldiers Field, Harvard built a stadium there. Engineering professors, including Ira Hollis, designed the arena with assistance from architect Charles Follen McKim (named after the physical culture proponent) and landscape architect Frederick Law Olmsted, who had designed New York's Central Park and Chicago's

Midway Plaisance, as well as campuses at Stanford and Berkeley. Initially, Harvard Stadium accommodated 21,000 spectators, with 13,000 additional temporary seats for big games.[7] At the time, this was a huge facility; in 1903 only baseball fields like the Polo Grounds seated so many. Since the stadium had to support the weight of the crowd, resist fire, require limited maintenance, and be constructed as cheaply as possible, the designers chose reinforced concrete. Even though concrete was untested in New England's harsh climate, Hollis considered it worth a try. But while concrete was clearly more durable, some worried that the stadium would make football a permanent part of university life. Hollis privately conceded as much, and in an engineering journal he admitted that the stadium implied a "willingness . . . to put athletic sports upon a permanent basis." Yet he minimized this problem by stressing football's benefits. Sport was now regulated by committees resembling those of other university departments, and the games facilitated gatherings of the university's far-flung "friends." All things considered, it did not seem so bad that spectator sport was becoming a permanent campus ritual, especially when an athletic department surplus of $33,000, accumulated from ticket sales, subsidized the project.[8]

Harvard Stadium demonstrated the feasibility of large, concrete arenas. Frederick W. Taylor, an engineer and rational time-management (Taylorism) proponent, even featured it prominently in a book about reinforced concrete. Additionally, the venue pioneered a new, multifaceted stadium-financing strategy. Besides ticket-sale revenues, Harvard Stadium was funded in part by private donations, including $100,000 from the class of 1879, which included economics professor F. W. Taussig.[9] This tactic foreshadowed the practice of building arenas with nonbudget monies, a boon for universities that hoped to maintain low-cost athletics. But it was also problematic. The use of gate revenue or donations allowed athletic departments to claim autonomy, or justify intercollegiate athletics as a self-funding university activity. Outside financing also pressured college sports impresarios to appeal to public desires. Sport was, in fact, becoming a lasting addition to modern universities, but its relationship to the academy appeared increasingly complicated as football became an integral part of popular culture.

Harvard Stadium kicked off a national stadium-building competition. Permanent stands were soon constructed at urban campuses such as Georgia Tech, or at traditional powers like Princeton. A $25,000 donation from Atlanta businessman John W. Grant spurred construction of Georgia Tech's athletic field in 1913, completed with $30,000 worth of labor provided by Fulton County convicts. Grant Field was designed by New York landscape architect Charles W. Leavitt, who also designed the Pittsburgh Pirates' Forbes Field (1909). The concrete stands initially seated 5,000, but this capacity was not enough for Tech's popular, Heisman-led teams. In 1915, the total number of seats was raised to 12,000, with plans for another grandstand. These additions, said the Atlanta press, made Grant Field the South's biggest stadium, comparable to fields at large East Coast universities.[10] This assertion was a stretch, since eastern universities were building especially large arenas at this time. In 1913, Yale began constructing a huge "bowl"; the next year Princeton rushed to complete its own concrete "horseshoe." Edgar Palmer, president of the New Jersey Zinc Company, donated $300,000 to build Palmer Memorial Stadium, which seated 41,000 (with a possible expansion to 55,000). Once the stadium was completed, a huge crowd descended on the small college town for the arena's first major game in 1914.[11]

Princeton saw the stadium as an endowment. Palmer, besides giving a "permanent football amphitheatre" to Princeton's athletic association, explicitly intended the facility to support the college. Its large capacity would negate the need to erect temporary stands for the vast Yale-game crowds and would therefore allow the athletic association to earn an annual profit and give the university $10,000 from gate receipts each year.[12] A different arrangement, however, took shape in New Haven, where Yale's Board of Athletic Control pioneered a new way to fund its 85-acre athletic complex, including a massive, 70,000-seat coliseum that would, by itself, cost at least $300,000. Yale enticed a large number of donors by promising them the option to buy tickets. Each $100 gift allowed a donor to buy two seats for fifteen years; each additional $100 added another seat. While Palmer Stadium was an endowment with virtually no strings attached, thousands of strings were attached to Yale's arena. Every donor who helped fund the bowl was entitled to buy entrance to the spectacle. Yale's Alumni Advisory Board explained the several reasons why the Yale Corporation was so determined to build a huge stadium that it utilized a strategy that seemed to cede athletic control to spectators. First, many Yale supporters were not able to attend the games, which had become major social events, at smallish Yale Field. Second, the concrete and earth stadium would be "fireproof" and therefore safe for large crowds. Third, the field, clubhouse, and stadium in the new athletic complex would unite "men of different [university] departments on common ground."[13]

Before a speck of dirt was moved or a drop of cement poured, the Yale Bowl was being asked to do a lot of work: please alumni and friends, unite a fragmented university, and accommodate huge crowds. It would even underwrite "athletic expenses for all Yale students."[14] Yale was neither the first nor last university to expect football to pay for physical culture, but it was the first to announce the construction of a huge stadium, solicit pledges in return for ticket options, and then expect the structure to turn a profit. Indeed, Yale's ambitions outstripped its benefactors. By 1912, the General Athletic Committee was already considering renting out the bowl to help pay for the athletic complex. The fundraising campaign fell short and the upper tier of stands was not finished until the 1920s, when the athletic association solicited donors for a "Bowl Completion Fund."[15] Nevertheless, in 1914, the Yale Bowl was a spectacular and awe-inspiring structure best comprehended through statistics: 35,000 cubic yards of concrete, 600,000 pounds of steel, and 75,000 square feet of turf covering twelve and a half acres. The first game, a 36–0 rout at the hands of Percy Haughton's Harvard squad, was viewed by 70,055 spectators with 300 reporters and telegraph operators. One writer explained the game by imagining a Martian's reaction. First, the extraterrestrial might have been surprised that a contest between two universities was not academic; second, he would have contrasted it with the Great War raging in Europe and seen football as a "friendly rivalry" in a noncombatant nation.[16]

In a few years, though, America would abandon neutrality and send young men off to actual war—not a moral equivalent of war. The global conflict changed life on both sides of the Atlantic, but it especially shaped American campuses. Early on, enrollments dropped when students joined the armed forces. But once the military and industry realized the need for trained experts, they encouraged young men to enroll, or "enlist," in college. Enrollment quickly climbed, especially at land-grant institutions with engineering and military drill programs. Universities created Reserve Officer Training Corps (ROTC) programs, and in 1918 the federal government created a Student Army Training Corps (SATC). Education became more democratic as federal funds supported 140,000 men at 525 colleges, but military discipline also dominated campuses that had basically become army training schools.[17] Some universities ceased intercollegiate football altogether, since spectator sport took too much time away from training, but others continued sport under SATC auspices. In 1918, the Big Ten granted athletic control to the military, while universities in the precursor to the Southeastern Conference (SEC) fielded teams composed of SATC men. The army even issued guidelines regarding eligibility, training, and season length.[18] In this context, several universities that had drifted away from football or athletic conferences in the Progressive Era returned during the war. Intercollegiate athletic competition became a way for universities to demonstrate their patriotism and their willingness to reenter the national mainstream. By 1915, California gave up rugby to resume the "American" game. In 1919 (after a 1918 SATC game against Cal), Stanford also returned to old-style football. Michigan rejoined the Big Nine in 1917, making it the Big Ten.[19]

Football was also a way to reunite postwar campuses around perceived traditions. The SATC dominated campus life during the war, and some worried that students might forget prewar life. Stanford's *Daily Palo Alto* was concerned that "old interests" were completely gone, and that many now merely saw campus as a backdrop for army training, not a college home. In Ann Arbor, students wondered how they would adjust to postwar life. After hastily constructed military buildings were torn down and khaki uniforms discarded, could campus ever return to normal? Certainly, men who had seen combat would not want to go back to "the old 'Rah! Rah!' days." Like other Americans, students both feared and hoped that life was permanently altered. They felt that the war to end all war had been won and it was time for a fresh start.[20] The desire for a new order, though, camouflaged a need to return to normalcy. Americans sought to bring back prewar spirit. One Stanford student colorfully urged that in order to do so, "the paint bucket of Cardinal 'pep' must be spilled all over the Quad" and old traditions reinstated. Athletics, it seemed, could help recover an imagined prewar status quo. Some Harvard students even celebrated football's 1919 return because it would help pull the university back together. Of course, critics had long complained that football could not unify Harvard (they even posited that perennial athletic losses to Yale were caused by the elective system and lack of college spirit), but in the postwar moment, many conveniently forgot this former pessimism.[21]

After the war football grew even bigger, in part because it held many implications for manliness—or, to use a term becoming more common in the early 1900s, masculinity. One Ann Arbor student wrote that returning to conference play would be even more significant than "extermination of the co-eds." Such rhetoric was not unusual at campuses where men were becoming alarmed at women's increased interest in athletics, or were trying to reclaim space from female students.[22] During and after the war, coaches even actively cultivated the idea that football was a manly, warlike struggle. Fielding Yost had clearly articulated this idea as early as 1905, when he analogized football to conflict by calling the other team the "enemy," dubbing players "missiles of human brawn," comparing the scrimmage to "human bombardment," and likening coaching to "generalship." Shortly before the 1918 armistice, Yost proclaimed, "The different drives made on the battle fronts are similar to the various positions and trick plays which occur on the gridiron. The Allies are bucking the line against the Hun, and when they succeed in breaking through it corresponds to a player, who carries the ball, smashing through for several yards." Likewise, in 1924, the University of Minnesota's President Marion Burton declared, "All healthy human beings love a combat. . . . No doubt this fact accounts in part for the widespread and rapidly growing interest of the public in intercollegiate football games." Antebellum educators would have chafed at the comparison between collegiate physical culture and armed conflict, but the Great War made athletic violence seem patriotic.[23]

Such comparisons made particular sense on campuses with SATC teams. All players on Purdue's 1918 football squad were enrolled in military training programs and the coach was Major Ed Jackson. After

Fielding Yost buys a Liberty Bond, Ferry Field, Ann Arbor, 1917. Fielding Harris Yost Papers, Box 8, Folder: Activities Football Related, Bentley Historical Library, University of Michigan.

the armistice, moreover, some army officers parlayed their experience into jobs as physical education teachers, military drill instructors, or coaches. Robert Neyland, a West Point graduate who served in France, was Professor of Military Science at the University of Tennessee before becoming the Volunteers' head coach in 1926. Throughout his career he saw football as a sort of "war game." Indiana University's mid-1920s coach was William "Navy Bill" Ingram, who previously coached at the Naval Academy and the Pacific Coast Fleet Service Team. "Navy Bill" Saunders coached at Clemson and Colorado.[24] Walter Camp, conversely, parlayed his football experience into a military position. To condition navy officers, Camp developed an exercise regimen for troops, later dubbed the "Daily Dozen." After the war, he published a do-it-yourself manual aimed at schoolboys, college players, and factory or office workers. Camp proudly cited football's wartime role, claiming that the American Expeditionary Force and fleet teams had found that "this game of mimic warfare developed the stalwart, courageous fighter." He said that after soldiers returned to America, army discipline permeated society and football became common throughout the nation.[25] Discipline was no longer about muscle control or manly honor and virtue; by the 1920s, it indicated ability to operate as part of a team. A modern man needed discipline because he was part of an army or industrial economy.

After the war, Major Frank Cavanaugh, who had been wounded in France, wrote football books and coached at Fordham. Unlike progressives, who had been concerned with athletes' minds, bodies, and morals, Cavanaugh stressed physical sacrifice. In *Inside Football* (1919), dedicated to football players who died in the war, Cavanaugh included a section on "The Warrior's Armor" (football helmets and pads) and claimed that he told his players that if they were "not willing to sacrifice an arm or a leg for the good of the cause," they should not be on the team. West Point coach Charles Daly, who coached Robert Neyland, wrote that football was a sustained battle or "war game." Daly cited Prussian military theorist Karl von Clausewitz and recommended the War Department's *Field Service Regulations* to players.[26] Such language permeated even football books by non–army veteran coaches, such as Bob Zuppke and Knute Rockne. In 1925, Rockne published a fictional account of his Notre Dame experiences, dedicated to a player killed at Château-Thierry. The novel portrayed Coach Brown of Dulac University as a kind teacher who said football was "just a game" yet compared athletes to soldiers, likening defenders to "the infantry trying to capture the grounds where the hangars are before the aeroplanes can leave the ground." Water boys equaled "commissary departments" and each coach acted as a defense secretary, "while the President and his cabinet can be likened to the chairman of the Board of Control and the faculty and alumni who make up th[ese] personnel."[27]

Militarism was rampant in American culture during the early 1920s—even though it was falling out of favor with many academic intellectuals—when campuses began to consecrate sites of memory to fallen soldiers. At first, universities erected modest memorials. In 1919, Michigan students collected $400 to erect a flagpole on Ferry Field. This patriotic symbol, including the ritual flag-raising at games, was intended to show that Michigan had not forgotten the sacrifices of its war dead. Yet some observers thought the flagpole too meager. Morbidly assuming the voice of a dead veteran, one student wrote, "There is a Harvard spirit, a constant companion of mine, who was killed by the same shell that put me on the 'flagpole list.' His alma mater is erecting a chapel to the Harvard dead, with their names carved on the walls." This fictional war veteran, forced to compete with Harvard even in the afterlife, was forever subject to his companion's haughtiness because Ann Arbor had not erected a suitable memorial. So some Michiganders suggested more suitable memorials, including a campanile, gateway, health building, or perhaps *two* flagpoles in front of the library.[28] But soon such plans would seem inadequate. In the 1920s, colleges competed with one another to build massive and expensive stadiums. In these arenas, generations of football players would supposedly display the physical and mental discipline that won wars, while perpetually inspiring spectators to take up manly physical culture. Yet no matter how strenuously colleges asserted patriotic reasons for stadiums, commercial or publicity-related motivations always lurked below the surface.

As we already saw, the earliest permanent football stadiums were built at elite or urban universities, mostly in the Northeast. This changed after 1919. Universities in the West and Midwest, which prospered due to the influx of wartime federal dollars, led the stadium-building frenzy. In 1921, Stanford raced to complete an arena so that it could continue dividing gate receipts equally and playing home games in Palo Alto against the University of California, which was then building a larger, and more profitable, California Memorial Stadium in Berkeley. One observer, who wanted to use war memorial funds, wrote that Stanford Stadium would demonstrate the permanence of athletics at a university that had only recently reinstituted football. The *Los Angeles Times* declared that the new stadium, seating 65,000 spectators and featuring the West Coast's largest scoreboard, would rival the Yale Bowl. To build this large facility so quickly, a team of Stanford engineering professors emulated Yale and carved the $210,000 arena out of the ground. Excavation began in June 1921, and by late October the earthquake-proof structure was complete and ready for the November dedication game. Planners had carefully taken into account the needs of the crowd that would flood Stanford's semirural campus on game

Construction of Stanford Stadium, 1921. Courtesy of Stanford University
Archives.

day. The arena was situated closer to Palo Alto than the previous field,
and it included a large parking lot for automobiles. Stanford's athletic
management even convinced the Southern Pacific Railroad to construct a new station nearby for the convenience of spectators traveling
by train. Unlike many other arenas, the massive and cheaply built
Stanford Stadium, funded in part by war memorial funds and infused
with the rhetoric of warfare at its groundbreaking ceremony, was
quickly paid off.[29]

By comparison, the University of California took its time. Its hillside stadium, first proposed in 1921 as a double-deck structure similar
to the Polo Grounds, was completed as a single-deck ellipse in 1923.
The $1.4 million arena, seating over 70,000, was dedicated to veter-
ans, yet it was also needed for the practical reason of seating the multitude of football fans. Berkeley, a major beneficiary of wartime federal
funding, had grown from 3,100 students in 1902 to 11,505 in 1922,
when it was America's largest university. Students wanted to watch
sports, but so did the increasingly prosperous general public: 62,000
applied for tickets for the 1920 Stanford game, and many were turned
away. The new stadium could accommodate this demand. Yet administrators tried to stress the project's pedagogical aspects. President
William Wallace Campbell saw Memorial Stadium as an "educational

force" for training men and demonstrating sportsmanship to students and the public. But the 80,000 spectators who attended the first game against Stanford, including over 5,000 perched on the hillside, may have had other matters in mind. One sportswriter observed, "Every one of the 73,423 seats was occupied by a blood-thirsty partisan, who would gladly sink his, or her, fangs in your tonsils if you dared let out a peep when the other side crashed through for a yard or so."[30] Sportsmanship, indeed.

Although California's stadium competition was intense, by the mid-1920s an even greater fervor captivated midwestern universities. By 1922, the University of Illinois, enrolling 9,084, was the nation's fourth largest university; Ohio State University (OSU) was sixth largest, with 7,521 students. By comparison, in 1905, Illinois had been only ninth (2,944 students), and OSU fourteenth (1,860 students). During the war these institutions built premier football programs to rival traditional powers like Michigan, Chicago, Harvard, Yale, and Princeton. Zuppke's Illinois squad racked up a combined 11–3 record in 1918 and 1919, while Ohio State won the 1920 Big Ten crown. By 1924, both universities had built arenas suited to their growing stature. According to fundraisers, stadiums would demonstrate patriotism, develop male bodies, imply institutional supremacy, and accommodate the multitude of consumers. The connection between sport and conflict was explicit. During the war, Ohio State planned a combined armory, drill field, and football stadium. While OSU never constructed this facility, after the war its supporters began raising funds for a large arena. Boosters, who echoed the arguments used to justify the Yale Bowl, argued that the Ohio Stadium complex would serve a diverse and ambitious array of purposes. It would improve student health by facilitating physical education courses and military drill; provide a space for intercollegiate football, which inspired students to exercise; enable football to advertise the university; and unify the diverse elements of a university fast becoming one of the nation's largest institutions of higher education and research.[31]

Ohio Stadium's 1921–1922 planning and construction were a massive project. This scope was fitting, since the resulting arena dwarfed Ohio Field's old stands and—if its promoters had their way—would last virtually forever. First, engineers had to redesign the site to con-

Preparing plaster models of the 60,000-plus–seat Ohio Stadium, 1920. The
Ohio State University Archives.

trol the flood-prone Olentangy River. Second, they had to choose construction materials. Physics professor Thomas Mendenhall tried to
persuade OSU trustees that a brick or stone stadium seating 45,000
spectators would serve the university better than a 63,000-seat stadium made of concrete. He argued that the stadium must last for centuries, and there was no guarantee that concrete was so durable. Ultimately, though, Ohio State ignored this warning and followed
Harvard's example by building a bigger, less expensive stadium of
concrete.[32] The huge number of seats also allowed more individuals to
subsidize construction. Like the prewar Yale Bowl and other 1920s arenas, Ohio Stadium was funded by a large number of small donations,
or subscriptions, gathered by an army of fundraisers throughout a
large geographical region. Stadium solicitors were instructed to tell
potential donors that each $100 contribution improved the health of
one of OSU's projected 10,000 students, while the games held there
would stimulate millions of spectators and draw attention to both the
university and the state. Ohioans, said fundraisers, had to beat Stan-

Construction of the reinforced-concrete grandstands of Ohio Stadium, circa 1922. The Ohio State University Archives.

ford, California, and Illinois in the stadium-building competition, or else lose out in the battle for national distinction.[33]

But not everyone agreed that Ohio State should build a stadium. In 1921, a potential donor in Wooster, Ohio, declared that he would not contribute because he believed the arena would exhibit a few players' "physical prowess" without contributing to overall student health. This critic thought that universities sponsored teams mainly for publicity, and he argued that colleges should not advertise themselves through athletics. In response, OSU president William Oxley Thompson was ambivalent. On the one hand, he supported the stadium as a place for both general physical education and military training. The public had been appalled at the condition of enlisted men during the war, and many now saw athletics as virtual military training. The stadium itself, moreover, might encourage nonathletes to engage in valuable physical activity. On the other hand, Thompson was not entirely convinced by such arguments and privately expressed skepticism about football's ability to keep thousands of students physically fit. He

Correct!

Billy Ireland, cartoonist for the Columbus Dispatch, conducts a spelling lesson.

Ohio Stadium fundraising, as characterized by a local newspaper cartoonist. The Ohio State University Archives.

conceded, though, that his opinion mattered little and he felt helpless in the face of "public demand."[34] As the leader of a major, state-funded university, Thompson could not afford to alienate the public. The people wanted intercollegiate sport because it seemed patriotic, so they would have sport. Yet Thompson may have also realized the stadium's long-term dangers. Although it might not always behoove the university to sponsor a militaristic sport—or at other times the people might want sport for other reasons—once the stadium was on campus, both it and football would be open to the desires of the ticket-buying, sport-consuming public.

Even though numerous individuals donated to the stadium campaign, by January 1923, OSU's athletic board still owed $550,000 on the arena. This was despite a net income of over $159,000 from the stadium's first season, when it hosted over 160,000 fans. Several seasons of such large returns may have paid construction costs, but the stadium did not just have to pay for itself. It was also expected to pay for Ohio State's "complete recreation program," which lost over $15,000 in 1922, not including coaches' salaries. Several very successful campaigns would be necessary to climb out of that financial hole. Ohioans, nonetheless, loved their "horseshoe," and students demonstrated tremendous enthusiasm. They had designated the 1921 *Makio* yearbook the "Stadium Number" and eagerly anticipated the new arena:

> Picture the Ohio Stadium, rearing its bulky towers high into the sky, moulded into long white classic curves—a triumph of architecture. Picture it, close-packed with cheering onlookers, afire with zeal for the fame of the Alma Mater—the tens of thousands of them. Picture those men of Scarlet and Gray, p[y]gmies on the green carpet of the playing field but their hearts athrob with a mighty loyalty and a fighting determination—crusaders of the college. Here is the spirit of Ohio State, glimpsed in a moment's emblazonment. Here, in a flash, the spirit of the Stadium Builders.[35]

This description captured the mentality of postwar football partisans. The men on the field were the university's "crusaders," demonstrating dedication to both alma mater and nation. Football was patriotic, but it also drew publicity and fueled institutional competition. A standing-room-only crowd of over 70,000 packed Ohio Stadium for the 1922 dedication game versus Michigan. The stadium, moreover, quickly inspired stadium builders around the globe. Milton Springer of the Philippine Amateur Athletic Association expressed his desire to build an arena just like Ohio Stadium, which he considered "the finest and most modern in the world."[36]

One did not have to look as far as Manila, though, to see Ohio Sta-

Artist's rendering of the façade and entryway to Ohio State's new stadium. The Ohio State University Archives.

dium's impact. The University of Illinois began planning its Memorial Stadium in 1921. Like counterparts in Columbus, students at Illinois understood the role stadiums played in the race for athletic and institutional supremacy. They hyperbolically proclaimed that the new stadium in Champaign would be "the greatest achievement ever known in the history of the universities of America" and noted that a successful fundraising campaign would mark Illinois "as the most progressive, the most virile and most enlightened school and student body in the country."[37] But fundraisers did not just rely on competitive spirit; they also drew upon Great War memory. The stadium would honor "Fighting Illini" who had fallen in combat, revive old traditions, and instill the spirit of the war dead by developing living students' bodies. A fundraising booklet even declared that if dead soldiers could speak, they would choose a magnificent athletic field. The stadium, as well as the large recreation field surrounding it, would "answer the call of *living* thousands" as well as "the imperious mandate of the dead hundreds."[38] Athletic director George Huff called Memorial Stadium a place where "Illini yet unborn" could "assemble to learn the traditions of a long-ago past, to measure their spirit of devotion with the

Ohio Stadium dedication game, OSU versus Michigan, October 21, 1922. The Ohio State University Archives.

spirits of [veterans], and to pledge their all to an enrichment of this spirit." Retired university president Edmund James also linked the commemoration with the needs of present and future bodies. He called upon alumni to support the stadium, which would improve student health and intercollegiate athletics, while instilling "future generations" with the memory of dead war heroes.[39]

Yet in reality there were other reasons for building Memorial Stadium. George Huff said that the arena would be a suitable venue for varsity athletics, and the need to stage big-time sport was obvious to anyone close to the fundraising drive, which stressed that old Illinois Field was simply not big enough for one of America's best football teams. Promotional literature personified the field as an old soldier who was graciously stepping aside to be replaced by a fresh fighter. Fundraisers professed nostalgia for Illinois Field (which could accommodate only 22,000, including standing room), but they desired a stadium holding at least 50,000. To underscore the modesty of Illinois's facilities compared with its grand aspirations, promoters juxtaposed a

LEST WE FORGET THOSE ILLINI WHO DIED IN THE WAR

THERE were nine thousand four hundred and forty-two of them in uniform when their country called. Trained they were, for in their four years at this University they had learned what it means to wear a uniform and they had caught something of the discipline of the soldier. Willing they were: 183 of them died, 158 of them were wounded, and 120 of them were decorated for distinguished service.

Nine thousand four hundred and forty-two . . . . and tomorrow, should their country call again, there would be probably fifteen thousand or even twenty thousand. And perhaps even more would be decorated—and, perhaps, even more killed and wounded.

But the spirit that sent them into action, the spirit which brought 183 of them forever out of our vision and understanding, is still with us. It is a living thing, and the Stadium will exist to keep that living thing before the eyes of future generations, of the hundreds of future generations who will walk through its archways, sit in its seats and move strenuously on its fields.

Each of the 183 will have a column erected to his memory. This column will be dedicated to him alone, so that Illini never will forget that Illini have made the supreme sacrifice.

And, that you who may not see the Stadium and be in it as frequently as the younger sons and daughters of Illinois who are here today, may have near you always the names of those who gave their lives in the war, we print these names.

. . . . . *"the spirit that sent them into action . . . is a living thing"*

"Lest we forget those Illini who died in the war." Great War memory and the promotion of University of Illinois Memorial Stadium. From University of Illinois, *The Story of the Stadium,* 1922.

ground-level view of Illinois Field against aerial photographs of the Yale Bowl and Harvard Stadium. The Illini, this photomontage implied, could never claim athletic superiority, or even parity, without a suitable stadium. When the *Chicago Tribune* reported in 1920 that Illinois's trustees had approved plans for a $1 million, 60,000-seat stadium, it did not mention a war memorial. It merely indicated that a new arena was needed because the old wooden stands did not allow the university to fulfill the 40,000 ticket requests for the 1920 Ohio State game.[40] If Illinois did not build a larger arena, fundraisers warned, it would decline in football importance. The best Big Ten teams, including Michigan, Chicago, and Wisconsin, would no longer come to Champaign when they could go to other schools and "receive three times the amount of money in gate receipts."[41] While promoters sold the stadium as a war-memorial facility that would improve students' physiques, they also knew it would serve the purposes of institutional competition and provide entertainment to Illinoisans who would travel from all over the state—especially by automobile, on Illinois's new network of good roads—to see football games there. In fact, fundraisers sometimes appealed blatantly to the public's desire for consumer spectacle. If the promise of a memorial or recreation field did not sway potential donors, canvassers were advised to stress that each $100 pledge was good for one seat option for ten years, or two for five years. The stadium, officially, was a memorial and educational facility. But it also provided a ritual space for leisure and entertainment for middle- and upper-class Illinoisans.[42]

The dangling of choice tickets before donors was a common fundraising tactic in the 1920s. No matter what reason, or mix of reasons, a university offered to build a stadium, it could always fall back on the promise of "preferred seating" to entice dollars out of donors' pockets. In 1920, the Yale Athletic Association returned to this strategy when it tried to raise $250,000 to complete its arena. The association argued that the Yale Bowl had to be finished so football games could inspire students to participate in physical culture. In return for a $100 donation to the Bowl Completion Fund, the association promised one "preferred ticket" for 15 years (up to 10 tickets for $1,000). Fundraisers insisted that this money would support physical education—not commercial spectacle. The promise of tickets in return for

Yale Bowl

Harvard Stadium

Present Illinois Field

Modest Illinois Field juxtaposed against grand, aerial views of the Yale Bowl and Harvard Stadium. From University of Illinois, *The Story of the Stadium*, 1922.

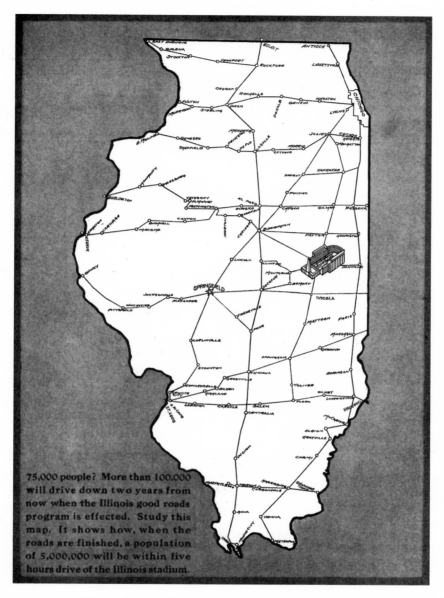

75,000 people? More than 100,000 will drive down two years from now when the Illinois good roads program is effected. Study this map. It shows how, when the roads are finished, a population of 5,000,000 will be within five hours drive of the Illinois stadium.

A diagram of Illinois's post–World War I system of good roads, which would make Illinois Memorial Stadium in Champaign accessible to millions of Illinoisans via automobile in the 1920s. From University of Illinois, *The Story of the Stadium,* 1922.

donations, however, sounded suspiciously like a quid pro quo: "We want the money for the best interest of Yale and you want to assure yourself good seats, which are hard to get with the increasing de- mand." So many spectators wanted to consume athletic spectacle that this was hardly an empty threat. Michigan athletic leaders were alarmed by the massive arenas being built in Columbus and Champaign. To replace Ferry Field's motley stands (capacity 42,000) with a modern earth, steel, and concrete bowl seating at least 70,000, they sold donors tickets as well as institutional pride. Michigan Stadium bondholders, as one clever illustration showed, were guaranteed seats inside the arena, not out on the street. California, likewise, warned that once the 20,000 seats allotted to Memorial Stadium contributors were gone, none would be available to the public for ten years.[43]

Even with the widespread usage of such fundraising tactics, universities could not afford to appear as though they were turning campuses into circuses or carnival midways. Stadiums were often built to resemble academic buildings. The stands at Chicago's Stagg Field (formerly Marshall Field) featured crenellated stone towers, mirroring the imposing gothic quadrangles located across 57th Street. The University of Illinois consciously designed its 60,000-seat stadium—one of America's largest sports venues at the time of construction—to fit the campus plan. Built with reinforced concrete, the façade incorporated red brick and stone so as to resemble the colonial-revival buildings then being constructed on the south side of campus. It was also intended to fit the university's governance structure. Although construction was funded through donations, Memorial Stadium became university property upon completion. Any profits reverted to the Athletic Board of Control to fund "Athletic developments." It was the university's cash cow, a way to tap popular culture to pay for physical education and intercollegiate sport.[44]

Fundraising campaigns, however, did not always meet their goals. While some football proponents responded to critics by asserting that student-athletes were not exploited to pay off stadium debts,[45] players probably were being exploited in some cases. After all, universities had to raise the money to pay the principal and interest on the bonds. Ohio Stadium, as we already saw, was not close to being paid off by 1923. Likewise, the debt for Nebraska's Memorial Stadium (1923) was

Detail sketch of fountain and entrance, showing memorial columns which will encircle the Stadium

The proposed commemorative columns at Illinois Memorial Stadium. Even after ambitious fundraising goals were not realized, the columns were retained; other features of the stadium complex, such as a Greek theater, were not. From University of Illinois, *The Story of the Stadium,* 1922.

not retired until 1940. In other cases, athletic departments reduced the scale of their ambitions to avoid the burden of debt. Illinois's extensive drive, which encompassed all forty-eight states and the District of Columbia, raised only $1.7 million of a projected $2.5 million. This shortfall led architects to scale back their ambitious designs. The completed structure included seating for 60,000 spectators, as well as 183 stone columns dedicated to the memory of students and alumni who died in the war. But since the facility's first priority was intercollegiate sport, other features were cut. The original plans included a Greek theater for plays and lectures, but this nonathletic—and, presumably, less profitable—space, unlike the magnificent grandstands for football competitions, were never constructed.[46]

In the 1920s, all of the Big Ten universities, including Minnesota, Indiana, and Michigan, constructed new stadiums or expanded older facilities through subscriptions, bonds, gate receipts, or some combination thereof. Meanwhile, some athletic leaders at the University of Chicago struggled unsuccessfully to replace their outdated facility. In 1921, Chicago turned away 30,000 who wanted to see the Maroons battle Wisconsin's Badgers, and by 1925 Stagg Field (capacity 34,000) was the conference's fifth smallest venue.[47] Amos Alonzo Stagg, head coach and athletic director, worked tirelessly to convince the administration and trustees to build a new 100,000-seat, state-of-the-art arena. Since the campus block where the old field was located was too small, the new arena might be located on land the university owned either north of campus or south of the Midway. Stagg was not bashful in his efforts. A new stadium, he said, could provide space for physical education, help Chicago retain athletic supremacy, and boost enrollment. It would also enlarge Chicago's donor pool and provide the university with up to $400,000 of revenue per year. This was roughly equivalent to a 5 percent return on $6 million, said Stagg, and he pointed out that a season's worth of gate receipts was easier to secure than a multimillion-dollar endowment. Some welcomed Stagg's overtures. Trustee Ernest Quantrell opined that a stadium was "becoming just as much a requisite of up-to-date University equipment as a gymnasium or physics lab[o]ratory."[48] But Stagg never got his new football arena. A new administration questioned the place of athletics in an institution that was becoming even more academic and shedding

William Rainey Harper's legacy of public engagement. Instead, Chicago made do with an addition to the grandstands. While Stagg continued his pleading, the old concrete stands were treated with pitch and sodium fluorsilicate ("Lapidolith"), and the aging coach corresponded with companies specializing in temporary seats.[49] In the late 1930s, after Stagg retired, Chicago eliminated football and abandoned the old field to other uses.

Chicago, as we will see in the next chapter, was changing its relationship to the nonacademic public by the 1930s. The stadiums constructed by its Big Ten counterparts, though, fully embodied the spirit of 1920s college football. Campus arenas like Ohio Stadium and Illinois Memorial Stadium supposedly educated thousands of students, not just a few players, yet also provided valuable national publicity through consumer spectacle, which aided institutional competition. Designed to fit campus plans, the arenas were funded with donations, not tuition dollars or state funds. This arrangement enabled universities to disclaim that they directly funded semiprofessional sporting events, but it would also come to limit the amount of control they had over the meaning of athletics. In addition, profits generated by these structures were not always funneled back into the university treasury. Rather, sometimes there were only vague promises, like Illinois's policy that gate receipts would fund athletics (a statement that may or may not have meant that the stadium would fund physical education). The athletic department was a semiautonomous unit at many universities by the 1930s, distributing revenue among sports programs and athletic facilities as its leaders, or university administrators, saw fit.

Although some argued that sport was an essential part of modern universities, stadiums were hardly the same as physics laboratories, lecture halls, or gymnasia. Once colleges built permanent structures for an athletic spectacle open to the ticket-buying public, they had become sponsors of popular culture. The athletic field was a space for consumers, whether or not the players were technically professionals. The games, therefore, had to be made legible, or visible, to the large crowds of spectators who bought tickets. By the 1890s, Penn, Princeton, Chicago, and other leading football programs installed scoreboards so that all spectators could follow and understand the game. While some writers argued that accurate scorekeeping and careful attention taught mental discipline, these strategies also helped spectators consume and enjoy the games. Athletic programs also profited from the more literal appetite for consumption displayed at concession stands. In 1921, the Georgia Tech Athletic Association conceded to local vendor R. J. Spiller "the right to sell soft drinks, cigars, peanuts, candies and other refreshments usually sold at athletic contests" at Grant Field for three years. Spiller, in turn, paid Tech's athletic program $1,000 per year. Apparently, Tech wanted to capitalize on the brisk business that Spiller's stand conducted, as this figure was almost double the rent stipulated in his contract for 1920–1921.[50]

Since so much money could be made (and lost) in sport, universities hoped to reduce the impact of chance, or risk, upon the lucrative spectacle. One way was through insurance policies. To protect against costly damage to the Marshall Field stands, Stagg, with guidance from the university legal counsel, insured them against $14,800 worth of damage in 1910. Universities also bought policies to protect against inclement weather. If more than one-tenth of an inch of rain fell at Grant Field on October 20, 1923, Hartford Fire Insurance would pay Georgia Tech's athletic association $5,000 to compensate for lost ticket revenue. Such weather conditions or property damage might be expensive, but the cost to life could be even greater. While critics had long charged that football could physically harm players, it was also becoming apparent that the many spectators who paid to see the games could die or be injured if someone was trampled by an excited mob, a fight broke out, or the stands collapsed under the weight of the crowd. This is why Chicago carefully regulated the crowd at the turn of the century, and it is also why Georgia Tech carried substantial insurance coverage against injury or death in the 1920s.[51]

While large universities and urban colleges were the main builders of campus arenas and purveyors of intercollegiate football in the 1920s, smaller schools also capitalized on spectator sport. In 1926, the Haskell Indian School in Lawrence, Kansas, dedicated its new stadium in a 36–0 victory over Bucknell. The grand structure, built with student labor, seated 10,500. For some critics, this arena demonstrated misplaced priorities, since the $250,000 raised in a national campaign might have been spent on new dormitories. Nevertheless, the stadium was built and the first game drew 20,000 white spectators, as well as

1,600 representatives of seventy Native American tribes who gathered for a powwow. Observers such as Secretary of the Interior Hubert Work saw Haskell's football success and stadium as evidence of a successful assimilation policy. Indian athletes, however, often saw sport in a different light. Football could demonstrate their strength and intelligence, or it could serve as a means of avenging centuries of violent, Anglo-American colonization. Haskell's administrators, writes one historian, could never "fully control the meaning that spectators, journalists, and the students themselves" ascribed to football. The game could signify pan-Indian spirit as much as it demonstrated assimilation. Likewise, while white spectators might have supported the imposition of white society's rational order upon Native Americans, they might have also embraced the supposedly savage anti-modernity—or apparent disorder—of Indian culture and football.[52]

Some white enthusiasts even appropriated a stereotypical view of Native American culture to celebrate the intercollegiate spectacle. Several universities, including Illinois, Stanford, and Miami (of Ohio), began using Indian mascots or nicknames in the 1920s. The Illinois Memorial Stadium campaign utilized Native American imagery, and soon after the arena's 1924 debut, students began putting on a red-face pageant during game-day ceremonies. A white student dressed in Indian-style clothing and wearing warpaint masqueraded as "Chief Illiniwek" and performed a dance to rouse the "Fighting Illini." This expression of whiteness occurred in a campus structure during a university activity, yet it was based on Wild West shows, popular lore, and circus performances, not academic scholarship. Eighty-plus years of these performances showed, perhaps better than any other example, how little control university intellectuals had over the athletic spectacle carried out on campus. The mascot was immensely popular among generations of students, townspeople, and Illinois sports fans, but by the 1980s some activists—including Native Americans and university professors—challenged it as insulting and misrepresentative of Indian culture. In turn, such critiques spawned a "Save the Chief" movement among students and townspeople, who claimed that Chief Illiniwek was a symbol honoring Native Americans and celebrating Illinois history. While scholars marshaled academic arguments to oppose the "Chief," their influence was limited. After all, arenas like Memorial Stadium were thrown open to the public every autumn Saturday, as were the rituals and meanings of college sport.[53]

By the late 1920s, college football was a popular-culture institution throughout America. This was especially apparent in southern universities, which were quickly approaching the athletic prestige of colleges in the Northeast, Midwest, and West. Many southern stadiums opened in the 1920s: Tennessee's Shields-Watkins Field (1921), Vanderbilt's Dudley Field (1922), LSU's Tiger Stadium (1924), North Carolina's Kenan Field (1927), and Duke Stadium (1929).[54] These stadiums were relatively small, usually seating 10,000 to 30,000. In one of the larger southern venues, the University of Georgia staged one of the most significant contests of the 1920s. Sanford Stadium in Athens replaced Sanford Field, both named for English professor and athletic director S. V. Sanford, who later served as university president. The old field was built in 1909 with the intention that it would last forever, but by 1926 it could no longer hold the big crowds that turned out for Georgia football. Completed in 1929, Sanford Stadium was financed with donations and $180,000 in loans. The new arena seated 32,000, less than half the size of the Yale Bowl or Michigan Stadium, but this was in a town with fewer than 15,000 residents. To dedicate the stadium, S. V. Sanford convinced Yale to send its football Bulldogs on their first trip outside the Northeast. It was not difficult to fill the new arena for this historic meeting. Ticket applications poured in from distant locales like New Hampshire; Chicago; Los Angeles; and Santiago, Cuba. On October 12, 1929, twenty-three special trains carried thousands of spectators from Atlanta to Athens. This "big iron parade" was joined by specials from Savannah, Raleigh, Birmingham, Montgomery, Louisville, Memphis, New Haven, and New York. Approximately 7,000 automobiles and 60 aircraft also made the trip to Athens.[55]

Staged two weeks before the 1929 stock market crash, Sanford Stadium's dedication game was the Athens social event of the year. An Atlanta newspaper wrote of the townwide celebration as "a salutation to the great god, Gridiron," that included many "luncheons . . . teas, dinners, and dances" for thousands of visitors. The state of Georgia declared the day an official holiday, and some predicted the game would be the "most brilliant event" the university had ever hosted.[56] Hotels and boardinghouses were packed. National Guardsmen directed traffic. Vendors hawked balloons on streets or in hotel lobbies; scalpers sold tickets illicitly; and florists peddled red roses to Georgians, or violets to Yale's rooters. Some in the crowd flouted Prohibition by purchasing quarts at local establishments; others were entranced by a novelty toy, the yo-yo. Many spectators stopped by the Georgia Hotel to listen to Yale's band play "Dixie" as it marched to the stadium. Ralph McGill of the *Atlanta Constitution* marveled at the spectacle: "There never was a day like this in the history of all Dixie football. Never was there such a parade before. It was a great bizarre crowd bent on a good time, and it was having it. There was no disorder—just a great, good-natured mob in a fine little city that was setting a record for fine and unadulterated hospitality and good sense."[57] Early 1800s educators and Progressive Era social scientists would have been horrified by McGill's carefree statement about the "mob" and "disorder," but it was a different time and place, and southern football was becoming a big deal.

The game was a triumph for Georgia and a disaster for Yale. According to the *New York Times*, Georgia's 15–0 victory "put the crowning touch to a perfect day for southern football." To call this contest an upset was an understatement; Yale was still one of the nation's premier teams and it had just routed Vermont the prior Saturday. The *Times* noted that this game was one of several that demonstrated the growing football parity between various regions (as well as the possible effects of the warm southern climate on players used to chilly New England autumns). Sportswriter Allison Danzig even pointed out that the vast numbers of spectators attending the games demonstrated the logic of building bigger or newer stadiums.[58] Football attracted attention and made money, and the universities that provided large arenas on campus for the spectacle seemed to be the biggest winners. Of course, this would change after the stock market crash. But for the time being, few worried about the economy or its effects upon college sport.

Historian John Sayle Watterson writes that huge football arenas, which became a standard variety of campus architecture in the 1920s, were "a sign that big-time football had drowned out all hopes for more modest athletic programs."[59] The massive, reinforced-concrete stadiums, no doubt, created a visible and permanent presence for big-time football on post–World War I campuses. Whether built for war memory, publicity, fundraising, interinstitutional competition, or a desire to accommodate the public demand for athletic spectacle—or some combination of these factors—stadiums welcomed popular culture to campus. But it is also important to remember that arenas were concrete representations of the fragmentation of the modern mind and the inaccessible nature of the intellectual work carried out in an ivory tower filled with academic disciplines. College athletics, a popular and consumable ritual, had become ensconced within a semiautonomous department located between the academy and the cultural marketplace. This department fulfilled the public's desire for consumerism and provided a way for universities to maintain visibility in a public sphere from which many intellectuals had become disengaged, often by necessity. College sport, unlike the abstract intellectual spaces occupied by professional academics, inhabited a visible university unit that welcomed the American people's dollars and cultural desires. While football may have seemed like middlebrow culture, it was really lowbrow culture wedged between the university and society and enjoyed by spectators who saw it as a respectable pastime. By the 1920s, as academics became more critical of both America's love affair with football and the growing divide between intellectuals and the public, they tried, with only limited success, to do something about it.

CHAPTER 7

Academic Backlash in the Post–World War I Era

G. T. W. Patrick, who published "The Psychology of Football" in the *American Journal of Psychology* in 1903, taught at the University of Iowa until 1922, when chronic neurasthenia prompted him to retire to Los Altos, California, near Stanford. During his long retirement, Patrick remained a perceptive, if cranky, observer of the academy and the American public. In October 1929, just five months after the Big Ten suspended Iowa for running an athletic slush fund, President Walter Jessup, later head of the Carnegie Foundation for the Advancement of Teaching, sent Patrick a copy of a new Carnegie report, *American College Athletics*. In November, soon after the stock market crash, Patrick commented that the report suggested "sensible reforms." Patrick recounted with dismay the recent Stanford-California game in Palo Alto, a spectacle that drew an overwhelming 89,000 spectators and $500,000 in gate receipts. He conceded, "The American people evidently must have sports . . . but I am wondering whether it is the function of our institutions of learning to furnish them."[1] Patrick and other Progressive Era scholars had once been optimistic that football might provide an accessible counterpoint to hyperspecialized research and help teach all Americans. But by the 1920s they were less sanguine. Consumerism, new communications technology, and militaristic nationalism had turned football into a hugely popular cultural spectacle located largely beyond academic control. Well-intentioned progressives had, in essence, made sport permanent by creating athletic departments, constructing concrete stadiums, and hiring a corps of professional athletic experts. This was at roughly the same time that university scholars had erected professional safeguards to protect themselves from the market and the society located outside the college walls—the same market within which big-time college athletics prospered. By the 1920s, although they did try, there was little that disaffected academics could do to abolish, or to reform significantly, big-time football.

While early 1900s coaches and players became skilled at producing

G. T. W. Patrick, early 1930s, around the time he was living
near Stanford and openly questioning the place of big-time
athletics in American universities. Frederick W. Kent
Photograph Collection, University of Iowa Libraries, Iowa
City, Iowa.

a popular spectacle, the era's scholars produced specialized knowledge
that was not always appreciated by the larger public. As universities
operated as industrial, knowledge-producing corporations and put
professors on trial or fired them for making unpopular statements,
some academics fought back by crafting reforms, including academic
freedom and tenure. Scholars argued that they were credentialed, pro-

fessional experts whose ideas resulted from careful study, training, and immersion within a community of specialists—not mere hired help. As a committee formed jointly in 1913 by several social science organizations contended, universities were inherently public institutions, and professors served a public role. But each new scholarly breakthrough could be a "shock to existing opinion." In private universities, harsh reactions might come from rich benefactors, while in state universities they might come from voters or politicians. Scholars had to be able to speak their minds freely in order to produce impartial, sound, and valuable knowledge. But they could not do so if they worked or lived in fear of untutored public opinion. Scholars needed academic freedom. Hoping to avoid comparisons to labor unions, academic freedom's proponents stressed that this was a public reform, not simply an occupational one.[2] For academic freedom to work, scholars also needed job security, or permanent tenure. In *University Control* (1913), Columbia psychologist and public intellectual James McKeen Cattell argued that tenure was typically associated with public offices *not* performed as wage labor. He scorned domineering administrators as well as alumni who were more concerned with football victories than with scholarship. While Cattell acknowledged that professors should not totally control universities, he did insist that their posts should be secure enough that they could write and speak freely without making "dishonorable compromises."[3] Implemented together, academic freedom and tenure could facilitate intellectuals' public roles and allow them to enlighten society.

Progressives even founded an organization to protect academic freedom and tenure, the American Association of University Professors (AAUP), in 1915. Faculty members throughout the nation had previously called for a broad professional association like the American Medical Association (formed 1847) or American Bar Association (1878). The AAUP's main goal was to ensure that universities followed academic standards and conventions. Early AAUP leaders included Columbia pragmatic philosopher John Dewey, as well as Arthur O. Lovejoy, a Johns Hopkins philosopher who had resigned from Stanford in 1900 to protest E. A. Ross's firing. The AAUP's founders saw themselves primarily as guardians of higher education, not just advocates for better academic working conditions. The new organization examined questionable dismissals of university scholars and urged the creation of guidelines and procedures regarding tenure and academic freedom.[4] It intended to protect scholars from the thumbs-up or thumbs-down mentality of the unthinking mob. In this role, as we will see, during the 1920s the AAUP became a loud critic of the institutional spirit that trumpeted athletics over academics, and some of its members portrayed football as an activity that, if unchecked, could corrupt universities.

Yet World War I proved that academic freedom, tenure, and the AAUP were not enough to protect professors. The range of acceptable faculty behavior, activities, and politics narrowed during the global conflict, when some universities punished professors for speaking out against American involvement in the war. Most notably, Nicholas Murray Butler tried to demonstrate Columbia's patriotism in 1917 by ordering the faculty to stop criticizing national foreign policy. Butler subsequently fired several professors, including J. McKeen Cattell, for opposing the military draft. These dismissals were also, in part, a way for the university to settle old scores. Cattell had long grated on colleagues, and his antiwar statements provided a convenient excuse to send him packing.[5] In 1918, a Chicago court indicted W. I. Thomas— the anthropologist who envisioned football as a kind of university extension in 1901—for violating the Mann Act (a Progressive Era measure intended to stop underage prostitution rings but which, in practice, was often used to persecute controversial individuals). The charges were eventually dropped, but the indictment cost Thomas his job. His bohemian lifestyle certainly helped bring about the charges, but historians suspect that some Chicagoans and the Federal Bureau of Investigation may have been more concerned with Harriet Thomas's antiwar activities than with her husband's moral indiscretions. Thomas later taught at the New School for Social Research and at Harvard, but he never again held a permanent faculty post.[6]

Although intellectual specialization had thrived in the Progressive Era, the final bars in the academic iron cage were cast during World War I. While some professors were dismissed for opposing the war, others found niches as producers of wartime knowledge in the new scholarly gridiron. First of all, industry and the federal government discovered additional practical applications for engineering and the sciences. In addition, psychology became particularly useful when the armed forces began using the Stanford-Binet intelligence test, developed by Stanford's Lewis Terman, to sort enlistees by mental aptitude. The government even tapped historians and political scientists to write propaganda. In turn, specialization increased as more ties were forged between universities, government, and industry. Yet although the war made some academics useful, it did not necessarily give them greater latitude to engage the public. Soon, many scholars found themselves addressing narrow audiences or beholden to funding agencies. Some also came to regret their former pro-war stance and retreated into silence. Many academics subsequently became locked into a fragmented intellectual culture located in a world apart from the public sphere. This situation was diametrically opposed to the hopes of progressives, who had sought to make publicly useful knowledge.[7] As disciplinary scholarship became increasingly narrow, however, football became even more important to the burgeoning consumer society. While college football suffered a brief setback at the beginning of the war, when many students entered the military, it was more popular than ever by the early 1920s. The postwar athletic boom, fueled by media advances, allowed more Americans to enjoy the popular spectacle, even if they had no formal ties to the universities for which they rooted.[8]

Football's growing popularity led to more criticism. Considering the progressive origins of football reform, it was only appropriate that one 1920s football critic was Upton Sinclair, the muckraker who had famously taken on Chicago's meat packers in *The Jungle* (1906). Sinclair turned his critical gaze toward the academy in *The Goose-Step* (1923). Using Progressive Era rhetoric, Sinclair lamented that too few students got too much exercise from the "gladiatorial combats" of football, while others merely exercised "vocal cords and the gambling instincts." College sport, he implied, fostered the irrational, disorderly crowd—not the rational, educated public. It also represented the perversion of academic ideals and the cutthroat nature of industrial competition. To make matters worse, some men made a living by the violent ritual. Rival colleges were carrying out "little wars" on the athletic field, which spawned "an elaborate cult of loyalties and heroisms." The recruiting, training, and exploitation of athletes had "become an enormous industry, absorbing the services not merely of students and alumni, but of a whole class of professional coaches, directors, press agents and promoters," who were quickly "coming to dominate college life and put the faculty on the shelf." For Sinclair, a writer steeped in progressive reform, this turn of events was disgraceful. Faculty should be in the public eye, not hidden behind a flashy but empty spectacle that appealed to crass consumerism.[9]

At a time when many scholars produced useful knowledge, yet struggled to maintain professional identity and public relevance, football's popularity and moneymaking potential also started upsetting academics. This backlash resulted, in part, from one of the most infamous scandals in the history of college football. In November 1921, two small southern Illinois towns—Carlinville and Taylorville, located east of St. Louis—hired ringers for an annual rivalry game played for both municipal pride and tens of thousands of dollars in wagers. Carlinville paid $2,700 to a group of athletes from Notre Dame. When the people of Taylorville discovered the plan, they hired University of Illinois players for their team. The latter town trotted out its ringers in the second half, winning the game (and $50,000 in bets) by a score of 16–7. Two months later, the Associated Press broke the story. The college players were quickly disqualified and the tainted game became a rallying cry for opponents of professional football.[10]

This scandal resulted in a period of national soul-searching regarding the place of sport in America's universities, and the AAUP asked its members to formulate suggestions for reform. A special committee of Northwestern University's AAUP chapter, like many turn-of-the-century scholars, upheld sport's many benefits but deplored the way universities conducted the spectacle and exploited athletes. Even though the performers were not paid outright, big-time college athletics resembled show business. The committee lamented, "The public, having paid vast sums of money for this entertainment, rightly or wrongly assumes that colleges are obligated to put up great stadiums, to hire an army of coaches and trainers at prices comparable to those paid to other skillful directors of entertainment, and provide another army of officials for games who must receive fees on a similar scale." Teams might advertise universities, said the Northwestern committee, but sport was more effective at publicizing itself than in disseminating the lessons of higher education. To correct this situation, they contended, universities should terminate paid coaches, shorten the football season, cut ticket prices, and cede control over athletics to students. Northwestern's full AAUP chapter just barely voted down the resolution, which was not forwarded to the national organization. Nevertheless, the suggestions created a flurry of opinion. Some Chicagoans, echoing progressive ideals, thought the professors were right—the proposed reforms, if implemented, would keep "graft and gambling" out of colleges. Others disagreed. One observer thought the United States needed a "national board to uniformly regulate the athletic activities" of its member universities; this suggestion, essentially, described the NCAA, which had existed for almost seventeen years at that point. Another critic, who disdained regulation by anyone who was not an athletic expert, liked the "thrill" of football and credited "well paid coaches" for the stimulating level of play and for the valuable publicity that they brought to universities.[11]

Hugh Fullerton of the *Chicago Tribune* placed the controversy in national perspective. While he overstated faculty opposition, Fullerton correctly noted that many anti-football professors were associated with the AAUP. He also observed that some traditional powers, such as Harvard, Yale, and Princeton, were looking to de-emphasize football. Soon, it seemed, colleges would cut the length of the season and "curb" professional coaches. Once this happened, universities would stop building 100,000-seat arenas and eliminate football as an "entertaining enterprise" that funded physical education. Princeton coach Bill Roper was particularly alarmed. Even though just two years earlier (in *Winning Football*) he had recommended that athletics be supported through undergraduate fees or endowment funds, he claimed in 1922 that Princeton's football team annually brought in $400,000 that was necessary to fund physical culture in the athletic department. Major universities everywhere seemed to be plotting football's demise. Harvard, said the *Tribune*, clearly favored laboratories over athletics, and administrators seemed willing to smother athletics "under the lava and ashes of scholasticism." Closer to home, even the University of Chicago might dethrone King Football.[12]

While some big universities planned to mute sport, a few smaller New England colleges, like Amherst and Williams, considered cutting it altogether.[13] Many small-college football critics did not merely oppose commercialism. Rather, they opposed big-time intercollegiate athletics as part of a broader critique of modern, intellectually fragmented universities focused on research. American higher education, they argued, had become stultifying and operated on an inhumane scale since the late 1800s. Academics—producing specialized knowledge in small fields at large universities—had become incapable of teaching students to think big thoughts. For education to regain social utility, colleges had to refocus attention on critical reflection. They had to abandon the idea that universities could expand indefinitely, or that any subject could be construed as a field deserving its own department. These thinkers rejected the pragmatic, instrumentalist orientation of turn-of-the-century academics who had designed a university system to instruct a whole population and produce socially useful knowledge. Colleges should teach students as individuals, not as parts of a population. Higher education should be based on traditional ideals of discipline, character, mental acumen, and morality—and reduce athletics to a subsidiary role.

Alexander Meiklejohn, who served as president of Amherst College from 1912 until his controversial 1923 dismissal, was one of these college reformers. During his tenure, Meiklejohn kept Amherst's enrollment small and alienated alumni by rejecting the applications of lightly qualified sons. He also hired some controversial young professors and was a pacifist, not a popular stance in the early 1920s. To Meiklejohn, a small college that created disciplined minds by challenging students to think was better than a larger institution that made old grads happy by teaching accepted facts to aspiring gentlemen. He used his position as a pulpit from which to expound a new kind of education. In *The Liberal College* (1920), Meiklejohn argued that athletics and other student activities were just one part of a residential campus life that included chapel services and student-teacher interaction. Students should learn music, drama, literature, as well as "careful training of the body" and "strength of character." Meiklejohn rejected the apparent credo of most universities in his "pragmatic" era, which was to study any subject one pleased. By contrast, he wanted a college to serve its community by educating whole individuals. While students should be able to play sports at college, too

Alexander Meiklejohn—a proponent of the liberal arts curriculum and the Great Books, as well as a critic of big-time college athletics—in the early 1900s. Photo courtesy of UW Madison Archives.

many extracurricular activities could prove a distraction from mental training. A liberal college had a duty to counteract the "trivial and vulgar amusements" of society. It was not true that all subjects were equally important. The elective system was fine if it generated student enthusiasm, but not if it merely led to the proliferation of departments. The nation should resemble a single "mind," not a "mob" or "crowd" whose speech was "an incoherent clash and clatter of unrelated groans, and shouts and yells." Meiklejohn also offered his own take on academic freedom. He supported the concept, yet believed that the AAUP merely pitted faculty and administrators against one another (like laborers and management) rather than uniting them as coadjudicators in a common, educational enterprise.[14]

Meiklejohn, who resembled other mid-1920s anti-modernists by criticizing John Dewey's pragmatic educational philosophy, employed rhetoric similar to that which antebellum Whig educators had used to promote manual labor education and gymnastics. He basically wanted colleges to return to a preindustrial educational ideal, to a time when educators shaped the morals of individuals instead of teaching specialized knowledge to large groups. Though he conceded that experimental psychology had proven Whig-style faculty psychology obsolete, Meiklejohn still defended a "gymnastic" theory of mind in a way that recalled the Yale Report. In both thought and sport, he asserted, one learned "best by practice in fast company." For a mind to succeed in modern life's economic, political, and educational tasks, it should possess specialized knowledge, but must also be trained in "discipline."[15] Big-time intercollegiate sport, played by highly trained, semiprofessional players before thousands of paying spectators in a massive stadium, was antithetical to the liberal arts, even if it was conducive to relieving the mental stresses of modern society or contributing to the formation of communal bonds. There was no need to pay a professional coach a large salary to orchestrate a spectacle that claimed to teach young men the ways of mental, moral, and physical self-control. All college teachers were engaged in the process of teaching such things, insisted Meiklejohn, so there was no need for a special ritual that sold this activity to the nonacademic community. Furthermore, there was no need to use sport to advertise a college—it was a public institution insofar as it trained young men (Amherst then had no female students) to be moral citizens. His ideas sounded anachronistic in the 1920s because, to a certain extent, they were. Yet Meiklejohn was intentionally anachronistic. He and other interwar curricular innovators, like the Whigs a century earlier, advocated the liberal arts as a way to cope with the stress, fragmentation, and greed of a modern society that seemed to be falling apart at the seams as it expanded.

Meiklejohn was particularly critical of professional coaches. In 1922, when Harvard, Yale, and Princeton were starting to de-emphasize sport, he called on these institutions to eliminate professional coaches. He observed that many universities, by creating athletic departments, had given competitive sport institutional autonomy. Meiklejohn warned Harvard's President A. Lawrence Lowell about the ramifications of this shift in university structure:

> The general effect of these changes has been to build up in each of our colleges an independent body responsible for the accomplishment of a definite task, in serious conflict with the other interests of the institution, and yet with no provision for keeping that body or its activities within proper limitation or control. Our games are no longer the play of undergraduates. The players tend to become puppets in the hands of coaches and boards of control who represent the "institutions" in their public contests for victory. These coaches and systems are, to say the best of them, highly specialized in point of view. In general they have very little understanding of the genuine purposes of a college. And yet they tend, more and more, to become independent bodies, responsible only to the public[,] which is interested in the winning of victories.[16]

An efficient, independent athletic department was no improvement over a less official structure. The new order represented the unwanted influence of commercial popular culture, which threatened liberal education. The public was not always a rational, orderly body that held colleges' best interests in mind. Sometimes, Meiklejohn implied, it just wanted to have fun.

Not all, of course, agreed. Some saw athletics, led by professional coaches, as the meal ticket for an important university department. Big-time football, they said, bankrolled the other sports that developed bodies and minds. Michigan's Fielding Yost asked, "Is it a crime for athletics to pay [its] own costs?" Sport had become a "big business" only because such a "health-building program" that benefited thousands of college students required efficient methods. Where would the money come, if not from football? The game was the "backbone" of collegiate physical culture; it just needed better supervision. Clarence Mendell, a Yale Latin professor and chair of that university's Athletic Board of Control, adamantly opposed Meiklejohn's call for eliminating coaches as well as his proposal for undergraduate control of athletics. Mendell argued that coaches taught football and directed the spectacle, the same way professors taught academic subjects and conducted research. Sport needed professional management. He wrote, "In the field of scholarship we try to give the undergraduate the very best that we have, and then we count on him to make use of it on his own initiative. Just so in football we should give the benefit of the best possible training to all the men who can be brought out to play one of the best games ever invented." Mendell argued that the athletic department should be taken as seriously as other university departments. It had "become too important a factor in our college training of today to make it wise, or even possible," he warned, "to return to the haphazard methods of management which result from leaving its affairs entirely in the hands of the undergraduates."[17]

Meiklejohn clearly held a minority opinion. And while his criticism of athletics may have been one reason Amherst's trustees forced his resignation in June 1923, it was a small part of his larger curricular program. Like other academic refugees, including E. A. Ross, Meiklejohn departed for Madison, where he established the University of Wisconsin's Experimental College. In this college, students studied a liberal arts core curriculum for two years before beginning specialized studies. He saw this innovation as a way to return to pre–Civil War pedagogy, before science and industry had fragmented intellectual life and obliterated the central place of religion and morality in modern society.[18] Meiklejohn believed that better teaching methods would benefit from the elimination of big-time sport. In 1925 he lamented that because thrilling football plays drove large crowds to insanity, coaches seemed like the world's greatest teachers. By contrast, society would shun a young man inspired by a rigorous philosophy course to question the world around him. Meiklejohn thought that sport found a more receptive audience than philosophy because it was more easily understood by more people, but he thought the problem went even deeper. America's colleges had lost their sense of purpose and relied too greatly upon lectures. The lecture method of teaching—a late 1800s educational innovation intended to replace dull recitations with exciting revelations of original, cutting-edge scholarship—just injected students with knowledge without making them ponder its meanings. Students thus learned facts without being inspired to engage critically history's greatest minds. In 1926, at the National Student Federation meeting in Ann Arbor—at which there was great enthusiasm for newly founded colleges like Bennington in Vermont and Claremont in Southern California—Meiklejohn contended that universities had become too large to be effective. The elective system fractured knowledge "and sent fragments of each Faculty far adrift so that [intellectual] unity was impossible."[19]

For some higher education critics, big-time football seemed appropriate for universities with big-time research goals, but a more subdued program was a better fit for smaller colleges focused on undergraduate, liberal arts education. The world had moved on since the Progressive Era, a time when many professed faith in the social utility of specialized knowledge. Some professors in the 1920s and 1930s, rather than stressing the social utility of specialized research, emphasized the broad meaning of timeless ideas and hoped to make the humanities relevant to the public. As historian Joan Shelley Rubin writes, John Erskine, Stringfellow Barr, Scott Buchanan, and Mortimer Adler used radio or popular periodicals to craft a "middlebrow" culture located between the highbrow culture of social elites and the lowbrow culture of the masses. Through book-of-the-month clubs, book reviews, and popularization of the so-called Great Books— works by classical philosophers like Plato and Aristotle or modern thinkers like Darwin or Hobbes—twentieth-century intellectuals might appropriate the lowly means of popular culture for the high-minded ends of teaching scholarly ideals to American society.[20] This was not an entirely new concept. After all, some Progressive Era scholars, especially in the social sciences and psychology, had seen football as a sort of middlebrow culture, a way of conveying modern truths to the public. Great Books proponents, in other words, were not inventing middlebrow culture in the interwar period. They were reshaping it for a new era.

Nevertheless, some aging progressives maintained that college sport, when carefully regulated, was a valuable social and cultural ritual. In 1925, an AAUP committee led by Thomas Moran, the Purdue economist who touted professional coaches sixteen years earlier, issued a report on athletics. The report, likely authored by Moran himself, used language straight out of the Progressive Era. Colleges had to cultivate "a vigorous and enlightened public opinion" in order to keep athletics educationally useful. Even though the AAUP committee acknowledged that reform would be difficult, its progressive optimism shone through. University alumni—who seemed willing to "hire" athletes outright in an attempt to win football victories—might be harder to win over than students, but this was a challenge, not a roadblock. "If the pressure of a wholesome alumni public opinion can be made effective in removing this rather widespread evil," said the report, "a very great and positive good will have been accomplished for intercollegiate athletics and for the boys who participate."[21]

Not all educators, though, bought the 1925 AAUP report's upbeat tone. Some colleges abandoned the idea that a few reforms and the right "public opinion" could make athletics safe for higher education. As early as the Progressive Era, the founders of Reed College in Portland, Oregon, had banned intercollegiate athletics. In the 1920s, Swarthmore, once a burgeoning East Coast university with a mighty football team, began envisioning itself as a smaller, more scholarly institution. Under President Frank Aydelotte, Swarthmore implemented an academic honors program and de-emphasized athletics by funding it through the regular budget. Some other, less well-endowed colleges felt obligated to eliminate football because they did not gain all the benefits sport supposedly provided and they could not compete in an athletic world ruled by large universities. In 1925, the University of Dubuque's President Karl Wettstone explained his decision to ban football by blaming public universities for implementing an athletic arms race. Always seeking publicity and athletic victory, state-funded institutions had dictated policies to smaller, privately run schools, often affiliated with Christian denominations (Dubuque was Presbyterian). Public universities built formidable teams by sending scouts to recruit the most talented high school students in the state. In turn, "the smaller schools of the land realized that they must follow suit or lose their hold on their young people." By 1924, Dubuque had no chance of beating "the strong machines" that scoured the region, attracted players from all over, and paid coaches huge salaries. From 1925 to 1928 it stopped playing what had become a losing game. Similarly, Kentucky's Centre College (whose "Praying Colonels" famously defeated Harvard in 1921) felt pressured to give up football or sacrifice accreditation.[22]

Even the AAUP could not maintain Moran's optimism. In April 1926, a committee dedicated to improving undergraduate intellect, which consisted of faculty members drawn from a broad range of academic disciplines and universities, issued a bulletin critiquing athletics. Employing standard Progressive Era rhetoric, this report said that properly regulated football could aid college education through recreation. But at present, the sport was corrupted by drinking, gambling, and ticket scalping. The game had grown out of proportion and had become distracting, producing "hysteria" and perverting collegiate ideals. Coaches often earned larger salaries than professors or college presidents, and the stadium both literally and figuratively outshadowed "the library, laboratory and lecture hall." This AAUP committee made several recommendations. First, each student should be limited to one year of eligibility. Even though this innovation would reduce the level of play, it would also help football remain a way to stimulate "college spirit and alumni enthusiasm." Second, the season should be limited to four games per year. Third, graduates, paid the same as professors, should replace professional coaches.[23] The response was mixed. Some deans, like those at Princeton, Columbia, and Brown, saw virtually nothing wrong with football, or they noted that coaches were staff members who cooperated with administrators. President Walter Jessup of Iowa and Big Ten commissioner Major John Griffith simply noted that midwestern athletic conferences had purified sport long ago. Only a few, such as the president of small Coe College in Iowa—who endorsed the report and could not see why others did not—disagreed. But even then, most dissenters simply stressed moderation. The dean of New York's City College, on the one hand, blamed alumni for commercialism, but on the other hand, he criticized faculty who wanted to regulate college sport to death. His solution was a "sane middle course" that did not go to either extreme. Others saw the case as closed. Columbia's Nicholas Murray Butler, referring to Progressive Era reforms, simply decreed, "We dealt with this situation twenty years ago."[24]

At this time, the Carnegie Foundation for the Advancement of Teaching, an organization founded in the same era as the NCAA, was conducting a study on college athletics. On October 24, 1929, "Black Thursday" of the stock market crash—less than two weeks after Georgia's stunning defeat of Yale and a month before G. T. W. Patrick offered his ambivalent assessment of college sport—the Carnegie Foundation released its famous report, *American College Athletics* ("Bulletin Number Twenty-Three"). The national press widely cited and discussed its findings. Written by a team of staffers led by Howard Savage, the Carnegie Report argued that universities should eliminate "commercialism" from sport, but it also conceded that athletics had become an essential part of America's universities.[25] The large tome's preface, composed by Carnegie Foundation president Henry Pritchett, briefly summarized the underlying tension between the problems the investigators had observed and the solutions they suggested. Pritchett posed two main questions. First, "What relation has this astonishing athletic display to the work of an intellectual agency like a university?" While a university was certainly an academic institution, he said, it was "also a social, a commercial, and an athletic agency" whose nonacademic activities had recently eclipsed teaching and research in the public mind. Second, he asked how students had found "the time or the money to stage so costly a performance." Pritchett answered that coaches, not students, were responsible for the entertaining spectacle that turned students into pawns who obeyed orders so that universities could subsidize athletic programs or fund the construction of new facilities like football stadiums or academic buildings. He wrote that the academy's intellectual and athletic components were connected, insofar as the administrators who oversaw scholarly research were also responsible for stadiums, coaches, and ticket sales.[26]

Such observations were correct, at least on the surface, but Pritchett's allusion to institutional unity showed that he ignored a fundamental truth of American universities. Each campus had common administrators, trustees, students, faculty, and teams, but often little else held a particular institution together. Individual universities were responsible for producing intellectual knowledge as well as staging athletic spectacles, but by the 1920s most had become fragmented into a multitude of departments with different methodologies and professional organizations. Each department held academic authority over one realm of knowledge—or, in the case of the athletic department, over one university activity. Administrators might speak for professors, students, and coaches, but their main goal was to make the university function as a collection of successful, specialized entities. The captains of erudition did not necessarily have to ensure that each unit complemented others. In a modern academic landscape, each department had to engage in a Darwin-style struggle for existence. Professors in the psychology department competed with experts in the sociology department for institutional resources, while research interests made them identify intellectually with psychology specialists at other universities, with whom they competed for academic prestige in their field. This was roughly analogous to the athletic department. The football team's main job was to win games against other universities, not necessarily to uphold the research or teaching of the psychology or sociology departments.

By underemphasizing the fragmented nature of America's universities, the Carnegie Report's authors posited less than adequate solutions. Pritchett and Savage contended that athletic commercialism simply had to be scaled back. Americans, especially college presidents, could achieve this goal by ensuring that universities provided enough intellectual challenges for students who had become too enamored with the "pageantry of college life."[27] This was a watered-down version of Meiklejohn's proposal to organize small colleges around the liberal arts. It also ignored the fact that universities rarely pursued a single intellectual or pedagogical purpose. By making a facile recommendation about the need to quell commercialism, the Carnegie Report disregarded essential truths of modern higher education. It was difficult for a big-time university to jettison big-time sport without damaging its reputation and shuttering a powerful publicity- and revenue-producing department. By recommending decommercialization without proposing serious changes to academic structure or athletic supervision, the Carnegie Report also failed to address adequately the growing influence of the coaching profession. A passage buried deep within the report itself even hinted that coaches were gaining a professional autonomy that might limit the effectiveness of outside reforms.[28] Any university that fielded an intercollegiate team, built a stadium, and created an athletic department needed professional coaches. As Meiklejohn's critics had observed in 1922, the days when big-time athletics could be managed by undergraduates or alumni had long since passed.

Since the 1910s, the NCAA had urged its members to bring sport under faculty control, so it is not surprising that athletic departments developed autonomy in the 1920s and many coaches gained faculty status for supervising a cultural ritual played in permanent campus arenas. Yet this new order represented only a superficial form of institutional control. First, not all coaches were tenured, so even honest, permanent coaches had to compete against corrupt journeymen (Moran noted this problem in 1909). Second, an athletic department had different goals from most other academic units. It, or at least the part of the department that supervised competitive athletics, was designed to provide publicity and earn revenue—not produce knowledge or teach students in credit-earning courses. The Carnegie Report pointed out that many times alumni groups, athletic associations, or athletic directors chose coaches. Since their services were perceived as being highly valuable, coaches often earned salaries higher than most professors; in some instances, their compensation equaled that of deans or university presidents. The Carnegie Report even commented that the greedy showmen (or "business men") who comprised part of the coaching profession were "not above accepting or even demanding increases of salary."[29]

The Carnegie Report overlooked the ways that coaches masked lucrative cultural roles with pedagogical claims. But at least one coach openly stated that football should make more money, not less. Notre Dame's Knute Rockne contended in 1930 that football was "not commercialized enough." He admitted that even though only a few colleges profited from football, if it were decommercialized, none would make money from it. As historian Murray Sperber notes, Rockne knew that big-time football's decline would hurt coaches at the same time it cut into the athletic department's ability to pay for its other activities.[30] Here was the rub, and the market-savvy Rockne was among the few honest enough to discuss it openly. One of the game's stated raisons d'être was to make money. Although coaches cast themselves as mentors skilled at teaching disciplined self-control to both players and spectators, they ultimately had to please the desires of paying spectators—regardless of whether or not those spectators wanted to learn to behave in a certain way. Coaches claimed they could do it all: teaching, publicity, community outreach, and fundraising. They even underwrote their own departmental budget. But, truth be told, they taught fewer students than the typical professor or physical education instructor and were paid much more to do so. And colleges could only measure coaches' success through victories and ticket sales—not the lessons absorbed by the crowd or the student body.

Considered in this light, the Carnegie Foundation's proposal to limit commercialism was a legitimate goal for athletic reform, and its widespread implementation may have changed college sport. But the report's assumption of the ease with which decommercialization could happen demonstrated its own naïveté. This was no longer the Progressive Era, and it would have been difficult to make such changes in the late 1920s. True, intercollegiate athletics had become part of the university, but that truth cut both ways. Administrators had some control over sport, but it would not be easy to eliminate an established department with its own experts (some of them tenured) and potential monetary value. Cutting ticket sales would only make things worse, since colleges would then have to find another way to fund the athletic department, such as endowments or student fees. In addition, athletics had become an integral part of popular culture, as well as of the academy. Americans loved college sport, in large part, because it rendered universities—if not academic research itself—visible and legible. By the 1920s, most disciplinary intellectuals could not maintain a connection to commercial culture like that which coaches had developed. Moreover, agencies such as the NCAA helped to institutionalize big-time athletics, eventually (by the 1950s) creating a business monopoly, or cartel, that essentially shunned amateurism in favor of semi-professional sport.[31]

Most universities were hesitant to meddle with a semi-academic unit that provided publicity and revenue, but the Great Depression prompted a few institutions to make dramatic changes in the 1930s. Johns Hopkins, for one, dropped ticket sales and let the public attend games for free. More famously, the University of Chicago—led by the precocious Great Books proponent Robert Maynard Hutchins—abolished football altogether in 1939. Chicago's elimination of big-time sport originated in the same back-to-basics, anti-pragmatist movement that spawned Meiklejohn's 1920s critiques. One historian has perceptively portrayed Hutchins as an educator who resembled Jeremiah

Day, primary author of the 1828 Yale Report. Hutchins openly critiqued, in his biting, witty style, his early 1900s education at Oberlin and Yale, where professors forced him to read boring textbooks, attend stultifying lectures, and conduct meaningless experiments. He complained that modern professors worked in "narrow fields" that made sense to other scholars, but were often incomprehensible to the modern student, who had to navigate a "multifarious collection of disconnected courses" that actually became less comprehensible over time. Like Meiklejohn, Hutchins said that America's "intellectual tradition" had become unintelligible at universities, where "its scattered and disjointed fragments [were] strewn from one end of the campus to the other." Hutchins hoped to put the modern mind back together. Rather than trying to strengthen Chicago by building more academic departments and using football to publicize them, as Harper had done forty years earlier, Hutchins wanted to make the university relevant to undergraduates by making its curriculum practically irrelevant. Students would recover timeless truth by reading thousands of years of Western intellectual thought—not construct timely, pragmatic truths by sorting through the minutiae of the latest, cutting-edge research. Hutchins and his intellectual sidekick, Mortimer Adler, built a liberal arts curriculum upon the Great Books canon. They stopped short, however, at dismantling Chicago's famous graduate research programs and specialized departments.[32]

Football, needless to say, was not a Great Book. It was a Progressive Era spectacle intended to strengthen individual nervous systems while advertising and disseminating the lessons of the collective, pragmatic mind that the academic gridiron of disciplinary scholarship was creating at big universities in places like Chicago and Madison. Even though sport was not necessarily academic, early-1900s professors and administrators had seen it as essential because athletics might make disciplinary universities relevant to industrial society. For Hutchins, who infuriated his critics by claiming that whenever he felt the urge to exercise he would lie down until it passed, physical activity was just a distraction from more serious mental endeavors.[33] In this way, even though Hutchins rejected the pragmatic orientation of William Rainey Harper, he only superficially resembled antebellum educators who viewed gymnastics as essential to college education

Robert Maynard Hutchins, president of the University of Chicago, in the early 1950s. Here he is pictured with promotional "dummies" of Encyclopedia Britannica's "Great Books of the Western World" series. Special Collections Research Center, University of Chicago Library.

(and even Alexander Meiklejohn, who was less critical of physical activity). Hutchins did, however, share antebellum educators' distaste for intercollegiate athletics, and by the late 1930s, Chicago was at a point where it could seriously consider eliminating big-time football.

Since 1925, Chicago's athletic luster had faded. Stagg regularly lost recruits to other midwestern football powers, causing Chicago to win fewer victories and lose many fans. He was also unable to convince the university to construct a massive new arena. Moreover, Chicago's 1931 "New Plan" of study yielded a more academic-minded student body and fewer football players, while it also led to the enrollment of a greater number of transfer students who could not play varsity football after moving to a new campus (the result of a Big Ten reform intended to thwart tramp athletes). When the university forced Stagg to retire at age seventy in 1932, the "Grand Old Man" went to the University of the Pacific and Chicago replaced him with Thomas Nelson Metcalf, who sympathized with Hutchins's intellectual goals and did not produce winning teams. The university fielded its last team with a winning record in 1935, when the Maroons' Jay Berwanger won the first Heisman Trophy (then the Downtown Athletic Club Trophy). From 1936 to 1939, Big Ten opponents frequently shut out Chicago's overmatched squad, and it won only six games, mostly against small colleges like Beloit and Wabash. Most of Stagg Field's seats went unfilled, and Maroons football had become an embarrassment. Few endorsed Hutchins's plan to eliminate football, but by the late 1930s he had surrounded himself with supportive trustees and administrators and helped his own cause by letting sport decline through poor management. Endorsing the idea that football competition indicated academic rank, Hutchins refused to shift from the Big Ten to a smaller conference, which was one of the few options remaining. Finally, in December 1939, the trustees voted to eliminate football.[34]

According to historian Robin Lester, Hutchins imagined an intellectual, "utopian" higher education institution "unaffected by the needs and tastes of the public." Hutchins, unlike Harper, was not attuned to the voice of the city. Yet the elimination of big-time college athletics had a drawback that Hutchins would barely acknowledge. He noted, albeit condescendingly, that alumni who conceded the logic of his football critiques made an argument with its own, nonintellectual

logic: their sons would not want to attend Chicago if it abolished football.[35] Publicity and visibility were major reasons Harper had adopted
football in the 1890s, and Stagg had claimed in the 1920s that successful athletic teams would increase both Chicago's enrollment and endowment. Such claims, while perhaps extravagant, may have held a
grain of truth. Although the educated public's reaction to Chicago's
decision to abolish football was fairly positive, fans and sportswriters
lambasted it. Lester suggests that this move limited Chicago's post-
1940 fundraising, and some observers argued that the university
needed new ways to gain publicity. William McNeil, a 1930s student
and *Daily Maroon* editor, later critiqued Hutchins for failing to affili-
ate with the NFL's Chicago Bears, which might have maintained the
university's ties to popular sport without turning students into
celebrity-athletes. This, wrote McNeil, was a "lost opportunity" to
maintain Harper's desire to exploit the public's interest in football.
McNeil made an interesting point, but he missed a more significant
one. Hutchins did not crave publicity. He wanted to build Chicago's
reputation as a place for serious, intellectual pursuits, not return to
the gridiron circus that Harper, the academy's own P. T. Barnum, had
pioneered in the 1890s.[36]

One of the few major universities to eliminate big-time football,
Chicago's undergraduate college eventually developed an exclusive
reputation as a place focused on the life of the mind. It was no longer a
destination for intellectually unambitious sons and daughters of middle-class Chicagoans. Ironically, though, Hutchins did not carry his
athletic reforms to their apparent, logical conclusion. He did not raze
Stagg Field's stands and convert the city block into the site of an experimental college like the one Meiklejohn founded at Wisconsin, nor
did he construct a center for study and popular dissemination of the
Great Books. The stadium lay empty and the field sprouted weeds until the Manhattan Project, the secret federal program to create nuclear
weapons, turned it into an atomic laboratory during World War II.
Under the stands, a research team led by Enrico Fermi initiated the
world's first controlled nuclear reaction in 1942. Subsequently, the
stands were torn down in the 1960s and the massive Regenstein Library, with space for 3.5 million volumes, opened on the site in 1970.
The ground where the Maroons once played football had come full cir-

Regenstein Library, University of Chicago, constructed on the former site of Stagg Field and the secret Manhattan Project laboratory that initiated the first controlled nuclear reaction in 1942. Special Collections Research Center, University of Chicago Library.

cle. The huge, reinforced-concrete and limestone library was very different from Stagg Field, yet the structures might once have complemented each other. Harper had envisioned a modern university that produced specialized research and used football to publicize academic work. By the mid-1900s, researchers still created specialized knowledge at the University of Chicago, but without big-time college sports, the campus seemed inaccessible to many Americans. The gothic quadrangles were cloisters for geniuses, not playgrounds for average people. No doubt, great books occupied the shelves, yet Regenstein's collection was intended primarily for faculty and graduate students (with undergraduates also allowed access). As problematic as football turned out to be, Harper and others had meant for sport to balance the university. Hutchins, by eliminating the quasi-lowbrow popular spectacle, may have been mostly successful in securing Chicago's identity as an elite, highbrow research institution.[37]

By the 1930s, some university intellectuals, especially those in the humanities and social sciences, had become conscious of their alienation from the public sphere. While the Carnegie Report cited the vast amounts of money that sports garnered during the 1920s, many professors occupied a world located far from the crowded stadium. The Great Depression did revive progressive notions of scholars' utility, yet at least some professors thought that their fellow academics, abetted by the trappings of professionalism, were out of touch. Columbia sociologist Robert Lynd lamented that a scholar worked "in a long, leisurely world in which the hands of the clock crawl slowly over a vast dial . . . and one simply works ahead within study walls relatively sound-proofed against the clamorous urgencies of the world outside." Lynd, like Progressive Era professors who fought for tenure and founded the AAUP, saw that younger scholars, "hired by businessmen trustees," often received small salaries and had to produce cutting-edge scholarship, while maintaining a patina of disinterested objectivity. He called upon older scholars with permanent tenure and job security to craft socially significant scholarship.[38] Lynd's call to action, though, implied a paradox. By the time most scholars were in a position to produce riskier scholarship that took advantage of tenure and academic freedom, they had grown accustomed to secure jobs in soundproof offices. Although he did not make this comparison, Lynd's portrait of academic intellectuals offered a striking contrast with the coaches or players who raced against the clock to secure victory and bowed to the cheers of the crowd.

Professors could (and did) register their distaste for big-time college athletics. But there was only so much they could do. On the one hand, sport seemed indispensable. It was widely perceived as a way to gain publicity, and ticket sales supposedly subsidized everything from physical education to academic facilities. On the other hand, academics could hardly compete with football. The creation of departments at increasingly large universities turned many scholars into cogs in the machinery of the erudition industry. They had gained some control over their labor through progressive reforms, but at the cost of alienating themselves from society. The climate of research and professional advancement first cultivated in the late 1800s had bred a kind of specialized academic laborer who produced knowledge that was often both scientifically accurate and socially useful, yet occupied a world located on the margins of the public sphere. Robert Herrick noted this irony in *Chimes* (1926), a parody of the William Rainey Harper–era University of Chicago. At fictional Eureka University, football was a central ring of "Barnum's Show," but professors seemed to occupy an academic sideshow. At the faculty club, intellectual fragmentation and alienation were palpable. Young professors gathered to "play billiards, read the magazines, and write letters"—but the club was a space disconnected from the public, and it did not foster wide-ranging intellectual discourse:

> Around the billiard tables they gossiped a little, talked shop: they were too tired or bored to discuss much else. With the increasing degree of specialization they were cut off from each other in little provinces of thought and interest: knowledge had become an archipelago of small islands instead of a single continent. One popular idea about university life,—that there were "stimulating contacts" among so many exceptional men,—was largely an illusion. Either they were too busy or too narrow in their culture and their interest to give much in general conversation.[39]

Academic knowledge was narrow and fragmented. Even when professional intellectuals participated in leisure activities or consumed popular writings, they were still located on an academic shop floor, its fatiguing specialization stifling their lives and limiting the scope of intellectual endeavor. The university was a workplace and, as in other industries, its laborers had specific jobs. Academic labor held the potential to facilitate discourse beyond a narrow field of specialists, but wearisome duties, professional decorum, and the dangerous currents of the market ensured that many intellectuals operated outside the cultural mainstream. In sports arenas and the popular media, though, athletic amusements provided a cultural space focused on physical spectacle, a space where meaning was not mediated by academics or produced via mental labor. Herrick's analogy to work was not coincidental. Modern intellectual culture's fragmentation resulted when late 1800s universities applied industrial methods to education and intellectual life. Unlike other early 1900s workers—especially those located on more physically taxing or dangerous shop floors and beholden to demanding foremen—intellectuals benefited from professional status and safeguards they invented in the Progressive Era. Reasonable and necessary innovations like tenure and academic freedom protected academics from the same market forces that had elevated college sport to a popular-culture ritual. Ironically, though, at the same time scholars sought safe professional spaces to ply their meticulous crafts, athletic specialists had also created university departments of athletics devoted to a popular-culture spectacle that exploited Americans' desire for consumer entertainment.

Football's 1920s commercialization left such a bad taste in the mouths of academics that some tried to rewrite their opinions of college sports. Recall that in 1893, Stanford's E. A. Ross promoted sport as a way for college men to strengthen themselves for social reform; fifteen years later, in Madison, he touted it as a way for students to learn to resist the crowd and the "mob mind." However, in his 1936 memoir, *Seventy Years of It*, Ross changed his tune drastically. He claimed that over thirty years earlier, while teaching at Nebraska, he had become disillusioned with football and decided it was a "farce." Yet Ross left Lincoln in 1906, at a time when he was still touting sport's progressive, educational value.[40] This was revisionism, not reminiscence. But it was a kind of revisionism that made sense, considering the change in historical context. In the 1930s, many academics lamented the fact that athletic programs had raked in football profits during the so-called Roaring Twenties, when coaches signed rich contracts or endorsement deals, and players were subsidized under the table. With the loss of income during the Great Depression, stadiums were no longer filled, yet universities, beginning in the South, legitimized athletic scholarships, which had long been attacked by critics as a form of blatant athletic commercialism and professionalism.[41]

Ross was not alone. G. T. W. Patrick also became more cynical about sport over the years, and he also became more critical of universities as he revised his opinions. A football apologist who promoted sport in the Progressive Era, by 1929 Patrick questioned his former stance. When he neared his ninetieth birthday in 1946, at the dawn of the post–World War II nuclear age, he became even more bitter. The retired philosophy professor lamented the modern academy's focus on science, especially atomic physics, at the expense of other important subjects, including psychology. He also posited sport's apparent relationship to America's declining morals, noting with disfavor that football gambling had recently reached an annual figure of $100 million. It is not surprising that Patrick reacted this way in the late 1940s. This was a time when a multitude of veterans returning to college on the GI Bill muddied eligibility requirements. Soon, elite colleges in the Northeast would create the Ivy League athletic conference. By 1951, basketball recruiting fiascos and point-shaving wagering scandals dominated the headlines and led to new national regulations. In comparison to such rampant corruption, the half-million-dollar Stanford-Cal Big Game payday that Patrick had critiqued in 1929 seemed like petty cash.[42]

While Upton Sinclair exaggerated when he complained that the faculty had been replaced by sport in the 1920s, he had a point. By the interwar decades, faculty members produced practical and useful knowledge, but they were much less culturally visible than intercollegiate football heroes. Scholarship was mostly located beyond the modern public's consumerist grasp, while football was a popular, entertaining commodity. Big-time sport had become so successful because it was one of the few popular aspects of America's ivory tower. Its purpose had once been (according to some) a way to represent and complement the ideas crafted in academic scholarship, but it had come to flout many aspects of academic life. Although some Progressive Era academics had seen football as a kind of middlebrow culture, sport actually fulfilled a very different role. It was the seemingly irrational anti-structure that reinforced academic structure—a lowbrow cultural activity that helped highbrow intellectual culture stay elevated.[43] Modern academic scholars had become precise observers of narrow natural or social phenomena who produced technically accurate scholarship with useful applications, but they were not flashy celebrities in a society that valued entertainment and strenuous sport. In some cases, like the Ross controversy in 1900, they were forced to defend themselves and even vow alienation from the public sphere. While progressive inventions like tenure, academic freedom, and the AAUP helped make life easier for some scholars—and allowed them to keep creating accurate, useful knowledge—these reforms did not necessarily help professors reach out to the public. Football players and coaches more easily found a public audience, and they could make lots of money doing it.

Big-time college sport, while seemingly at odds with academics, was a product of modern culture. As educators, lawmakers, and philanthropists crafted modern American higher education, academics established a framework for creating knowledge and dispensing professional rewards. Football games, carried out on fields called gridirons, emulated the logic of interinstitutional competition and provided publicity for a virtual gridiron of interconnected universities. Athletic departments, based in commercial popular culture in a way that increasingly specialized academic departments were not, made the academy seem relevant. Sport gained a permanent place in America's academic ivory tower because the goals of higher education had shifted in the 1800s. Once a cloistered world of philosophical deduction where teachers instructed students in moral, mental, and physical discipline, universities became practical realms of scientific rigor where scholars produced and disseminated knowledge in cloistered academic disciplines, graduating a mass of students versed in a wide range of practical subjects. Although some 1920s educators and critics challenged both football and the narrowness of academic fields, even strenuous athletic sport—present at the creation of modern intellectual culture—had gained its own special place in the university. Once considered a sideshow to the academic circus, it had become, for many Americans, the main event.

A Circus or a Sideshow?

The sideshows are so numerous, so diverting—so important, if you will—that they have swallowed up the circus, and those who perform in the main tent must often whistle for their audiences, discouraged and humiliated.

—Woodrow Wilson, "What Is a College For?" (1909)

More than a century of controversies notwithstanding, intercollegiate athletics' immense popularity has not faded into the past. Nor has it ceased serving as a basis for critiques like G. T. W. Patrick's 1929 question about whether or not institutions of learning should furnish sports, or Woodrow Wilson's 1909 lament about the academic circus and its extracurricular sideshows. At the beginning of the twenty-first century, media outlets like cable television networks and Internet sites magnify college sport's visibility and moneymaking potential, keeping the athletic circus's rings humming. Meanwhile, critical observers point to the controversial role that big-time sports play in American culture and university life. Between the university and the athletic field, which, we might ask, is the circus and which is the sideshow? Athletics, after all, often inspires large and questionable expenditures on many campuses. In particular, huge amounts of money, often provided by donors who are promised luxurious seats, are dedicated to stadium renovations. Many of the big, concrete campus stadiums built in the early 1900s are still around, and university athletic departments are constantly modernizing and expanding them to fit today's needs. America's largest stadiums, indeed, are not professional sports venues—they are football arenas at Michigan, Ohio State, Tennessee, and other universities. In the early 2000s, the athletic departments at major universities such as Stanford, Nebraska, and Illinois even undertook multimillion-dollar renovation projects to maintain 1920s stadiums as spaces for lucrative consumer spectacle.[1]

It is clear that since the late 1800s many institutions have perceived sport as a dubious form of alchemy, a nonacademic activity that might draw publicity, increase revenue, and build institutional spirit. Since

1980, at least ninety-two colleges and universities have started big-time football programs. The University of Buffalo (SUNY) moved up to big-time intercollegiate athletics in the early 1990s as a way to augment its public profile. In 2010, likewise, Georgia State University in Atlanta launched its football program to attract publicity, raise the number of applicants, and retain students. Universities, noted one observer in the *New York Times*, added football as a way "to fuse the disparate segments of a university . . . through an activity appealing to eggheads, blockheads, and all those in between."[2] Meanwhile, legislators routinely cut support for public higher education, with the result that some universities rely heavily upon cheap labor, in the form of contingent faculty (itinerant adjuncts and visiting professors), or raise the cost of tuition and fees. Though football revenue is typically pumped back into athletics, the never-ending, perhaps foolhardy, hope is that athletics will enhance prestige and attract tuition dollars, alumni donations, or grants that will keep institutions of higher education nationally competitive. Perhaps this magical transformation does happen for some lucky schools with gigantic fan bases and media outlets, but Murray Sperber has convincingly argued that alumni donations (except those given strictly to the athletic department) are not always tied to athletic success.[3]

In an era when society is rolling back Progressive Era reforms designed to counteract the capitalist excesses of the late 1800s Gilded Age, abstract market forces are once again being allowed to take control of American higher education. The AAUP president, among others, writes about how administrators and policymakers have allowed academic freedom and tenure to erode so that universities can maintain flexibility and minimize costs by allowing academic labor—especially contingent labor—to compete on an open market.[4] Meanwhile, the big-time coaches who orchestrate the spectacle are able to command an increasingly large portion of the profits—even though it is hard to tell if athletic programs are actually turning a profit on the football circus. Since the 1970s, fewer college coaches have been granted tenured positions,[5] and as a result they run the risk of losing their jobs if they go a season or two without a bowl game appearance. But such risks can also pay off in the lucrative world of popular sport. Every season, university athletic departments engage with one another and professional sports franchises in a costly race to hire coaches who will, presumably, produce victorious programs and bring glory to campus. In 2007, for example, former NFL coach Nick Saban landed a $32 million contract to lead the University of Alabama's Crimson Tide football squad. Saban, along with Billy Donovan, Rich Rodriguez, and others who annually climb onto the lavish coaching carousel resemble nothing less than the greedy businessmen-coaches whom the Carnegie Foundation criticized in 1929.[6] In the sports media, to say nothing of the coaching profession, this reality tends to be seen less as a problem for reform than as a way of life. Reinforcing this situation, athletic departments are often maintained as units with budget lines that, like sports facilities, are relatively permanent and can even be extravagant.

Yet despite massive and controversial paychecks, coaches continue to endear themselves to the public, the same way Rockne, Heisman, and Zuppke did almost a century ago. They win games and provide feathers for the caps of alumni and students. Some coaches, commendably, are active in their local communities and participate in charity fundraising efforts, like the American Cancer Society's "Coaches vs. Cancer" program. Coaches also create good publicity by using the rhetoric of discipline, pedagogy, and leadership. Saban, for one, has capitalized on his image as a leader by cowriting a book on management.[7] Although some team leaders claim they teach character, critical observers might conclude that coaches—along with university administrators and athletic departments—are actually in the business of training a handful of semiprofessional athletes. When the University of Illinois hired Ron Zook to coach the Illini football team in 2004, it promoted Illinois's newest (and richest) state employee by plastering the catchphrase "Leader, Teacher, Recruiter" on billboards. But pronouncements about the educational role of sport do not change the fact that big-time coaches are rewarded primarily for recruiting a handful of semiprofessional athletes, preparing them to win big games consumed by millions, and providing institutional publicity. Whether or not they teach discipline to a few young men is largely irrelevant— or, at the very least, does not justify their large salaries. Needless to say, it is virtually impossible to measure whether coaches teach discipline to the tens of thousands of spectators who pack the grandstands on Saturday afternoon or to the millions who watch from afar on television or the Internet.

College athletics, moreover, still provides an excruciatingly visible stage for some of Americans' ugliest beliefs and worst prejudices—including the kind that might have been acceptable in the Progressive Era, a time when segregation was considered one variety of progress. In 1909, Albert Shaw lamented the press's distasteful ability to place middle-class, white college athletes in the company of supposedly less respectable figures like African American boxer Jack Johnson. Today one laments the media's tendency to put student-athletes in a spotlight where they can be judged by talking heads, like talk-show host Don Imus, whose views on race or gender might remind us of Shaw. And despite Title IX, the 1970s Civil Rights Act amendment that guaranteed equality for women's intercollegiate athletics, Americans still pay more attention to men's sports (which bring in more revenue) than to women's teams.[8] Meanwhile, debates rage about racially charged mascots, such as the University of North Dakota Sioux, Illinois's now-retired Chief Illiniwek, or Ole Miss's undead "Colonel Reb." Sportswriters, community members, students, and faculty contribute to passionate exchanges even as the NCAA has tried to quell such controversies via institutional sanctions. Yet once again, it all makes sense when we realize that intercollegiate athletics—and the arenas that host it—comprises a cultural space where meaning is not dictated by professional standards of academic intellectual discourse. The interpretations of intercollegiate athletics are open to the public.

Outspoken critics of big-time college athletics like Sperber are probably right when they deplore the popular spectacles as little more than "beer and circus." Commercial sponsors, coaches, and the media make a tidy profit from an activity that at best teaches a few students character and sportsmanship, and at worst distracts millions from academics. However, like the authors of the 1929 Carnegie Report, present-day critics are only half right when they heap blame on rampant commercialism and decry sport as an enterprise contradictory to the university's goals. Once upon a time, progressive professors even cautiously lauded football, protecting it from its harshest critics and helping to make it the prototypical big-time college sport. By creating a professional bureaucracy and a national coaching corps, reformers

A student portraying "Chief Illiniwek" at Illinois Memorial Stadium, circa 1950. The university formally retired the "Chief" in early 2007. Courtesy of the University of Illinois at Urbana-Champaign Archives, Record Series number 39/2/20.

gave sport an integral and permanent, not marginal, place in the academy. Considering the fact that big-time football had become big business and a fixture in American universities by the late 1920s, it is not surprising that many academics started to question the educational role of college athletics more critically at that time. Yet there was little they could do, unless they tried—as did Robert Maynard Hutchins and Alexander Meiklejohn in the 1930s—to eliminate big-time sport and replace it with a different form of collegiate curriculum and middlebrow culture that would return American higher education to an imagined, premodern collegiate ideal of "Great Books" and liberal arts studies. Small colleges even became recognized as a distinct institutional type in the twentieth century. The NCAA's 1973 restructuring into three divisions—representing varying degrees of big-time and small-time athletics programs—echoed this change.[9]

The question G. T. W. Patrick asked after reading the 1929 Carnegie Report still resonates: Americans clearly desire popular spectacle, but should academic institutions sponsor the cultural ritual of big-time sport? Patrick implied they should not; universities were places of scholarship, not providers of physical display and consumerism. While his argument had merit, and its logic might seem irrefutable to many critics of college athletics, such idealism ignores the historical realities of America's ivory tower. Progressive Era administrators and intellectuals created universities that hosted an expanding array of specialized academic disciplines. These pragmatic institutions, and the knowledge produced therein, were increasingly removed from mainstream culture. To smooth out the rough, inaccessible contours of the newly constructed ivory tower, and thus make them accessible to the American people, reformers offered regulated games as the savior of the university. Sport was seen as good because it was a ritual located between the academy and the public. If supervised correctly, said reformers, sport could train young men's bodies, minds, and morals; provide useful lessons to the assembled crowd; advertise academic institutions to the nonacademic public; and even pay for physical education programs or campus facilities. Such expectations were too high, but football, nonetheless, seemed a cure-all panacea, a counterbalance to the top-heavy intellectual culture of modern universities. Just as the people in the stands could find in football any meaning they desired, apparently so could college leaders. Progressive Era reforms, though, gave sport a life of its own and a permanent space on campus. Academic meanings for football ceased to matter as big-time athletics became a public ritual with a multitude of devotees and a wide variety of cultural meanings.

In order to comprehend the way sport has situated itself within the rarefied halls of academia as well as the lucrative spaces of popular culture, we must examine changes in society and academic life from the 1820s to the 1930s. Seen in this light, college sport is not a wholly nonacademic cultural activity, nor is the university an ivory tower inevitably separate from society. Rather, sport and the academy are two sides of a currency minted in a society with an immense, relatively unregulated higher education system that has tried to play many diverse roles. Even when scholars embrace scientific specialization and aspire to professional status, the institutions of modern intellectual culture where they work must find a way to appeal to the public located beyond the college walls. Big-time college athletics, which comprise the one department of the modern university devoted to staging popular spectacle, has dubiously filled that role since the early 1900s. In order to create universities that find new ways to engage a rational public sphere—while still maintaining invaluable traditions of free inquiry and social responsibility—we must understand the history and cultural rationale of intercollegiate athletics, a seemingly irrational element of higher education.

Notes

ABBREVIATIONS USED IN NOTES

AAS   Amos Alonzo Stagg Papers, UCA

AC   *Atlanta Constitution*

AJP   *American Journal of Psychology*

ALL   A. Lawrence Lowell Presidential Papers, HUA

ATH   Arthur Twining Hadley Papers, YUA

AUC   Archives, Robert W. Woodruff Library of the Atlanta University Center, Atlanta, Georgia

BHL   Bentley Historical Library, University of Michigan, Ann Arbor, Michigan

CRVH   Charles R. Van Hise Papers, UWA

CT   *Chicago Tribune/Chicago Daily Tribune*

CWE   Charles William Eliot Presidential Papers, HUA

DPA   *Daily Palo Alto*, microfilm copy in Stanford University Green Library

DSJ   David Starr Jordan Papers (microfilm copy in SUA)

FHY   Fielding Harris Yost Papers, BHL

GTA   Georgia Institute of Technology Archives and Records Division, Atlanta, Georgia

HA   (Harvard) *Advocate*, HUA

HC   (Harvard) *Crimson*

HGM   *Harvard Graduates Magazine*

HM   (Harvard) *Monthly*, HUA

HUA   Harvard University Archives, Cambridge, Massachusetts

IUB   Indiana University Archives, Bloomington, Indiana

JBA   James B. Angell Papers, BHL

LAT   *Los Angeles Times*

MA   (Michigan) *Argonaut*, BHL

MD   *U. of Michigan Daily/Michigan Daily*, BHL

MI   (Michigan) *Inlander*, BHL

MUC   (Michigan) *University Chronicle*, BHL

NYT   *New York Times/New-York Daily Times*

OSU   Ohio State University Archives, Columbus, Ohio

PSM   *Popular Science Monthly*

RCP   (Edward Alsworth) Ross Controversy Papers, SUA

RCZ   Robert C. Zuppke Papers, UIUC

RNC   Robert N. Corwin Correspondence (Department of Athletics, Physical Education, and Recreation Records), YUA

SFC   *San Francisco Chronicle*

SS   (Stanford) *Sequoia*, SUA

SUA   Stanford University Special Collections and Archives, Stanford, California

UCA   University of Chicago Special Collections, Chicago, Illinois

UIA   University of Iowa Archives, Iowa City, Iowa

UIUC   University of Illinois Archives, Urbana-Champaign, Illinois

UWA   University of Wisconsin Archives, Madison, Wisconsin

WCP   Walter Chauncey Camp Papers, YUA (microfilm copy in University of Illinois Library, Urbana-Champaign, Illinois)

WDC   *Wisconsin Daily Cardinal*

WHS   Wisconsin Historical Society, Madison, Wisconsin

WLB   William Lowe Bryan Papers, IUB

WOT   William Oxley Thompson Papers, OSU

WP   *Washington Post*

WPL   Warren P. Lombard Papers, BHL

WRH   William Rainey Harper Papers, UCA

WTR   William T. Reid, Jr. Correspondence and Related Papers, HUA

YUA   Yale University Manuscripts and Archives Division, New Haven, Connecticut

INTRODUCTION: THE CULTURAL CORNERSTONE OF THE IVORY TOWER

1. "Leland Stanford Junior University," *SFC*, Oct. 2, 1891, 6. See also Kevin Starr, *Americans and the California Dream, 1850–1915* (New York: Oxford University Press, 1973), 307–344, and *Inventing the Dream: California through the Progressive Era* (New York: Oxford University Press, 1985), 224–225.

2. "New University," *SFC*, Oct. 2, 1891, 4.

3. "Palo Alto on Top," *SFC*, Mar. 20, 1892, 24.

4. The term "intellectual culture" is based on the premise that intellectuals, those who produce academic knowledge, have their own culture. They do not just possess ideas or objectively seek truth; rather, they are intellectual

laborers grounded in "epistemic communities" or "communities of discourse." See Thomas Kuhn, *The Structure of Scientific Revolutions* (1962; Chicago: University of Chicago Press, 1970); David Hollinger, *In the American Province: Studies in the History and Historiography of Ideas* (Bloomington: Indiana University Press, 1985), 105–151; Thomas Bender, *Intellect and Public Life: Essays on the Social History of Academic Intellectuals in the United States* (Baltimore: Johns Hopkins University Press, 1993), 3–46; Burton J. Bledstein, *The Culture of Professionalism: The Middle Class and the Development of Higher Education in America* (New York: Norton, 1976). On the rise of academic disciplines, see Bruce Kuklick, *The Rise of American Philosophy: Cambridge, Massachusetts, 1860–1930* (New Haven, CT: Yale University Press, 1977); Peter Novick, *That Noble Dream: The "Objectivity Question" and the American Historical Profession* (Cambridge, UK: Cambridge University Press, 1988); Dorothy Ross, *The Origins of American Social Science* (Cambridge, UK: Cambridge University Press, 1991).

5. This was well before the quasi-academic radio programs, book clubs, and periodicals of the 1920s. On the origins of middlebrow culture, see Joan Shelley Rubin, *The Making of Middlebrow Culture* (Chapel Hill: University of North Carolina Press, 1992); on the history of cultural hierarchy, see Lawrence Levine, *Highbrow/Lowbrow: The Emergence of Cultural Hierarchy in America* (Cambridge, MA: Harvard University Press, 1988); Kathryn J. Oberdeck, *The Evangelist and the Impresario: Religion, Entertainment, and Cultural Politics in America, 1884–1914* (Baltimore: Johns Hopkins University Press, 1999). On 1900s intellectuals' attitudes about popular culture, see Paul Gorman, *Left Intellectuals and Popular Culture in Twentieth-Century America* (Chapel Hill: University of North Carolina Press, 1996).

6. The Progressive Era, dating roughly from the 1890s to 1910s, was a time when Americans searched for order, tried to tame chance, and looked to experts for guidance and leadership in social reform. Intercollegiate football was one Progressive Era crusade. Key works on the Progressive Era that inform this study include Robert H. Wiebe, *The Search for Order, 1877–1920* (New York: Hill and Wang, 1967); David W. Noble, *The Paradox of Progressive Thought* (Minneapolis: University of Minnesota Press, 1958); Michael McGerr, *A Fierce Discontent: The Rise and Fall of the Progressive Movement in America* (New York: Oxford University Press, 2003); Robin F. Bachin, *Building the South Side: Urban Space and Civic Culture in Chicago, 1890–1919* (Chicago: University of Chicago Press, 2004); Shelton Stromquist, *Reinventing the "Peo-

ple": *The Progressive Movement, the Class Problem, and the Origins of Modern Liberalism* (Urbana: University of Illinois Press, 2006); Daria Frezza, *The Leader and the Crowd: Democracy in American Public Discourse*, trans. Martha King (Athens: University of Georgia Press, 2007). On the ways that Progressive Era reformers, university administrators, and social scientists tried to make universities relevant to the public without letting the public corrupt these progressive institutions of higher education and research, see Brian M. Ingrassia, "Public Influence inside the College Walls: Progressive Era Universities, Social Scientists, and Intercollegiate Football Reform," *Journal of the Gilded Age and Progressive Era* 10:1 (Jan. 2011): 59–88.

7. See Robert W. Snyder, *The Voice of the City: Vaudeville and Popular Culture in New York* (New York: Oxford University Press, 1989), 84.

8. Sport history helps scholars focus attention on cultural rituals that illuminate important social issues. For example, histories of baseball and prizefighting illustrate the meanings of work, gender, and race in 1800s America, while studies of urban stadiums expose political and cultural debates. See Donald J. Mrozek, *Sport and American Mentality, 1880–1910* (Knoxville: University of Tennessee Press, 1983); Elliott J. Gorn, *The Manly Art: Bare-Knuckle Prize Fighting in America* (Ithaca, NY: Cornell University Press, 1986); Steven A. Riess, *City Games: The Evolution of American Urban Society and the Rise of Sports* (Urbana: University of Illinois Press, 1989); George B. Kirsch, *The Creation of American Team Sports: Baseball and Cricket, 1838–1872* (Urbana: University of Illinois Press, 1989); Warren Goldstein, *Playing for Keeps: A History of Early Baseball* (Ithaca, NY: Cornell University Press, 1989); Jules Tygiel, *Past Time: Baseball as History* (New York: Oxford University Press, 2000); Adrian Burgos, Jr., *Playing America's Game: Baseball, Latinos, and the Color Line* (Berkeley: University of California Press, 2007); Bruce Kuklick, *To Every Thing a Season: Shibe Park and Urban Philadelphia, 1909–1976* (Princeton, NJ: Princeton University Press, 1991); Neil J. Sullivan, *The Diamond in the Bronx: Yankee Stadium and the Politics of New York* (New York: Oxford University Press, 2001); Bachin, *Building the South Side,* 205–246; Daniel Rosensweig, *Retro Ball Parks: Instant History, Baseball, and the New American City* (Knoxville: University of Tennessee Press, 2005). Nevertheless, it is important to note that athletic games are not just professional ventures; rather, amateur sport, especially intercollegiate athletics, is an important part of American life. On the history of sport in relation to university life, see Frederick Rudolph, *The American College and University: A History* (1962; Athens: Uni-

versity of Georgia Press, 1990), 373–393; Laurence R. Veysey, *The Emergence of the American University* (Chicago: University of Chicago Press, 1965), 276–277; Ronald A. Smith, *Sports and Freedom: The Rise of Big-Time Intercollegiate Athletics* (New York: Oxford University Press, 1988). On the history of college football, see John Sayle Watterson, *College Football: History, Spectacle, Controversy* (Baltimore: Johns Hopkins University Press, 2000); Michael Oriard, *Reading Football: How the Popular Press Created an American Spectacle* (Chapel Hill: University of North Carolina Press, 1993), and *King Football: Sport and Spectacle in the Golden Age of Radio and Newsreels, Movies and Magazines, the Weekly and the Daily Press* (Chapel Hill: University of North Carolina Press, 2001); John M. Carroll, *Red Grange and the Rise of Modern Football* (Urbana: University of Illinois Press, 1999). Such studies, though, often focus on college football's cultural or social meanings without exploring its institutional or intellectual roles. One notable exception is Robin Lester's important case study of the University of Chicago: *Stagg's University: The Rise, Decline, and Fall of Big-Time Football at Chicago* (Urbana: University of Illinois Press, 1995).

9. Clifford Geertz is cited in analyses of college football by Michael Oriard, in works such as *Reading Football* and *King Football*, as well as by John Pettegrew, *Brutes in Suits: Male Sensibility in America, 1890–1920* (Baltimore: Johns Hopkins University Press, 2007), 160–163. See also Clifford Geertz, "Deep Play: Notes on the Balinese Cockfight," in *The Interpretation of Cultures: Selected Essays* (New York: Basic, 1973), 412–453.

10. For an argument that supports college athletics, see J. Douglas Toma, *Football U: Spectator Sports in the Life of the American University* (Ann Arbor: University of Michigan Press, 2003). For a more critical appraisal, see Murray Sperber, *Beer and Circus: How Big-Time College Sports Is Crippling Undergraduate Education* (New York: Henry Holt, 2000).

11. Helen Lefkowitz Horowitz, *Campus Life: Undergraduate Cultures from the End of the Eighteenth Century to the Present* (New York: Knopf, 1987), 98–117, Wilson quoted at 102.

12. See Rudolph, *American College*, 399–401; Veysey, *Emergence*, 320–324; Bledstein, *Culture of Professionalism*, 287–331; John R. Thelin, *A History of American Higher Education* (Baltimore: Johns Hopkins University Press, 2004), 103–107. On transatlantic aspects of Progressive Era scholarship, see Daniel T. Rodgers, *Atlantic Crossings: Social Politics in a Progressive Age* (Cambridge, MA: Harvard University Press, 1998), 76–111; James Turner, *The*

Liberal Education of Charles Eliot Norton (Baltimore: Johns Hopkins University Press, 1999). On the meanings of "discipline," see Michel Foucault, *Discipline and Punish: The Birth of the Prison*, trans. Alan Sheridan (1975; New York: Vintage, 1977). Although "discipline" has denoted a branch of scholarship or field of learning since the 1300s, its usage in reference to professional intellectual communities spread over a broad geographical range is specific to modern society.

13. On "communities of discourse," see Hollinger, *In the American Province*, 130–151. On "epistemic communities," see Bender, *Intellect and Public Life*, 10. On modern intellectual fragmentation, see Carl Schorske, *Fin de Siècle Vienna: Politics and Culture* (New York: Vintage, 1979). On the public sphere, see Jürgen Habermas, *The Structural Transformation of the Public Sphere: An Inquiry into a Category of Bourgeois Society*, trans. Thomas Burger with Frederick Lawrence (1962; Cambridge, MA: Massachusetts Institute of Technology Press, 1989); on the alienation of modern American intellectuals, see Bender, *Intellect and Public Life*, 30–46. On the impact of Darwinian thought, see Louis Menand, *The Metaphysical Club: A Story of Ideas in America* (New York: Farrar, Straus and Giroux, 2001); Philip P. Wiener, *Evolution and the Founders of Pragmatism* (Cambridge, MA: Harvard University Press, 1949). On the importance of the nervous system for creating a "sound mind in a sound body" (*mens sana in corpore sano*), see Bruce Haley, *The Healthy Body and Victorian Culture* (Cambridge, MA: Harvard University Press, 1978).

14. The sources examined in this study, mostly generated by middle-class white males, used terms like *manly* or *manliness* almost exclusively, rather than *masculine* or *masculinity*. The former term, which connoted honor and maturity, began yielding to the latter term, which implied brute physicality, in the 1890s; nonetheless, terms such as *masculinity* were not common in academic sources until the 1910s. On gender and manliness, see Joan Wallach Scott, *Gender and the Politics of History*, rev. ed. (1998; New York: Columbia University Press, 1999), 28–50; E. Anthony Rotundo, *American Manhood: Transformations in Masculinity from the Revolution to the Modern Era* (New York: Basic, 1993); Mark C. Carnes, *Secret Ritual and Manhood in Victorian America* (New Haven, CT: Yale University Press, 1989); Gail Bederman, *Manliness and Civilization: A Cultural History of Gender and Race in the United States, 1880–1917* (Chicago: University of Chicago Press, 1995).

15. On the circus, see Janet M. Davis, *The Circus Age: Culture and Society under the American Big Top* (Chapel Hill: University of North Carolina Press,

2002); Gregory J. Renoff, *The Big Tent: The Traveling Circus in Georgia, 1820–1930* (Athens: University of Georgia Press, 2008). On amusement parks, see John F. Kasson, *Amusing the Million: Coney Island at the Turn of the Century* (New York: Hill and Wang, 1978). On vaudeville, see Snyder, *Voice*; Oberdeck, *Evangelist*. On baseball, see Benjamin G. Rader, *Baseball: A History of America's Game,* 2nd ed. (Urbana: University of Illinois Press, 2002). On world's fairs, see Robert W. Rydell, *All the World's a Fair: Visions of Empire at American International Expositions, 1876–1916* (Chicago: University of Chicago Press, 1984); James Gilbert, *Perfect Cities: Chicago's Utopias of 1893* (Chicago: University of Chicago Press, 1991).

16. On the public relevance of early 1900s scholarship, see Rodgers, *Atlantic Crossings*, 76–111; John Louis Recchiuti, *Civic Engagement: Social Science and Progressive-Era Reform in New York City* (Philadelphia: University of Pennsylvania Press, 2007); Ian Tyrell, *Historians in Public: The Practice of American History, 1890–1970* (Chicago: University of Chicago Press, 2006); Rubin, *Making of Middlebrow Culture.*

17. On the intersection of sport, media, and celebrity in the 1920s, see Charles J. Shindo, *1927 and the Rise of Modern America* (Lawrence: University Press of Kansas, 2009).

18. On *liminality*, see Victor Turner, *The Ritual Process: Structure and Anti-Structure* (Ithaca, NY: Cornell University Press, 1969), 94–130, and *Dramas, Fields, and Metaphors: Symbolic Action in Human Society* (Ithaca, NY: Cornell University Press, 1974), 87; Jean-Christophe Agnew, *Worlds Apart: The Market and the Theater in Anglo-American Thought, 1550–1750* (Cambridge, UK: Cambridge University Press, 1986).

19. On transnational history, see, for example, Thomas Bender, *A Nation among Nations: America's Place in World History* (New York: Hill and Wang, 2006); Kristin L. Hoganson, *Consumers' Imperium: The Global Production of American Domesticity, 1865–1920* (Chapel Hill: University of North Carolina Press, 2007); Rodgers, *Atlantic Crossings.*

20. This study cites archival collections located at Harvard and Yale in the Northeast; Stanford in the West; Georgia Tech and Clark Atlanta University in the South; and numerous universities in the Midwest, including Michigan, Chicago, Wisconsin, Illinois, and Indiana.

1. PHYSICAL CULTURE, DISCIPLINE, AND HIGHER EDUCATION
IN 1800S AMERICA

1. Francis A. Walker, "College Athletics: Oration Delivered before the Phi Beta Kappa Society, in Sanders Theatre, Thursday, June 29, 1893," *HGM* 2:5 (Sept. 1893), 2, 5–7.

2. On the history of American higher education, see Frederick Rudolph, *The American College and University: A History* (1962; Athens: University of Georgia Press, 1990); John R. Thelin, *A History of American Higher Education* (Baltimore: Johns Hopkins University Press, 2004); Laurence R. Veysey, *The Emergence of the Modern University* (Chicago: University of Chicago Press, 1965). On moral philosophy, see Stewart Davenport, *Friends of the Unrighteous Mammon: Northern Christians and Market Capitalism, 1815–1860* (Chicago: University of Chicago Press, 2008), 36–37; D. H. Meyer, *The Instructed Conscience: The Shaping of the American National Ethic* (Philadelphia: University of Pennsylvania Press, 1972). On natural philosophy, see George M. Marsden, *The Soul of the American University: From Protestant Establishment to Established Nonbelief* (New York: Oxford University Press, 1994); Stanley M. Guralnick, "Sources of Misconception on the Role of Science in the Nineteenth-Century American College," *Isis* 65:228 (Sept. 1974): 352–366. On colleges' involvement in local communities, see Thomas Bender, *Intellect and Public Life: Essays on the Social History of Academic Intellectuals in the United States* (Baltimore: Johns Hopkins University Press, 1993), 3–46. On the market revolution and its cultural effects, see Daniel Walker Howe, *What Hath God Wrought: The Transformation of America, 1815–1848* (New York: Oxford University Press, 2007); Charles Sellers, *The Market Revolution: Jacksonian America 1815–1846* (New York: Oxford University Press, 1991); Jean-Christophe Agnew, *Worlds Apart: The Market and the Theater in Anglo-American Thought, 1550–1750* (Cambridge, UK: Cambridge University Press, 1986). On sentimentalism, see Karen Halttunen, *Confidence Men and Painted Women: A Study of Middle-Class Culture in America, 1830–1870* (New Haven, CT: Yale University Press, 1982); Richard F. Teichgraeber III, *Sublime Thoughts/Penny Wisdom: Situating Emerson and Thoreau in the American Market* (Baltimore: Johns Hopkins University Press, 1995).

3. Richard B. Sher, *Church and University in the Scottish Enlightenment: The Moderate Literati of Edinburgh* (Princeton, NJ: Princeton University Press, 1985), 175–212; Daniel Walker Howe, *Political Culture of the American Whigs* (Chicago: University of Chicago Press, 1979), 22–42, and *Making the American*

Self: Jonathan Edwards to Abraham Lincoln (Cambridge, MA: Harvard University Press, 1997), 157–185; David Hogan, "Modes of Discipline: Affective Individualism and Pedagogical Reform in New England, 1820–1850," *American Journal of Education* 99 (1990): 1–56.

4. The Yale Report, originally published in the *American Journal of Science and Arts* (1829), was republished in 1830: Yale College, "Report of the Faculty" in *Reports on the Course of Instruction in Yale College; by a Committee of the Corporation, and the Academical Faculty* (New Haven, CT: Hezekiah Howe, 1830), 5–7 (original emphasis), 27–30, 7–10, 15–16. The remark about steamboats anticipated the setting of Herman Melville's *The Confidence-Man* (1857). On the Yale Report, see Rudolph, *American College*, 130–135; Louise L. Stevenson, *Scholarly Means to Evangelical Ends: The New Haven Scholars and the Transformation of Higher Learning in America, 1830–1890* (Baltimore: Johns Hopkins University Press, 1986), 16–19, 31.

5. On early college athletics in America, see Ronald A. Smith, *Sports and Freedom: The Rise of Big-Time College Athletics* (New York: Oxford University Press, 1988), 8–21. On Jahn's *Turner* movement in Prussia, see Horst Ueberhorst and Wolfgang Stump, *Friedrich Ludwig Jahn and His Time, 1778–1852*, trans. Timothy Nevill (1978; Munich: Moos, 1982), 27–46; Emmett A. Rice, John L. Hutchinson, and Mabel Lee, *A Brief History of Physical Education*, 5th ed. (New York: Ronald, 1969), 70–75; Fred Eugene Leonard, "Friedrich Ludwig Jahn, and the Development of Popular Gymnastics (*Vereinsturnen*) in Germany," *Mind and Body* 12:137 (July 1905): 133–139. On Follen and Beck, see Charles Follen, *The Works of Charles Follen, with a Memoir of His Life*, ed. Harrison Gray, 5 vols. (Boston: Hilliard, Gray, 1842); George W. Spindler, *Karl Follen: A Biographical Study* (Chicago: University of Chicago Press, 1917); Fred Eugene Leonard, "First Introduction of the Jahn Gymnastics into America (1825–1830)," *Mind and Body* 12:139–144 (Oct. 1905–Feb. 1906): 193–198, 217–223, 249–254, 281–292, 313–319, 345–351; Harvey Green, *Fit for America: Health, Fitness, Sport, and American Society* (New York: Pantheon, 1986), 89–90. On Follen and Beck's involvement in gymnastics, see Leonard, "The First Introduction of the Jahn Gymnastics," parts 2, 5, and 6 (Oct. 1905, Jan. 1906, Feb. 1906); Follen, *Works of Charles Follen*, 1:16, 25, 55, 126, 135–137, 149–161. On Bancroft and Ticknor, see David B. Tyack, *George Ticknor and the Boston Brahmins* (Cambridge, MA: Harvard University Press, 1967).

6. Stephen D. Rice, *Minding the Machine: Languages of Class in Early Industrial America* (Berkeley: University of California Press, 2004), 69–95, 145–155;

Jonathan A. Glickstein, *Concepts of Free Labor in Antebellum America* (New Haven, CT: Yale University Press, 1991), 78–79. On manual labor colleges and race, see Milton C. Sernett, *Abolition's Axe: Beriah Green, Oneida Institute, and the Black Freedom Struggle* (1986; Syracuse, NY: Syracuse University Press, 2004).

7. Charles Beck, *A Treatise on Gymnasticks, Taken Chiefly from the German of F. L. Jahn* (Northampton, MA: Simeon Butler, 1828), iv, 151–157; see also Rice, Hutchinson, and Lee, *Brief History of Physical Education*, 162–163. On the moral implications of the European Turner movement, see George L. Mosse, *Nationalism and Sexuality: Respectability and Abnormal Sexuality in Modern Europe* (New York: Howard Fertig, 1985), 78–79; see also Michel Foucault, *History of Sexuality; Volume I: An Introduction*, trans. Robert Hurley (1978; New York: Vintage, 1990), 27–30.

8. Charles Follen to Boston Gymnasium Committee, July 3, 1827, quoted in Follen, *Works of Charles Follen*, 1:180. On early gymnasia, see Green, *Fit for America*, 90; Stephen Hardy, *How Boston Played: Sport, Recreation, and Community, 1865–1915* (Boston: Northeastern University Press, 1982), 108; Helen Lefkowitz Horowitz, *Rereading Sex: Battles over Sexual Knowledge and Suppression in Nineteenth-Century America* (New York: Vintage, 2002), 46.

9. Charles Follen, *Address, Introductory to the Fourth Course of the Franklin Lectures, Delivered at the Masonic Temple, Nov. 3, 1834* (Boston: Tuttle and Weeks, 1835), 7–8, 12. On the history of ideas about labor and management, see Rice, *Minding the Machine*, 42–68; Daniel T. Rodgers, *The Work Ethic in Industrial America, 1850–1920* (1974; Chicago: University of Chicago Press, 1978), 91–92; Glickstein, *Concepts of Free Labor*, 38, 113–121. On the transgressive potential of women's gymnastics, see Alison Piepmeier, *Out in Public: Configurations of Women's Bodies in Nineteenth-Century America* (Chapel Hill: University of North Carolina Press, 2004), 18–19, 37–45.

10. Beck, *Treatise on Gymnasticks*, 165–167, 157.

11. Michel Foucault, *Discipline and Punish: The Birth of the Prison*, trans. Alan Sheridan (1975; New York: Vintage, 1977), 170–228; David J. Rothman, *The Discovery of the Asylum: Social Order and Disorder in the New Republic* (Boston: Little, Brown, 1971), xiii, 81–88, 150. For the Yale Report's promotion of discipline, see Yale College, "Report of the Faculty," 21–23, 9–12. On Lieber and Wayland, see Frank Freidel, *Francis Lieber: Nineteenth-Century Liberal* (Baton Rouge: Louisiana State University Press, 1947), 20, 50–62, 96–105;

Francis Wayland and H. L. Wayland, *A Memoir of the Life and Labors of Francis Wayland*, 2 vols. (New York: Sheldon, 1867), 2:339–350.

12. Steven A. Riess, *City Games: Evolution of American Urban Society and the Rise of Sports* (Urbana: University of Illinois Press, 1989); George B. Kirsch, *The Creation of American Team Sports: Baseball and Cricket, 1838–1872* (Urbana: University of Illinois Press, 1989); Melvin L. Adelman, *A Sporting Time: New York City and the Rise of Modern Athletics, 1820–70* (1986; Urbana: University of Illinois Press, 1990), 97, 110–116; Green, *Fit for America*, 90; Elliott J. Gorn, *The Manly Art: Bare-Knuckle Prize Fighting in America* (Ithaca, NY: Cornell University Press, 1986).

13. On the Turners' resurgence, see Elliott J. Gorn and Warren Goldstein, *A Brief History of American Sports* (1993; Urbana: University of Illinois Press, 2004), 66; Rice, Hutchinson, and Lee, *Brief History of Physical Education*, 74–75, 169; Bruce Levine, *The Spirit of 1848: German Immigrants, Labor Conflict, and the Coming of the Civil War* (Urbana: University of Illinois Press, 1992), 91–94; Don Harrison Doyle, *The Social Order of a Frontier Community: Jacksonville, Illinois, 1825–70* (Urbana: University of Illinois Press, 1978), 133–134. On early college gymnasia, see Rudolph, *American College*, 151–153. On the Yale game, see "Yale Foot Ball Game," *NYT*, Oct. 18, 1852, 2. On antebellum interclass football, see Smith, *Sports and Freedom*, 8, 13, 22.

14. Nathan Allen, *Physical Culture in Amherst College* (Lowell, MA: Stone & House, 1869), 6–13, 16, 30–37; Hitchcock quoted on p. 13. On Allen, see John D. Davies, *Phrenology: Fad and Science; A 19th-Century American Crusade* (New Haven, CT: Yale University Press, 1955), 57; Patricia A. Vertinsky, *The Eternally Wounded Woman: Women, Doctors, and Exercise in the Late Nineteenth Century* (1989; Urbana: University of Illinois Press, 1994), 123; Heather Munro Prescott, *Student Bodies: The Influence of Student Health Services in American Society and Medicine* (Ann Arbor: University of Michigan Press, 2007), 35–37; Rice, Hutchinson, and Lee, *Brief History of Physical Education*, 166–167. On Hitchcock and spectatorship at the Amherst gymnasium, see J. Edmund Welch, *Edward Hitchcock, M.D.: Founder of Physical Education in the College Curriculum* (1962; Greenville, NC: East Carolina College, 1966), 79–80, 92.

15. Smith, *Sports and Freedom*, 14–25.

16. Andrew Warwick, *Masters of Theory: Cambridge and the Rise of Mathematical Physics* (Chicago: University of Chicago Press, 2003), 176–226; Paul

R. Deslandes, *Oxbridge Men: British Masculinity and the Undergraduate Experience, 1850–1920* (Bloomington: Indiana University Press, 2005), 1–3, 180.

17. On crew, see Smith, *Sports and Freedom*, 4, 13–66. On baseball, see George B. Kirsch, *Baseball in Blue and Gray: The National Pastime during the Civil War* (Princeton, NJ: Princeton University Press, 2003), 4–11, 73–74, and *Creation of American Team Sports*, 54–56, 69–72. Bascom quoted in Benjamin G. Rader, *Baseball: A History of America's Game*, 2nd ed. (Urbana: University of Illinois Press, 2002), 11. On the 1860 gymnastics exhibition, see Smith, *Sports and Freedom*, 33.

18. Russell L. Johnson, *Warriors into Workers: The Civil War and the Formation of Urban-Industrial Society in a Northern City* (New York: Fordham University Press, 2003), 169–171, 222–224; W. J. Rorabaugh, *The Craft Apprentice: From Franklin to the Machine Age in America* (New York: Oxford University Press, 1986), 201; Todd DePastino, *Citizen Hobo: How a Century of Homelessness Shaped America* (Chicago: University of Chicago Press, 2003), 16–18. On modern and premodern time, see Herbert C. Gutman, *Work, Culture, and Society in Industrializing America: Essays in American Working-Class and Social History* (New York: Vintage, 1977), 3–78.

19. Dudley A. Sargent, *Dudley Allen Sargent: An Autobiography*, ed. Ledyard Sargent (Philadelphia: Lea & Febiger, 1927), 60–62, 119–126. On wartime physical culture, see Johnson, *Warriors into Workers*, 235–236; Adelman, *Sporting Time*, 282; Allen, *Physical Culture in Amherst*, 17. Two institutions that combined physical and military training were Bowdoin College and the University of Iowa; see Jeremiah E. Goulka, "Introduction," in *The Grand Old Man of Maine: Selected Letters of Joshua Lawrence Chamberlain, 1865–1914*, ed. Jeremiah E. Goulka (Chapel Hill: University of North Carolina Press, 2004), xv–xxxviii; "Faculty Minutes, 1864–1874," Manuscript File, Box 21, Folder: "1860–1890 Faculty: Minutes," UIA.

20. On postwar industrialism, see Eric Foner, *Reconstruction: America's Unfinished Revolution, 1863–1877* (New York: Harper & Row, 1988), 460–511; Edward L. Ayers, *The Promise of the New South: Life after Reconstruction* (New York: Oxford University Press, 1992), 104–131. On Civil War–era thought, see George M. Fredrickson, *The Inner Civil War: Northern Intellectuals and the Crisis of the Union* (New York: Harper & Row, 1965), 166–180, 199–216; Louis Menand, *The Metaphysical Club: A Story of Ideas in America* (New York: Farrar, Straus and Giroux, 2001); T. J. Jackson Lears, *Something for Nothing: Luck in America* (New York: Viking, 2003), 178–186.

21. On the rise of professional baseball and its meanings, see Warren Goldstein, *Playing for Keeps: A History of Early Baseball* (Ithaca, NY: Cornell University Press, 1989), 17–31, 43–53, 84–100; Riess, *City Games*; Kirsch, *Creation of American Team Sports*, 99–101. On boxing, see Gorn, *Manly Art*, 66, 131, 137. On working-class leisure in 1800s America, see Roy Rosenzweig, *Eight Hours for What We Will: Workers and Leisure in an Industrial City, 1870–1920* (Cambridge, UK: Cambridge University Press, 1983), 1–5; Kathy Peiss, *Cheap Amusements: Working Women and Leisure in Turn-of-the-Century New York* (Philadelphia: Temple University Press, 1986). On the importance of streetcars and railroads for the development of sports, see David Nasaw, *Going Out: The Rise and Fall of Public Amusements* (New York: Basic Books, 1993), 96–97; Bruce Kuklick, *To Every Thing a Season: Shibe Park and Urban Philadelphia, 1909–1976* (Princeton, NJ: Princeton University Press, 1991), 19–22; Smith, *Sports and Freedom*, 3–4, 27–29, 52–55. Good examples of railroads taking spectators to campus parks are "In the Football World: Yale Confident of Victory over Princeton Today," *NYT*, Nov. 14, 1903, 7, and "Princeton Wins Big Football Game," *NYT*, Nov. 15, 1903, 1. On the centrality of trains in post–Civil War society, see Alan Trachtenberg, *The Incorporation of America: Culture and Society in the Gilded Age* (New York: Hill and Wang, 1982), 3–10; Mark R. Wilson, *The Business of Civil War: Military Mobilization and the State, 1861–1865* (Baltimore: Johns Hopkins University Press, 2006), 1–4, 191–225.

22. Riess, *City Games*, 53–92; Adelman, *Sporting Time*, 145–83; Kirsch, *Creation of American Team Sports*, 8–11; Rader, *Baseball*, 20–30.

23. Sargent, *Autobiography*, 60–72. On the nineteenth-century circus, see Janet M. Davis, *The Circus Age: Culture and Society under the American Big Top* (Chapel Hill: University of North Carolina Press, 2002); Gregory J. Renoff, *The Big Tent: The Traveling Circus in Georgia, 1820–1930* (Athens: University of Georgia Press, 2008). On vaudeville, including Keith's circus years, see Robert W. Snyder, *The Voice of the City: Vaudeville and Popular Culture in New York* (New York: Oxford University Press, 1989), 26–27, 104–129. On billiards as working-class sport, see Riess, *City Games*, 17–19.

24. On the Morrill Act colleges, see Coy F. Cross, *Justin Smith Morrill: Father of the Land-Grant Colleges* (East Lansing: Michigan State University Press, 1999), 77–89; Earle Ross, *Democracy's College: The Land-Grant Movement in the Formative Stage* (Ames: Iowa State University Press, 1942), 122–128, 136–166. On "free labor," see Eric Foner, *Free Soil, Free Labor, Free Men: The Ideology of the Republican Party before the Civil War* (1970; New York: Oxford University

Press, 1995). One proponent of technical higher education was Jonathan Baldwin Turner; for his attitudes on social mobility, see Turner, "A State University for the Industrial Classes" (1851), quoted in Mary Turner Carriel, *The Life of Jonathan Baldwin Turner* (1911; Urbana: University of Illinois Press, 1961), 69–85. On the general impact of the Morrill Act on American higher education, see Christopher Newfield, *Ivy and Industry: Business and the Making of the American University, 1880–1980* (Durham, NC: Duke University Press, 2003), 26–28. On the switch from disciplines to discipline, see Veysey, *Emergence*, 22–179, 263–341; Roger L. Geiger, *To Advance Knowledge: The Growth of American Research Universities, 1900–1940* (New York: Oxford University Press, 1986), 1–57; Rudolph, *American College*, 264–306, 395–402.

25. On Eliot, see Pusey, "Introduction," in Charles William Eliot, *A Turning Point in Higher Education: The Inaugural Address of Charles William Eliot as President of Harvard College, October 19, 1869*, with an introduction by Nathan Pusey (Cambridge, MA: Harvard University Press, 1969), v–xi; Hugh Hawkins, *Between Harvard and America: The Educational Leadership of Charles W. Eliot* (New York: Oxford University Press, 1972), 48–49. On "captains of erudition," see Rudolph, *American College*, 290–295; Thorstein Veblen, *The Higher Learning in America: A Memorandum on the Conduct of Universities by Business Men* (1918; New York: Hill and Wang, 1957), 62–97.

26. Eliot, *Turning Point*, 2–3, 9–10, 21. On earlier versions of the elective system in the 1820s (Harvard and Virginia), see Rudolph, *American College*, 118–121; George Ticknor, *Remarks on Changes Lately Proposed or Adopted in Harvard University* (Boston: Cummings, Hilliard, 1825).

27. James McCosh, *Inauguration of James McCosh, D.D., LL.D, as President of the College of New Jersey, Princeton; October 27, 1868* (New York: Robert Carter, 1868), 41, 48, 51–52; J. David Hoeveler, Jr., *James McCosh and the Scottish Intellectual Tradition: From Glasgow to Princeton* (Princeton, NJ: Princeton University Press, 1981), 235–237. Noah Porter, *The American Colleges and the American Public* (New Haven, CT: Charles C. Chatfield, 1870), 270–273.

28. Eliot, *Turning Point*, 3–4, 9, 14, 17–18, 21. On contemporary opinion of Eliot, especially John Fiske's reaction to Eliot's inaugural, see Hawkins, *Between Harvard and America*, 49. The Harvard Annex for women (Radcliffe College) opened in 1879, ten years after Eliot said that women might one day study at Harvard.

29. Eliot, *Turning Point*, 5, 11, 17, 21. See also Hamilton Cravens, *The Tri-*

umph of Evolution: The Heredity-Environment Controversy, 1900–1941 (1978; Baltimore: Johns Hopkins University Press, 1988), 20; T. J. Jackson Lears, *Rebirth of a Nation: The Making of Modern America, 1877–1920* (New York: HarperCollins, 2009), 297; Hawkins, *Between Harvard and America*, 15.

30. McCosh, "Academic Teaching in Europe," 41.

31. Hawkins, *Between Harvard and America*, 43.

32. On the historic origins of disciplines in America, see Bender, *Intellect and Public Life*, ix–xix, 1–46; Veysey, *Emergence*, 142–143, 320–324; Burton J. Bledstein, *The Culture of Professionalism: The Middle Class and the Development of Higher Education in America* (New York: Norton, 1976), 287–331; Lears, *Rebirth of a Nation*, 234. On the rise of specific disciplines, see Bruce Kuklick, *The Rise of American Philosophy: Cambridge, Massachusetts, 1860–1930* (New Haven, CT: Yale University Press, 1977); Peter Novick, *That Noble Dream: The "Objectivity Question" and the American Historical Profession* (Cambridge, UK: Cambridge University Press, 1988); Dorothy Ross, *The Origins of American Social Science* (Cambridge, UK: Cambridge University Press, 1990).

33. Andrew D. White, extract from "Reminiscences & Suggestions" (c. 1902); DSJ, Reel 35, Frames 860–873; White to Jordan, March 7, 1903; DSJ: Reel 36, Frames 401–408, SUA; David Starr Jordan, "Are Fellowships Almsgiving or Investments?" *PSM* 61 (1902), 565, and "Comrades in Zeal," *PSM* 64 (1904), 312; William Rainey Harper, *The Prospects of the Small College* (Chicago: University of Chicago Press, 1900), 31–32.

34. David Starr Jordan, "Evolution of the College Curriculum," in *The Care and Culture of Men: A Series of Addresses on the Higher Education* (San Francisco: Whitaker & Ray, 1896), 24–56; Jordan, "School and the State," in *Care and Culture*, 109–110. On Jordan, see Edward McNall Burns, *David Starr Jordan: Prophet of Democracy* (Palo Alto, CA: Stanford University Press, 1953); Jordan, *The Days of a Man: Being Memories of a Naturalist, Teacher and Minor Prophet of Democracy*, 2 vols. (Yonkers, NY: World, 1922); Kevin Starr, *Americans and the California Dream, 1850–1915* (New York: Oxford University Press, 1973), 307–344; Alexandra Minna Stern, *Eugenic Nation: Faults and Frontiers of Better Breeding in Modern America* (Berkeley: University of California Press, 2005), 22, 50–52, 84, 106–108, 133.

35. William James, "The Ph.D. Octopus," *HM*, Mar. 1903, 1–9.

36. "University Games," (Michigan) *Oracle*, Mar. 9, 1867, 4 (quote). "Model University in Dakota" and "Propriety of Admitting Women into Our

College," *HA*, Feb. 11, 1866, 81–83, 91; "Survival of the Fittest," *MA*, May 16, 1885, 262; "Small Colleges," *MA*, Feb. 10, 1883, 172–173. Editorials, *MA*, Apr. 21, 1888, 180; *MA*, Nov. 9, 1889, 41; *MA*, May 17, 1890, 201.

37. "Local News in Brief," *NYT*, Nov. 9, 1869, 8; Guy Maxton Lewis, "The American Intercollegiate Football Spectacle, 1869–1917" (Ph.D. diss., University of Maryland, 1964), 12; David Goldblatt, *The Ball Is Round: A Global History of Football* (New York: Viking, 2006), 97; Smith, *Sports and Freedom*, 69–72.

38. Kirsch, *Baseball in Blue and Gray*, 33, 40–41; Gorn and Goldstein, *Brief History*, 159; Donald J. Mrozek, *Sport and American Mentality, 1880–1910* (Knoxville: University of Tennessee Press, 1983), 28–66.

39. "University Games," *Oracle*, 4.

40. On "rational recreation," see Riess, *City Games*, 67, 84, 151–152; Allen Guttmann, *From Ritual to Record: The Nature of Modern Sports* (New York: Columbia University Press, 1978), 40–44.

41. University leaders who used the rhetoric of manliness in an attempt to exclude women from universities included David Starr Jordan of Stanford and G. Stanley Hall of Clark; see, for example, Hall to Jordan, Feb. 23, 1892, DSJ, Reel 3, Frames 530–531, SUA; David Starr Jordan, "Higher Education of Women" in *Care and Culture*, 123–124, 131. See also Julie Des Jardins, *Women and the Historical Enterprise in America: Gender, Race, and the Politics of Memory, 1880–1945* (Chapel Hill: University of North Carolina Press, 2003), 30–51; Gail Bederman, *Manliness & Civilization: A Cultural History of Gender and Race in the United States, 1880–1917* (Chicago: University of Chicago Press, 1995), 103; Cynthia Eagle Russett, *Sexual Science: The Victorian Construction of Womanhood* (Cambridge, MA: Harvard University Press, 1989), 61–62, 122–123, 148. On the debate over coeducation at Michigan, see Howard H. Peckham, *Making of the University of Michigan: 1817–1992,* ed. Margaret Steneck and Nicholas Steneck (1967; Ann Arbor, MI: Bentley Historical Library, 1994), 64.

42. John Sayle Watterson, *College Football: History, Spectacle, Controversy* (Baltimore: Johns Hopkins University Press, 2000), 18–20.

43. Robert H. Wiebe, *The Search for Order, 1877–1920* (New York: Hill and Wang, 1967); Lears, *Something for Nothing*, 187–227. On Taylor, see Trachtenberg, *Incorporation of America*, 69; Robert Kanigel, *The One Best Way: Frederick Winslow Taylor and the Enigma of Efficiency* (New York: Viking, 1997), 215; Lears, *Rebirth of a Nation*, 258–265.

44. On Camp's orderliness and the transformation of American football,

see Michael Oriard, *Reading Football: How the Popular Press Created an American Spectacle* (Chapel Hill: University of North Carolina Press, 1993), 40–56; Richard P. Borkowski, "The Life and Contributions of Walter Camp to American Football" (Ed.D. diss., Temple University, 1979), 57–58, 71–73; John Pettegrew, *Brutes in Suits: Male Sensibility in America, 1890–1920* (Baltimore: Johns Hopkins University Press, 2007), 135; Watterson, *College Football*, 20. On football's similarity to war, see Guttmann, *Ritual to Record*, 121–125; Michael Mandelbaum, *The Meaning of Sports: Why Americans Watch Baseball, Football, and Basketball and What They See When They Do* (New York: PublicAffairs, 2004), 119–143.

45. Untitled, *MA*, Nov. 2, 1889, 36. On sport and work in the late 1800s, see Rodgers, *Work Ethic*, 108–109.

46. See Carl E. Schorske, *Fin-de-Siècle Vienna: Politics and Culture* (New York: Vintage, 1979), xvii–xxx, 3–23.

47. George Fitch, *At Good Old Siwash* (1910; New York: Grosset & Dunlap, 1911), 196–197.

2. PROGRESSIVE ERA UNIVERSITIES AND FOOTBALL REFORM

1. On university extension, see Thomas Wakefield Goodspeed, *William Rainey Harper: First President of the University of Chicago* (Chicago: University of Chicago Press, 1928), 67–108; Richard J. Storr, *Harper's University: The Beginnings* (Chicago: University of Chicago Press, 1966), 196–209, 327–328; Merle Curti and Vernon Carstensen, *The University of Wisconsin: A History, 1848–1925*, 2 vols. (Madison: University of Wisconsin Press, 1949), 1:640, 711–731; 2:88, 109–110, 474–475, 549–590; Joseph F. Kett, *The Pursuit of Knowledge under Difficulties: From Self-Improvement to Adult Education in America, 1750–1990* (Stanford, CA: Stanford University Press, 1994), 182–189, 277–283. On Chicago, see Steven J. Diner, *A City and Its Universities: Public Policy in Chicago, 1892–1919* (Chapel Hill: University of North Carolina Press, 1980); Robin F. Bachin, *Building the South Side: Urban Space and Civic Culture in Chicago, 1890–1919* (Chicago: University of Chicago Press, 2004), 73–124. On the state of Wisconsin, whose progressives pioneered the "Wisconsin Idea" of university–state government cooperation, see Maureen A. Flanagan, *America Reformed: Progressives and Progressivisms, 1890s–1920s* (New York: Oxford University Press, 2007), 86–87; Curti and Carstensen, *University of Wisconsin*, 2:3–4, 23–24, 132; Charles McCarthy, *The Wisconsin Idea* (New York: Macmillan, 1912).

2. Edward L. Ayers, *The Promise of the New South: Life after Reconstruction* (New York: Oxford University Press, 1992), 313–315; Leo Andrew Doyle, "Causes Won, Not Lost: Football and Southern Culture, 1892–1983" (Ph.D. diss., Emory University, 1998), 1–63; Paul K. Conkin, *Gone with the Ivy: A Biography of Vanderbilt University* (Knoxville: University of Tennessee Press, 1985), 214–217. On football ritual and institutional status, see John Pettegrew, *Brutes in Suits: Male Sensibility in America, 1890–1920* (Baltimore: Johns Hopkins University Press, 2007), 143–146.

3. Edmund James, untitled report (c. 1912), 36–37, Edmund Janes James Presidential Papers (RG 2/5/3), Box 26, Folder "Athletics 1912," UIUC. On Chicago, see Robin Lester, *Stagg's University: The Rise, Decline, and Fall of Big-Time Football at Chicago* (Urbana: University of Illinois Press, 1995), 21–22. On presidents' relationship to intercollegiate football reform, see Ronald A. Smith, *Pay for Play: A History of Big-Time College Athletic Reform* (Urbana: University of Illinois Press, 2011), 34–41.

4. "Football at the Georgia-Carolina Fair," *Bulletin of Atlanta University* 186 (Dec. 1908), Atlanta University Published and Printed Materials, 1867–1992, Box 2, Folder 95, AUC. See also Frances Clemmer, "Negro Football" (Dec. 17, 1900), Horace Bumstead Papers, Box 21, Folder "Atlanta University Football Game Report," AUC. On black college football in Atlanta, see Hasan Kwame Jeffries, "Fields of Play: The Mediums through Which Black Athletes Engaged in Sports in Jim Crow Georgia," *Journal of Negro History* 86:3 (Summer 2001): 265.

5. On Yale, see "Yale's Big Football Balance," *NYT*, Feb. 23, 1894, 6; "Yale's Athletic Finances," *NYT*, Feb. 19, 1904, 6. On Harvard, see "Athletic Expenses 1894–95," *HGM* 4:15 (Mar. 1896), 460; "Athletic Expenses 1900–01," *HGM* 10:38 (Dec. 1901), 276–282. On the demographics of spectatorship (and readership) at the turn of the century, see Michael Oriard, *Reading Football: How the Popular Press Created an American Spectacle* (Chapel Hill: University of North Carolina Press, 1993), 74–75.

6. While I have not been able to ascertain the extent of this phenomenon, it is apparent that at many universities revenues gained from intercollegiate ticket sales were pumped back into the athletic department, which often was responsible for physical education as well as athletics. As later chapters show, commentators (including journalists and coaches, such as Knute Rockne of Notre Dame and Bill Roper of Princeton) frequently countered football critics

by asserting that if big-time sport was decommercialized, there would be no way to pay for physical education.

7. Ronald A. Smith, "Introduction" and "Afterword," in *Big-Time Football at Harvard, 1905: The Diary of Coach Bill Reid*, ed. Ronald A. Smith (Urbana: University of Illinois Press, 1994), 323.

8. Oriard, *Reading Football*, 179–180; John Sayle Watterson, *College Football: History, Spectacle, Controversy* (Baltimore: Johns Hopkins University Press, 2000), 9; Lester, *Stagg's University*, 68; "Palo Alto on Top," *SFC*, Mar. 20, 1892, 24; "Yale Celebrates Victory, *NYT*, Nov. 17, 1914, 11; Albert Shaw, "College Reform—And Football," *American Review of Reviews*, Dec. 1909, 724–726; John Griffith, Memorandum to Western Conference of Athletics RE Betting (Oct. 19, 1923), AAS, Folder 2-22, UCA.

9. "With the Educators," *LAT*, June 19, 1908, II4. On tramp athletes, see Watterson, *College Football*, 46–47. On tramps in American society, see Todd DePastino, *Citizen Hobo: How a Century of Homelessness Shaped America* (Chicago: University of Chicago Press, 2003), xx–xxi, 32–38.

10. On risk and injury, see "Change the Football Rules," *NYT*, Dec. 2, 1893, 2. On naval strategy, see "New Publications—Hamilton Williams, *Britain's Naval Power*," *NYT*, Feb. 2, 1895, 3. On the history of the wedge, see Watterson, *College Football*, 12–13. On Deland, see "Harvard, 22; Cornell, 12," *NYT*, Oct. 28, 1894, 6. Deland cited Napoleon on the first page of his business book: *Imagination in Business*, rev. ed. (New York: Harper, 1909), 1.

11. On the reforms, see "To Modify Football Rules: First Step Will be Taken at the University Club," *NYT*, Feb. 3, 1894, 6; "To Change Football Rules," *NYT*, Feb. 4, 1894, 3; "To Modify Football Rules: First Meeting of the University Committee," *NYT*, Feb. 24, 1894, 6. On evasion of the new rules, see "Harvard, 22; Cornell, 12," *NYT*, Oct. 28, 1894, 6.

12. On Eliot and the overseers, see "Reform in College Sports," *NYT*, Feb. 22, 1894, 3. Two of Eliot's critics were Theodore Roosevelt and Frank Angell; see Frederick Rudolph, *The American College and University: A History* (1962; Athens: University of Georgia Press, 1990), 377; Angell, "President Eliot on College Athletic Sports," *SS*, Apr. 26, 1894, 390. On Eliot's support of athletics, see Charles William Eliot, *University Administration* (Boston: Houghton Mifflin, 1908), 22; Hugh Hawkins, *Between Harvard and America: The Educational Leadership of Charles W. Eliot* (New York: Oxford University Press, 1972), 113–116.

13. For Baldwin, see "Athletes Crowded Out Literary Men," *NYT*, Feb. 23, 1894, 6. For Wilder and Wilson, see "Football or No Football," *NYT*, Feb. 18, 1894, 24.

14. "Yale Again Triumphant," *NYT*, Nov. 25, 1894, 1.

15. "Bahen's Condition Serious," *WP*, Dec. 1, 1894, 3; "Football Matches Prohibited," *WP*, Dec. 5, 1894, 6; "No Hope for Poor Bahen," *WP*, Dec. 8, 1894, 2; "Sporting News and Comment," *WP*, Dec. 11, 1894, 6; "Bahen's Surgical Ordeal," *WP*, Dec. 23, 1894, 3; "Bahen Benefit," *WP*, Mar. 8, 1895, 3; "Summoned to Bahen's Bedside," *WP*, Mar. 25, 1895, 7; "Could Not Fix Blame," *WP*, Mar. 28, 1895, 2; "Football Player Bahen Dead," *NYT*, Mar. 27, 1895, 1. Watterson erroneously reports that Bahen died in January; *College Football*, 36.

16. "Football Unfit for College Use," *NYT*, Jan. 31, 1895, 6; Watterson, *College Football*, 27–31.

17. Watterson, *College Football*, 27–31; Walter Camp, *Football Facts and Figures: A Symposium of Expert Opinions on the Game's Place in American Athletics* (New York: Harper, 1894), 1–10, 15–16. Yale captain Frank Hinkey was one defender; see "Getting Recruits for Yale," *NYT*, Feb. 18, 1895, 10.

18. Harper quoted in Lester, *Stagg's University*, 19; David Starr Jordan, "Policy of Stanford University," *SS*, Apr. 26, 1894, 388–390.

19. James Angell, D. B. St. John Roosa, J. G. Schurman, and Ethelbert Warfield, "Are Football Games Educative or Brutalizing?" *Forum*, Jan. 1894, 634–654.

20. Eugene Lamb Richards, "The Football Situation," *PSM* 45 (1894), 721–724; Richards, "Foot-Ball and Its Opponents," *Yale Medical Journal* 1 (1894–1895): 221–222. On manliness and imperialism, see Kristin L. Hoganson, *Fighting for American Manhood: How Gender Politics Provoked the Spanish-American and Philippine-American Wars* (New Haven, CT: Yale University Press, 1998).

21. W. M. Conant, "Educational Aspect of College Athletics," *Boston Medical and Surgical Journal* 131 (1894): 380–386; John T. Bowen, "Reports of Societies: Boston Society for Medical Improvement," *Boston Medical and Surgical Journal* 131 (1894): 393–397. See also Camp, *Football Facts and Figures*, 14.

22. "From Gridiron to the Grave" and "Georgia Falls before Virginia," *AC*, Oct. 31, 1897, 7; "Death Knell of Football," *AC*, Nov. 1, 1897, 1; "Atlanta Pastors Condemn the Game," *AC*, Nov. 2, 1897, 7; "Professor Herty on Athletic Sports," *AC*, Nov. 2, 1897, 3; "A Letter from Gammon's Mother," *AC*, Nov. 5,

1897, 5; "The Day in the House," AC, Nov. 9, 1897, 3; "Governor Atkinson and the Anti-Football Bill," *AC*, Dec. 4, 1897, 6; "A Good Place for a Veto," *AC*, Dec. 5, 1897, 18; "Gov. Atkinson's Reasons for Football Bill Veto," *AC*, Dec. 8, 1897, 5. See also Watterson, *College Football*, 36–37.

23. Angell, Roosa, Schurman, and Warfield, "Are Football Games Educative or Brutalizing?" 646–648. On changes in spectatorship and football's meanings, see Oriard, *Reading Football*, 97–101. By the 1920s Notre Dame attracted many working-class urban fans known as the "Subway Alumni"; see Murray Sperber, *Shake Down the Thunder: The Creation of Notre Dame Football* (New York: Henry Holt, 1993), 264.

24. Watterson, *College Football*, 48–53. Lake Forest College attended the 1895 meeting but was later replaced by Michigan. On the power of large associations in late 1800s America, see Alan Trachtenberg, *The Incorporation of America: Culture and Society in the Gilded Age* (New York: Hill and Wang, 1982).

25. Stagg to Wallace Heckman, Nov. 18, 1903 (copy), and Lane to Angell, Feb. 20, 1904 (copy), in AAS, Folder 9-13, UCA. See also JBA, Box 6, Folders 210–211, BHL. See also Lester, *Stagg's University*, 78.

26. On Wheeler's defense of football, see "Berkeley's New President," *LAT*, Nov. 1, 1899, 8. For Jordan's critiques, see Jordan, "University Tendencies in America," *PSM* 63 (1903), 147; Jordan, *The Days of a Man: Being Memories of a Naturalist, Teacher and Minor Prophet of Democracy*, 2 vols. (Yonkers, NY: World, 1922), 2:193–194. On Annapolis, see Park Benjamin, "Public Football vs. Naval Education: In Defense of the Naval Academy," *Independent*, Nov. 26, 1903, 2777–2780.

27. William Rainey Harper, *The Trend in Higher Education* (Chicago: University of Chicago Press, 1905), 175–176, 277–282; Angell to Van Hise, Dec. 24, 1903 (copy), JBA, Box 6, Folder 201, BHL; *Harper's Weekly*, Sept. 3, 1904, 1358, 1367; Editor *Harper's Weekly* to Harper, Jan. 15, 1904, WRH, Folder 7-5, UCA.

28. "Doubt Free Sport Plan," *CT*, Oct. 27, 1903, 8.

29. "Fourteen Football Victims this Year," *LAT*, Dec. 6, 1903, B3. Charles William Eliot, "Evils of College Football" (1905), in Eliot, *The Man and His Beliefs*, ed. William Nelson (New York: Harper, 1926), 115–120. On the 1905 football crisis and Progressive Era reform, see Watterson, *College Football*, 80–98; Rudolph, *American College*, 375–377; John S. Watterson, "The Gridiron Crisis of 1905: Was It Really a Crisis?" *Journal of Sport History* 27:2 (Summer

2000): 291–298; Elliott J. Gorn and Warren Goldstein, *Brief History of American Sports* (1993; Urbana: University of Illinois Press, 2004), 157–158. On the 1906 Pure Food and Drug Act, see Michael McGerr, *A Fierce Discontent: The Rise and Fall of the Progressive Movement in America* (New York: Oxford University Press, 2003), 160–163.

30. "Roosevelt Campaign for Football Reform," *NYT*, Oct. 10, 1905, 1; "T. Roosevelt, Jr., Injured," *NYT*, Oct. 6, 1905, 1.

31. "Hard Job to Reform It, Eliot Says," *NYT*, Oct. 11, 1905, 7; "Football Congress, Schurman Suggests," *NYT*, Oct. 12, 1905, 9; "For a Supreme Court of Amateur Sport," *NYT*, Oct. 22, 1905, X4; "New Athletic Board Generally Favored," *NYT*, Oct. 29, 1905, 12.

32. "Abolition of Football or Immediate Reforms," *NYT*, Nov. 28, 1905, 11; "Half Back Moore Buried," *NYT*, Nov. 29, 1905, 11. Watterson, *College Football*, 71–72.

33. Henry Beach Needham, "The College Athlete: How Commercialism Is Making Him a Professional," *McClure's Magazine*, June 1905, 115–128; Needham, "The College Athlete; His Amateur Code: Its Evasion and Administration," *McClure's Magazine*, July 1905, 260–272. Edward S. Jordan, "Buying Football Victories: The Universities of Chicago, Illinois, and Northwestern," *Collier's* 36:7, Nov. 11, 1905, 19–23; "Buying Football Victories: The University of Wisconsin," *Collier's* 36:8, Nov. 18, 1905, 22–23; "Buying Football Victories: University of Michigan," *Collier's* 36:9, Nov. 25, 1905, 21–23; "Buying Football Victories: The University of Minnesota," *Collier's* 36:10, Dec. 2, 1905, 19–20. Lincoln Steffens's articles were originally published in *McClure's Magazine* in 1902–1903 and published in 1904 as *Shame of the Cities*.

34. Intercollegiate Athletic Association of the United States, *Proceedings of the First Annual Meeting Held at New York City, New York December 29, 1906* [New York: Intercollegiate Athletic Association of the United States, 1906], 12 (Pierce), 23 (Stagg). See also Watterson, *College Football*, 68–79; Smith, *Pay for Play*, 42–51.

35. Palmer Pierce, Untitled Address, Intercollegiate Athletic Association of the United States, *Proceedings*, 27–28 (original emphasis).

36. On football's progressive reform, see Rudolph, *American College*, 375–377; Watterson, *College Football*, 66–67, 98, 100–104, 108; Ronald A. Smith, *Sports and Freedom: The Rise of Big-Time College Athletics* (New York: Oxford University Press, 1988), 203.

37. "Football," *Outlook*, Dec. 5, 1908, 762–763.

38. Ibid.; "Harvard and Yale Battle on Gridiron," *NYT*, Nov. 21, 1914, 14. On meatpacking and trust-busting, see McGerr, *Fierce Discontent*, 155–163.

39. Walter Camp, "Influence of the Tackle Play: A Development Which Has Changed the Character of Football," *Collier's* 46, Oct. 15, 1910, 24–25. On the transition to the new rules committee, see Watterson, *College Football*, 120–129; Smith, "Afterword," in *Big-Time Football at Harvard*, 321–322.

40. Pierce, Untitled Address, Intercollegiate Athletic Association of the United States, *Proceedings*, 29. On Progressive Era educational reform institutions, see Hugh Hawkins. *Banding Together: The Rise of National Associations in American Higher Education, 1887–1950* (Baltimore: Johns Hopkins University Press, 1992). Hawkins only mentions the NCAA in passing.

41. Robert H. Wiebe, *The Search for Order, 1877–1920* (New York: Hill and Wang, 1967), xiii–xiv.

42. "Want Colleges to Play Football with Feet, Not Hands," *NYT*, Oct. 15, 1905, SM5; "Football for President," *NYT*, Oct. 16, 1905, 10; "New Football League Planned for Colleges," *NYT*, Oct. 18, 1905, 12; "Want Roosevelt's Support," *NYT*, Oct. 19, 1905, 11.

43. Benjamin I. Wheeler to Arthur T. Hadley, Nov. 28, 1905, and Dec. 11, 1905, ATH, RU 25, YRG 2-A, Series 1, Box 91, Folder 1796, YUA; Wheeler to Charles William Eliot, Nov. 29, 1905, CWE, Box 131, Folder "Wheeler, Benjamin I., 1903–1908," HUA; "No More Football," *LAT*, Nov. 29, 1905, 11.

44. Benjamin Ide Wheeler, "Shall Football Be Ended or Mended?" (1906), in *The Abundant Life: Benjamin Ide Wheeler*, ed. Monroe E. Deutsch (Berkeley: University of California Press, 1926), 113–115. On Wheeler's early career, see "Harvard, 22; Cornell, 12," *NYT*, Oct. 28, 1894, 6; Monroe E. Deutsch, "Introduction," in *Abundant Life*, ed. Deutsch, 5.

45. Wheeler, "Rugby Game Is Popular," *LAT*, Sept. 23, 1906, III2.

46. "Rugby Game Is Finally Adopted," *DPA* 28:52 (Mar. 22, 1906), 1; "Reach Quick Decision," *DPA* 28:53 (Mar. 23, 1906), 4.

47. William James to David Starr Jordan, c. Apr. 20, 1906, DSJ, Reel 49, Frame 168; "Jordan Addresses Students," *DPA* 28:69 (Apr. 21, 1906), 4; Archie Rice, "Veteran Football Critic Says Make New Game for the West," *SFC*, Nov. 18, 1906, 2. On natural disasters, see Kevin Rozario, *Culture of Calamity: Disaster and the Making of Modern America* (Chicago: University of Chicago Press, 2007), 101–133.

48. Wheeler, "Shall Football Be Ended or Mended?," 113–115.

49. Jordan, *Days of a Man*, 2:193; H. Chesney White to Jordan, June 1,

1907, DSJ, Reel 55, Frame 015, SUA. On resistance to rugby, see "Oppose the Game," *LAT*, Dec. 20, 1907, I6; "Jordan Meets Chill Silence," *LAT*, Dec. 21, 1907, I6; "High Schools Reject Rugby," *LAT*, Sept. 23, 1906, III2. In an open letter to Los Angeles high schools, Wheeler argued that rugby was better than football because it did not require specialized training or coaches; see "Rugby Game Is Popular," *LAT*, Sept. 23, 1906, III2.

50. "Anxious to Quit Big Nine," *CT*, Jan. 14, 1907, 10; "Referee," *CT*, Feb. 3, 1907; "Michigan Now at Parting of Ways," *CT*, Feb. 4, 1907, 10; "Michigan Votes for Withdrawal," *CT*, Jan. 14, 1908, 6; Howard Roberts, *The Big Nine: The Story of Football in the Western Conference* (New York: G. P. Putnam's Sons, 1948), 23.

51. David Starr Jordan to Charles R. Van Hise, Feb. 5, 1908, CRVH, RG 4/10/01, Folder 6-76, UWA. On the responses, see Alston Ellis to Jordan, Dec. 14, 1909, DSJ, Reel 65, Frames 687–688; William Black to Jordan, Jan. 3, 1910, DSJ, Reel 66, Frame 13, SUA.

52. Van Hise to Jordan, Feb. 13, 1908, CRVH, Folder 6-76, UWA. See also LeBaron R. Briggs to Jordan, Jan. 4, 1910, DSJ, Reel 66, Frame 27, SUA.

53. Van Hise to Jordan, Feb. 13, 1908, CRVH, Folder 6-76, UWA; Jordan to Van Hise, Feb. 18, 1908, CRVH, Folder 6-76, UWA.

54. "Football Rules May Not Be Changed," *NYT*, Dec. 30, 1910, 9.

55. Walter Camp to David Starr Jordan, Jan. 8, 1908, DSJ, Reel 58, Frames 81–85; Baskerville to Jordan, Dec. 10, 1906, DSJ, Reel 52, Frames 482–485, SUA. A. H. Baskerville authored *Modern Rugby Football: New Zealand Methods; Points for the Beginner, the Player, the Spectator* (1907; Christchurch, NZ: Kiwi, 1995). On the importation of rugby players from the British Empire, see "Rugby Match Saturday," *DPA*, Feb. 7, 1906, 1; "Experts Play Rugby," *DPA*, Feb. 12, 1906, 1; Frank Angell, "Rugby Football on the Pacific Coast," *Independent* 68:3191, Jan. 27, 1910, 196.

56. T. M. Williams, "The Old and New Game," *SS*, Nov. 1907, 71–73. On peace eugenics, see Paul Crook, *Darwinism, War and History: The Debate over the Biology of War from the "Origin of Species" to the First World War* (Cambridge, UK: Cambridge University Press, 1994), 119–124. On rugby reform, see Jordan, *Days of a Man*, 2:194–195; Orrin Leslie Elliott, *Stanford University: The First Twenty-Five Years* (Stanford, CA: Stanford University Press, 1937), 234–235; Watterson, *College Football*, 93–98.

57. Watterson, *College Football*, 110–114; William Everett Hicks, "The Mil-

itary Worthlessness of Football," *The Independent*, Nov. 25, 1909, 1201–1204. This critique was echoed in 1913; Watterson, *College Football*, 136..

58. Woodrow Wilson to Arthur T. Hadley, Dec. 6, 1909, ATH, Box 93, Folder 1846; A. Lawrence Lowell to Hadley, Dec. 1, 1909, Dec. 21, 1909, Jan. 13, 1910, ATH, Box 55, Folders 1056–1057; Hadley to Lowell, Dec. 19, 1909 (copy), ATH, Box 55, Folder 1056; Lowell to Hadley, Dec. 21, 1909, ATH, Box 55, Folder 1056, YUA. Faunce and Thompson quoted in Caspar Whitney, ed., "Is Football Worth While: A Symposium of Opinion from the Presidents of Representative Educational Institutions in the United States," *Colliers* 44:13, Dec. 18, 1909, 13, 24.

59. Watterson, *College Football*, 117–132.

3. PSYCHOLOGISTS: BODY, MIND, AND THE CREATION OF DISCIPLINE

1. George Thomas White Patrick, "A Further Study of Heraclitus," *AJP* 1 (1887–1888), 638.

2. See Jay W. Fay, *American Psychology before William James* (1939; New York: Octagon, 1966), 18, 90–128. Philosophers who pioneered the "science of the soul" included Noah Porter, *The Human Intellect: With an Introduction upon Psychology and the Soul*, 4th ed. (New York: Charles Scribner's Sons, 1868), 5. On physiology, see Everett Mendelsohn, "Revolution and Reduction: The Sociology of Methodological and Philosophical Concerns in Nineteenth Century Biology," in *The Interaction between Science and Philosophy*, ed. Y. Elkana (Atlantic Highlands, NJ: Humanities Press, 1974), 407–426, 418; Anson Rabinbach, *The Human Motor: Energy, Fatigue, and the Origins of Modernity* (New York: Basic, 1990), 50.

3. George M. Fredrickson, *The Inner Civil War: Northern Intellectuals and the Crisis of the Union* (New York: Harper & Row, 1965), 74, 192–193; Louis Menand, *The Metaphysical Club: A Story of Ideas in America* (New York: Farrar, Straus and Giroux, 2001); Bruce Kuklick, *The Rise of American Philosophy: Cambridge, Massachusetts, 1860–1930* (New Haven, CT: Yale University Press, 1977), 47–54; Philip P. Wiener, *Evolution and the Founders of Pragmatism* (Cambridge, MA: Harvard University Press, 1949), 18–30, 97–128; John M. O'Donnell, *The Origins of Behaviorism: American Psychology, 1870–1920* (New York: New York University Press, 1985), 1–105.

4. See Silas Weir Mitchell, George Read Morehouse, and William Williams Keen, *Gunshot Wounds and Other Injuries of Nerves* (1864; San Francisco: Nor-

man, 1989); Mitchell, *Injuries of Nerves and Their Consequences* (1872; New York: Dover, 1965), 11; Mitchell, *Wear and Tear; or, Hints for the Overworked*, 5th ed. (1887; New York: Arno, 1973), 11–17. On the rest cure, see Richard D. Walter, *S. Weir Mitchell, M.D.—Neurologist: A Medical Biography* (Springfield, IL: Charles C. Thomas, 1970), 47–61, 127–140; Lisa A. Long, *Rehabilitating Bodies: Health, History, and the American Civil War* (Philadelphia: University of Pennsylvania Press, 2003), 29–57; Patricia A. Vertinsky, *The Eternally Wounded Woman: Women, Doctors, and Exercise in the Late Nineteenth Century* (1989; Urbana: University of Illinois Press, 1994), 204–233. On Beard, see George M. Beard, *American Nervousness: Its Causes and Consequences; A Supplement to Nervous Exhaustion (Neurasthenia)* (New York: G. P. Putnam's Sons, 1881), vi; John S. Haller and Robin M. Haller, *The Physician and Sexuality in Victorian America* (Urbana: University of Illinois Press, 1974), 5–43; Tom Lutz, *American Nervousness, 1903: An Anecdotal History* (Ithaca, NY: Cornell University Press, 1991), 1–30; F. G. Gosling, *Before Freud: Neurasthenia and the American Medical Community, 1870–1910* (Urbana: University of Illinois Press, 1987), 9–29; Janet Oppenheim, *"Shattered Nerves": Doctors, Patients, and Depression in Victorian England* (New York: Oxford University Press, 1991), 79–109. On 1800s comparisons of bodies and machines, see Rabinbach, *Human Motor*; Mark Seltzer, *Bodies and Machines* (New York: Routledge, 1992), 3–21.

5. Gail Bederman, *Manliness and Civilization: A Cultural History of Gender and Race in the United States* (Chicago: University of Chicago Press, 1995), 77–120; Bruce Haley, *The Healthy Body and Victorian Culture* (Cambridge, MA: Harvard University Press, 1978), 4.

6. G. Mercer Adam, *Sandow on Physical Training* (New York: J. Selwin, 1894), 1; "Football Reform," *Outlook*, Nov. 18, 1906, 649. Sandow and Roosevelt met in the early 1900s; David Chapman, *Sandow the Magnificent: Eugen Sandow and the Beginnings of Bodybuilding* (Urbana: University of Illinois Press, 1994), 151. On the relationship between education, mental fatigue, and physical culture, see Rabinbach, *Human Motor*, 146–153.

7. "Gymnasium," *Yale Courant*, Oct. 31, 1866, 68; "Out-Door Sports," *HA*, Oct. 22, 1867, 28; "Gymnasiums," *MUC*, Nov. 16, 1867, 4. See also "Over-Worked Brain," *MUC*, Oct. 5, 1872, 3.

8. "Shall We Have a Gymnasium?" *MUC*, Oct. 17, 1868, 12.

9. Harvard's gymnasium, established before the Civil War, charged a $2 annual fee (raised to $4 in 1872–1873); see *Harvard University Catalogue* from 1861, 1869, 1873, and 1874. Students wanted "an accomplished gymnast" to

staff the facility; "Week," *HA*, Jan. 31, 1879, 110. On Hemenway Gymnasium, see Samuel Eliot Morison, *Three Centuries of Harvard, 1636–1936* (1936; Cambridge, MA: Harvard University Press, 1986), 408–409. On Yale's gymnasium, see "Again the College Man," *NYT*, Sept. 25, 1892, 10; "To Measure the Muscles," *NYT*, Feb. 12, 1894, 8. On Chicago, see "Corner-Stone of Bartlett Gymnasium to Be Laid Thanksgiving," *CT*, Nov. 23, 1901, 2; "Corner-Stone of New 'Gym' Laid," *CT*, Nov. 29, 1901, 9. On Michigan, see Howard H. Peckham, *The Making of the University of Michigan, 1817–1992*, ed. Margaret L. Steneck and Nicholas H. Steneck (1967; Ann Arbor, MI: Bentley Historical Library, 1994), 107. On Stanford, see Orrin Leslie Elliott, *Stanford University: The First Twenty-Five Years, 1891–1925* (Stanford, CA: Stanford University Press, 1937), 189.

10. Edward H. Clarke, *Sex in Education; or, A Fair Chance for the Girls* (Boston: Osgood, 1873), and *Building of a Brain* (Boston: Osgood, 1874); Mitchell, *Wear and Tear*, 43–47. See also Cynthia Eagle Russett, *Sexual Science: The Victorian Construction of Womanhood* (Cambridge, MA: Harvard University Press, 1989), 104–129, 146–147, 206; Vertinsky, *Eternally Wounded Woman*, 39–68; Rosalind Rosenberg, *Beyond Separate Spheres: Intellectual Roots of Modern Feminism* (New Haven, CT: Yale University Press, 1982), 1–28; Heather Munro Prescott, *Student Bodies: The Influence of Student Health Services in American Society and Medicine* (Ann Arbor: University of Michigan Press, 2007), 12–14. On female physical education, see Barbara Miller Solomon, *In the Company of Educated Women: A History of Women and Higher Education in America* (New Haven, CT: Yale University Press, 1985), 103–104.

11. Mitchell, *Wear and Tear*, 75, 45. Prince quoted in Walter Camp and Lorin Deland, *Football* (Boston: Houghton Mifflin, 1896), 44–45; Camp to Deland, Oct. 26, 1896; WCP, Reel 7, Frame 234. Morton Prince played football in 1875; he and his brother (Charlie Prince) served on the Harvard University Foot Ball Club committee that outlined the club's rules before it started playing rugby in 1874; Morison, *Three Centuries*, 404. On railway spine, see Barbara Young Welke, *Recasting American Liberty: Gender, Race, Law, and the Railroad Revolution, 1865–1920* (Cambridge, UK: Cambridge University Press, 2001), 139–170; Eric Caplan, "Trains and Trauma in the American Gilded Age," in *Traumatic Pasts: History, Psychiatry, and Trauma in the Modern Age, 1870–1930*, ed. Mark S. Micale and Paul Lerner (Cambridge, UK: Cambridge University Press, 2001), 57–77.

12. Prince surveyed Harvard, Princeton, Michigan, Cornell, Williams, and

Dartmouth; "Accident Neuroses and Foot-Ball Playing," *Boston Medical and Surgical Journal* 138 (1898): 393. He reasoned that football players felt no imminent danger, while military personnel keenly felt danger; yet he excused sailors who experienced mental trauma in the 1898 explosion of the battleship *Maine* by commenting that it might have been an exception to his parameters, since the explosion surprised them. In addition, Prince noted that injured railroad employees rarely experienced mental trauma, whereas passengers were more often mentally injured—especially women, who tended to faint because they were unprepared for traumatic situations.

13. Kristin L. Hoganson, *Fighting for American Manhood: How Gender Politics Provoked the Spanish-American and Philippine-American Wars* (New Haven, CT: Yale University Press, 1998), 107–132; Donald J. Mrozek, *Sport and American Mentality, 1880–1910* (Knoxville: University of Tennessee Press, 1983), 28–66; Theodore Roosevelt, *The Strenuous Life: Essays and Addresses* (New York: Century, 1905), 1–24. On Crane, see E. Anthony Rotundo, *American Manhood: Transformations in Masculinity from the Revolution to the Modern Era* (New York: Basic, 1993), 240–241.

14. Wilhelm Wundt studied with Emil DuBois-Reymond and Helmholtz; he published *Principles of Physiological Psychology* in 1873–1874; Solomon Diamond, "Wundt before Leipzig," in *Wilhelm Wundt in History: The Making of a Scientific Psychology*, ed. Robert W. Rieber and David K. Robinson (New York: Kluwer Academic, 2001), 1–68. On the relationship among psychology, physiology, and physical culture, see Roberta J. Park, "'Taking Their Measure' in Play, Games, and Physical Training: The American Scene, 1870s to World War I," *Journal of Sport History* 33:2 (Summer 2006): 193–217.

15. Hugo Münsterberg, "New Psychology, and Harvard's Equipment for Teaching It," *HGM* 1:2 (Jan. 1893), 201–209; Morison, *Three Centuries*, 377.

16. G. Stanley Hall, *Adolescence: Its Psychology and Its Relation to Physiology, Anthropology, Sociology, Sex, Crime, Religion, and Education* (New York: D. Appleton, 1904), 1:221; Dorothy Ross, *G. Stanley Hall: The Psychologist as Prophet* (Chicago: University of Chicago Press, 1972), 314–315, 326; Bederman, *Manliness and Civilization*, 77–120; Vertinsky, *Eternally Wounded Woman*, 171–203.

17. G. Stanley Hall, July 15, 1887, Manuscript File, Box 21, "Faculty M-P," UIA. On his studies at Johns Hopkins, see George Thomas White Patrick, *George Thomas White Patrick: An Autobiography* (Iowa City: University of Iowa Press, 1947), 73.

18. Patrick, "Further Study of Heraclitus," 635–642. On scholarly boundaries at the turn of the century, see Francesca Bordogna, *William James at the Boundaries* (Chicago: University of Chicago Press, 2008), 4–5, 26–29.

19. On Patrick's training and the psychology laboratory, see Stow Persons, *The University of Iowa in the Twentieth Century: An Institutional History* (Iowa City: University of Iowa Press, 1990), 13, 107, 116; Patrick, *Autobiography*, 116, 122–123. G. T. W. Patrick to Henry Schaeffer, May 9, 1894, Manuscript File, Box 21, Folder "Faculty M-P"; Patrick to William Haddock, July 7, 1894, July 12, 1894, and Aug. 3, 1897, Manuscript File, Box 9, Folder "Psychology—General"; Edward Kunkel to Carl Seashore, Mar. 22, 1901, and Patrick, Philosophy Department Report, May 16, 1898, Manuscript File, Box 9, Folder "Organizations—Publications," UIA.

20. George Thomas White Patrick, "The Psychology of Football," *AJP* 14 (1903): 368, 373, 378–379. Patrick was commenting on Herbert Spencer's essay "Physical Education" (1859) and Karl Groos's book *Play of Man* (1896). Walter Camp admitted he was not aware of any articles on the psychology of football; Camp to Patrick, Aug. 1, 1902, WCP, Reel 14, Frames 78–79.

21. Patrick, "Psychology of Football," 373, 380.

22. On Indian boarding schools, see David W. Adams, *Education for Extinction: American Indians and the Boarding School Experience, 1875–1928* (Lawrence: University Press of Kansas, 1995). On Carlisle football, see Michael Oriard, *Reading Football: How the Popular Press Created an American Spectacle* (Chapel Hill: University of North Carolina Press, 1993), 233–247.

23. On Patrick's account of Germany, see Richard T. Hull, ed., *Presidential Addresses of the American Philosophical Association, 1901–1910* (Dordrecht: Kluwer Academic, 1999), 95–96, 99; Patrick, *Autobiography*, 126–130.

24. Paul van Dyke, "Athletics and Education," *Outlook*, Feb. 11, 1905, 392.

25. "Foot-Ball," *HA*, May 14, 1875, 80; A. G. Newcomer, "Mind or Muscle?" *SS*, Jan. 6, 1892, 89.

26. William Lowe Bryan, "Capital in Nerves: A Chapel Sermon, Delivered at Indiana University in 1893," WLB, Folder 69.6, IUB; "Capital in Nerves: A Practical Suggestion," *SS*, Mar. 22, 1894, 332–333. Jordan so admired this advice that he repeated it to Stanford freshmen; "Lecture to Freshmen," *DPA*, Sept. 11, 1901, 1. On Bryan's academic biography, see Eliot Hearst and James H. Capshew, *Psychology at Indiana University: A Centennial Review and Compendium* (Bloomington: Indiana University Department of Psychology, 1988), 6–15.

27. Hoganson, *Fighting for American Manhood*, 88–106; Oriard, *Reading Football*, 189–276, 204–205.

28. Edward S. Jordan, "Buying Football Victories: The University of Wisconsin," *Collier's* 36:8, Nov. 18, 1905, 22, 23; "Buying Football Victories: The Universities of Chicago, Illinois, and Northwestern," *Collier's* 36:9, Nov. 11, 1905, 19.

29. Warren Plympton Lombard, "The Variations of the Normal Knee-Jerk and Their Relation to the Activity of the Central Nervous System," *AJP* 1 (1887–1888): 9, 40, 61. On Lombard's training and career, see Horace W. Davenport, *Not Just Any Medical School: The Science, Practice, and Teaching of Medicine at the University of Michigan, 1850–1941* (Ann Arbor: University of Michigan Press, 1999), 62–64; Warren P. Lombard, "The Life and Work of Carl Ludwig," *Science* 44 (1916): 363–375; Lombard to Hall (copy, undated), WPL, Box 1, Folder 1, BHL. Lombard was on the 1874 Harvard team; "McGill vs. Harvard," *HA*, May 15, 1874, 103.

30. S. Weir Mitchell to Warren P. Lombard, Sept. 28, 1908, WPL, Box 1, Folder 4; Lombard, Report to Biology Club, Jan. 20, 1894, WPL, Box 2, Folder 54; W. Davis to Lombard, Jan. 26, 1899, WPL, Box 2, Folder 56, BHL.

31. Warren Lombard, "Some Musings of an Old Man," Scientific Club speech, Nov. 19, 1938, WPL, Box 1, Folder 2; Lombard, "Acc[ount] of life since graduation," WPL, Box 1, Folder 1, BHL. "Rousing Meeting," *MD*, Oct. 6, 1894, 1.

32. "Rousing Meeting," 1; "Jollification," *MD*, Nov. 27, 1894, 1; "For Unity and Strength," *MD*, Oct. 5, 1895, 1; "Football Enthusiasm," *MD*, Oct. 10, 1896, 1; "Dr. Nancr[è]de's Generosity," *MD*, Dec. 13, 1894, 1; "Present Outlook for Athletics at the University of Michigan—A Symposium," *MI*, Jan. 1894, 244–245. A specialist on abdominal gunshot wounds, Nancrède served on Michigan's Athletic Board in the 1890s and often attended athletic matches; "Dr. Charles B. Nancrède—Eminent Specialist in Gunshot and Bullet Wounds" (undated newspaper clipping); David A. Bloom, Gretchen Uznis, Darrell A. Campbell, Jr., "Charles B. G. de Nancrède: Academic Surgeon at the *Fin de Siècle*," *World Journal of Surgery* 22 (1998): 1175–1181; unidentified newspaper clipping (c. May 9, 1898), DB Faculty Vertical File, Charles Beylard Guerard de Nancrède, Folder 1, BHL; "Board in Control," *MD* 7:12 (Oct. 14, 1896), 1.

33. "Monster Rally for Varsity Rugby," *DPA*, Nov. 11, 1908, 1; "Rousing Rugby Rally Will Open Season Tomorrow," *DPA*, Sept. 1, 1915, 1; "Rousing

Rally Initiates 1915 Rugby Season" *DPA,* Sept. 3, 1915, 1. On a similar debate over women's attendance at University of Chicago rallies, see "Girls' Team," *Daily Maroon* 1:34 (Nov. 14, 1902), 2.

34. "Football Rally," *DPA* 19:46 (Nov. 7, 1901), 1.

35. "Athletic Education for Women," *MI,* Apr. 1896, 291–301; "Women Hold Athletic Rally," *DPA,* Sept. 9, 1915, 1.

36. Winton U. Solberg, *The University of Illinois, 1894–1904: The Shaping of the University* (Urbana: University of Illinois Press, 2000), 74.

37. Edwin G. Dexter, "Accidents from College Football," *Educational Review* 25 (1904): 415–428; Edwin Dexter biography file, UIUC; Solberg, *University of Illinois, 1894–1904,* 372–373.

38. Edwin G. Dexter, "Newspaper Football," *PSM* 68 (1906), 261–265.

39. Dexter, "Accidents from College Football," 422–425.

40. Edwin G. Dexter, "The Survival of the Fittest in Motor Training," *Educational Review* 23 (1902): 81–91; Karl Groos, *The Play of Man,* trans. Elizabeth Baldwin (1896; New York: D. Appleton, 1898).

41. Dexter, "Newspaper Football," 265.

42. William James, "The Moral Equivalent of War" (1906), in *Memories and Studies* (London: Longmans, Green, 1911), 267–291. Historians who have interpreted James's article as referring to football include Mrozek, *Sport and American Mentality,* 63–64; James B. Gilbert, *Work without Salvation: America's Intellectuals and Industrial Alienation, 1880–1910* (Baltimore: Johns Hopkins University Press, 1977), 77–78.

43. On Angell's biography, see the Frank Angell Biographical File, SUA, and Elliott, *Stanford University,* 223–242. On David Starr Jordan's pronouncements, see Jordan, "Policy of Stanford University," *SS,* Apr. 26, 1894, 389–390.

44. Frank Angell, "President Eliot on College Athletic Sports," *SS,* Apr. 26, 1894, 390.

45. Frank Angell, "Rugby Football on the Pacific Coast," *Independent* 68:3191, Jan. 27, 1910, 195–198. See also Angell, "Rugby vs. Intercollegiate Football," *SS,* Dec. 1908, 113–114; Angell, "Passing of the Paid Coach," *SS,* Mar. 1911, 183–184; Angell to Jordan, July 22, 1915, DSJ, Reel 92, Frame 1087, SUA. For Jordan's opinion of rugby, see Jordan to Walter Camp, Jan. 20, 1908, WCP, Reel 11, Frame 322. On Angell's career as a track timer, see Angell Biographical File, SUA. His articles included Angell, "Note on Some of the Physical Factors Affecting Reaction Time Together with a Description of a

New Reaction Key," *AJP* 22:1 (1911): 86–93, and "Duration, Energy and Extent of Reaction Movements—Simple and Flying Reactions," *AJP* 30:2 (Apr. 1919): 224–236.

46. Charles Baird, "Harvard Game," *MI*, Nov. 1895, 70; C[olbert] Searles, "Sports and Work," *SS*, Oct. 1904, 150–151.

47. On the 1902 Rose Bowl, see "Aftermath of Defeat," *DPA*, Jan. 7, 1902, 1. On Lanagan's retreats at Stanford, see "Team to Leave Campus," *DPA*, Nov. 9, 1905, 1. On Stagg's treatment of his players at Chicago, see Robin Lester, *Stagg's University: The Rise, Decline, and Fall of Big-Time Football at Chicago* (Urbana: University of Illinois Press, 1995), 54; "Outing for Stagg's Men," *CT*, Nov. 27, 1905, 10; "Off for Country," *Daily Maroon*, Nov. 13, 1902, 1. On the 1905 Big Game, see "Stanford Eleven Triumphs over the California Team," *DPA*, Nov. 13, 1905, 1.

48. *DPA*, Oct. 16, 1908, 2; Sedley Peck, "Abolish the Game?" *SS*, Feb. 1912, 170–171.

49. H. Addington Bruce, "The Psychology of Football," *Outlook* 96, Nov. 5, 1910, 543–544. On Bruce, see P. M. Dennis, "Psychology's First Publicist: H. A. Bruce," *Psychological Reports* 68 (1991): 755–765; Nathan G. Hale, Jr., *Freud and the Americans: The Beginnings of Psychoanalysis in the United States, 1876–1917* (New York: Oxford University Press, 1971), 3–23.

50. On Jordan's offer to Bryan (who later became president of Indiana University), see correspondence between Bryan and Jordan, Apr. 5, 1892, to May 3, 1892; WLB, Folder 69.3, IUB. On the situation at Illinois, see Solberg, *University of Illinois 1894–1904*, 76–78.

51. On Harvard, see Bruce Kuklick, *Rise of American Philosophy*, 461, 475; Ralph Barton Perry, "Psychology, 1876–1929," in *The Development of Harvard University since the Inauguration of President Eliot, 1869–1929*, ed. Samuel Eliot Morison (Cambridge, MA: Harvard University Press, 1930), 216. On Michigan, see Peckham, *Making of the University of Michigan*, 181; on Iowa, see Persons, *University of Iowa*, 104–116, 133–135.

52. Bordogna, *William James at the Boundaries*, 7–8.

4. SOCIAL SCIENTISTS: MAKING SPORT SAFE FOR A RATIONAL PUBLIC

1. Edward A. Ross, *Social Psychology: An Outline and Source Book* (New York: Macmillan, 1908), 86–87. On the "mob" in Progressive Era discourse, see Daria Frezza, *The Leader and the Crowd: Democracy in American Public Discourse*, trans. Martha King (Athens: University of Georgia Press, 2007), 3,

12–13, 20–24, 59–60; David A. Zimmerman, *Panic! Markets, Crises, and Crowds in American Fiction* (Chapel Hill: University of North Carolina Press, 2006), 1–33, 165.

2. On Ely and early social science, see Daniel T. Rodgers, *Atlantic Crossings: Social Politics in a Progressive Age* (Cambridge, MA: Harvard University Press, 1998), 76–111; Benjamin G. Rader, *The Academic Mind and Reform: The Influence of Richard T. Ely in American Life* (Lexington: University of Kentucky Press, 1966), 32–40; Paul K. Conkin, *Prophets of Prosperity: America's First Political Economists* (Bloomington: Indiana University Press, 1980), 311. On the academic division of labor, see Thomas L. Haskell, *The Emergence of Professional Social Science: The American Social Science Association and the Nineteenth-Century Crisis of Authority* (Urbana: University of Illinois Press, 1977), vi–vii.

3. On social scientists and Darwinian thought, see Stow Persons, ed., *Evolutionary Thought in America* (New Haven, CT: Yale University Press, 1950), 160–266. On the shift away from A PRIORI social science, see Dorothy Ross, *The Origins of American Social Science* (Cambridge, UK: Cambridge University Press, 1991), 53, 59. A good example of the mixing of religion and social science is Edward Alsworth Ross, *Sin and Society: An Analysis of Latter-Day Iniquity* (Boston: Houghton Mifflin, 1907). On the Social Gospel, see Henry F. May, *Protestant Churches and Industrial America* (1949; New York: Harper & Row, 1967); Shelton Stromquist, *Reinventing "The People": The Progressive Movement, the Class Problem, and the Origins of Modern Liberalism* (Urbana: University of Illinois Press, 2006), 38–39.

4. Francis A. Walker, "College Athletics: Oration Delivered before the Phi Beta Kappa Society, in Sanders Theatre, Thursday, June 29, 1893," *HGM* 2:5 (Sept. 1893), 2, 5–7, 9, 12–13. On Walker, see Bernard Newton, *The Economics of Francis Amasa Walker: American Economics in Transition* (New York: Augustus M. Kelley, 1968), 5–15; James Phinney Munroe, *A Life of Francis Amasa Walker* (New York: Henry Holt, 1923), 27–29.

5. Frank W. Taussig, "A Professor's View of Athletics," *HGM* 3:11 (Mar. 1895), 306–310.

6. On late 1800s capitalists, politics, and reform, see Alan Trachtenberg, *The Incorporation of America: Culture and Society in the Gilded Age* (New York: Hill and Wang, 1982), 78–86; Michael E. McGerr, *The Decline of Popular Politics: The American North, 1865–1928* (New York: Oxford University Press, 1986), 138–183; McGerr, *A Fierce Discontent: The Rise and Fall of the Progres-*

sive Movement in America (New York: Oxford University Press, 2003), 77–117, 147–181. On "best men" reformers, see John G. Sproat, *"The Best Men": Liberal Reformers in the Gilded Age* (New York: Oxford University Press, 1968).

7. E. A. Ross, "Reform Spirit," *SS*, Jan. 25, 1893, 226–231. On Ross, see Julius Weinberg, *Edward Alsworth Ross and the Sociology of Progressivism* (Madison: State Historical Society of Wisconsin, 1972), 21–55.

8. "Football Rally," *DPA*, Nov. 7, 1901, 1; "Football Dinner," *DPA*, November 7, 1901, 4; Burt Estes Howard, *Education and Democracy* (Los Angeles: B. R. Baumgardt, 1901), 18–19, 37–42, 45. On Stanford and California progressivism, see Philip J. Ethington, *The Public City: The Political Construction of Urban Life in San Francisco, 1850–1900* (Cambridge, UK: Cambridge University Press, 1994), 349–352.

9. On Roosevelt's visit, see "They Discussed Athletics," *MD*, Jan. 14, 1895, 1; "Teddy on Football," *MD*, Apr. 14, 1899, 1. See also Andrew C. McLaughlin in "Symposium on Professionalism in Western Athletics," *MI*, Jan. 1894, 166–168. "In Retrospect," (Michigan) *Wolverine*, Jan. 10, 1902, 10; Noah Cheever, "Football and Character," *MI*, Dec. 1902, 101–103; "Prof. Charles Cooley on College Athletics," *MD*, Mar. 13, 1906, 1; "Prof. A. C. M'Laughlin Defends Athletics," *MD*, Feb. 15, 1906, 1; Louis Whitehead, "Foot-Ball Controversy," *MI*, Jan. 1894, 184–186; James Leroy, "Spirit of Michigan," *MI*, June 1903, 309–311. Similar pronouncements were made in mainstream journals; see "Football," *Outlook*, Dec. 5, 1908, 763.

10. M. W. Greer, "Athletics," *SS*, Dec. 9, 1891, 39; Jack Reynolds, "Football Outlook," *SS*, Sept. 11, 1900, 4; Delos Wilcox, "Dishonesty in College Work," *MI*, Jan. 1894, 189–192. Elsewhere, Wilcox warned that football wagering, like gambling at bucket shops, races, and elections, led to unhealthy competition and actually stifled democracy; Delos F. Wilcox, *The American City: A Problem in Democracy* (1904; New York: Macmillan, 1909), 144.

11. Walker, "College Athletics," 9, 12–13; Isaac Loos, *Quill* (Feb. 10, 1894), quoted in Karl Loos and Helen Loos Whitney, *Isaac Althaus Loos* (Iowa City: University of Iowa Press, 1947), 57; Ross, *Social Psychology*, 84, 86–87. See also Andrew C. McLaughlin in "Symposium on Professionalism in Western Athletics," *MI*, Jan. 1894, 166–168. On Sumner, see Richard Hofstadter, *Social Darwinism in American Thought* (1944; Boston: Beacon, 1992), 51–66; Robert C. Bannister, *Social Darwinism: Science and Myth in Anglo-American Thought* (Philadelphia: Temple University Press, 1979), 98–113.

12. Thorstein Veblen, *The Theory of the Leisure Class* (1899; New York: Pen-

guin, 1979), 255–256, 261–263. On Veblen's views of masculinity, evolution, and football, see John Pettegrew, *Brutes in Suits: Male Sensibility in America, 1890–1920* (Baltimore: Johns Hopkins University Press, 2007), 131–133.

13. William I. Thomas, "The Gaming Instinct," *American Journal of Sociology* 6 (May 1901): 750–753, 758–761. On Thomas, see James B. Gilbert, *Work without Salvation: America's Intellectuals and Industrial Alienation, 1880–1910* (Baltimore: Johns Hopkins University Press, 1977), 69–70; Donald J. Mrozek, *Sport and American Mentality, 1880–1910* (Knoxville: University of Tennessee Press, 1983), 28–31; Morris Janowitz, "Introduction," in *W. I. Thomas on Social Organization and Social Personality: Selected Papers*, ed. Morris Janowitz (Chicago: University of Chicago Press, 1966), xi–xxix.

14. Thomas, "Gaming Instinct," 750–753, 758–761. On discourses of whiteness and "civilization," see Gail Bederman, *Manliness and Civilization: A Cultural History of Gender and Race in the United States, 1880–1917* (Chicago: University of Chicago Press, 1995), 88–101.

15. Ira Howerth to William Rainey Harper, with Harper's handwritten note to Amos Alonzo Stagg, Oct. 15, 1897, AAS, Folder 9-2, UCA. On Harper and the early days of the University of Chicago, see Thomas Wakefield Goodspeed, *William Rainey Harper: First President of the University of Chicago* (Chicago: University of Chicago Press, 1928), 67–108; Richard J. Storr, *Harper's University: The Beginnings* (Chicago: University of Chicago Press, 1966), 19, 327–328; Robin F. Bachin, *Building the South Side: Urban Space and Civic Culture in Chicago, 1890–1919* (Chicago: University of Chicago Press, 2004), 1–6, 23–72. On the 1893 fair, see James Gilbert, *Perfect Cities: Chicago's Utopias of 1893* (Chicago: University of Chicago Press, 1991). On social settlements, see Allen F. Davis, *Spearheads for Reform: The Social Settlements and the Progressive Movement, 1890–1914* (1967; New Brunswick, NJ: Rutgers University Press, 1984); Steven J. Diner, *A City and Its Universities: Public Policy in Chicago, 1892–1919* (Chapel Hill: University of North Carolina Press, 1980), 119–129; Robert M. Crunden, *Ministers of Reform: The Progressives' Achievement in American Civilization, 1889–1920* (1982; Urbana: University of Illinois Press, 1984), 16–25; Judith Ann Trolander, *Professionalism and Social Change: From the Settlement House Movement to Neighborhood Centers, 1886 to the Present* (New York: Columbia University Press, 1987), 1–29; Rivka Shpak Lissak, *Pluralism and Progressives: Hull House and the New Immigrants, 1890–1919* (Chicago: University of Chicago Press, 1989); Mina Carson, *Settlement Folk: Social Thought and the American Settlement Movement, 1885–*

1930 (Chicago: University of Chicago Press, 1990). On social work and social science at Chicago, see Bachin, *Building the South Side*, 73–124; Stow Persons, *Ethnic Studies at Chicago, 1905–1945* (Urbana: University of Illinois Press, 1987). On extension, see Storr, *Harper's University*, 61, 196–209.

16. Paul Van Dyke, "Athletics and Education," *Outlook* 79, Feb. 11, 1905, 389–393; Van Dyke's article was cited widely; see, for example, J. William White, "Football and Its Critics," *Outlook* 81, Nov. 18, 1905, 662–669. On Van Dyke, see his obituary, *NYT*, Aug. 31, 1933, 17. On Ross's nativism, see Weinberg, *Edward Alsworth Ross*, 149–176. On Progressive Era fears of chance and anti-gambling crusades, see Jackson Lears, *Something for Nothing: Luck in America* (New York: Viking, 2003), 194–197.

17. Van Dyke, "Athletics and Education," 390–393. On gendered implications of "hysteria," see Carroll Smith-Rosenberg, "The Hysterical Woman: Sex Roles and Role Conflict in Nineteenth-Century America," in *Disorderly Conduct: Visions of Gender in Victorian America* (New York: Knopf, 1985), 197–216.

18. Edward S. Jordan, "Buying Football Victories: The Universities of Chicago, Illinois and Northwestern," *Collier's* 36:7, Nov. 11, 1905, 19, 23; "Buying Football Victories: The University of Michigan," *Collier's* 36:9, Nov. 25, 1905, 21; "Buying Football Victories: The University of Minnesota," *Collier's* 36:10, Dec. 2, 1905, 19; "Buying Football Victories: The University of Wisconsin," *Collier's* 36:8, Nov. 18, 1905, 22–23. For the accusation against Jordan, see "Jordan's Frenzied Athletics Received with Contempt," *MD*, Nov. 21, 1905, 2. On the Australian ballot, see Eldon Cobb Evans, *A History of the Australian Ballot System in the United States* (Chicago: University of Chicago Press, 1917), 17–21.

19. On the Wisconsin Idea, see Merle Curti and Vernon Carstensen, *The University of Wisconsin: A History, 1848–1925*, 2 vols. (Madison: University of Wisconsin Press, 1949), 2:3–4, 23–24, 132; Nancy C. Unger, *Fighting Bob LaFollette: The Righteous Reformer* (Chapel Hill: University of North Carolina Press, 2000), 121–122; Maureen A. Flanagan, *America Transformed: Progressives and Progressivisms, 1890s–1920s* (New York: Oxford University Press, 2007), 86–87; Charles McCarthy, *The Wisconsin Idea* (New York: Macmillan, 1912); Frederick Jackson Turner, quoted in McCarthy, *Wisconsin Idea*, 124–125, 139–140. Frederic C. Howe, *Wisconsin: An Experiment in Democracy* (New York: Charles Scribner's Sons, 1912). On extension, see Curti and Carstensen, *University of Wisconsin*, 1:640, 711–731; 2:88, 109–110, 474–475,

549–590; Joseph F. Kett, *The Pursuit of Knowledge under Difficulties: From Self-Improvement to Adult Education in America, 1750–1990* (Stanford, CA: Stanford University Press, 1994), 182–189, 277–283. On the scholarship of crowd psychology at the turn of the century, see Zimmerman, *Panic!* 30–32; Robert A. Nye, *The Origins of Crowd Psychology: Gustave Le Bon and the Crisis of Mass Democracy in the Third Republic* (London: Sage, 1975).

20. Frederick Jackson Turner, "Speech at Alumni Banquet," Frederick Jackson Turner Papers, Box 2, Folder "Football," WHS. On Turner's Big Nine proposal and the reaction, see Curti and Carstensen, *University of Wisconsin*, 2:536–540; John Sayle Watterson, *College Football: History, Spectacle, Controversy* (Baltimore: Johns Hopkins University Press, 2000), 85–92. On the "strenuous life," see Theodore Roosevelt, *The Strenuous Life: Essays and Addresses* (1899; New York: Century, 1905), 1–21. Turner's conclusions about character were not surprising, considering his "frontier thesis," which argued that America's democratic character emerged on the frontier; Turner, "Significance of the Frontier in American History," in *The Frontier in American History* (1920; New York: Dover, 1996), 1–38. One of Turner's graduate students even wrote about sport's relationship to the closing of the frontier; Frederic L. Paxson, "The Rise of Sport," *Mississippi Valley Historical Review* 4 (Sept. 1917): 143–168.

21. Woodrow Wilson, "What Is a College For?" in Wilson, *The Papers of Woodrow Wilson*, ed. Arthur S. Link, 69 vols. (Princeton, NJ: Princeton University Press, 1975), 19:334–337. On Wilson's relation to Ely, see Clifford F. Thies and Gary M. Pecquet, "The Shaping of a Future President's Economic Thought: Richard T. Ely and Woodrow Wilson at 'The Hopkins,'" *Independent Review* 15:2 (Fall 2010): 257–277.

22. Albert Shaw, "College Reform—And Football," *American Review of Reviews*, Dec. 1909, 724–726. On Shaw, see Lloyd J. Graybar, *Albert Shaw of the* Review of Reviews: *An Intellectual Biography* (Lexington: University of Kentucky Press, 1974). On Ely, see Rader, *Academic Mind*, 26–27; Rodgers, *Atlantic Crossings,* 97–101, 132–136. For Shaw's correspondence with Wilson, see Wilson, *Papers of Woodrow Wilson*, 19:606.

23. Shaw, "College Reform—And Football," 724, 726–728. On Jack Johnson, see Geoffrey C. Ward, *Unforgivable Blackness: The Rise and Fall of Jack Johnson* (New York: Knopf, 2004).

24. On segregation and nativism in the Progressive Era, see McGerr, *Fierce Discontent*, 182–218. On the dubious "whiteness" of new immigrants, see

David R. Roediger, *Working toward Whiteness: How America's Immigrants Became White* (New York: Basic Books, 2005), and Thomas A. Guglielmo, *White on Arrival: Italians, Race, Color, and Power in Chicago, 1890–1945* (New York: Oxford University Press, 2003). On fears of consumerism and celebrity in the early 1900s, see Warren Susman, *Culture as History: The Transformation of American Society in the Twentieth Century* (New York: Pantheon, 1984), 122–149, 271–285.

25. Ross, *Social Psychology*, 84, 87.

26. Josiah Royce, "Some Relations of Physical Training to the Present Problems of Moral Education in America," in *Race Questions, Provincialism, and Other American Problems* (New York: Macmillan, 1908), 229–287. On the philosophy of "loyalty," see John Clendenning, *The Life and Thought of Josiah Royce* (Madison: University of Wisconsin Press, 1985), 321–328. Early 1900s playground proponents used similar arguments; see Dominick Cavallo, *Muscles and Morals: Organized Playgrounds and Urban Reform, 1880–1920* (Philadelphia: University of Pennsylvania Press, 1981), 1–8.

27. "College Sports to Be Discussed," *NYT*, Oct. 23, 1909, 13. On Moran, see Stanley Coulter, "Thomas Francis Moran: An Appreciation," *Indiana Magazine of History* 25:1 (Mar. 1929): 47–51; William Murray Hepburn and Louis Martin Sears, *Purdue University: Fifty Years of Progress* (Indianapolis: Hollenbeck 1925), 166.

28. Thomas F. Moran, "Courtesy and Sportsmanship in Intercollegiate Athletics" (originally delivered Dec. 28, 1909, at the IAAUS annual meeting in New York), *American Physical Education Review* 15 (Feb. 1910): 118–124.

29. Moran, "Courtesy and Sportsmanship," 1–3, 6–7. On the history of the coaching profession, see Watterson, *College Football*, 40–43, 55–56; Mrozek, *Sport and American Mentality*, 67–68, 73–75.

30. On Arthur Woodford, see "Editorial," *Indiana Daily Student* 11:7 ([May] 1885), 154, Reference File, IUB; "Johns Hopkins University," *NYT*, June 14, 1891, 11; Arthur B. Woodford, "On the Use of Silver Money in the United States," *Annals of the American Academy of Political and Social Science* 4 (1893): 91–149; "Special Labor Agents," *AC*, May 16, 1885, 1. On George Petrie, as well as the origins of the Georgia-Auburn rivalry, see Leo Andrew Doyle, "Causes Won, Not Lost: Football and Southern Culture, 1892–1983" (Ph.D. diss., Emory University, 1998), 1–63; Brenda Harper Mattson, "George Petrie: The Early Years, 1866–1892" (M.A. thesis, Auburn University, 1983); "Athletes of Auburn," *AC*, Apr. 17, 1892, 16; "Football Man Tells of Game,"

AC, Nov. 13, 1898, 22. On McCarthy, see "University Throws Open Its Doors," *AC*, Sept. 16, 1897, 4; "First Game of Varsity Teams," *AC*, Oct. 4, 1897, 7; "Vanderbilt Will Play University," *AC*, Oct. 23, 1898, 9; "Georgia Goes Home in Triumph," *AC*, Oct. 31, 1898, 5; "Points by the Way," *AC*, Nov. 17, 1897, 4.

31. David Starr Jordan, draft of letter to S. F. Lieb (c. 1900), RCP, Box 1, Folder 1; J. M. Stillman to Josiah Royce (c. March 1901) and Royce to Stillman, March 17, 1901, Stillman scrapbook, RCP, Box 3, SUA. On Ross's dismissal, see Weinberg, *Edward Alsworth Ross*, 42–55.

32. Jordan to Ross, June 15, 1900, RCP, Box 1, Folder 4; Jordan to Ray L. Wilbur (c. 1903), RCP, Box 1, Folder 2, SUA; Jordan to Hadley, Nov. 19, 1900, ATH, RU 25, YRG 2-A, Series I, Box 49, Folder 0958, YUA.

33. E. A. Ross to Jane Stanford, May 19, 1900, DSJ, Reel 26, Frames 413–419; David Starr Jordan to Stanford, May 21, 1900, DSJ, Reel 26, Frames 431–437; Jordan to Stanford, Oct. 4, 1900, RCP, Box 1, Folder 4, SUA.

34. See Richard Hofstadter and Walter P. Metzger, *The Development of Academic Freedom in the United States* (New York: Columbia University Press, 1955), 441–442.

35. Ellen W. Schrecker, *No Ivory Tower: McCarthyism and the Universities* (New York: Oxford University Press, 1986), 15–16, 23. On Ely's trial, see Rader, *Academic Mind*, 130–158; Hofstadter and Metzger, *Development of Academic Freedom*, 426–436. On the downfall of Wisconsin progressivism, see Curti and Carstensen, *University of Wisconsin*, 2:71.

36. Thorstein Veblen, *The Higher Learning in America: A Memorandum on the Conduct of Universities by Business Men* (1918; New York: Hill and Wang, 1957), 90–92, 97. On Veblen's tempestuous career, see Rick Tilman, *The Intellectual Legacy of Thorstein Veblen: Unresolved Issues* (Westport, CT: Greenwood Press, 1996), 21–24; Stephen Edgell, *Veblen in Perspective: His Life and Thought* (Armonk, NY: M. E. Sharpe, 2001), 19–20, 24–25; Julie A. Reuben, *The Making of the Modern University: Intellectual Transformation and the Marginalization of Morality* (Chicago: University of Chicago Press, 1996), 195–200.

37. Edward Alsworth Ross, *Seventy Years of It: An Autobiography* (New York: D. Appleton, 1936), 101–103.

5. COACHES: IN THE DISCIPLINARY ARENA

1. Heather Munro Prescott, *Student Bodies: The Influence of Student Health Services in American Society and Medicine* (Ann Arbor: University of Michigan Press, 2007), 34–37; J. Edmund Welch, *Edward Hitchcock, MD: Founder*

of Physical Education in the College Curriculum (1962; Greenville, NC: East Carolina College, 1966), 140–146. On anthropometry's origins, see Ann Fabian, *The Skull Collectors: Race, Science, and America's Unburied Dead* (Chicago: University of Chicago Press, 2010), 178–183.

2. Jay W. Seaver, *Anthropometry and Physical Examination: A Book for Practical Use in Connection with Gymnastic Work and Physical Education* (New Haven, CT: Tuttle, Morehouse, and Taylor, 1890), 121, 9–15.

3. Prescott, *Student Bodies*, 35–37; Edward Cummings, "The Harvard Exhibit at the World's Fair," *HGM* 2:5 (Sept. 1893), 61–62. On the Midway, see Robert W. Rydell, *All the World's a Fair: Visions of Empire at American International Expositions, 1876–1916* (Chicago: University of Chicago Press, 1984), 40–41, 57, 60–68; James Gilbert, *Perfect Cities: Chicago's Utopias of 1893* (Chicago: University of Chicago Press, 1991), 109–114.

4. Dudley A. Sargent to Charles William Eliot, July 26, 1888, CWE, UAI 5.150, Box 16, Folder "1888, P-T"; Charles Eliot Norton to Charles William Eliot, Sept. 1, 1884, CWE, Box 11, Folder "1884, J-Pl," HUA; Kim Townsend, *Manhood at Harvard: William James and Others* (New York: Norton, 1996), 101. On Norton's involvement on Harvard's athletic committee, see Kermit Vanderbilt, *Charles Eliot Norton: Apostle of Culture in a Democracy* (Cambridge, MA: Harvard University Press, 1959), 135.

5. Dudley A. Sargent to Charles William Eliot, Sept. 6, 1892, CWE, Box 22, Folder "1892, S-Sh," HUA. In 1907 President Eliot and the Harvard Corporation asked Sargent to give up his salary yet maintain his summer school at the Hemenway Gymnasium; Eliot to Sargent, July 6, 1907, CWE, Box 119, Folder "Sargent . . . 1904–1908," HUA. On Sargent and Sullivan, see John F. Kasson, *Houdini, Tarzan, and the Perfect Man: The White Male Body and the Challenge of Modernity in America* (New York: Hill and Wang, 2001), 41–46.

6. Robin Lester, *Stagg's University: The Rise, Decline, and Fall of Big-Time Football at Chicago* (Urbana: University of Illinois Press, 1995). On the negotiations, see Amos Alonzo Stagg to William Rainey Harper, Nov. 25, 1890, and Nov. 28, 1891, WRH, Folder 13-38, UCA.

7. On competition, see Stagg to Harper, March 8, 1892, WRH, Folder 13-38 (original emphasis), UCA. On Williams, see Stagg to Harper, March 30, 1892, WRH, Folder 13-38 (original emphasis), UCA.

8. Emmett Angell to Charles Van Hise, Dec. 31, 1909, CRVH, RG 4/10/01, Folder 17-241, UWA. See also C. L. Brewer to E. B. Norris, Dec. 30, 1909, CRVH, Folder 17-241; Edward Cochems to Van Hise, Dec. 27, 1909, CRVH, 17-

241, UWA. Angell's book was *Play: Comprising Games for the Kindergarten, Playground, Schoolroom and College* (Boston: Little, Brown, 1910).

9. On temperate habits and gentlemanliness, see Frank Haggerty to Van Hise, Dec. 27, 1909; W. G. Anderson to Van Hise, Jan. 25, 1910; Geo[rge] Liscomb to Van Hise, Mar. 3, 1910; Harold Burton to Van Hise; CRVH, Folder 17-241, UWA. On military discipline, see John Corbett to Van Hise, Jan. 4, 1910, CRVH, Folder 17-241, UWA.

10. Gulick to Van Hise, Feb. 8, 1910; Sargent to Van Hise, Jan. 11, 1910, CRVH, Folder 18-268, UWA. One professor said that Hetherington could "purify athletics" because he was "physically vigorous, active and aggressive, and . . . strong with his dealing with men and events"; Charles Greene to Van Hise, Jan. 10, 1910, CRVH, Folder 18-268, UWA.

11. Hall to Van Hise, Jan. 15, 1910, CRVH, Folder 18-268; Hetherington to Van Hise, Apr. 22, 1910, CRVH, Folder 17-241, UWA. On Hall, see Gail Bederman, *Manliness and Civilization: A Cultural History of Gender and Race in the United States, 1880–1917* (Chicago: University of Chicago Press, 1995), 77–120; Dorothy Ross, *G. Stanley Hall: The Psychologist as Prophet* (Chicago: University of Chicago Press, 1972), 279–340.

12. Amos Alonzo Stagg to William Rainey Harper, July 6, 1905, AAS, 9-10, UCA.

13. Corwin to Frederic Allen, Dec. 22, 1914 (copy), RNC, YRG 38-A, Series I, Department of Athletics, Physical Education and Recreation Records 1912–1919, RU 507, Box 1, Folder 2; Corwin to Vance McCormick, Dec. 12, 1915 (copy), RNC, Box 9, Folder 100; Corwin to John Field, Feb. 28, 1917 (copy), RNC, Box 8, Folder 97, YUA. On amateurism in New England, see Townsend, *Manhood at Harvard*, 107–108, 115–116.

14. H. Shindle Wingert to William O. Thompson, Jan. 4, 1912, WOT, Folder 3/e/7/2; Wingert to Thompson, Mar. 20, 1915, WOT, 3/e/7/3, OSU (original emphasis). On the OSU athletic department, see James E. Pollard, *History of the Ohio State University: The Story of Its First Seventy-Five Years, 1873–1948* (Columbus: Ohio State University Press, 1952), 193, 209.

15. Ira Hollis, Report on Athletic Sports, Nov. 18, 1899, CWE, Box 27, Folder "Athletic Committee, 1894–1903," HUA.

16. William T. Reid, Jr., to Christine Reid, Jan. 6, 1905, WTR, HUG 4736.14, Box 6, Folder "Christine Lincoln . . . 1905," HUA.

17. William T. Reid, Sr., to Dean Ames, Apr. 13, 1899 (copy), Correspondence and Related Papers: Reid Family, 1863–1970, HUG 4736.12, Box 1,

Folder "William T. Reid, Sr. 1900—Correspondence"; Reid, Sr., to Reid, Jr., Mar. 31, 1901, WTR, Box 5, Folder "William T. Reid, Sr., 1901 (2 of 2)"; Reid, Sr., to LeBaron Briggs, Dec. 3, 1901 (copy), WTR, Box 5, Folder "William T. Reid, Sr., 1902"; Reid, Sr., to Reid, Jr., May 1, 1906, WTR, Box 6, Folder "William T. Reid, Sr., 1906 (1 of 2)," HUA.

18. William T. Reid, Jr., "Football and Coaching," *HGM* 15:59 (Mar. 1907), 401. Ronald A. Smith, "Afterword," in *Big-Time Football at Harvard, 1905: The Diary of Coach Bill Reid*, ed. Ronald A. Smith (Urbana: University of Illinois Press, 1994), 324.

19. "Football Situation—Explanation of Report by Coach Reid," *HGM* 14:55 (Mar. 1906), 489 (quote); "Reid Condemns Football," *HGM* 14:54 (Dec. 1905), 300; Charles William Eliot, "Topics from the President's Report," *HGM* 14:55 (Mar. 1906), 406; R. B. Merriman, "Football Reform," *HGM* 14:55 (Mar. 1906), 426–427. On Reid's life as a journeyman coach, see correspondence between Bill and Christine Reid, WTR, Box 6, HUA; Smith, "Afterword," 326–329. For critiques of the reforms, see J. William White, "Football and Its Critics," *Outlook*, Nov. 18, 1905, 666; Eliot, "Rational College Sports," *HGM* 15:59 (Mar. 1907), 385.

20. Amos Alonzo Stagg to Walter Camp, Mar. 4, 1911, WCP, Reel 16, Frame 616.

21. Parke H. Davis to Walter Camp, Jan. 23, 1913, WCP, Reel 7, Frame 181; Herbert Reed, *Football for Public and Player* (New York: Frederick A. Stokes, 1913), 188, 198–199, 200–207. See also Alex Ishkanian to Camp, Jan. 30, 1915, WCP, Reel 11, Frame 10. On Davis's "Record Office," see his correspondence with Stagg, 1931–1932, AAS, Folders 1a-16 and 1a-17, UCA. Davis wrote *Football: The American Intercollegiate Game* (New York: Scribner's, 1911).

22. Clifford Putney, *Muscular Christianity: Manhood and Sports in Protestant America, 1880–1920* (Cambridge, MA: Harvard University Press, 2001), 60–61; Lester, *Stagg's University*, 8–20; Williams to Minnesota Football Candidates, Sept. 5, 1916 (copy), RNC, Box 8, Folder 96, YUA. Williams quoted Luke 9:62: "He who having put his hand to the plow, and turneth back, is not fit for the Kingdom of Heaven" (King James Version of the Christian Bible).

23. Morris Gray to A. Lawrence Lowell, Mar. 11, 1912; ALL, UAI 5.160, Series 1919–1914, Folder 83, HUA.

24. Brown's President William H. P. Faunce, without intended irony, proclaimed, "There is no bigger white man on the team than Fred Pollard." See John M. Carroll, *Fritz Pollard: Pioneer in Racial Advancement* (Urbana: Uni-

versity of Illinois Press, 1992), 41–127, 59, 67–68, 100–106. On Paul Robeson, see Martin Bauml Duberman, *Paul Robeson* (New York: Knopf, 1988), 19–25.

25. Sport historians have virtually ignored these manuals, especially those published in the 1900s. Oriard discusses 1890s manuals by Camp and Deland in *Reading Football: How the Popular Press Created an American Spectacle* (Chapel Hill: University of North Carolina Press, 1993); he does not discuss manuals by Haughton, Heisman, Jones, Rockne, Yost, and Zuppke in *King Football: Sport and Spectacle in the Golden Age of Radio and Newsreels, Movies and Magazines, the Weekly and the Daily Press* (Chapel Hill: University of North Carolina Press, 2001), 437–470 (bibliography).

26. Walter Camp, *American Football* (1891; New York, 1974), 69, 158, 167–173. Amos Alonzo Stagg, with Henry L. Williams, *A Scientific and Practical Treatise on American Football for Schools and Colleges* (Hartford, CT: Case, Lockwood & Branard, 1893), 3–4, 11, 50–55, 264; a condensed version was titled *Simple Explanations of the Great Game of Football, with Diagrams for Spectators.* Walter Camp and Lorin Deland, *Football* (Boston: Houghton Mifflin, 1896), 46–48, 33; chapter 4 (32–39) is titled "How to Watch a Game."

27. See correspondence among Walter Camp, Lorin Deland, and Houghton Mifflin, Sept. 1899 to Apr. 1901, Houghton Mifflin Company Records, Folder "Camp . . . Deland—Football: contract, copyright records, 1896," MS Am 2346 (475), Houghton Library, Harvard University, Cambridge, MA. See also Deland to Camp, Sept. 23, 1899, WCP, Reel 7, Frames 244–246. In 1906, Deland even recommended abolishing ticket sales; "Football Situation—Additional Report by Lorin F. Deland" *HGM* 14:55 (Mar. 1906), 488.

28. Fielding H. Yost, *Football for Player and Spectator* (Ann Arbor, MI: University Publishing Company, 1905), 10–13.

29. "Yost's Football Text-Book Makes Big Hit," *MD*, Sept. 28, 1905, 1; Editorial, *MD*, Sept. 28, 1905, 2.

30. Fielding Yost, "Winning Plays in Football" (c. 1920s), 2, and "Sportsmanship" (c. 1920s), 1, FHY, Box 7, Folder "Miscellaneous Papers on Athletics," BHL. See also Yost, untitled address (c. 1926), 3, and "Sign Boards along the Highway of Life to the Goal of Success, Victory and Happiness" (c. early 1930s), 1, FHY, Box 7, Folder "Miscellaneous Papers on Athletics," BHL. For his views on race and "eugenics," see Yost, "Race Betterment" (c. 1920s), 2, 3, 6, FHY, Box 7, Folder "Miscellaneous Papers on Athletics," BHL; Yost, *Football for Player and Spectator*, 14. On eugenics, see Daniel J. Kevles, *In the Name of Eugenics: Genetics and the Uses of Human Heredity* (1985; Cambridge,

MA: Harvard University Press, 1995). In the 1920s Yost did cowrite an obscure pamphlet: Fielding Yost and George Little, *Football Notes: A Series of Lectures Delivered to the Classes in Football at the University of Michigan* (Ann Arbor, MI: Elton E. Wieman/O. D. Morrill, 1924).

31. William W. Roper, *Winning Football* (New York: Dodd, Mead, 1920), vii, 15–16, 19. Roper also published *Football, Today and Tomorrow* (New York: Duffield, 1927). Michael Oriard notes that 1920s coaches usually belonged to one of two broad categories: Pop or Biff. Pop was a "father figure" who earned respect and adoration, while the Biff coach was usually "profane" and ruthless; see Oriard, *King Football*, 146–151. Bill Reid even claimed that he pumped valuable information and "fatherly advice" from Fielding Yost simply by acting like a good son; see Reid, Jr., to Christine Reid, Aug. 29, 1905, and Aug. 30, 1905, WTR, Box 6, Folder "Christine Lincoln . . . 1905," HUA.

32. John W. Heisman, *Principles of Football* (St. Louis: Sports Publishing Bureau, 1922), 1–3, 5–6, 16–18.

33. "Clemson Comes to Meet Tech," *AC*, Oct. 17, 1903, 8; "Coach Heisman Tells Why His Teams Are Successful," *AC*, Oct. 19, 1903, 7; "Coach Heisman Writes about Sewanee's Charges," *AC*, Nov. 19, 1903, 6.

34. Percy D. Haughton, *Football and How to Watch It*, introduction by Heywood Broun (Boston: Marshall Jones, 1922), 3, 6, 10, 26, 85–86, 89–90. See also Reed, *Football for Public and Player*, 186–187.

35. Heisman, *Principles*, 7–8; Roper, *Winning Football*, vii, 15–16, 19; James Harrison, "Sports of the Times," *NYT*, Dec. 2, 1927, 29.

36. "Haughton Is Chosen Coach at Columbia," *NYT*, March 11, 1923, S1; Mark F. Bernstein, *Football: The Ivy League Origins of an American Obsession* (Philadelphia: University of Pennsylvania Press, 2001), 126–127.

37. Howard H. Jones, *How to Coach and Play Football* (Iowa City: Clio Press, 1923), 9, 122–128. Haughton's title page in *Football and How to Watch It* read "Harvard Coach, 1908–1916."

38. "Name Howard Jones Coach at U.S.C.," *LAT*, Feb. 4, 1925, B1; Bill Henry, "Observations," *LAT*, Feb. 4, 1925, B2; "Eckersall Asserts Coast Sports on Par with America's Foremost College Athletics," *LAT*, Feb. 15, 1925, A8; "Howard Jones Made Coach of Trojan Eleven," *CT*, Feb. 4, 1925, 18; Raymond Schmidt, *Shaping College Football: The Transformation of an American Sport, 1919–1930* (Syracuse, NY: Syracuse University Press, 2007), 17–18; Oriard, *King Football*, 79–80.

39. Knute K. Rockne, *Coaching: The Way of the Winner*, rev. ed. (1925; New York: Devin-Adair, 1928), vii–ix; Knute K. Rockne and Walter E. Meanwell, *Training, Conditioning, and the Care of Injuries* (Madison, WI, 1931), 16, 34; Glenn Scobey Warner, *A Course in Football for Players and Coaches* (Carlisle, PA, 1912), 14–19.

40. Murray Sperber, *Shake Down the Thunder: The Creation of Notre Dame Football* (New York: Henry Holt, 1993), 139–148, 194–195, 237–238, 270–285, 328–333, 350–352.

41. Glenn Scobey Warner, *Football for Coaches and Players* (Stanford, CA: Stanford University Press, 1927), vii–viii. On Carlisle's success under Warner, see John S. Steckbeck, *Fabulous Redmen: The Carlisle Indians and Their Famous Football Teams* (Harrisburg, PA: J. Horace McFarland, 1951), 127–130. On federal Indian boarding schools, see David W. Adams, *Education for Extinction: American Indians and the Boarding School Experience, 1875–1928* (Lawrence: University Press of Kansas, 1995).

42. He said his book was "a faithful reflection of the Illinois system of football with no childish holding back of 'pet' ideas and plays"; Robert C. Zuppke, assisted by Milton M. Olander, *Coaching Football* (Champaign, IL: Bailey & Himes, 1930), "Foreword."

43. Robert C. Zuppke, *Football Technique and Tactics*, 2nd rev. ed. (1922; Champaign, IL: Bailey & Himes, 1924), "Introductory Note"; Zuppke asst. Olander, *Coaching Football*, "Foreword." On Zuppke's biography, see "Brains, Not Brawn Gets Zuppke to Top," (Champaign) *News-Gazette*, Mar. 7, 1920, RCZ, RG 28/3/20, Box 6, Folder "Clippings 1920"; Athletic Publicity Office press release, Nov. 1957, undated biography, Box 8, Folder "Zuppke Biographical Materials (including contracts)," UIUC. For assertions of Zuppke's abilities and devotion to teach young men discipline, see, for example, Frank Menke, "Bob Zuppke—Maker of Men and Master Football Coach" ("From King Features Syndicate; for Release at WILL"), Feb. 22, 1930, RCZ, Box 1, Folder "1930," UIUC.

44. On sportsmanship, see Robert Zuppke, "Playing the Game," *Executives' Club News*, Jan. 24, 1930, 5–6, RCZ, Box 6, Folder "Newspaper & Magazine Articles . . . by Zuppke," UIUC. On his endorsements, see Rawlings poster, 1928; with Zuppke to Walter Bischoff (Rawlings Sales Manager), Apr. 1, 1928, RCZ, Box 1, Folder "1928," UIUC. See also "'Still a Chatterbox': Zuppke," *CT*, Jan. 12, 1956, B1.

45. Robert Zuppke, "Follow the Ball," *Chicago Daily News*, Sept. 25, 1925,

RCZ, Box 6, Folder "Newspaper & Magazine Articles . . . *by* Zuppke," UIUC. Later, Zuppke claimed to unite "theoretical, practical, and psychological aspects of the game"; *Coaching Football,* "Foreword."

46. J. W. Wilce, *Football: How to Play It and How to Understand It* (New York: Charles Scribner's Sons, 1923), 63.

47. On the shift to Freud in the early 1900s, see Nathan G. Hale, Jr., *Freud and the Americans: The Beginnings of Psychoanalysis in the United States, 1876–1917* (New York: Oxford University Press, 1971).

48. John M. Carroll, *Red Grange and the Rise of Modern Football* (Urbana: University of Illinois Press, 1999), 92–99. On 1920s coaches' hatred of professional sports, see Schmidt, *Shaping College Football,* 62–81.

49. Wiley Lee Umphlett, *Creating the Big Game: John W. Heisman and the Invention of American Football* (Westport, CT: Greenwood Press, 1992); Nat Brandt, *When Oberlin Was King of the Gridiron: The Heisman Years* (Kent, OH: Oberlin College, distributed by Kent State University Press, 2001); contract (Nov. 25, 1904), in Georgia Tech Athletic Association Records (UA #300), Series 2, Box 1, Folder 21 (Heisman Contracts), GTA. On the pamphlet, see Gerald Gems, "John William Heisman," *American National Biography,* 24 vols. (New York: Oxford University Press, 1999), 10:524–525. On Heisman's hiring at Rice, see Umphlett, *Creating the Big Game,* 191. In Rice's catalog, Heisman was listed among "Faculty"; Rice Institute, *Announcements for the Academic Year Beginning September Fourteenth Nineteen Hundred and Twenty-Five* ([Houston, 1925]). On coaches' salaries, see Ronald A. Smith, *Pay for Play: A History of Big-Time College Athletic Reform* (Urbana: University of Illinois Press, 2011), 64–66.

50. Many professors felt that Yost had muscled his way into the faculty; John Richard Behee, *Fielding Yost's Legacy to the University of Michigan* (Ann Arbor, MI: Ulrich's Books, 1971), 196–197, 204–205.

51. On OSU, see Pollard, *History of Ohio State,* 210, 215; on Iowa, see State University of Iowa, *Catalogue 1924–1925; Including Announcements for 1925–1926* (Iowa City, [1925]), 147; on Illinois, see University of Illinois, *Annual Register, 1933–1934* (Urbana-Champaign, IL, 1934), 167, 169. On the "Gates Plan" at Penn, see Smith, *Pay for Play,* 72–73.

52. Yost, "Future Trends in Varsity Athletics" (c. 1920s), 2, 3, FHY, Box 7, Folder "Speeches (2)"; James O. Murfin to Charles Baird, Dec. 2, 1907, Box 1, Folder "July–Dec. 1907," Charles Baird Papers, BHL.

53. LeBaron R. Briggs to A. Lawrence Lowell, Mar. 27, 1922, ALL, Series

1919–1922, Folder 96; Bingham to Lowell, Feb. 26, 1927, ALL, Series 1925–1928, Folder 598, HUA.

6. STADIUMS: BETWEEN CAMPUS AND CULTURE

1. Ira N. Hollis to Charles William Eliot (1900–01 Athletic Report), Jan. 2, 1902, CWE, UAI 5.150 (CWE), Box 46, Folder "Hollis, Ira N., 1893–1903 1 of 2," HUA. On Harvard Stadium, see Ronald A. Smith, "Commercialized Intercollegiate Athletics and the 1903 Harvard Stadium," *New England Quarterly* 78:1 (Mar. 2005): 40–46; Robert C. Trumpbour, *The New Cathedrals: Politics and Media in the History of Stadium Construction* (Syracuse, NY: Syracuse University Press, 2007), 15–16. On stadiums in general, see Raymond Schmidt, *Shaping College Football: The Transformation of an American Sport, 1919–1930* (Syracuse, NY: Syracuse University Press, 2007), 39–61; Ronald A. Smith, "Far More Than Commercialism: Stadium Building from Harvard's Innovations to Stanford's 'Dirt Bowl,'" *International Journal of the History of Sport* 25:11 (Sept. 2008): 1455–1467; John Sayle Watterson, *College Football: History, Spectacle, Controversy* (Baltimore: Johns Hopkins University Press, 2000), 143–157; Michael Oriard, *King Football: Sport and Spectacle in the Golden Age of Radio and Newsreels, Movies and Magazines, the Weekly and the Daily Press* (Chapel Hill: University of North Carolina Press, 2001), 6–7; John M. Carroll, *Red Grange and the Rise of Modern Football* (Urbana: University of Illinois Press, 1999), 59–76; Robert M. Soderstrom, *The Big House: Fielding H. Yost and the Building of Michigan Stadium* (Ann Arbor, MI: Huron River Press, 2005). On the ties among sport, nationalism, and militarism, see S. W. Pope, *Patriotic Games: Sporting Traditions in the American Imagination, 1876–1926* (New York: Oxford University Press, 1997).

2. On urban intercollegiate contests, see Ronald A. Smith, *Sports and Freedom: The Rise of Big-Time College Athletics* (New York: Oxford University Press, 1988), 78–82. On Chicago, see Horace Butterworth, "Athletic Field," AAS, Folder 20-5, UCA; Amos Alonzo Stagg to Wallace Heckman, Nov. 2, 1910 (copy), AAS, Folder 9-13, UCA. On Yale Field, see "Yale Preparing for Big Football Year," *NYT*, Sept. 1, 1912, S4.

3. William Rainey Harper to Amos Alonzo Stagg, Apr. 7, 1896, AAS, Folder 9-2; Harper to Stagg, Apr. 29, 1902, AAS, 9-5; Harper to Stagg, Nov. 21, 1905, and Stagg to Harper, Nov. 22, 1905 (copy), AAS, Folder 9-10, UCA. On the 1902 grandstand collapse, see correspondence among Stagg, Harper, Heckman et al., in AAS, Folder 9-13, UCA.

4. [Stagg] to Heckman, Nov. 23, 1905, and Nov. 29, 1905 (copies); Heckman to Stagg, Dec. 1, 1905, AAS, 9-13. On a 1902 crowd control problem, see Horace Butterworth to William Rainey Harper, Oct. 12, 1902, AAS, 9-6, UCA.

5. Henry Lee Higginson, "Soldiers' Field," in *Four Addresses* (Boston: Merrymount, 1902), 3–32. On Civil War memory, see David W. Blight, *Race and Reunion: The Civil War in American Memory* (Cambridge, MA: Harvard University Press, 2001).

6. "Mass Meeting," *WDC*, Mar. 27, 1893, 1; "Fair Grounds," *WDC*, Feb. 9, 1893, 1; "Students en Masse," *WDC*, Mar. 29, 1893, 1; "Are Wide Awake," *WDC*, Apr. 14, 1893, 1; "Randall Field or Camp Randall," *WDC*, Sept. 25, 1894), 3. On the GAR, see Stuart McConnell, *Glorious Contentment: The Grand Army of the Republic, 1865–1900* (Chapel Hill: University of North Carolina Press, 1992), 125–205; Camp Randall Subject File, Folder 1, UWA. See also John Pettegrew, "'The Soldier's Faith': Turn-of-the-Century Memory of the Civil War and the Emergence of Modern American Nationalism," *Journal of Contemporary History* 31:1 (Jan. 1996): 70 n.4.

7. "Proposed Stadium," *HGM*, June 1903, 647–648; Ira N. Hollis, "Stadium," *HGM*, Mar. 1904, 344–346. Some students semi-seriously suggested the name "Holliseum"; "Prof. Hollis's Retirement," *HGM* 12:45 (Sept. 1903), 78–89. On Olmsted, see Witold Rybczynski, *A Clearing in the Distance: Frederick Law Olmsted and America in the Nineteenth Century* (New York: Scribner, 1999), 423–426.

8. Ira N. Hollis, "Origin of the Harvard Stadium," *Harvard Engineering Journal* 3:2 (June 1904): 97; Hollis to Charles William Eliot (1900–01 Athletic Report), Jan. 2, 1902, CWE, Box 46, Folder "Hollis, Ira N., 1893–1903 1 of 2," HUA; Hollis, "Stadium," 341–343.

9. Frederick W. Taylor and Sanford E. Thompson, *A Treatise on Concrete Plain and Reinforced: Materials, Construction, and Design of Concrete and Reinforced Concrete* (New York: John Wiley, 1905), frontispiece, 466–471. "Seventy-Nine's Great Gift," *HGM* 11:43 (Mar. 1903), 486.

10. Robert C. McMath et al., *Engineering the New South: Georgia Tech, 1885–1985* (Athens: University of Georgia Press, 1985), 111; "John W. Grant . . . Makes Possible Gigantic Stadium at the Georgia Tech at Cost of $100,000," *AC*, Apr. 1, 1913, 11; "New Tech Stadium to be Named for Hugh Inman Grant," *AC*, Apr. 14, 1913, 7; "Grant Field Will Seat 12,000 Fans with New Stands," *AC*, Aug. 15, 1915, A3.

11. "Gives to Princeton a $300,000 Stadium," *NYT*, Mar. 29, 1914, 2; "To

Rush Work on Stadium," *NYT*, Apr. 2, 1914, 9; "No Trouble with Crowd," *NYT*, Nov. 15, 1914, S2; "Tigers' Brace Comes Too Late," *NYT*, Nov. 15, 1914, S1.

12. "Gives to Princeton a $300,000 Stadium"; "To Open Tigers' Stadium," *NYT*, Oct. 19, 1914, 7.

13. "Yale's $700,000 Athletic Centre, with Sunken Stadium," *NYT*, June 9, 1912, SM5.

14. "New Yale Coliseum," *NYT*, May 25, 1912, 12.

15. "May Rent New Stadium," *NYT*, Dec. 29, 1912, 34; "Yale University Athletic Association—Finish the Bowl," AAS, Folder 20-4, UCA.

16. "Harvard and Yale Battle on Gridiron," *NYT*, Nov. 21, 1914, 14; "War in the Yale Bowl," *NYT*, Nov. 21, 1914, 12; "Harvard Beats Yale by 36 to 0," *NYT*, Nov. 22, 1914, 1.

17. On the SATC, see Carol S. Gruber, *Mars and Minerva: World War I and the Uses of the Higher Learning in America* (Baton Rouge: Louisiana State University Press, 1975), 213–252; David O. Levine, *The American College and the Culture of Aspiration, 1915–1940* (Ithaca, NY: Cornell University Press, 1986), 23–32. On campus military discipline, see "Faculty Approves Military Training," *MD*, Feb. 18, 1917, 1; *MI*, Nov. 1918, frontispiece. On the war's cultural effects, see Paul Fussell, *The Great War and Modern Memory* (1975; New York: Oxford University Press, 2000), 7–35. On postwar students, see Paula S. Fass, *The Damned and the Beautiful: American Youth in the 1920s* (New York: Oxford University Press, 1977), 370.

18. Carl D. Voltmer, *A Brief History of the Intercollegiate Conference of Faculty Representatives, with Special Consideration of Athletic Problems* (New York: Western Intercollegiate Conference, 1935), 28–31; Melvin Henry Gruensfelder, "A History of the Origin and Development of the Southeastern Conference" (M.S. thesis, University of Illinois, 1964), 16. On Harvard's choice to cease football, see "Athletics Adjourned," *HC*, Nov. 1, 1918, 2.

19. On Stanford's return to football, see "Fighting Spirit of Stanford Flares at Rally," *DPA*, Nov. 12, 1915, 1, 3; "Football Schedule Includes American and Rugby with California," *DPA*, Oct. 23, 1918, 1; Editorial, *DPA*, Oct. 23, 1918, 3; "American Football Is Decided by the Athletic Board," *DPA*, Feb. 12, 1919, 1. Trustee Herbert Hoover supported the return to football; see "Herbert Hoover Accepts Responsibility for Tuition Ruling and Supports Move," *DPA*, Oct. 16, 1919, 1. For student reactions to Michigan's return to the Big Nine, see "Athletic Board Votes 8–1 for Re-entering Conference," *MD*, Nov. 23,

1917, 1, 6; "Fortunate Step for Michigan," *MD*, Nov. 23, 1917, 2; Voltmer, *Brief History of the Intercollegiate Conference*, 27.

20. Editorials, *DPA*, Sept. 28, 1918, 2, and *DPA*, Oct. 25, 1918, 2; "Rah! Rah! Days Again?" *MI*, Feb. 1919, 31; "Problems of Returning Peace," *DPA*, Nov. 8, 1918, 2. See also David M. Kennedy, *Over Here: The First World War and American Society* (New York: Oxford University Press, 1980), 245–258.

21. On pep, see "Stanford and Pride," *DPA*, Aug. 8, 1919, 2. See also "Customs Committee Makes Report on Traditions," *DPA*, Nov. 18, 1919, 1, 2; "Why No Block 'M'?" *MD*, Nov. 5, 1919, 2. On Harvard's return to intercollegiate sport, see "Football," *HC*, Sept. 22, 1919, 2. For the critique of Harvard's lack of campus unity, see Editorial, *HM*, 13:1 (Oct. 1891), 38; Editorial, *HM* 17:1 (Oct. 1893), 36; Editorial, *HM* 33:3 (Dec. 1901), 124–125; H. M. Kallen, "The Honor System—A Symposium," *HM* 52:4 (June 1911), 128; Charles Merrill Rogers, Jr., "Harvard Indifference—A Homily for Freshmen," *HM* 57:1 (Oct. 1913), 2–4.

22. Maurice Dunne, quoted in "Campus Approves Conference Move," *MD*, Nov. 23, 1917, 6. On women's athletics at Stanford, see "Registration in Women's Athletics Reaches 300 Mark," *DPA*, Oct. 2, 1919, 2. On male students reclaiming space after the war, see "Law Steps," *DPA*, Nov. 13, 1918, 2; "Women and the Law Steps," *DPA*, Nov. 12, 1919, 2. On sex-segregated seating at football rallies, see "Annual Big Game Rally Will Be Held Tomorrow," *DPA*, Nov. 25, 1918, 1; "Reserved Seats," *DPA*, Nov. 25, 1918, 2; W. C. Palmer, "Explains Michigan Spirit," *MD*, Nov. 2, 1919, 4. On the shift from *manliness* to *masculinity*, see Gail Bederman, *Manliness and Civilization: A Cultural History of Gender and Race in the United States, 1880–1917* (Chicago: University of Chicago Press, 1995), 17–19.

23. Fielding H. Yost, *Football for Player and Spectator* (Ann Arbor, MI: University Publishing Company, 1905), 10–11, 21–22, 27–49; "Coach Yost Believes War Is Like Football," *MD*, Oct. 26, 1918, 1; Marion Burton, "To Our Guests," *Official Athletic Program* (Mich. vs. Minn., 1924), 5, Milton Starr Scrapbook, BHL. Herbert Reed also compared football to warfare; *Football for Public and Player* (New York: Frederick A. Stokes, 1913), v, 15–30.

24. On Jackson, see "Commandant at Purdue Is Aid in Building Eleven," *MD*, Oct. 22, 1918, 3. On Neyland, see James Montgomery, Stanley Folmsbee, and Lee Greene, *To Foster Knowledge: A History of the University of Tennessee, 1794–1970* (Knoxville: University of Tennessee Press, 1984), 356–359; Robert Neyland, *Football as a War Game: The Annotated Journals of General R. R.*

Neyland, ed. Andy Kozar (Nashville: Falcon Press, 2002). On Ingram, see E. O. Stiehm to Bryan, c. 1923, WLB, Folder "Stiehm E.O. 19——," IUB. On Saunders, see James Whiteside, *Colorado: A Sports History* (Niwot: University Press of Colorado, 1999), 204.

25. Walter Camp, *Football without a Coach* (New York: D. Appleton, 1920), vi, 2, 20–21. On the "Daily Dozen," see Franklin D. Roosevelt to Camp, June 2, 1917, WCP, Reel 15, Frame 263. See also Camp's correspondence with Herbert Hoover, May 22–28, 1917, WCP, Reel 10, Frames 521–524. On Camp's military service, see Richard P. Borkowski, "The Life and Contributions of Walter Camp to American Football" (Ed.D. diss., Temple University, 1979), 234–256.

26. Major Frank Cavanaugh, *Inside Football* (Boston: Small, Maynard, 1919), frontispiece, dedication, 1–2, 12–13. On Cavanaugh, see Oriard, *King Football*, 150–151. Charles O. Daly, *American Football: How to Play It* (New York: Harper, 1921), ix–x, frontispiece, "Football Axioms," 1, 30. On Daly, see Schmidt, *Shaping College Football*, 84.

27. Knute K. Rockne, *The Four Winners—The Head, the Hands, the Foot, the Ball* (New York: Devin-Adair, 1925), dedication, 36–38. See also Robert Zuppke, "10 Things a Boy Should Know How to Do!" rev. ed. (Milwaukee, 1934), 6, 18, RCZ, RG 28/3/20, Box 8, Folder "Zuppke Biographical Materials," UIUC.

28. On the flagpole, see "Commemorating Michigan's Heroes," *MD*, Oct. 7, 1919, 2; "Flagpole to Honor Dead," *MD*, Oct. 9, 1919, 1; "For Michigan Heroes," *MD*, Oct. 15, 1919, 2. On the rivalry with Harvard, see "Communication from 'Spirit' Scores Flagpole Plan; Urges Campus Gateway" (signed, "One Who Died Over There"), *MD*, Oct. 16, 1919, 1, 6. On proposals for new memorials, see "Memorial Problem," *MD*, Oct. 21, 1919, 2.

29. "Begin Excavations for Stanford Stadium," *LAT*, June 10, 1921, III2; "Stanford Stadium Almost Finished," *LAT*, August 19, 1921, III1; "Build Station for Big Football Game," *LAT*, October 24, 1921, I5; "Stanford Stadium is Almost Ready," *LAT*, October 24, 1921, I5; "Grid Plans to be Marked on Board," *LAT*, Nov. 2, 1921, I7; Bertha Vaughan, "Stadium, Ready for Game, is Great Accomplishment," *DPA*, Nov. 18, 1921, 7; "Ready by November 19!" *Stanford Pictorial*, Oct. 1921, 11. For the proposed use of memorial funds, see "From a Stanford Viewpoint," *Stanford Pictorial*, Dec. 1920, 69. See also Smith, "Far More than Commercialism," 1462–1464. On the groundbreaking, see John Pettegrew, *Brutes in Suits: Male Sensibility in America, 1890–1920* (Baltimore: Johns Hopkins University Press, 2007), 175.

30. "Huge Stadium to Be Built at Berkeley," *LAT*, Sept. 17, 1921, I4; "Stadium Built Like Theater," *LAT*, Sept. 24, 1921, I4; W. W. Campbell, "Annual Report of the President of the University, 1923–1924," *University of California Bulletin*, Third Series 18:6 (Berkeley, CA, 1924), 7; Bill Henry, "Golden Bears Dedicate New Stadium by Crushing Cardinals, 9 to 0," *LAT*, Nov. 25, 1923, 113. On Berkeley's enrollment figures, see "Where We Stand," *University of Illinois Memorial Stadium Notes*, July 1922, 1, "Stadium Drive, 1921–1927" (RG 2/6/0/5), Box 1, Folder "Notes 1922," UIUC; "Michigan Is Now Largest American University," *MD*, Oct. 19, 1905, 1.

31. *Ohio Stadium*, 2–5, WOT, 3/e/35/5, OSU. Drawings for the earlier, projected complex are in WOT, Folder 3/e/7/3, OSU. On campus enrollment numbers, see "Where We Stand"; "Michigan is Now Largest American University," *MD*, Oct. 19, 1905, 1.

32. Thomas C. Mendenhall, "Some Thoughts Regarding the Proposed Stadium" (report to trustees), c. Apr. 1921, WOT, 3/e/35/5, OSU. On flood control, see William Oxley Thompson, "Foreword," *Ohio Stadium*, 1, WOT, 3/e/35/5, OSU. On the stadium's eventual construction, see Osman C. Hooper, *History of the Ohio State University; Volume II: 1910 to 1925*, ed. Thomas C. Mendenhall ([Columbus]: Ohio State University Press, [1925]), 41–44.

33. On the stadium's advertising ability, see Trustee J. R. Lovejoy to E. S. Johnson, Nov. 23, 1920, WOT, 3/e/35/4, OSU. On how the stadium would bring together the university's "constituency," see Thompson's speech to faculty and students, Aug. 30, 1920, WOT, 3/e/35/5, OSU. On the claims of fundraisers, see "Selling Ohio Stadium—A Handbook for Canvassers" (Columbus: Ohio Stadium Committee, Ohio Union, Ohio State University), 5, 16, WOT, 3/e/35/5, OSU; "We Started Something," *Magnet*, Dec. 17, 1920, 2, WOT, 3/e/35/5, OSU.

34. C. C. Hayden to William Oxley Thompson, Mar. 25, 1921, WOT, 3/e/35/5; Thompson to Hayden, Mar. 28, 1921, and Thompson to L. S. Goddard, Apr. 14, 1921, and Thompson to Arthur Cunningham, Apr. 5, 1921, WOT, 3/e/35/5, OSU. On wartime concern about male physique, see Thomas Fleming, *The Illusion of Victory: America in World War I* (New York: Basic, 2003), 87; Pope, *Patriotic Games*, 121–138.

35. "Ohio Stadium," *Makio* 40 ([Columbus], 1921), [12]. On Ohio Stadium's finances, see "Ohio Plays to 200,000 who Pay $159,063 Net," *CT*, Jan. 21, 1923, A3.

36. Hugh Fullerton, "Ohio Dedicates Stadium Today with Wolverines,"

CT, Oct. 21, 1922, 11; Milton Springer to OSU Athletic Director, Mar. 14, 1921, WOT, 3/e/35/6, OSU.

37. *"Go Get That Stadium, Illini"* (handbill, c. 1922), Papers of Alumni Association–Executive Director's Office (RG 26/1/0/14), Box 1, Folder "Stadium Drive 1920–1924," UIUC.

38. University of Illinois, *The Story of the Stadium* (Urbana: University of Illinois, 1922), [28]. Students argued that they should make financial sacrifices to honor dead soldiers; *"Only through Sacrifice Are Great Deeds Accomplished"* (handbill, c. 1922), RG 26/1/0/14, Box 1, Folder "Stadium Drive, 1920–1924," UIUC.

39. George Huff quoted in "Presentation to the University," *University of Illinois Memorial Football Stadium Dedication Exercises* (Oct. 17, Oct. 18, 1924), 16, RG 26/1/0/14, Box 1, Folder "Stadium Drive 1920–1924," UIUC. Edmund J. James quoted in University of Illinois, *Story of the Stadium*, [35].

40. University of Illinois, *Story of the Stadium*, [17, 20]; "Trustees Favor Illini Stadium," *CT*, Dec. 16, 1920, 18.

41. "Facts about the University of Illinois, the Alumni Association and the Memorial Stadium and Recreation Field" ([Urbana], 1921), 11; see also "How Foreign Students at the University of Illinois Distinguished Themselves in the Great Drive for Stadium Funds," 9, RG 26/1/0/14, Box 1, Folder "Stadium Drive 1920–1924," UIUC.

42. "Stadium Captain—His Book," 6, 8–9, RG 26/1/0/14, Box 1, Folder "Stadium Campaign 1921," UIUC.

43. "Yale University Athletic Association—Finish the Bowl," 1920, AAS, Folder 20-4, UCA. On Michigan, see Soderstrom, *Big House*, 135–212, 318. On California, see "For Athletic Stadium," *LAT*, Oct. 1, 1921, II14.

44. "Trustees Fix Site of Stadium," "Plan Monster Athletic Field near Stadium," and "Stadium Organization," *University of Illinois Memorial Stadium Notes*, July 1922, 1–2, RG 2/6/0/5, Box 1, Folder *"Notes 1922,"* UIUC. On Chicago, see Robin Lester, *Stagg's University: The Rise, Decline, and Fall of Big-Time Football at Chicago* (Urbana: University of Illinois Press, 1995), 99.

45. See "Dykstra Defends Western Conference Football," *CT*, Jan. 3, 1940, 23; "Northwestern President Calls Football an Asset," *CT*, Jan. 5, 1940, 23; "Indiana Obeys Big 10 Code—President Wells," *CT*, Jan. 6, 1940, 17; "Iowa Wins with Honest Football—Gilmore," *CT*, Jan. 8, 1940, 19.

46. "Facts about . . . Memorial Stadium and Recreation Field," 13; University of Illinois, *Story of the Stadium*, [25]; Carroll, *Red Grange*, 3. For the

records of the campaign, see "Stadium Drive Record, 1921," RG 26/1/14, UIUC. On Nebraska, see McLaren Sawyer, *Centennial History of the University of Nebraska*, 2 vols. (Lincoln: University of Nebraska Press, 1973), 2:106.

47. On the relative size of Chicago's stadium, see "Huge Crowd to See Maroon-Badger Tilt," *CT*, Nov. 15, 1921, 23; "In the Wake of the News," *CT*, Nov. 15, 1925, A5. Minnesota's 55,000-seat, $2 million Memorial Stadium opened in 1924; "Gopher Football Coach Guest of Alumni Here," *CT*, June 6, 1923, 17; "Notre Dame to Make Minnesota Turnstiles Spin," *CT*, Oct. 4, 1925, A3. Indiana dedicated its Memorial Stadium (25,000 seats) in November 1925; "Indiana," *CT*, Nov. 19, 1925, 22. Michigan's 72,000-seat bowl opened in 1927; Soderstrom, *Big House*. On Big Ten stadium building in the 1920s, see Smith, "Far More than Commercialism," 1459–1460.

48. Amos Alonzo Stagg to Ernest Quantrell, Dec. 9, 1922 (copy), AAS, Folder 20-5; Stagg to William Harman, Jan. 31, 1922 (copy), AAS, Folder 20-5; Quantrell to Stagg, Dec. 5, 1922, AAS, Folder 20-5, UCA.

49. Lester, *Stagg's University*, 128–131; Stagg to Wallace Heckman, Sept. 14, 1923, AAS, 20-5; D. L. Christopher to UC Athletic Director, Apr. 25, 1933, AAS, 20-5; UCA.

50. On the Georgia Tech concession stand, see contracts between Spiller and J. B. Crenshaw, June 24, 1920, and May 24, 1921, Athletic Association Records, UA 300, Series 1, Box 1, Folder 8 ("Grant Field, 1915–1927"), GTA. On scoreboards, see William Rainey Harper to Amos Alonzo Stagg, Nov. 22, 1897, AAS, Folder 9-2, UCA.

51. On Marshall Field insurance, see Stagg to Wallace Heckman, Jan. 26, 1910 (copy); Heckman to Stagg, Feb. 15, 1910, and Feb. 23, 1910, AAS, Folder 9-13, UCA. On Georgia Tech, see policies in UA 300, Series 1, Box 1, Folder 10 ("Insurance Policies, 1921–1923"), GTA.

52. Myriam Vučković, *Voices from Haskell: Indian Students between Two Worlds, 1884–1928* (Lawrence: University Press of Kansas, 2008), 153–159. On Indians as symbols of anti-modernism, see Philip J. Deloria, *Playing Indian* (New Haven, CT: Yale University Press, 1998).

53. On Chief Illiniwek, see Carol Spindel, *Dancing at Halftime: Sports and the Controversy over American Indian Mascots* (New York: New York University Press, 2000), 83–95, 108–119; on pseudo-Indian sports pageantry, see Oriard, *King Football*, 291. On Native American mascots, see Jennifer Guiliano, "An American Spectacle: Collegiate Mascots and the Performance of Tradition" (Ph.D. diss., University of Illinois, 2010).

54. Paul K. Conkin, *Gone with the Ivy: A Biography of Vanderbilt University* (Knoxville: University of Tennessee Press, 1985), 309–310; Montgomery, Folmsbee, and Greene, *To Foster Knowledge*, 354; Peter Finney, *The Fighting Tigers, 1893–1993: One Hundred Years of LSU Football* (Baton Rouge: Louisiana State University Press, 1993), 78–79; Pamela Grundy, *Learning to Win: Sports, Education, and Social Change in Twentieth-Century North Carolina* (Chapel Hill: University of North Carolina Press, 2001), 102.

55. Charles Gurr, *The Personal Equation: A Biography of Steadman Vincent Sanford* (Athens: University of Georgia Press, 1999), 42, 88–96; Thomas Dyer, *University of Georgia: A Bicentennial History, 1785–1985* (Athens: University of Georgia Press, 1985), 183–184, 206. On the 1909 field, see "Want Athletic Field," *AC*, July 1, 1909, 7. On the stadium and Yale game, see "University's Need of a Stadium Stressed at Annual Banquet," *AC*, Dec. 16, 1926; "U. of Georgia Seeks to Bring Yale South," *AC*, Oct. 18, 1928, 11; "Georgia-Yale Game Has 'It,'" *AC*, Aug. 28, 1929, 15; "Game with Yale Will Dedicate Georgia Stadium," *AC*, Sept. 29, 1929, F1; "Great Iron Parade Will Move on Athens," *AC*, Oct. 6, 1929, A4; "Deeds of a Great Day," AC, Oct. 14, 1929, 4; "Yale Squad Begins Georgia Trip Today," *NYT*, Oct. 10, 1929, 37; "Cheers Speed Yale as Squad Entrains," *NYT*, Oct. 11, 1929, 42.

56. "University of Georgia News of Interest," *AC*, Sept, 29, 1929, D6; "'On to Athens' Is Slogan of Sports-Loving Atlantans," *AC*, Oct. 12, 1929, 9; "Holiday for Football," *NYT*, Oct. 13, 1929, E2.

57. "Joyous Hysteria Holds Athens in Happy Thralldom," *AC*, Oct. 13, 1929, 1.

58. "Yale Beaten, 15–0, by Georgia Eleven in a Stirring Game," *NYT*, Oct. 13, 1929, S1; Danzig, "Football's Growth Is Shown in Upsets," *NYT*, Oct. 14, 1929, 32.

59. Watterson, *College Football*, 143, 156.

7. ACADEMIC BACKLASH IN THE POST–WORLD WAR I ERA

1. G. T. W. Patrick to Dean Kay, Nov. 24, 1929; G. T. W. Patrick Faculty File (01.15.03), UIA. On Iowa's suspension, see Raymond Schmidt, "The 1929 Iowa Football Scandal: Paying Tribute to the Carnegie Report?" *Journal of Sport History* 34:3 (Fall 2007): 343–351.

2. Edwin R. A. Seligman et al., "Preliminary Report of the Joint Committee on Academic Freedom and Academic Tenure," *American Political Science Review* 9:2 (May 1915): 374–378. On the history of American academic freedom

and its European antecedents, see Frederick Rudolph, *The American College and University: A History* (1962; Athens: University of Georgia Press, 1990), 410–416; Laurence R. Veysey, *The Emergence of the American University* (Chicago: University of Chicago Press, 1965), 355–356, 416; Richard Hofstadter and Walter P. Metzger, *The Development of Academic Freedom in the United States* (New York: Columbia University Press, 1955), 396, 474–475; Ellen W. Schrecker, *No Ivory Tower: McCarthyism and the Universities* (New York: Oxford University Press, 1985), 14–23.

3. J. McKeen Cattell, *University Control* (New York: Science Press, 1913), 32–39, 47.

4. Philo A. Hutcheson, *A Professional Professoriate: Unionization, Bureaucratization, and the AAUP* (Nashville: Vanderbilt University Press, 2000), 1–9; Hofstadter and Metzger, *Development of Academic Freedom*, 476–495; "Report of the Committee of Inquiry on Conditions at the University of Utah, 1915," in *Professors on Guard: The First AAUP Investigations*, ed. Walter P. Metzger (New York: Arno, 1977).

5. Progressive historian Charles Beard famously resigned from Columbia in protest. See Hofstadter and Metzger, *Development of Academic Freedom*, 499–502; David S. Brown, *Beyond the Frontier: The Midwestern Voice in American Historical Writing* (Chicago: University of Chicago Press, 2009), 58–59; Michael Rosenthal, *Nicholas Miraculous: The Amazing Career of the Redoubtable Dr. Nicholas Murray Butler* (New York: Farrar, Straus and Giroux, 2006), 234–239.

6. Morris Janowitz, "Introduction," in *W. I. Thomas on Social Organization and Social Personality: Selected Papers*, ed. Morris Janowitz (Chicago: University of Chicago Press, 1966), xi ff. On the Mann Act, see David J. Langum, *Crossing over the Line: Legislating Morality and the Mann Act* (Chicago: University of Chicago Press, 1994).

7. On science and engineering, see David O. Levine, *The American College and the Culture of Aspiration, 1915–1940* (Ithaca, NY: Cornell University Press, 1986), 32–38; Daniel J. Kevles, *The Physicists: The History of a Scientific Community in Modern America* (1971; New York: Vintage, 1979), 102–184. On psychology and mental testing, see Henry L. Minton, *Lewis M. Terman: Pioneer in Psychological Testing* (New York: New York University Press, 1986), 62–126. On philosophical specialization, see Bruce Kuklick, *The Rise of American Philosophy: Cambridge, Massachusetts, 1860–1930* (New Haven, CT: Yale University Press, 1977), 451–452, 565–566. On historians' propaganda and postwar

silence, see Peter Novick, *That Noble Dream: The "Objectivity Question" and the American Historical Profession* (Cambridge, UK: Cambridge University Press, 1988), 112–132. On postwar social science, see Dorothy Ross, *Origins of American Social Science* (Cambridge, UK: Cambridge University Press, 1991), 390–470; Mark C. Smith, *Social Science in the Crucible: The American Debate over Objectivity and Purpose, 1918–1941* (Durham, NC: Duke University Press, 1994), 23–48.

8. John Sayle Watterson, *College Football: History, Spectacle, Controversy* (Baltimore: Johns Hopkins University Press, 2000), 155–156; Michael Oriard, *King Football: Sport and Spectacle in the Golden Age of Radio and Newsreels, Movies and Magazines, the Weekly and the Daily Press* (Chapel Hill: University of North Carolina Press, 2001), 23–64.

9. Upton Sinclair, *The Goose-Step: A Study of American Education* (Pasadena, CA: published by the author, 1923), 370–371.

10. Watterson, *College Football*, 151–152; Raymond Schmidt, *Shaping College Football: The Transformation of an American Sport, 1919–1930* (Syracuse, NY: Syracuse University Press, 2007), 67–69; "Two Towns Bet $100,000 upon 'Ringer' Game," *CT*, Jan. 29, 1922, 1; "Pro Fans Resent Stagg's Tirade at Game," *CT*, Nov. 3, 1923, 12.

11. "Northwestern Keeps Football after Big Fight," *CT*, Dec. 8, 1922, 1. On reactions to the report, see "Inquiring Reporter," *CT*, Dec. 10, 1922, A1.

12. Hugh Fullerton, "College Gridiron Game of East on Trial for Its Life," *CT*, Dec. 22, 1922, 21; "Princeton Men Divided on Cut for Grid Sport," *CT*, Dec. 23, 1922, 10; "Yale Football Tangle Is Hard One to Unravel," *CT*, Dec. 25, 1922, 33; "Sports at Harvard Gone If Lowell Volcano Erupts," *CT*, Dec. 26, 1922, 15. On earlier statements by Princeton's Bill Roper, see Roper, *Winning Football* (New York, 1920), 172–174.

13. Fullerton, "College Gridiron Game of East on Trial," *CT*, Dec. 22, 1922, 21.

14. Alexander Meiklejohn, *The Liberal College* (1920; New York: Arno, 1969), 6–7, 9, 15–16, 29, 33–35, 41–43, 64, 85–93, 97–104. On Meiklejohn's controversial career at Amherst, see "Amherst in Clash over Meiklejohn," *NYT*, June 15, 1923, 1; "Amherst Dispute Divides Faculty," *NYT*, June 16, 1923, 1.

15. Meiklejohn, *Liberal College*, 118–130. On Meiklejohn's opposition to John Dewey, see Adam R. Nelson, *Education and Democracy: The Meaning of Alexander Meiklejohn, 1872–1964* (Madison: University of Wisconsin Press,

2001), 233–260. Anti-modernism was especially evident in the 1925 Scopes Trial; Edward J. Larson, *Summer for the Gods: The Scopes Trial and America's Continuing Debate over Science and Religion* (1997; Cambridge, MA: Harvard University Press, 1998), 31–59.

16. Alexander Meiklejohn to A. Lawrence Lowell, Jan. 24, 1922, ALL, UAI 5.160, Series 1919–1922, Folder 96, HUA. See also "Amherst Head Assails Athletic Coach Ways," *NYT*, Feb. 18, 1922, 2.

17. Fielding H. Yost, "Future Trends in Varsity Athletics" (c. 1920s), 7–8, FHY, Box 7, Folder "Speeches (2)"; Yost, "Administration of Intercollegiate and Interscholastic Games" (undated, c. 1920s), 1–8, FHY, Box 7, Folder "Speeches (3)," BHL. On Clarence Mendell, see "Would Bar Coaches at College Games," *NYT*, Dec. 23, 1922, 7.

18. "Meiklejohn Resigns Amherst Headship; Gets Year Leave," *NYT*, June 20, 1923, 1; Alexander Meiklejohn, *The Experimental College* (1932; New York: Arno, 1971), xi, xiii.

19. "Students Attack Football Policies," *NYT*, Dec. 4, 1926; "Says Colleges Teach Only Football Well," *NYT*, Nov. 12, 1925, 2.

20. Joan Shelley Rubin, *The Making of Middlebrow Culture* (Chapel Hill: University of North Carolina Press, 1992).

21. "Find Evils Remain in College Sports," *NYT*, June 11, 1925, 16.

22. On Reed and Swarthmore, see Helen Lefkowitz Horowitz, *Campus Life: Undergraduate Cultures from the End of the Eighteenth Century to the Present* (New York: Knopf, 1987), 106–107, 113–114; Rudolph, *American College*, 456–458. On Dubuque, see Karl Frederick Wettstone, *"Dubuque's" Stand against Commercialized College Athletics* (Dubuque, IA: University of Dubuque, 1925), 8–12. On Centre, see Watterson, *College Football*, 149; "Would Oust College Head," *NYT*, Dec. 21, 1925, 25; "Centre Seeks Dr. Rogers," *NYT*, Nov. 26, 1926, 35.

23. "Professors Assail College Football as a Moral Menace," *NYT*, Apr. 26, 1926, 1.

24 ."College Officials Split on Football," *NYT*, Apr. 27, 1926, 3; "Butler Upholds Sport at Columbia," *NYT*, Apr. 28, 1926, 6. See also Watterson, *College Football*, 156–157.

25. Howard J. Savage, Harold Bentley, John T. McGovern, and Dean F. Smiley; with a preface by Henry S. Pritchett, *American College Athletics* [Bulletin no. 23] (New York: Carnegie Foundation for the Advancement of Teaching, 1929). On the report, see John R. Thelin, *Games Colleges Play: Scandal and*

Reform in Intercollegiate Athletics (Baltimore: Johns Hopkins University Press, 1994), 13–14; Schmidt, *Shaping College Football*, 217–233; Howard J. Savage, *Fruit of an Impulse: Forty-Five Years of the Carnegie Foundation, 1905–1950* (New York: Harcourt, Brace, 1953), 157–158; Watterson, *College Football*, 157; "College Officials Split on Football," *NYT*, Apr. 27, 1926.

26. Henry Pritchett, "Preface," in Savage, Bentley, McGovern, and Smiley, *American College Athletics*, v–vi, viii, xii.

27. Savage, Bentley, McGovern, and Smiley, *American College Athletics*, xxi, 306–311; Thelin, *Games Colleges Play*, 25; Ronald A. Smith, *Pay for Play: A History of Big-Time College Athletic Reform* (Urbana: University of Illinois Press, 2011), 68–70.

28. Savage, Bentley, McGovern, and Smiley, *American College Athletics*, 162–166.

29. Ibid., 164–165, 171–175.

30. Knute Rockne quoted in Dec. 17, 1930, AP report; see Murray Sperber, *Shake Down the Thunder: The Creation of Notre Dame Football* (New York: Henry Holt, 1993), 310.

31. On the NCAA as a cartel, see Paul R. Lawrence, *Unsportsmanlike Conduct: The National Collegiate Athletic Association and the Business of College Football* (New York: Praeger, 1987), xii–xv; W. Burlette Carter, "The Age of Innocence: The First 25 Years of the National Collegiate Athletic Association, 1906 to 1931," *Vanderbilt Journal of Entertainment and Technology Law* 8:2 (2006): 211–291.

32. Robert Maynard Hutchins, *Education for Freedom* (Baton Rouge: Louisiana State University Press, 1943), 3–13, 25. On Hutchins and Mortimer Adler, see Rubin, *Middlebrow Culture*, 186–197; Tim Lacy, "Making a Democratic Culture: The Great Books Idea, Mortimer J. Adler, and Twentieth-Century America" (Ph.D. diss., Loyola University Chicago, 2006). On Hutchins's resemblance to Day, see Rudolph, *American College*, 479. On athletics at Johns Hopkins, see John Calvin French, *A History of the University Founded by Johns Hopkins* (Baltimore: Johns Hopkins University Press, 1946), 296–297.

33. William H. McNeil, *Hutchins' University: A Memoir of the University of Chicago, 1929–1950* (Chicago: University of Chicago Press, 1991), 97; Lester, *Stagg's University: The Rise, Decline, and Fall of Big-Time Football at Chicago* (Urbana: University of Illinois Press, 1995), 170.

34. Lester, *Stagg's University*, 125–186, 209–210; "Graduates Hope Big 10

Will Let Chicago Remain," *CT*, Dec, 23, 1939, 15. On the New Plan, see McNeil, *Hutchins' University*, 27–33.

35. Lester, *Stagg's University*, 162; Hutchins, *Education for Freedom*, 21.

36. McNeil, *Hutchins' University*, 98. Robin Lester critiques McNeil, although he probably reads McNeil's proposal that the Bears could have been a "graduate football team for a graduate university" too literally; *Stagg's University*, 284 n.27. On post-1940 fundraising, see Lester, *Stagg's University*, 187–195.

37. On Regenstein Library, see "U. of C. Library Building Is Stone Jigsaw Puzzle," *CT*, Nov. 2, 1969, D1; "U. of C. Consolidates Library Facilities," *CT*, Aug. 23, 1970, SCL5; "$21 Million U. of C. Library," *CT*, Oct. 28, 1970, C16; "U. of C. Consolidates Library Facilities," *CT*, Aug. 23, 1970, SCL5. On the atomic laboratory, see Stephane Groueff, *Manhattan Project: The Untold Story of the Making of the Atomic Bomb* (Boston: Little, Brown, 1967), 68–75. On Chicago's changing reputation, see Lester, *Stagg's University*, 193–195; McNeil, *Hutchins' University*, 168–169.

38. Robert S. Lynd, *Knowledge for What? The Place of Social Science in American Culture* (Princeton, NJ: Princeton University Press, 1939), 2, 7, 10. On Lynd, see Smith, *Social Science in the Crucible*, 120–158. On the revival of progressive scholarship in the 1930s, especially President Franklin Roosevelt's "Brain Trust," see Adam Cohen, *Nothing to Fear: FDR's Inner Circle and the Hundred Days That Created Modern America* (New York: Penguin, 2009), 6–7; David M. Kennedy, *Freedom from Fear: The American People in Depression and War, 1929–1945* (New York: Oxford University Press, 1999), 119–124.

39. Robert Herrick, *Chimes* (New York: Macmillan, 1926), 72.

40. Edward Alsworth Ross, *Seventy Years of It: An Autobiography* (New York: D. Appleton, 1936), 14.

41. Watterson, *College Football*, 183–191.

42. G. T. W. Patrick, "Journal 1945–47"; G. T. W. Patrick Papers, Box 1, 75 ff, 101 ff, UIA. On postwar scandals and reform efforts, see Murray Sperber, *Onward to Victory: The Crises That Shaped College Sports* (New York: Henry Holt, 1998), 285–343; Smith, *Pay for Play*, 99–120.

43. On "anti-structure," see Victor Turner, *The Ritual Process: Structure and Anti-Structure* (Ithaca, NY: Cornell University Press, 1969). On highbrow and lowbrow culture, see Lawrence Levine, *Highbrow/Lowbrow: The Emergence of Cultural Hierarchy in America* (Cambridge, MA: Harvard University Press, 1988).

EPILOGUE: A CIRCUS OR A SIDESHOW?

1. On Stanford's $100 million project, see "Stanford Stadium—Here, Here for a Site That Had It There," *SFC*, Nov. 27, 2005, C10; "New Stadium, with Sushi Bar, Wins Raves," *SFC*, Sept. 17, 2006, B3. On Illinois's $125 million project, see "Stadium Prepares for Makeover," *Daily Illini*, Feb. 10, 2006, 1A. On expansion projects at Nebraska and Ohio State, see Alva W. Stewart, *College Football Stadiums: An Illustrated Guide to NCAA Division I-A* (Jefferson, NC: McFarland, 2000), 121, 145.

2. On Buffalo, see Murray Sperber, *Beer and Circus: How Big-Time College Sports Is Crippling Undergraduate Education* (New York: Henry Holt, 2000), 65–68. On GSU, see "Georgia State Hoping Football Builds Community in a Football Town," *NYT*, Apr. 20, 2009, D1.

3. Sperber, *Beer and Circus*, 256–260.

4. On contingent labor, tenure, and academic freedom, see Cary Nelson, *No University Is an Island: Saving Academic Freedom* (New York: New York University Press, 2010), 79–106. On late twentieth-century understandings of the market as an abstract phenomenon located in a realm beyond human control, see Daniel T. Rodgers, *Age of Fracture* (Cambridge, MA: Harvard University Press, 2011), 41–76.

5. Michael Oriard, *Bowled Over: Big-Time College Football from the Sixties to the BCS Era* (Chapel Hill: University of North Carolina Press, 2009), 192.

6. On Nick Saban, see Charlie Nobles, "Saban Goes to Alabama—Miami Fans Turn Crimson," *NYT*, Jan. 4, 2007, D3; Andrew Zimbalist, "Looks Like a Business—Should Be Taxed Like One," *NYT*, Jan. 7, 2007, 9.

7. On "Coaches vs. Cancer," see http://www.cancer.org/Involved/Partici pate/CoachesvsCancer/about-coaches-vs-cancer (accessed Feb. 27, 2011); Nick Saban's book, written with Brian Curtis, is *How Good Do You Want to Be? A Champion's Tips on How to Lead and Succeed at Work and in Life* (New York: Ballantine, 2005), 125–192.

8. On Don Imus, see Kelli Anderson, "A Pillar of Strength," *Sports Illustrated*, Nov. 19, 2007, 70–74. On women's sports and Title IX, see Eileen McDonagh and Laura Pappano, *Playing with the Boys: Why Separate Is Not Equal in Sports* (New York: Oxford University Press, 2008), ix–x.

9. Sperber, *Beer and Circus*. On the origin of NCAA divisions, see Joseph N. Crowley, *In the Arena: The NCAA's First Century* (Indianapolis: National Collegiate Athletic Association, 2006), 220.

Bibliography

ARCHIVAL COLLECTIONS

Atlanta University Center Archives, Robert Woodruff Library, Atlanta, Georgia
> Atlanta University Published and Printed Materials
> Horace Bumstead Papers

Bentley Historical Library, University of Michigan, Ann Arbor, Michigan
> James B. Angell Papers
> Charles Baird Papers
> Board in Control of Intercollegiate Athletics Records
> Marion L. Burton Papers
> Victor Hugo Lane Papers
> Warren P. Lombard Papers
> Andrew Cunningham McLaughlin Papers
> James Orin Murfin Papers
> Fielding Harris Yost Papers

Boston Public Library, Boston, Massachusetts
> Hugo Münsterberg Collection

Brown University Archives, Providence, Rhode Island
> William Herbert Perry Faunce Papers

Georgia Institute of Technology Archives and Records Division, Atlanta, Georgia
> Athletic Association Records

Harvard University Archives, Cambridge, Massachusetts
> Athletic Committee Minutes
> Charles Beck Collection
> Dean LeBaron R. Briggs Papers
> Committee on the Regulation of Athletic Sports Records
> Charles William Eliot Presidential Papers
> A. Lawrence Lowell Presidential Papers
> Reid Family Correspondence and Related Papers
> William T. Reid, Jr., Correspondence and Related Papers

Dudley A. Sargent Papers

F. W. Taussig Papers

Houghton Library, Harvard University, Cambridge Massachusetts

Houghton-Mifflin Company Records

Indiana University Archives, Bloomington, Indiana

William Lowe Bryan Papers

David Starr Jordan Papers

Joseph Swain Papers

Library of Congress, Washington, DC

Silas Weir Mitchell Correspondence

Ohio State University Archives, Columbus, Ohio

Athletic Director Records

William Oxley Thompson Papers

Purdue University Archives, West Lafayette, Indiana

H. A. Huston Faculty Collection

Thomas A. Moran Faculty Collection

James H. Smart Papers

Stanford University Archives, Stanford, California

Frank Angell Biographical File

David Starr Jordan Papers

E. A. Ross Controversy Records

Ray Lyman Wilbur Papers

Tufts University Digital Collections and Archives, Medford, Massachusetts

Department of Physical Education/Athletics Records

University of Chicago Special Collections and Archives, Chicago, Illinois

William Rainey Harper Papers

Amos Alonzo Stagg Papers

University of Illinois Archives, Urbana, Illinois

Alumni Association Records

Edwin G. Dexter Biographical File

Andrew Sloan Draper Papers

Edmund Janes James Papers

Stadium Drive Records

Robert C. Zuppke Papers

University of Iowa Archives, Iowa City, Iowa

Faculty Minutes, 1860–1890

Walter Jessup Papers

Isaac A. Loos Faculty Collection

George T. W. Patrick Papers, Faculty Collection

Philosophy Department Manuscript File

Psychology Department Manuscript File

University of Wisconsin Archives, Madison, Wisconsin

Charles Kendall Adams Papers

Camp Randall Subject File

Charles R. Van Hise Papers

Wisconsin State Historical Society, Madison, Wisconsin

Edward Alsworth Ross Papers

Frederick Jackson Turner Papers

Yale University Archives and Manuscripts, New Haven, Connecticut

Walter Chauncey Camp Papers

Department of Athletics, Physical Education, and Recreation Records

Arthur T. Hadley Papers

NEWSPAPERS AND PERIODICALS

American Journal of Psychology

American Review of Reviews

Atlanta Constitution

Boston Medical and Surgical Journal

Century

Chicago Tribune

Collier's

Cosmopolitan

Daily Illini (University of Illinois)

Daily Maroon (University of Chicago)

Daily Palo Alto (Stanford)

The Forum

(Harvard) Advocate

(Harvard) Crimson

Harvard Graduates Magazine

(Harvard) Monthly

Harvard University Catalogue

The Independent

Living Age

Los Angeles Times

The Makio (Ohio State University)
McClure's Magazine
Michigan Alumnus
(Michigan) Argonaut
(Michigan) Inlander
Michigan Oracle
(Michigan) University Chronicle
New York Times
Nineteenth Century
North American
The Outing
The Outlook
Popular Science Monthly
Rice Institute Announcements
San Francisco Chronicle
St. Nicholas
Stanford Pictorial
(Stanford) Sequoia
U. of Michigan Daily/Michigan Daily
University of Illinois Annual Register
University of Iowa Catalogue
Washington Post
Wisconsin Daily Cardinal
Yale Courant

PUBLISHED PRIMARY SOURCES

Adam, G. Mercer. *Sandow on Physical Training*. New York: J. Selwin, 1894.

Addams, Jane. *Twenty Years at Hull-House, with Autobiographical Notes*. 1910; Urbana: University of Illinois Press, 1990.

Allen, Nathan. *Physical Culture in Amherst College*. Lowell, MA: Stone & House, 1869.

Anderson, Kelli. "A Pillar of Strength." *Sports Illustrated* (Nov. 19, 2007): 70–74.

Angell, Frank. "Duration, Energy and Extent of Reaction Movements—Simple and Flying Reactions." *American Journal of Psychology* 30:2 (1919): 224–236.

———. "Note on Some of the Physical Factors Affecting Reaction Time

Together with a Description of a New Reaction Key." *American Journal of Psychology* 22:1 (1911): 86–93.

———. "Rugby Football on the Pacific Coast." *The Independent* 68:3191 (Jan. 27, 1910): 195–198.

Angell, James Burrill. *The Higher Education: A Plea for Making It Accessible to All; An Address Delivered at the Annual Commencement of the University of Michigan, June 26, 1879.* Ann Arbor, MI: Board of Regents, 1879.

Angell, James B., D. B. St. John Roosa, Ethelbert Warfield, and J. G. Schurman. "Are Football Games Educative or Brutalizing?" *Forum* 16 (1894): 634–654.

Baskerville, A. H. *Modern Rugby Football: New Zealand Methods; Points for the Beginner, the Player, the Spectator.* 1907; Christchurch, NZ: Kiwi, 1995.

Beard, George M. *American Nervousness: Its Causes and Consequences; A Supplement to Nervous Exhaustion (Neurasthenia).* New York: G. P. Putnam's Sons, 1881.

Beck, Charles. *A Treatise on Gymnasticks, Taken Chiefly from the German of F. L. Jahn.* Northampton, MA: Simeon Butler, 1828.

Benjamin, Park. "Public Football vs. Naval Education: In Defense of the Naval Academy." *The Independent* 55 (Nov. 26, 1903): 2777–2780.

Bowen, John T. "Reports of Societies: Boston Society for Medical Improvement." *Boston Medical and Surgical Journal* 131 (1894): 393–397.

Bruce, H. Addington. "The Psychology of Football." *Outlook* 96 (Nov. 5, 1910): 541–545.

Camp, Walter. *American Football.* New York: Harper, 1891; New York: Arno, 1974.

———. *Football Facts and Figures: A Symposium of Expert Opinions on the Game's Place in American Athletics.* New York: Harper, 1894.

———. *Football without a Coach.* New York: D. Appleton, 1920.

———. "Influence of the Tackle Play: A Development Which Has Changed the Character of Football." *Collier's* 46 (Oct. 15, 1910): 24–25.

Camp, Walter, and Lorin F. Deland. *Football.* Boston: Houghton Mifflin, 1896.

Campbell, W. W. "Annual Report of the President of the University, 1923–1924." *University of California Bulletin*, Third Series 18:6 (Berkeley, CA, 1924).

Cattell, James McKeen. *University Control.* New York: Science Press, 1913.

Cavanaugh, Major Frank W. *Inside Football*. Boston: Small, Maynard, 1919.

Clarke, Edward H. *The Building of a Brain*. Boston: Osgood, 1874.

———. *Sex in Education; or, A Fair Chance for the Girls*. Boston: Osgood, 1873.

Conant, W. M. "Educational Aspect of College Athletics." *Boston Medical and Surgical Journal* 131 (1894): 380–386.

Cummings, Edward. "The Harvard Exhibit at the World's Fair." *Harvard Graduates Magazine* 2:5 (Sept. 1893): 50–63.

Daly, Charles O. *American Football: How to Play It*. New York: Harper, 1921.

Davis, Parke H. *Football: The American Intercollegiate Game*. New York: Scribner's, 1911.

Deland, Lorin. *Imagination in Business*, rev. ed. New York: Harper & Brothers, 1909.

Dexter, Edwin G. "Accidents from College Football." *Educational Review* 25 (1904): 415–428.

———. "Newspaper Football." *Popular Science Monthly* 68 (1906): 261–265.

———. "The Survival of the Fittest in Motor Training." *Educational Review* 23 (1902): 81–91.

Eliot, Charles William. *Education for Efficiency and the New Definition of the Cultivated Man*. Boston: Houghton Mifflin, 1909.

———. *The Man and His Beliefs*, ed. William Allen Nelson. New York: Harper, 1926.

———. "Rational College Sports." *Harvard Graduates Magazine* 15:59 (Mar. 1907): 385–388.

———. "Topics from the President's Report." *Harvard Graduates Magazine* 14:55 (Mar. 1906): 404–406.

———. *A Turning Point in Higher Education: The Inaugural Address of Charles William Eliot as President of Harvard College, October 19, 1869*. With an introduction by Nathan M. Pusey. Cambridge, MA: Harvard University Press, 1969.

———. *University Administration*. Boston: Houghton Mifflin, 1908.

Eliot, Charles William, Andrew F. West, William R. Harper, and Nicholas Murray Butler. *Present College Questions: Six Papers Read before the National Educational Association, at the Sessions Held in Boston, July 6 and 7, 1903*. New York: Appleton, 1903.

Emerson, Ralph Waldo. *English Traits*. London: G. Routledge, 1856.

Faunce, William H. P. *Facing Life*. New York: Macmillan, 1928.

Fitch, George. *At Good Old Siwash* (1910; New York: Grosset & Dunlap, 1911).

Follen, Charles. *An Address, Introductory to the Fourth Course of the Franklin Lectures, Delivered at the Masonic Temple, Nov. 3, 1834*. Boston: Tuttle and Weeks, 1835.

———. *The Works of Charles Follen, with a Memoir of His Life*, ed. Harrison Gray, 5 vols. Boston: Hilliard, Gray, and Company, 1842.

Groos, Karl. *The Play of Man*, trans. Elizabeth L. Baldwin. 1896; New York: D. Appleton, 1898.

Hall, G. Stanley. *Adolescence: Its Psychology and Its Relation to Physiology, Anthropology, Sociology, Sex, Crime, Religion, and Education*, 2 vols. New York: D. Appleton, 1904.

Harper, William Rainey. *The Prospects of the Small College*. Chicago: University of Chicago Press, 1900.

———. *Religion and the Higher Life: Talks to Students*. Chicago: University of Chicago Press, 1904.

———. *The Trend in Higher Education*. Chicago: University of Chicago Press, 1905.

Haughton, Percy D. *Football and How to Watch It*. With an introduction by Heywood Broun. Boston: Marshall Jones, 1922.

Haven, Joseph. *Mental Philosophy: Including the Intellect, Sensibilities, and Will*. 1857; Boston: Gould and Lincoln, 1868.

Heisman, John W. *Principles of Football*. St. Louis: Sports Publishing Bureau, 1922.

Herrick, Robert. *Chimes*. New York: Macmillan, 1926.

Hicks, William Everett. "The Military Worthlessness of Football." *The Independent* 67 (Nov. 25, 1909): 1201–1204.

Higginson, Henry Lee. *Four Addresses*. Boston: Merrymount, 1902.

Hitchcock, Edward, and Edward Hitchock, Jr. *Elementary Anatomy and Physiology: For Colleges, Academies, and Other Schools*. 1860; New York: American Book Company, 1866.

Hitchcock, Edward, Jr., and Hiram H. Seelye. *An Anthropometric Manual*. Amherst, MA: J. E. Williams, 1887.

Hollis, Ira N. "Origin of the Harvard Stadium." *Harvard Engineering Journal* 3:2 (June 1904): 90–108.

Hopkins, Mark. *An Outline Study of Man; or, The Body and Mind in One System: With Illustrative Diagrams, and a Method for Blackboard Teaching*. New York: Scribner, Armstrong, 1874.

———. *Teachings and Counsels: Twenty Baccalaureate Sermons*. New York: Charles Scribner's Sons, 1884.

Howard, Burt Estes. *Education and Democracy*. Los Angeles: B. R. Baumgardt, 1901.

Howe, Frederic C. *Wisconsin: An Experiment in Democracy*. New York: Charles Scribner's Sons, 1912.

Hutchins, Robert Maynard. *Education for Freedom*. Baton Rouge: Louisiana State University Press, 1943.

Intercollegiate Athletic Association of the United States. *Proceedings of the First Annual Meeting Held at New York City, New York December 29, 1906*. [New York: Intercollegiate Athletic Association of the United States, 1906].

James, William. *Memories and Studies*. London: Longmans, Green, 1911.

———. "The Ph.D. Octopus." *Harvard Monthly* (Mar. 1903): 1–9.

Johnson, Owen. *Stover at Yale*. New York: Frederick A. Stokes, 1911.

Jones, Howard H. *How to Coach and Play Football*. Iowa City, IA: Clio Press, 1923.

Jordan, David Starr. "Are Fellowships Almsgiving or Investments?" *Popular Science Monthly* 61 (1902): 565.

———. *The Blood of the Nation: A Study of the Decay of Races through the Survival of the Unfit*. 1899; Boston: American Unitarian Association, 1902.

———. *The Care and Culture of Men: A Series of Addresses on the Higher Education*. San Francisco: Whitaker & Ray, 1896.

———. "Comrades in Zeal." *Popular Science Monthly* 64 (1904): 304–315.

———. *The Days of a Man: Being Memories of a Naturalist, Teacher and Minor Prophet of Democracy*, 2 vols. Yonkers, NY: World, 1922.

———. *The Human Harvest: A Study of the Decay of Races through the Survival of the Unfit*. Boston: American Unitarian Association, 1907.

———. "University Tendencies in America." *Popular Science Monthly* 63 (1903): 141–148.

———. *War and the Breed: The Relation of War to the Downfall of Nations*. Boston: Beacon, 1915.

Jordan, David Starr, and Harvey Ernest Jordan. *War's Aftermath: A Preliminary Study of the Eugenics of War as Illustrated by the Civil War of the United States and the Late Wars in the Balkans*. Boston: Houghton Mifflin, 1914.

Jordan, Edward S. "Buying Football Victories: The Universities of Chicago, Illinois and Northwestern." *Collier's* 36:7 (Nov. 11, 1905): 19–23.

————. "Buying Football Victories: The University of Michigan." *Collier's* 36:9 (Nov. 25, 1905): 21–23.

————. "Buying Football Victories: The University of Minnesota." *Collier's* 36:10 (Dec. 2, 1905): 19–20.

————. "Buying Football Victories: The University of Wisconsin." *Collier's* 36:8 (Nov. 18, 1905): 22–23.

Lewis, Dio. *The New Gymnastics for Men, Women, and Children; With a Translation of Prof. Kloss's Dumb-Bell Instructor and Prof. Schreber's Pangymnastikon*. Boston: Ticknor and Fields, 1862.

Lombard, Warren Plympton. "The Variations of the Normal Knee-Jerk and Their Relation to the Activity of the Central Nervous System." *American Journal of Psychology* 1 (1887–1888): 5–71.

Loos, Isaac Althaus. *Studies in the Politics of Aristotle and the Republic of Plato; Bulletin of the University of Iowa* (New Series: Nos. 1 and 2). Iowa City, IA: The University Press, 1899.

Lowell, A. Lawrence. *What a University President Has Learned*. New York: Macmillan, 1923.

Lynd, Robert S. *Knowledge for What? The Place of Social Science in American Culture*. Princeton, NJ: Princeton University Press, 1939.

McCarthy, Charles. *The Wisconsin Idea*. New York: Macmillan, 1912.

McCosh, James. *Inauguration of James McCosh, D.D., LL.D, as President of the College of New Jersey, Princeton; October 27, 1868*. New York: Robert Carter, 1868.

McNeil, William H. *Hutchins' University: A Memoir of the University of Chicago, 1929–1950*. Chicago: University of Chicago Press, 1991.

Meiklejohn, Alexander. *The Experimental College*. 1932; New York: Arno, 1971.

————. *The Liberal College*. 1920; New York: Arno, 1969.

Merriman, R. B. "Football Reform." *Harvard Graduates Magazine* 14:55 (Mar. 1906): 426–427.

Mitchell, Silas Weir, George Read Morehouse, and William Williams Keen. *Gunshot Wounds and Other Injuries of Nerves*. 1864; San Francisco: Norman, 1989.

————. *Injuries of Nerves and Their Consequences*. New York: Dover, 1965.

————. *Wear and Tear; or, Hints for the Overworked*, 5th ed. 1887; New York: Arno, 1973.

Moran, Thomas F. "Courtesy and Sportsmanship in Intercollegiate Athletics." *American Physical Education Review* 15:2 (Feb. 1910): 118–124.

Münsterberg, Hugo. "The New Psychology, and Harvard's Equipment for Teaching It." *Harvard Graduates Magazine* 1:2 (Jan. 1893): 201–209.

Needham, Henry Beach. "The College Athlete: How Commercialism Is Making Him a Professional." *McClure's Magazine* 25 (June 1905): 115–128.

———. "The College Athlete; His Amateur Code: Its Evasion and Administration." *McClure's Magazine* 25 (July 1905): 260–272.

Neyland, Robert. *Football as a War Game: The Annotated Journals of General R. R. Neyland*, ed. Andy Kozar. Nashville: Falcon Press, 2002.

Nichols, Edward H., and Frank L. Richardson. "Football Injuries of the Harvard Squad for Three Years Under the Revised Rules." *Boston Medical and Surgical Journal* 160 (1909): 33–37.

Nichols, Edward H., and Homer B. Smith. "The Physical Aspect of American Football." *Boston Medical and Surgical Journal* 154 (1906): 1–8.

Patrick, George Thomas White. "A Further Study of Heraclitus." *American Journal of Psychology* 1 (1888): 557–690.

———. *George Thomas White Patrick: An Autobiography*. Iowa City: University of Iowa Press, 1947.

———. "The Psychology of Football." *American Journal of Psychology* 14 (1903): 368–381.

Paxson, Frederic L. "The Rise of Sport." *Mississippi Valley Historical Review* 4 (1917): 143–168.

Porter, Noah. *The American Colleges and the American Public*. New Haven, CT: Charles C. Chatfield, 1870.

———. *The Human Intellect: With an Introduction upon Psychology and the Soul*, 4th ed. New York: Charles Scribner's Sons, 1868.

Prince, Morton. "Accident Neuroses and Foot-Ball Playing." *Boston Medical and Surgical Journal* 138 (1898): 392–394.

Reed, Herbert. *Football for Public and Player*. New York: Frederick A. Stokes, 1913.

Reid, William T., Jr. "Football and Coaching." *Harvard Graduates Magazine* 15:59 (Mar. 1907): 401.

Richards, Eugene Lamb. "College Athletics, I. Advantages." *Popular Science Monthly* 24 (1884): 446–453.

———. "College Athletics, II. Evils and Their Remedies." *Popular Science Monthly* 24 (1884): 587–597.

———. "Foot-Ball and Its Opponents." *Yale Medical Journal* 1 (1894–1895): 221–224.

————. "The Football Situation." *Popular Science Monthly* 45 (1894): 721–733.

Rockne, Knute K. *Coaching: The Way of the Winner*, rev. ed. 1925; New York: Devin-Adair, 1928.

————. *The Four Winners—The Head, the Hand, the Foot, the Ball*. New York: Devin-Adair, 1925.

Rockne, Knute K., and Walter E. Meanwell. *Training, Conditioning, and the Care of Injuries*. Madison, WI, 1931.

Roosevelt, Theodore. *The Strenuous Life: Essays and Addresses*. 1899; New York: Century, 1905.

Roper, William W. *Football, Today and Tomorrow*. New York: Duffield, 1927.

————. *Winning Football*. New York: Dodd, Mead, 1920.

Ross, Edward Alsworth. *Seventy Years of It: An Autobiography*. New York: D. Appleton, 1936.

————. *Sin and Society: An Analysis of Latter-Day Iniquity*. Boston: Houghton Mifflin, 1907.

————. *Social Control: A Survey of the Foundations of Order*. 1901; New York: Macmillan, 1922.

————. *Social Psychology: An Outline and Source Book*. New York: Macmillan, 1908.

Royce, Josiah. *Race Questions, Provincialism, and Other American Problems*. New York: Macmillan, 1908.

Saban, Nick, with Brian Curtis. *How Good Do You Want to Be? A Champion's Tips on How to Lead and Succeed at Work and in Life*. New York: Ballantine, 2005.

Sargent, Dudley A. *Dudley Allen Sargent: An Autobiography*, ed. Ledyard W. Sargent. Philadelphia: Lea & Febiger, 1927.

————. *Physical Education*. Boston: Ginn, 1906.

Savage, Howard J. *Fruit of an Impulse: Forty-Five Years of the Carnegie Foundation, 1905–1950*. New York: Harcourt, Brace, 1953.

Savage, Howard J., Harold Bentley, John T. McGovern, and Dean F. Smiley. With a preface by Henry S. Pritchett. *American College Athletics* (Bulletin no. 23). New York: The Carnegie Foundation for the Advancement of Teaching, 1929.

Seaver, Jay W. *Anthropometry and Physical Examination: A Book for Practical Use in Connection with Gymnastic Work and Physical Education*. New Haven, CT: Tuttle, Morehouse, and Taylor, 1890.

Seligman, Edwin R. A., et al. "Preliminary Report of the Joint Committee on Academic Freedom and Academic Tenure." *American Political Science Review* 9:2 (May 1915): 374–381.

Shaw, Albert. "College Reform—And Football." *American Review of Reviews* 40 (1909): 726–728.

Sidis, Boris. "The Nature of the Mob." *Atlantic Monthly* 75:448 (Feb. 1895): 189–197.

———. *The Psychology of Suggestion: A Research into the Subconscious Nature of Man and Society*. With an introduction by William James. New York: D. Appleton, 1898.

Sinclair, Upton. *The Goose-Step: A Study of American Education*. Pasadena, CA: published by the author, 1923.

Spencer, Herbert. "Physical Education" in *Essays on Education and Kindred Subjects*. New York: Dutton, 1911.

Stagg, Amos Alonzo, with Wesley Winans Stout. *Touchdown!* New York: Longmans, Green, 1927.

Stagg, Amos Alonzo, with Henry L. Williams. *A Scientific and Practical Treatise on American Football for Schools and Colleges*. Hartford, CT: Case, Lockwood & Branard, 1893.

———. *Simple Explanations of the Great Game of Football, with Diagrams for Spectators*. Hartford, CT: Case, Lockwood & Branard, 1893.

Steffens, Lincoln. *The Shame of the Cities*. 1904; New York: Hill and Wang, 1957.

Taussig, F. W. "A Professor's View of Athletics." *Harvard Graduates Magazine* 3:11 (Mar. 1895): 306–310.

Taylor, Frederick W., and Sanford E. Thompson. *A Treatise on Concrete Plain and Reinforced: Materials, Construction, and Design of Concrete and Reinforced Concrete*. New York: John Wiley, 1905.

Thomas, William I. "The Gaming Instinct." *American Journal of Sociology* 6 (May 1901): 750–763.

Ticknor, George. *Remarks on Changes Lately Proposed or Adopted in Harvard University*. Boston: Cummings, Hilliard, 1825.

Turner, Frederick Jackson. *The Frontier in American History*. 1920; New York: Dover, 1996.

University of Illinois. *The Story of the Stadium*. Urbana: University of Illinois, 1922.

Van Dyke, Paul. "Athletics and Education." *Outlook* 79 (Feb. 11, 1905): 389–393.

Veblen, Thorstein. *The Higher Learning in America: A Memorandum on the Conduct of Universities by Business Men.* 1918; New York: Hill and Wang, 1957.

———. *The Theory of the Leisure Class.* 1899; New York: Penguin, 1979.

Walker, Francis Amasa. "College Athletics: Oration Delivered before the Phi Beta Kappa Society, in Sanders Theatre, Thursday, June 29, 1893." *Harvard Graduates Magazine* 2:5 (Sept. 1893): 1–8.

Warner, Glenn Scobey. *A Course in Football for Players and Coaches.* Carlisle, PA, 1912.

———. *Football for Coaches and Players.* Stanford, CA: Stanford University Press, 1927.

Wayland, Francis. *Thoughts on the Present Collegiate System in the United States.* Boston: Gould, Kendall & Lincoln, 1842.

Wayland, Francis, and H. L. Wayland. *A Memoir of the Life and Labors of Francis Wayland, D.D., LL.D.,* two volumes. New York: Sheldon, 1867.

Wettstone, Karl Frederick. *"Dubuque's" Stand against Commercialized College Athletics.* Dubuque, IA: University of Dubuque, 1925.

Wheeler, Benjamin Ide. *The Abundant Life,* ed. Monroe E. Deutsch. Berkeley: University of California Press, 1926.

White, Andrew Dickson. *A History of the Warfare of Science with Theology in Christendom,* 2 vols. 1896; New York: D. Appleton, 1898.

White, J. William. "Football and Its Critics." *Outlook* 81 (Nov. 18, 1905): 662–669.

Whitney, Caspar, ed. "Is Football Worth While: A Symposium of Opinion from the Presidents of Representative Educational Institutions in the United States." *Collier's* 44:13 (Dec. 18, 1909): 13, 24.

Wilce, J. W. *Football: How to Play It and How to Understand It.* New York: Charles Scribner's Sons, 1923.

Wilcox, Delos F. *The American City: A Problem in Democracy.* 1904; New York: Macmillan, 1909.

Wilson, Woodrow. *The Papers of Woodrow Wilson,* ed. Arthur S. Link, 69 vols. Princeton, NJ: Princeton University Press, 1975.

Woodford, Arthur B. "On the Use of Silver Money in the United States." *Annals of the American Academy of Political and Social Science* 4 (1893): 91–149.

Yale College. "Report of the Faculty" (1829) in *Reports on the Course of Instruction in Yale College; by a Committee of the Corporation, and the Academical Faculty.* New Haven, CT: Hezekiah Howe, 1830.

Yost, Fielding H. *Football for Player and Spectator*. Ann Arbor, MI: University Publishing Company, 1905.

Yost, Fielding H., and George E. Little. *Football Notes: A Series of Lectures Delivered to the Classes in Football at the University of Michigan*. Ann Arbor, MI: Elton E. Wieman/O. D. Morrill, 1924.

Zuppke, Robert C. *Football Technique and Tactics*, 2nd rev ed. 1922; Champaign, IL: Bailey & Himes, 1924.

Zuppke, Robert C., assisted by Milton M. Olander. *Coaching Football*. Champaign, IL: Bailey & Himes, 1930.

SECONDARY BOOKS AND ARTICLES

Adams, David W. *Education for Extinction: American Indians and the Boarding School Experience, 1875–1928*. Lawrence: University Press of Kansas, 1995.

Adelman, Melvin L. *A Sporting Time: New York City and the Rise of Modern Athletics, 1820–70*. 1986; Urbana: University of Illinois Press, 1990.

Agnew, Jean-Christophe. *Worlds Apart: The Market and the Theater in Anglo-American Thought, 1550–1750*. Cambridge, UK: Cambridge University Press, 1986.

Ashby, LeRoy. *With Amusement for All: A History of American Popular Culture since 1830*. Lexington: University Press of Kentucky, 2006.

Ayers, Edward L. *The Promise of the New South: Life after Reconstruction*. New York: Oxford University Press, 1992.

Bachin, Robin F. *Building the South Side: Urban Space and Civic Culture in Chicago, 1890–1919*. Chicago: University of Chicago Press, 2004.

Bannister, Robert C. *Social Darwinism: Science and Myth in Anglo-American Thought*. Philadelphia: Temple University Press, 1979.

Bederman, Gail. *Manliness and Civilization: A Cultural History of Gender and Race in the United States, 1880–1917*. Chicago: University of Chicago Press, 1995.

Behee, John Richard. *Fielding Yost's Legacy to the University of Michigan*. Ann Arbor, MI: Ulrich's Books, 1971.

Bender, Thomas. *Intellect and Public Life: Essays on the Social History of Academic Intellectuals in the United States*. Baltimore: Johns Hopkins University Press, 1993.

———. *A Nation among Nations: America's Place in World History*. New York: Hill and Wang, 2006.

Bernstein, Mark F. *Football: The Ivy League Origins of an American Obsession.* Philadelphia: University of Pennsylvania Press, 2001.

Blake, Casey Nelson. *Beloved Community: The Cultural Criticism of Randolph Bourne, Van Wyck Brooks, Waldo Frank & Lewis Mumford.* Chapel Hill: University of North Carolina Press, 1990.

Bledstein, Burton J. *The Culture of Professionalism: The Middle Class and the Development of Higher Education in America.* New York: Norton, 1976.

Blight, David W. *Race and Reunion: The Civil War in American Memory.* Cambridge, MA: Harvard University Press, 2001.

Bloom, David A., Gretchen Uznis, and Darrell A. Campbell, Jr. "Charles B. G. de Nancrède: Academic Surgeon at the *Fin de Siècle.*" *World Journal of Surgery* 22 (1998): 1175–1181.

Blumin, Stuart M. *The Emergence of the Middle Class: Social Experience in the American City, 1760–1900.* Cambridge, UK: Cambridge University Press, 1989.

Bordogna, Francesca. *William James at the Boundaries.* Chicago: University of Chicago Press, 2008.

Boring, Edwin G. *A History of Experimental Psychology.* New York: Century, 1929.

Borkowski, Richard P. "The Life and Contributions of Walter Camp to American Football." Ed.D. diss., Temple University, 1979.

Boyer, Paul. *Urban Masses and Moral Order in America, 1820–1920.* Cambridge, MA: Harvard University Press, 1978.

Brandt, Nat. *When Oberlin Was King of the Gridiron: The Heisman Years.* Kent, OH: Oberlin College, distributed by Kent State University Press, 2001.

Brown, David S. *Beyond the Frontier: The Midwestern Voice in American Historical Writing.* Chicago: University of Chicago Press, 2009.

Burgos, Adrian, Jr. *Playing America's Game: Baseball, Latinos, and the Color Line.* Berkeley: University of California Press, 2007.

Burns, Edward McNall. *David Starr Jordan: Prophet of Democracy.* Palo Alto, CA: Stanford University Press, 1953.

Cahn, Susan K. *Coming on Strong: Gender and Sexuality in Twentieth-Century Women's Sports.* New York: Free Press, 1994.

Carnes, Mark C. *Secret Ritual and Manhood in Victorian America.* New Haven, CT: Yale University Press, 1989.

Carriel, Mary Turner. *The Life of Jonathan Baldwin Turner.* With an introduction by David D. Henry. 1911; Urbana: University of Illinois Press, 1961.

Carroll, John M. *Fritz Pollard: Pioneer in Racial Advancement*. Urbana: University of Illinois Press, 1992.

———. *Red Grange and the Rise of Modern Football*. Urbana: University of Illinois Press, 1999.

Carson, Mina. *Settlement Folk: Social Thought and the American Settlement Movement, 1885–1930*. Chicago: University of Chicago Press, 1990.

Carter, W. Burlette. "The Age of Innocence: The First 25 Years of the National Collegiate Athletic Association, 1906 to 1931." *Vanderbilt Journal of Entertainment and Technology Law* 8:2 (2006): 211–291.

Cavallo, Dominick. *Muscles and Morals: Organized Playgrounds and Urban Reform, 1880–1920*. Philadelphia: University of Pennsylvania Press, 1981.

Chapman, David L. *Sandow the Magnificent: Eugen Sandow and the Beginnings of Bodybuilding*. Urbana: University of Illinois Press, 1994.

Chudacoff, Howard P. *The Age of the Bachelor: Creating an American Subculture*. Princeton, NJ: Princeton University Press, 1999.

Clendenning, John. *The Life and Thought of Josiah Royce*. Madison: University of Wisconsin Press, 1985.

Cleves, Rachel Hope. *The Reign of Terror in America: Visions of Violence from Anti-Jacobinism to Antislavery*. Cambridge, UK: Cambridge University Press, 2009.

Cohen, Adam. *Nothing to Fear: FDR's Inner Circle and the Hundred Days That Created Modern America*. New York: Penguin, 2009.

Conkin, Paul K. *Gone with the Ivy: A Biography of Vanderbilt University*. Knoxville: University of Tennessee Press, 1985.

———. *Prophets of Prosperity: America's First Political Economists*. Bloomington: Indiana University Press, 1980.

Cott, Nancy. *The Grounding of Modern Feminism*. New Haven, CT: Yale University Press, 1987.

Coulter, Stanley. "Thomas Francis Moran: An Appreciation." *Indiana Magazine of History* 25:1 (1929): 47–51.

Cravens, Hamilton. *The Triumph of Evolution: The Heredity-Environment Controversy, 1900–1941*. 1978; Baltimore: Johns Hopkins University Press, 1988.

Crook, Paul. *Darwinism, War and History: The Debate over the Biology of War from the "Origin of Species" to the First World War*. Cambridge, UK: Cambridge University Press, 1994.

Cross, Coy F. *Justin Smith Morrill: Father of the Land-Grant Colleges*. East Lansing: Michigan State University Press, 1999.

Crowley, Joseph N. *In the Arena: The NCAA's First Century*. Indianapolis: National Collegiate Athletic Association, 2006.

Crunden, Robert M. *Ministers of Reform: The Progressives' Achievement in American Civilization, 1889–1920*. 1982; Urbana: University of Illinois Press, 1984.

Currell, Susan, and Christina Cogdell, ed. *Popular Eugenics: National Efficiency and American Mass Culture in the 1930s*. Athens: Ohio University Press, 2006.

Curti, Merle, and Vernon Carstensen. *The University of Wisconsin: A History, 1848–1925*, 2 vols. Madison: University of Wisconsin Press, 1949.

Davenport, Horace W. *Not Just Any Medical School: The Science, Practice, and Teaching of Medicine at the University of Michigan, 1850–1941*. Ann Arbor: University of Michigan Press, 1999.

Davenport, Stewart. *Friends of the Unrighteous Mammon: Northern Christians and Market Capitalism, 1815–1860*. Chicago: University of Chicago Press, 2008.

Davies, John D. *Phrenology: Fad and Science; A 19th-Century American Crusade*. New Haven, CT: Yale University Press, 1955.

Davis, Allen F. *Spearheads for Reform: The Social Settlements and the Progressive Movement, 1890–1914*. 1967; New Brunswick, NJ: Rutgers University Press, 1984.

Davis, Janet M. *The Circus Age: Culture and Society under the American Big Top*. Chapel Hill: University of North Carolina Press, 2002.

Dawley, Alan. *Changing the World: American Progressives in War and Revolution*. Princeton, NJ: Princeton University Press, 2003.

Degler, Carl N. *In Search of Human Nature: The Decline and Revival of Darwinism in American Social Thought*. New York: Oxford University Press, 1991.

Deloria, Philip J. *Playing Indian*. New Haven, CT: Yale University Press, 1998.

Dennis, P. M. "Psychology's First Publicist: H. A. Bruce." *Psychological Reports* 68 (1991): 755–765.

DePastino, Todd. *Citizen Hobo: How a Century of Homelessness Shaped America*. Chicago: University of Chicago Press, 2003.

Des Jardins, Julie. *Women and the Historical Enterprise in America: Gender,*

Race, and the Politics of Memory, 1880–1945. Chapel Hill: University of North Carolina Press, 2003.

Deslandes, Paul R. *Oxbridge Men: British Masculinity and the Undergraduate Experience, 1850–1920*. Bloomington: Indiana University Press, 2005.

Diner, Steven J. *A City and Its Universities: Public Policy in Chicago, 1892–1919*. Chapel Hill: University of North Carolina Press, 1980.

Doyle, Don Harrison. *The Social Order of a Frontier Community: Jacksonville, Illinois, 1825–70*. Urbana: University of Illinois Press, 1978.

Doyle, Leo Andrew. "Causes Won, Not Lost: Football and Southern Culture, 1892–1983." Ph.D. diss., Emory University, 1998.

Duberman, Martin Bauml. *Paul Robeson*. New York: Alfred A. Knopf, 1988.

Dyer, Thomas. *The University of Georgia: A Bicentennial History, 1785–1985*. Athens: University of Georgia Press, 1985.

Edgell, Stephen. *Veblen in Perspective: His Life and Thought*. Armonk, NY: M. E. Sharpe, 2001.

Edwards, Rebecca. *New Spirits: Americans in the Gilded Age, 1865–1905*. New York: Oxford University Press, 2006.

Eksteins, Modris. *Rites of Spring: The Great War and the Birth of the Modern Age*. 1989; Boston: Houghton Mifflin, 2000.

Elkana, Y., ed. *The Interaction between Science and Philosophy*. Atlantic Highlands, NJ: Humanities Press, 1974.

Elliott, Orrin Leslie. *Stanford University: The First Twenty-Five Years, 1891–1925*. Stanford, CA: Stanford University Press, 1937.

Ethington, Philip J. *The Public City: The Political Construction of Urban Life in San Francisco, 1850–1900*. Cambridge, UK: Cambridge University Press, 1994.

Evans, Eldon Cobb. *A History of the Australian Ballot System in the United States*. Chicago: University of Chicago Press, 1917.

Fabian, Ann. *The Skull Collectors: Race, Science, and America's Unburied Dead*. Chicago: University of Chicago Press, 2010.

Falla, Jack. *NCAA: The Voice of College Sports*. Mission, KS: National Collegiate Athletic Association, 1981.

Fass, Paula S. *The Damned and the Beautiful: American Youth in the 1920s*. New York: Oxford University Press, 1977.

Fay, Jay W. *American Psychology before William James*. 1939; New York: Octagon, 1966.

Finney, Peter. *The Fighting Tigers, 1893–1993: One Hundred Years of LSU Football*. Baton Rouge: Louisiana State University Press, 1993.

Flanagan, Maureen A. *America Reformed: Progressives and Progressivisms, 1890s–1920s*. New York: Oxford University Press, 2007.

Fleming, Thomas. *The Illusion of Victory: America in World War I*. New York: Basic, 2003.

Foner, Eric. *Free Soil, Free Labor, Free Men: The Ideology of the Republican Party before the Civil War*. 1970; New York: Oxford University Press, 1995.

———. *Reconstruction: America's Unfinished Revolution, 1863–1877*. New York: Harper & Row, 1988.

Foucault, Michel. *Discipline and Punish: The Birth of the Prison*, trans. Alan Sheridan. 1975; New York: Vintage, 1977.

———. *The History of Sexuality; Volume I: An Introduction*, trans. Robert Hurley. 1978; New York: Vintage, 1990.

Fredrickson, George M. *The Inner Civil War: Northern Intellectuals and the Crisis of the Union*. New York: Harper & Row, 1965.

Freidel, Frank. *Francis Lieber: Nineteenth-Century Liberal*. Baton Rouge: Louisiana State University Press, 1947.

French, John Calvin. *A History of the University Founded by Johns Hopkins*. Baltimore: Johns Hopkins University Press, 1946.

Frezza, Daria. *The Leader and the Crowd: Democracy in American Public Discourse, 1880–1941*, trans. Martha King. Athens: University of Georgia Press, 2007.

Fussell, Paul. *The Great War and Modern Memory*. 1975; New York: Oxford University Press, 2000.

Geertz, Clifford. *The Interpretation of Cultures: Selected Essays*. New York: Basic, 1973.

Geiger, Roger L. *To Advance Knowledge: The Growth of American Research Universities, 1900–1940*. New York: Oxford University Press, 1986.

Gilbert, James B. *Perfect Cities: Chicago's Utopias of 1893*. Chicago: University of Chicago Press, 1991.

———. *Work without Salvation: America's Intellectuals and Industrial Alienation, 1880–1910*. Baltimore: Johns Hopkins University Press, 1977.

Ginger, Ray. *Altgeld's America: The Lincoln Ideal versus Changing Realities*. 1958; Chicago: Quadrangle, 1965.

Glickstein, Jonathan A. *Concepts of Free Labor in Antebellum America*. New Haven, CT: Yale University Press, 1991.

Goldblatt, David. *The Ball Is Round: A Global History of Football*. New York: Viking, 2006.

Goldstein, Warren. *Playing for Keeps: A History of Early Baseball*. Ithaca, NY: Cornell University Press, 1989.

Goodspeed, Thomas Wakefield. *William Rainey Harper: First President of the University of Chicago*. Chicago: University of Chicago Press, 1928.

Gorman, Paul R. *Left Intellectuals and Popular Culture in Twentieth-Century America*. Chapel Hill: University of North Carolina Press, 1996.

Gorn, Elliott J. *The Manly Art: Bare-Knuckle Prize Fighting in America*. Ithaca, NY: Cornell University Press, 1986.

Gorn, Elliott J., and Warren Goldstein. *A Brief History of American Sports*. 1993; Urbana: University of Illinois Press, 2004.

Gosling, F. G. *Before Freud: Neurasthenia and the American Medical Community, 1870–1910*. Urbana: University of Illinois Press, 1987.

Goulka, Jeremiah E., ed. *The Grand Old Man of Maine: Selected Letters of Joshua Lawrence Chamberlain, 1865–1914*. Chapel Hill: University of North Carolina Press, 2004.

Graybar, Lloyd J. *Albert Shaw of the* Review of Reviews: *An Intellectual Biography*. Lexington: University of Kentucky Press, 1974.

Green, Harvey. *Fit for America: Health, Fitness, Sport, and American Society*. New York: Pantheon, 1986.

Grossman, David Michael. "Professors and Public Service, 1885–1925: A Chapter in the Professionalization of the Social Sciences." Ph.D. diss., Washington University, St. Louis, 1973.

Groueff, Stephane. *Manhattan Project: The Untold Story of the Making of the Atomic Bomb*. Boston: Little, Brown, 1967.

Gruber, Carol S. *Mars and Minerva: World War I and the Uses of the Higher Learning in America*. Baton Rouge: Louisiana State University Press, 1975.

Gruensfelder, Melvin Henry. "A History of the Origin and Development of the Southeastern Conference." M.S. thesis, University of Illinois, 1964.

Grundy, Pamela. *Learning to Win: Sports, Education, and Social Change in Twentieth-Century North Carolina*. Chapel Hill: University of North Carolina Press, 2001.

Guglielmo, Thomas A. *White on Arrival: Italians, Race, Color, and Power in Chicago, 1890–1945*. New York: Oxford University Press, 2003.

Guiliano, Jennifer. "An American Spectacle: Collegiate Mascots and the Performance of Tradition." Ph.D. diss., University of Illinois, 2010.

Guralnick, Stanley M. "Sources of Misconception on the Role of Science in the Nineteenth-Century American College." *Isis* 65:228 (Sept. 1974): 352–366.

Gurr, Charles. *The Personal Equation: A Biography of Steadman Vincent Sanford*. Athens: University of Georgia Press, 1999.

Gutman, Herbert C. *Work, Culture, and Society in Industrializing America: Essays in American Working-Class and Social History*. New York: Vintage, 1977.

Guttmann, Allen. *From Ritual to Record: The Nature of Modern Sports*. New York: Columbia University Press, 1978.

———. *Women's Sports: A History*. New York: Columbia University Press, 1991.

Habermas, Jürgen. *The Structural Transformation of the Public Sphere: An Inquiry into a Category of Bourgeois Society*, trans. Thomas Burger with Frederick Lawrence. 1962; Cambridge, MA: Massachusetts Institute of Technology Press, 1989.

Hale, Nathan G., Jr. *Freud and the Americans: The Beginnings of Psychoanalysis in the United States, 1876–1917*. New York: Oxford University Press, 1971.

Haley, Bruce. *The Healthy Body and Victorian Culture*. Cambridge, MA: Harvard University Press, 1978.

Haller, John S., and Robin M. Haller. *The Physician and Sexuality in Victorian America*. Urbana: University of Illinois Press, 1974.

Halttunen, Karen. *Confidence Men and Painted Women: A Study of Middle-Class Culture in America, 1830–1870*. New Haven, CT: Yale University Press, 1982.

Hardy, Stephen. *How Boston Played: Sport, Recreation, and Community, 1865–1915*. Boston: Northeastern University Press, 1982.

Harris, Neil. *Humbug: The Art of P.T. Barnum*. Boston: Little, Brown, 1973.

Haskell, Thomas L. *The Emergence of Professional Social Science: The American Social Science Association and the Nineteenth-Century Crisis of Authority*. Urbana: University of Illinois Press, 1977.

Hawkins, Hugh. *Banding Together: The Rise of National Associations in American Higher Education, 1887–1950*. Baltimore: Johns Hopkins University Press, 1992.

————. *Between Harvard and America: The Educational Leadership of Charles W. Eliot.* New York: Oxford University Press, 1972.

Hearst, Eliot, and James H. Capshew. *Psychology at Indiana University: A Centennial Review and Compendium.* Bloomington: Indiana University Department of Psychology, 1988.

Hepburn, William Murray, and Louis Martin Sears. *Purdue University: Fifty Years of Progress.* Indianapolis: Hollenbeck, 1925.

Hoeveler, J. David, Jr. *James McCosh and the Scottish Intellectual Tradition: From Glasgow to Princeton.* Princeton, NJ: Princeton University Press, 1981.

Hofstadter, Richard. *Social Darwinism in American Thought.* 1944; Boston: Beacon, 1992.

Hofstadter, Richard, and Walter P. Metzger. *The Development of Academic Freedom in the United States.* New York: Columbia University Press, 1955.

Hogan, David. "Modes of Discipline: Affective Individualism and Pedagogical Reform in New England, 1820–1850." *American Journal of Education* 99 (1990): 1–56.

Hoganson, Kristin L. *Consumers' Imperium: The Global Production of American Domesticity, 1865–1920.* Chapel Hill: University of North Carolina Press, 2007.

————. *Fighting for American Manhood: How Gender Politics Provoked the Spanish-American and Philippine-American Wars.* New Haven, CT: Yale University Press, 1998.

Hollinger, David A. *In the American Province: Studies in the History and Historiography of Ideas.* Bloomington: Indiana University Press, 1985.

Hooper, Osman C. *History of the Ohio State University; Volume II: 1910 to 1925,* ed. Thomas C. Mendenhall. [Columbus]: Ohio State University Press, [1925].

Horowitz, Helen Lefkowitz. *Campus Life: Undergraduate Cultures from the End of the Eighteenth Century to the Present.* New York: Knopf, 1987.

————. *Rereading Sex: Battles over Sexual Knowledge and Suppression in Nineteenth-Century America.* New York: Vintage, 2002.

Howe, Daniel Walker. *Making the American Self: Jonathan Edwards to Abraham Lincoln.* Cambridge, MA: Harvard University Press, 1997.

————. *The Political Culture of the American Whigs.* Chicago: University of Chicago Press, 1979.

————. *The Unitarian Conscience: Harvard Moral Philosophy, 1805–1861.* 1970; Middletown, CT: Wesleyan University Press, 1988.

————. *What Hath God Wrought: The Transformation of America, 1815–1848.* New York: Oxford University Press, 2007.

Hull, Richard T., ed. *Presidential Addresses of the American Philosophical Association, 1901–1910.* Dordrecht: Kluwer, 1999.

Hutcheson, Philo A. *A Professional Professoriate: Unionization, Bureaucratization, and the AAUP.* Nashville: Vanderbilt University Press, 2000.

Ingrassia, Brian M. "Public Influence inside the College Walls: Progressive Era Universities, Social Scientists, and Intercollegiate Football Reform." *Journal of the Gilded Age and Progressive Era* 10:1 (Jan. 2011): 59–88.

Janowitz, Morris, ed. *W. I. Thomas on Social Organization and Social Personality: Selected Papers.* Chicago: University of Chicago Press, 1966.

Jeffries, Hasan Kwame. "Fields of Play: The Mediums through Which Black Athletes Engaged in Sports in Jim Crow Georgia." *Journal of Negro History* 86:3 (Summer 2001): 264–275.

Johnson, Russell L. *Warriors into Workers: The Civil War and the Formation of Urban-Industrial Society in a Northern City.* New York: Fordham University Press, 2003.

Kanigel, Robert. *The One Best Way: Frederick Winslow Taylor and the Enigma of Efficiency.* New York: Viking, 1997.

Karabel, Jerome. *The Chosen: The Hidden History of Admission and Exclusion at Harvard, Yale, and Princeton.* Boston: Houghton Mifflin, 2005.

Kasson, John F. *Amusing the Million: Coney Island at the Turn of the Century.* New York: Hill and Wang, 1978.

————. *Houdini, Tarzan, and the Perfect Man: The White Male Body and the Challenge of Modernity in America.* New York: Hill and Wang, 2001.

Kennedy, David M. *Freedom from Fear: The American People in Depression and War, 1929–1945.* New York: Oxford University Press, 1999.

————. *Over Here: The First World War and American Society.* New York: Oxford University Press, 1980.

Kett, Joseph F. *The Pursuit of Knowledge under Difficulties: From Self-Improvement to Adult Education in America, 1750–1990.* Stanford, CA: Stanford University Press, 1994.

Kevles, Daniel J. *In the Name of Eugenics: Genetics and the Uses of Human Heredity.* 1985; Cambridge, MA: Harvard University Press, 1995.

————. *The Physicists: The History of a Scientific Community in Modern America.* 1971; New York: Vintage, 1979.

Kirsch, George B. *Baseball in Blue and Gray: The National Pastime during the Civil War*. Princeton, NJ: Princeton University Press, 2003.

————. *The Creation of American Team Sports: Baseball and Cricket, 1838–1872*. Urbana: University of Illinois Press, 1989.

Kloppenberg, James T. *Uncertain Victory: Social Democracy and Progressivism in European and American Thought, 1870–1920*. New York: Oxford University Press, 1986.

Kuhn, Thomas. *The Structure of Scientific Revolutions*, 2nd ed. 1962; Chicago: University of Chicago Press, 1970.

Kuklick, Bruce. *A History of Philosophy in America, 1720–2000*. New York: Oxford University Press, 2001.

————. *The Rise of American Philosophy: Cambridge, Massachusetts, 1860–1930*. New Haven, CT: Yale University Press, 1977.

————. *To Every Thing a Season: Shibe Park and Urban Philadelphia, 1909–1976*. Princeton, NJ: Princeton University Press, 1991.

Lacy, Tim. "Making a Democratic Culture: The Great Books Idea, Mortimer J. Adler, and Twentieth-Century America." Ph.D. diss., Loyola University Chicago, 2006.

Langum, David J. *Crossing over the Line: Legislating Morality and the Mann Act*. Chicago: University of Chicago Press, 1994.

Larson, Edward J. *Summer for the Gods: The Scopes Trial and America's Continuing Debate over Science and Religion*. Cambridge, MA: Harvard University Press, 1997.

Lawrence, Paul R. *Unsportsmanlike Conduct: The National Collegiate Athletic Association and the Business of College Football*. New York: Praeger, 1987.

Lears, T. J. Jackson. *No Place of Grace: Antimodernism and the Transformation of American Culture, 1880–1920*. New York: Pantheon, 1981.

————. *Rebirth of a Nation: The Making of Modern America, 1877–1920*. New York: HarperCollins, 2009.

————. *Something for Nothing: Luck in America*. New York: Viking, 2003.

Leonard, Fred Eugene. "The First Introduction of the Jahn Gymnastics into America (1825–1830)." *Mind and Body* 12:139–144 (Oct. 1905–Feb. 1906): 193–198, 217–223, 249–254, 281–292, 313–319, 345–351.

————. "Friedrich Ludwig Jahn, and the Development of Popular Gymnastics (*Vereinsturnen*) in Germany." *Mind and Body* 12:137 (July 1905): 133–139.

Lester, Robin. *Stagg's University: The Rise, Decline, and Fall of Big-Time Football at Chicago*. Urbana: University of Illinois Press, 1995.

Levine, Bruce. *The Spirit of 1848: German Immigrants, Labor Conflict, and the Coming of the Civil War*. Urbana: University of Illinois Press, 1992.

Levine, David O. *The American College and the Culture of Aspiration, 1915–1940*. Ithaca, NY: Cornell University Press, 1986.

Levine, Lawrence. *Highbrow/Lowbrow: The Emergence of Cultural Hierarchy in America*. Cambridge, MA: Harvard University Press, 1988.

Lewis, Guy Maxton. "The American Intercollegiate Football Spectacle, 1869–1917." Ph.D. diss., University of Maryland, 1964.

Lissak, Rivka Shpak. *Pluralism and Progressives: Hull House and the New Immigrants, 1890–1919*. Chicago: University of Chicago Press, 1989.

Lombard, Warren P. "The Life and Work of Carl Ludwig." *Science* 44 (1916): 363–375.

Long, Lisa A. *Rehabilitating Bodies: Health, History, and the American Civil War*. Philadelphia: University of Pennsylvania Press, 2003.

Loos, Karl D., and Helen Loos Whitney; foreword by H. G. Plum. *Isaac Althaus Loos*. Iowa City: University of Iowa Press, 1947.

Lowen, Rebecca S. *Creating the Cold War University: The Transformation of Stanford*. Berkeley: University of California Press, 1997.

Lutz, Tom. *American Nervousness, 1903: An Anecdotal History*. Ithaca, NY: Cornell University Press, 1991.

Mandelbaum, Michael. *The Meaning of Sports: Why Americans Watch Baseball, Football, and Basketball and What They See When They Do*. New York: PublicAffairs, 2004.

Marsden, George M. *Fundamentalism and American Culture*, 2nd ed. 1980; New York: Oxford University Press, 2006.

———. *The Soul of the American University: From Protestant Establishment to Established Nonbelief*. New York: Oxford University Press, 1994.

Mattson, Brenda Harper. "George Petrie—The Early Years, 1866–1892." M.A. thesis, Auburn University, 1983.

May, Henry F. *Protestant Churches and Industrial America*. 1949; New York: Harper & Row, 1967.

McConnell, Stuart. *Glorious Contentment: The Grand Army of the Republic, 1865–1900*. Chapel Hill: University of North Carolina Press, 1992.

McDonagh, Eileen, and Laura Pappano. *Playing with the Boys: Why Separate Is Not Equal in Sports*. New York: Oxford University Press, 2008.

McGerr, Michael E. *The Decline of Popular Politics: The American North, 1865–1928*. New York: Oxford University Press, 1986.

————. *A Fierce Discontent: The Rise and Fall of the Progressive Movement in America*. New York: Oxford University Press, 2003.

McGuigan, Dorothy. *A Dangerous Experiment: 100 Years of Women at the University of Michigan*. Ann Arbor, MI: Center for Continuing Education of Women, 1970.

McMath, Robert C., et al. *Engineering the New South: Georgia Tech, 1885–1985*. Athens: University of Georgia Press, 1985.

McPherson, James M. *Battle Cry of Freedom: The Civil War Era*. New York: Oxford University Press, 1988.

Menand, Louis. *The Marketplace of Ideas*. New York: Norton, 2010.

————. *The Metaphysical Club: A Story of Ideas in America*. New York: Farrar, Straus and Giroux, 2001.

Metzger, Walter P., ed. *Professors on Guard: The First AAUP Investigations*. New York: Arno, 1977.

Meyer, D. H. *The Instructed Conscience: The Shaping of the American National Ethic*. Philadelphia: University of Pennsylvania Press, 1972.

Micale, Mark S., and Paul Lerner, eds. *Traumatic Pasts: History, Psychiatry, and Trauma in the Modern Age, 1870–1930*. Cambridge, UK: Cambridge University Press, 2001.

Minton, Henry L. *Lewis M. Terman: Pioneer in Psychological Testing*. New York: New York University Press, 1986.

Montgomery, James, Stanley Folmsbee, and Lee Greene. *To Foster Knowledge: A History of the University of Tennessee, 1794–1970*. Knoxville: University of Tennessee Press, 1984.

Morison, Samuel Eliot. *Three Centuries of Harvard 1636–1936*. Cambridge, MA: Harvard University Press, 1936.

Morison, Samuel Eliot, ed. *The Development of Harvard University since the Inauguration of President Eliot, 1869–1929*. Cambridge, MA: Harvard University Press, 1930.

Mosse, George L. *Nationalism and Sexuality: Respectability and Abnormal Sexuality in Modern Europe*. New York: Howard Fertig, 1985.

Mrozek, Donald J. *Sport and American Mentality, 1880–1910*. Knoxville: University of Tennessee Press, 1983.

Munroe, James Phinney. *A Life of Francis Amasa Walker*. New York: Henry Holt, 1923.

Nasaw, David. *Children of the City: At Work and at Play*. Garden City, NY: Anchor, 1985.

————. *Going Out: The Rise and Fall of Public Amusements*. New York: Basic Books, 1993.

Nelson, Adam R. *Education and Democracy: The Meaning of Alexander Meiklejohn, 1872–1964*. Madison: University of Wisconsin Press, 2001.

Nelson, Cary. *No University Is an Island: Saving Academic Freedom*. New York: New York University Press, 2010.

Nevius, Blake. *Robert Herrick: The Development of a Novelist*. Berkeley: University of California Press, 1962.

Newfield, Christopher. *Ivy and Industry: Business and the Making of the American University, 1880–1980*. Durham, NC: Duke University Press, 2003.

Newton, Bernard. *The Economics of Francis Amasa Walker: American Economics in Transition*. New York: Augustus M. Kelley, 1968.

Noble, David W. *The Paradox of Progressive Thought*. Minneapolis: University of Minnesota Press, 1958.

Novick, Peter. *That Noble Dream: The "Objectivity Question" and the American Historical Profession*. Cambridge, UK: Cambridge University Press, 1988.

Numbers, Ronald L. *Darwinism Comes to America*. Cambridge, MA: Harvard University Press, 1998.

Nye, Robert A. *The Origins of Crowd Psychology: Gustave Le Bon and the Crisis of Mass Democracy in the Third Republic*. London: Sage, 1975.

O'Donnell, John M. *The Origins of Behaviorism: American Psychology, 1870–1920*. New York: New York University Press, 1985.

Oberdeck, Kathryn J. *The Evangelist and the Impresario: Religion, Entertainment, and Cultural Politics in America, 1884–1914*. Baltimore: Johns Hopkins University Press, 1999.

Okun, Mitchell. *Fair Play in the Marketplace: The First Battle for Pure Food and Drugs*. Dekalb: Northern Illinois University Press, 1986.

Oppenheim, Janet. *"Shattered Nerves": Doctors, Patients, and Depression in Victorian England*. New York: Oxford University Press, 1991.

Oriard, Michael. *Bowled Over: Big-Time College Football from the Sixties to the BCS Era*. Chapel Hill: University of North Carolina Press, 2009.

————. *King Football: Sport and Spectacle in the Golden Age of Radio and Newsreels, Movies and Magazines, the Weekly and the Daily Press*. Chapel Hill: University of North Carolina Press, 2001.

————. *Reading Football: How the Popular Press Created an American Spectacle.* Chapel Hill: University of North Carolina Press, 1993.

Owens, Larry. "Pure and Sound Government: Laboratories, Playing Fields, and Gymnasia in the Nineteenth-Century Search for Order." *Isis* 76 (1985): 182–194.

Park, Roberta J. "'Taking Their Measure' in Play, Games, and Physical Training: The American Scene, 1870s to World War I." *Journal of Sport History* 33:2 (Summer 2006): 193–217.

Peckham, Howard H. *The Making of the University of Michigan: 1817–1992,* ed. Margaret L. Steneck and Nicholas H. Steneck. 1967; Ann Arbor, MI: Bentley Historical Library, 1994.

Peiss, Kathy. *Cheap Amusements: Working Women and Leisure in Turn-of-the-Century New York.* Philadelphia: Temple University Press, 1986.

Persons, Stow. *Ethnic Studies at Chicago, 1905–1945.* Urbana: University of Illinois Press, 1987.

————. *The University of Iowa in the Twentieth Century: An Institutional History.* Iowa City: University of Iowa Press, 1990.

Persons, Stow, ed. *Evolutionary Thought in America.* New Haven, CT: Yale University Press, 1950.

Peterson, Theodore. *Magazines in the Twentieth Century,* 2nd ed. Urbana: University of Illinois Press, 1964.

Pettegrew, John. *Brutes in Suits: Male Sensibility in America, 1890–1920.* Baltimore: Johns Hopkins University Press, 2007.

————. "'The Soldier's Faith': Turn-of-the-Century Memory of the Civil War and the Emergence of Modern American Nationalism." *Journal of Contemporary History* 31:1 (Jan. 1996): 49–73.

Piepmeier, Alison. *Out in Public: Configurations of Women's Bodies in Nineteenth-Century America.* Chapel Hill: University of North Carolina Press, 2004.

Pittenger, Mark. *American Socialists and Evolutionary Thought, 1870–1920.* Madison: University of Wisconsin Press, 1993.

Pollard, James E. *History of the Ohio State University: The Story of Its First Seventy-Five Years, 1873–1948.* Columbus: Ohio State University Press, 1952.

Pope, S. W. *Patriotic Games: Sporting Traditions in the American Imagination, 1876–1926.* New York: Oxford University Press, 1997.

Prescott, Heather Munro. *Student Bodies: The Influence of Student Health*

Services in American Society and Medicine. Ann Arbor: University of Michigan Press, 2007.

Putney, Clifford. *Muscular Christianity: Manhood and Sports in Protestant America, 1880–1920*. Cambridge, MA: Harvard University Press, 2001.

Rabinbach, Anson. *The Human Motor: Energy, Fatigue, and the Origins of Modernity*. New York: Basic Books, 1990.

Rader, Benjamin G. *The Academic Mind and Reform: The Influence of Richard T. Ely in American Life*. Lexington: University of Kentucky Press, 1966.

———. *Baseball: A History of America's Game*, 2nd ed. Urbana: University of Illinois Press, 2002.

Recchiuti, John Louis. *Civic Engagement: Social Science and Progressive-Era Reform in New York City*. Philadelphia: University of Pennsylvania Press, 2007.

Renoff, Gregory J. *The Big Tent: The Traveling Circus in Georgia, 1820–1930*. Athens: University of Georgia Press, 2008.

Repplier, Agnes. *J. William White, M.D.: A Biography*. Boston: Houghton Mifflin, 1919.

Reuben, Julie A. *The Making of the Modern University: Intellectual Transformation and the Marginalization of Morality*. Chicago: University of Chicago Press, 1996.

Rice, Emmett A., John L. Hutchinson, and Mabel Lee. *A Brief History of Physical Education*, 5th ed. New York: Ronald, 1969.

Rice, Stephen D. *Minding the Machine: Languages of Class in Early Industrial America*. Berkeley: University of California Press, 2004.

Rieber, Robert W., and David K. Robinson, eds. *Wilhelm Wundt in History: The Making of a Scientific Psychology*. New York: Kluwer Academic, 2001.

Riess, Stephen A. *City Games: The Evolution of American Urban Society and the Rise of Sports*. Urbana: University of Illinois Press, 1989.

Roberts, Howard. *The Big Nine: The Story of Football in the Western Conference*. New York: G. P. Putnam's Sons, 1948.

Robinson, Ray. *Rockne of Notre Dame: The Making of a Football Legend*. New York: Oxford University Press, 1999.

Rodgers, Daniel T. *Age of Fracture*. Cambridge, MA: Harvard University Press, 2011.

———. *Atlantic Crossings: Social Politics in a Progressive Age*. Cambridge, MA: Harvard University Press, 1998.

————. *The Work Ethic in Industrial America, 1850–1920*. 1974; Chicago: University of Chicago Press, 1978.

Roediger, David R. *The Wages of Whiteness: Race and the Making of the American Working Class*, rev. ed. 1991; London: Verso, 1999.

————. *Working toward Whiteness: How America's Immigrants Became White*. New York: Basic Books, 2005.

Rorabaugh, W. J. *The Craft Apprentice: From Franklin to the Machine Age in America*. New York: Oxford University Press, 1986.

Rosenberg, Rosalind. *Beyond Separate Spheres: Intellectual Roots of Modern Feminism*. New Haven, CT: Yale University Press, 1982.

Rosensweig, Daniel. *Retro Ball Parks: Instant History, Baseball, and the New American City*. Knoxville: University of Tennessee Press, 2005.

Rosenthal, Michael. *Nicholas Miraculous: The Amazing Career of the Redoubtable Dr. Nicholas Murray Butler*. New York: Farrar, Straus and Giroux, 2006.

Rosenzweig, Roy. *Eight Hours for What We Will: Workers and Leisure in an Industrial City, 1870–1920*. Cambridge, UK: Cambridge University Press, 1983.

Ross, Dorothy. *G. Stanley Hall: The Psychologist as Prophet*. Chicago: University of Chicago Press, 1972.

————. *The Origins of American Social Science*. Cambridge, UK: Cambridge University Press, 1991.

Ross, Earle D. *Democracy's College: The Land-Grant Movement in the Formative Stage*. Ames: Iowa State University Press, 1942.

Rothman, David J. *The Discovery of the Asylum: Social Order and Disorder in the New Republic*. Boston: Little, Brown, 1971.

Rotundo, E. Anthony. *American Manhood: Transformations in Masculinity from the Revolution to the Modern Era*. New York: Basic, 1993.

Rozario, Kevin. *The Culture of Calamity: Disaster and the Making of Modern America*. Chicago: University of Chicago Press, 2007.

Rubin, Joan Shelley. *The Making of Middlebrow Culture*. Chapel Hill: University of North Carolina Press, 1992.

Rudolph, Frederick. *The American College and University: A History*. 1962; Athens: University of Georgia Press, 1990.

————. *Curriculum: A History of the American Undergraduate Course of Study since 1636*. San Francisco: Jossey-Bass, 1977.

————. *Mark Hopkins and the Log: Williams College, 1836–1872*. New Haven, CT: Yale University Press, 1956.

Russett, Cynthia Eagle. *Sexual Science: The Victorian Construction of Womanhood*. Cambridge, MA: Harvard University Press, 1989.

Rybczynski, Witold. *A Clearing in the Distance: Frederick Law Olmsted and America in the Nineteenth Century*. New York: Scribner, 1999.

Rydell, Robert W. *All the World's a Fair: Visions of Empire at American International Expositions, 1876–1916*. Chicago: University of Chicago Press, 1984.

Sandage, Scott A. *Born Losers: A History of Failure in America*. Cambridge, MA: Harvard University Press, 2005.

Sawyer, McLaren. *Centennial History of the University of Nebraska*, 2 vols. Lincoln: University of Nebraska Press, 1973.

Schmidt, Raymond. "The 1929 Iowa Football Scandal: Paying Tribute to the Carnegie Report?" *Journal of Sport History* 34:3 (Fall 2007): 343–351.

————. *Shaping College Football: The Transformation of an American Sport, 1919–1930*. Syracuse, NY: Syracuse University Press, 2007.

Schorske, Carl E. *Fin-de-Siècle Vienna: Politics and Culture*. New York: Vintage, 1979.

Schrecker, Ellen W. *No Ivory Tower: McCarthyism and the Universities*. New York: Oxford University Press, 1985.

Scott, Joan Wallach. *Gender and the Politics of History*, rev. ed. 1988; New York: Columbia University Press, 1999.

Sellers, Charles. *The Market Revolution: Jacksonian America 1815–1846*. New York: Oxford University Press, 1991.

Seltzer, Mark. *Bodies and Machines*. New York: Routledge, 1992.

Sernett, Milton C. *Abolition's Axe: Beriah Green, Oneida Institute, and the Black Freedom Struggle*. 1986; Syracuse, NY: Syracuse University Press, 2004.

Sher, Richard B. *Church and University in the Scottish Enlightenment: The Moderate Literati of Edinburgh*. Princeton, NJ: Princeton University Press, 1985.

Shindo, Charles J. *1927 and the Rise of Modern America*. Lawrence: University Press of Kansas, 2009.

Smith, Mark C. *Social Science in the Crucible: The American Debate over*

Objectivity and Purpose, 1918–1941. Durham, NC: Duke University Press, 1994.

Smith, Ronald A. "Commercialized Intercollegiate Athletics and the 1903 Harvard Stadium." *New England Quarterly* 78:1 (Mar. 2005): 26–48.

———. "Far More Than Commercialism: Stadium Building from Harvard's Innovations to Stanford's 'Dirt Bowl.'" *International Journal of the History of Sport* 25:11 (Sept. 2008): 1453–1474.

———. *Pay for Play: A History of Big-Time College Athletic Reform*. Urbana: University of Illinois Press, 2011.

———. *Sports and Freedom: The Rise of Big-Time Intercollegiate Athletics*. New York: Oxford University Press, 1988.

Smith, Ronald A., ed. *Big-Time Football at Harvard, 1905: The Diary of Coach Bill Reid*. Urbana: University of Illinois Press, 1994.

Smith-Rosenberg, Carroll. *Disorderly Conduct: Visions of Gender in Victorian America*. New York: Knopf, 1985.

Snyder, Robert W. *The Voice of the City: Vaudeville and Popular Culture in New York*. New York: Oxford University Press, 1989.

Soderstrom, Robert M. *The Big House: Fielding H. Yost and the Building of Michigan Stadium*. Ann Arbor, MI: Huron River Press, 2005.

Solberg, Winton U. *The University of Illinois, 1867–1894: An Intellectual and Cultural History*. Urbana: University of Illinois Press, 1968.

———. *The University of Illinois, 1894–1904: The Shaping of the University*. Urbana: University of Illinois Press, 2000.

Solomon, Barbara Miller. *In the Company of Educated Women: A History of Women and Higher Education in America*. New Haven, CT: Yale University Press, 1985.

Sperber, Murray. *Beer and Circus: How Big-Time College Sports Is Crippling Undergraduate Education*. New York: Henry Holt, 2000.

———. *College Sports Inc.: The Athletic Department vs. the University*. New York: Henry Holt, 1990.

———. *Onward to Victory: The Crises That Shaped College Sports*. New York: Henry Holt, 1998.

———. *Shake Down the Thunder: The Creation of Notre Dame Football*. New York: Henry Holt, 1993.

Spindel, Carol. *Dancing at Halftime: Sports and the Controversy over American Indian Mascots*. New York: New York University Press, 2000.

Spindler, George W. *Karl Follen: A Biographical Study*. Chicago: University of Chicago Press, 1917.

Sproat, John. *"The Best Men": Liberal Reformers in the Gilded Age*. New York: Oxford University Press, 1968.

Stagg, Paul. "The Development of the National Collegiate Athletics Association in Relationship to Intercollegiate Athletics in the United States." Ph.D. diss., New York University, 1946.

Starr, Kevin. *Americans and the California Dream, 1850–1915*. New York: Oxford University Press, 1973.

———. *Inventing the Dream: California through the Progressive Era*. New York: Oxford University Press, 1985.

Steckbeck, John S. *Fabulous Redmen: The Carlisle Indians and Their Famous Football Teams*. Harrisburg: J. Horace McFarland, 1951.

Stern, Alexandra Minna. *Eugenic Nation: Faults and Frontiers of Better Breeding in Modern America*. Berkeley: University of California Press, 2005.

Stevenson, Louise L. *Scholarly Means to Evangelical Ends: The New Haven Scholars and the Transformation of Higher Learning in America, 1830–1890*. Baltimore: Johns Hopkins University Press, 1986.

Stewart, Alva W. *College Football Stadiums: An Illustrated Guide to NCAA Division I-A*. Jefferson, NC: McFarland, 2000.

Stocking, George W. *Victorian Anthropology*. New York: Free Press, 1987.

Storr, Richard J. *Harper's University: The Beginnings*. Chicago: University of Chicago Press, 1966.

Stromquist, Shelton. *Reinventing "The People": The Progressive Movement, the Class Problem, and the Origins of Modern Liberalism*. Urbana: University of Illinois Press, 2006.

Sullivan, Neil J. *The Diamond in the Bronx: Yankee Stadium and the Politics of New York*. New York: Oxford University Press, 2001.

Susman, Warren. *Culture as History: The Transformation of American Society in the Twentieth Century*. New York: Pantheon, 1984.

Teichgraeber, Richard F., III. *Sublime Thoughts/Penny Wisdom: Situating Emerson and Thoreau in the American Market*. Baltimore: Johns Hopkins University Press, 1995.

Tewksbury, Donald G. *The Founding of American Colleges and Universities before the Civil War*. New York: Columbia University Teachers College Bureau of Publications, 1932.

Thelin, John R. *Games Colleges Play: Scandal and Reform in Intercollegiate Athletics*. Baltimore: Johns Hopkins University Press, 1994.

———. *A History of American Higher Education*. Baltimore: Johns Hopkins University Press, 2004.

Thies, Clifford F., and Gary M. Pecquet. "The Shaping of a Future President's Economic Thought: Richard T. Ely and Woodrow Wilson at 'The Hopkins.'" *Independent Review* 15:2 (Fall 2010): 257–277.

Tilman, Rick. *The Intellectual Legacy of Thorstein Veblen: Unresolved Issues*. Westport, CT: Greenwood Press, 1996.

Toma, J. Douglas. *Football U: Spectator Sports in the Life of the American University*. Ann Arbor: University of Michigan Press, 2003.

Townsend, Kim. *Manhood at Harvard: William James and Others*. New York: Norton, 1996.

Trachtenberg, Alan. *The Incorporation of America: Culture and Society in the Gilded Age*. New York: Hill and Wang, 1982.

Trolander, Judith Ann. *Professionalism and Social Change: From the Settlement House Movement to Neighborhood Centers, 1886 to the Present*. New York: Columbia University Press, 1987.

Trumpbour, Robert C. *The New Cathedrals: Politics and Media in the History of Stadium Construction*. Syracuse, NY: Syracuse University Press, 2007.

Turner, James. *The Liberal Education of Charles Eliot Norton*. Baltimore: Johns Hopkins University Press, 1999.

Turner, Victor. *Dramas, Fields, and Metaphors: Symbolic Action in Human Society*. Ithaca, NY: Cornell University Press, 1974.

———. *The Ritual Process: Structure and Anti-Structure*. Ithaca, NY: Cornell University Press, 1969.

Tyack, David B. *George Ticknor and the Boston Brahmins*. Cambridge, MA: Harvard University Press, 1967.

Tygiel, Jules. *Past Time: Baseball as History*. New York: Oxford University Press, 2000.

Tyrell, Ian. *Historians in Public: The Practice of American History, 1890–1970*. Chicago: University of Chicago Press, 2006.

Ueberhorst, Horst, and Wolfgang Stump. *Friedrich Ludwig Jahn and His Time, 1778–1852*, trans. Timothy Nevill. 1978; Munich: Moos, 1982.

Umphlett, Wiley Lee. *Creating the Big Game: John W. Heisman and the Invention of American Football*. Westport, CT: Greenwood, 1992.

Unger, Nancy C. *Fighting Bob LaFollette: The Righteous Reformer.* Chapel Hill: University of North Carolina Press, 2000.

Vanderbilt, Kermit. *Charles Eliot Norton: Apostle of Culture in a Democracy.* Cambridge, MA: Harvard University Press, 1959.

Vertinsky, Patricia A. *The Eternally Wounded Woman: Women, Doctors, and Exercise in the Late Nineteenth Century.* 1989; Urbana: University of Illinois Press, 1994.

Veysey, Laurence R. *The Emergence of the American University.* Chicago: University of Chicago Press, 1965.

Voltmer, Carl D. *A Brief History of the Intercollegiate Conference of Faculty Representatives, with Special Consideration of Athletic Problems.* New York: Western Intercollegiate Conference, 1935.

Vučković, Myriam. *Voices from Haskell: Indian Students between Two Worlds, 1884–1928.* Lawrence: University Press of Kansas, 2008.

Wallach, Stephanie. "Luther Halsey Gulick and the Salvation of the American Adolescent." Ph.D. diss., Columbia University, 1989.

Walter, Richard D. *S. Weir Mitchell, M.D.—Neurologist: A Medical Biography.* Springfield, IL: Charles C. Thomas, 1970.

Ward, Geoffrey C. *Unforgivable Blackness: The Rise and Fall of Jack Johnson.* New York: Knopf, 2004.

Warwick, Andrew. *Masters of Theory: Cambridge and the Rise of Mathematical Physics.* Chicago: University of Chicago Press, 2003.

Watterson, John Sayle. *College Football: History, Spectacle, Controversy.* Baltimore: Johns Hopkins University Press, 2000.

———. "The Gridiron Crisis of 1905: Was It Really a Crisis?" *Journal of Sport History* 27:2 (Summer 2000): 291–298.

Weinberg, Julius. *Edward Alsworth Ross and the Sociology of Progressivism.* Madison: State Historical Society of Wisconsin, 1972.

Welch, J. Edmund. *Edward Hitchcock, M.D.: Founder of Physical Education in the College Curriculum.* 1962; Greenville, NC: East Carolina College, 1966.

Welke, Barbara Young. *Recasting American Liberty: Gender, Race, Law, and the Railroad Revolution, 1865–1920.* Cambridge, UK: Cambridge University Press, 2001.

Westby, David L., and Allen Sack. "The Commercialization and Functional Rationalization of College Football: Its Origins." *Journal of Higher Education* 47 (1976): 625–647.

Whiteside, James. *Colorado: A Sports History*. Niwot: University Press of Colorado, 1999.

Wiebe, Robert H. *The Search for Order, 1877–1920*. New York: Hill and Wang, 1967.

Wiener, Philip P. *Evolution and the Founders of Pragmatism*. Cambridge, MA: Harvard University Press, 1949.

Wilentz, Sean. *Chants Democratic: New York City and the Rise of the American Working Class, 1788–1850*. New York: Oxford University Press, 1984.

Wilson, Mark R. *The Business of Civil War: Military Mobilization and the State, 1861–1865*. Baltimore: Johns Hopkins University Press, 2006.

Woodward, C. Vann. *Origins of the New South, 1877–1913*. 1951; Baton Rouge: Louisiana State University Press, 1971.

Young, Frank Ripley McDonald. "Football in the Gilded Age: The Origin and Social Meaning of American Football." M.A. thesis, University of Maryland, 1972.

Young, James Harvey. *Pure Food: Securing the Federal Food and Drugs Act of 1906*. Princeton, NJ: Princeton University Press, 1989.

Zimbalist, Andrew. *Unpaid Professionals: Commercialism and Conflict in Big-Time College Sports*. Princeton, NJ: Princeton University Press, 1999.

Zimmerman, David A. *Panic! Markets, Crises, and Crowds in American Fiction*. Chapel Hill: University of North Carolina Press, 2006.

Index